PUBLIC BORROWING

PUBLIC BORROWING

Critical Concepts in Finance

Edited by
Tehreem Husain and D'Maris Coffman

Volume IV
Market Microstructure, Creditor Action, and Contagion

Routledge
Taylor & Francis Group

LONDON AND NEW YORK

First published 2022
by Routledge
2 Park Square, Milton Park, Abingdon, Oxon OX14 4RN

and by Routledge
52 Vanderbilt Avenue, New York, NY 10017

Routledge is an imprint of the Taylor & Francis Group, an informa business

British Library Cataloguing-in-Publication Data
A catalogue record for this book is available from the British Library

Library of Congress Cataloging-in-Publication Data
A catalog record has been requested for this book

ISBN: 978-1-138-90553-5 (set)
ISBN: 978-1-138-90558-0 (volume IV)

Typeset in Times New Roman
by Deanta Global Publishing Services, Chennai, India

Publisher's Note
References within each chapter are as they appear in the original complete work

CONTENTS

VOLUME IV ACKNOWLEDGEMENTS

The Publishers would like to thank the following for permission to reprint their material:

University of Chicago Press for permission to reprint F. Allen and D. Gale, 'Financial Contagion', *Journal of Political Economy* 108, 1, 2000, 1–33.

The Bank for International Settlements for permission to reprint J. D. Amato, 'Risk Aversion and Risk Premia in the CDS Market', *BIS Quarterly Review* Part 5, December, 2005, 55–68.

John Wiley & Sons for permission to reprint M. G. Arghyrou and J. D. Tsoukalas, 'The Greek Debt Crisis: Likely Causes, Mechanics and Outcomes', *World Economy* 34, 2011, 173–191.

Elsevier for permission to reprint J. Beirne and M. Fratzscher, 'The Pricing of Sovereign Risk and Contagion During the European Sovereign Debt Crisis', *Journal of International Money and Finance* 34, 2013, 60–82.

John Wiley & Sons for permission to reprint A. Karolyi, 'Does International Finance Contagion Really Exist?', *International Finance* 6, 2003, 179–199.

Oxford University Press for permission to reprint Fabio Fornari and Livio Stracca, 'What Does a Financial Shock Do? First International Evidence'. *Economic Policy* 27, 71, 2012, pp. 407–445.

The IMF for permission to reprint Nicola Gennaioli, Alberto Martin and Stefano Rossi, 'Banks, Government Bonds, and Default: What Do the Data Say?', (July 2014). IMF Working Paper No. 14/120.

John Wiley & Sons for permission to reprint N. M. Boyson, C. W. Stahel and R. Stulz, 'Hedge Fund Contagion and Liquidity Shocks', *Journal of Finance* 65, 5, 2010, 1789–1816.

Oxford University Press for permission to reprint M. Brunnermeier and L.H. Pedersen, 'Market Liquidity and Funding Liquidity', *Review of Financial Studies* 22, 6, 2009, 2201–2238.

John Wiley & Sons for permission to reprint G. Dell'Ariccia, I. Schnabel and J. Zettelmeyer, 'How do Official Bailouts Affect the Risk of Investing in Emerging Markets?', *Journal of Money, Credit and Banking* 38, 7, 2006, 1689–1714.

Oxford University Press for permission to reprint R. Pitchford and M. L. J. Wright, 'On the Contribution of Game Theory to the Study of Sovereign Debt and Default', *Oxford Review of Economic Policy* 29, 4, 2013, 649–667.

Disclaimer

VOLUME IV INTRODUCTION
Market Microstructure, Creditor Action, and Contagion

A full discussion of public borrowing would be incomplete without an examination of developments in the market microstructure, the manner in which public debt is traded, the growth of credit derivatives (especially credit default swaps and interest rate swaps), and the attendant possibilities for creditor action and financial market contagion. In the aftermath of the Eurozone crisis, these debates became much more frequent and more nuanced. This volume explores these debates. Our discussion also focuses on the changing regulatory climate and the renewed spectre of creditor action that erode traditional concepts of sovereign immunity. The volume also explores in detail the literature on sovereign debt crises and their contagion effects.

We start the volume with Allen and Gale (2000) who provide microeconomic foundations for financial contagion. The authors identify a critical 'channel of contagion', which they describe in terms of 'the overlapping claims that different regions or sectors of the banking system have on one another'. With liquidity shocks imperfectly correlated across regions, banks hold interregional claims on other banks to provide insurance against liquidity preference shocks. They conclude that: 'in the absence of uncertainty, the first-best allocation of risk sharing can be achieved. However, this arrangement is financially fragile. A small liquidity preference shock in one region can spread by contagion throughout the economy.' Results show that contagion is dependent on two concepts, completeness of the interbank network and the degree of connectedness.

Concepts of completeness and interconnectedness of networks, advocated by Allen and Gale (2000) manifest in several episodes of contagion (Affinito & Pozzolo, 2017). In the summer of 2002, WorldCom, the USA's second largest long-distance telephone company at that time, filed for bankruptcy causing a market-wide contagion effect on credit default swaps (CDS) spreads. Large changes in spreads on CDS occurred in 2002. Amato (2005) investigates this phenomenon and explores whether the large widening of credit spreads in 2002 was a result of rapid deterioration in outlook or because of investors suddenly becoming more risk averse. The chapter constructs measures of risk premia and risk aversion in credit markets using data from the credit default swap market from 2002–05. Results show that risk premia are highly volatile over time. Default risk premia and risk aversion relate strongly to fundamental factors such as indicators of real economic activity, monetary policy announcements, and technical market factors such as issuance of collateralized debt obligations (CDOs). Hence, this chapter confirms Allen and Gale's (2000) findings that in a financially integrated world, with a high degree of connectedness, contagion effects can have severe consequences.

These themes of contagion, risk aversion, and the role of fundamental factors are brought together in Arghyrou and Tsoukalas's (2011) study of the Greek sovereign debt crisis. Using literature on the currency crisis, the authors explore the Greek crisis and find its likely causes in two factors. First, a key factor behind the crisis was the steady deterioration of Greek macroeconomic fundamentals over the period 2001–09 inconsistent with long-term Economic and Monetary Union (EMU) participation. Second, the crisis can also be attributed to a shift in markets' expectations, from a regime of credible commitment to future EMU participation under an implicit EMU/German guarantee of Greek fiscal liabilities, to a regime of non-credible EMU commitment without fiscal guarantees. The authors show that the risk of contagion to other periphery EMU countries was significant; and that without extensive structural reforms the sustainability of the EMU is in question. The chapter reiterates the importance of market fundamentals and perceptions on policy credibility for the occurrence of a sovereign debt crisis.

In the aftermath of the Global Financial Crisis of 2007, Greece was not the only European nation embroiled in a sovereign debt crisis. Beirne and Fratzscher (2013) analyse the drivers of sovereign risk for 31 advanced and emerging economies during the European sovereign debt crisis. Similar to Amato (2005) and Arghyrou and Tsoukalas (2011), deterioration in macroeconomic fundamentals is crucial in explaining the sovereign debt crisis. This was possibly due to the failure of empirical models to explain the market pricing of sovereign risk in the pre-crisis period. Moreover, fundamentals contagion – a sharp rise in the sensitivity of financial markets to fundamentals – is also an important factor in the rise in sovereign yield spreads and CDS spreads during the crisis. In contrast to Arghyrou and Tsoukalas (2011), regional spill-overs and contagion have been less important, including for euro-area countries. The chapter also finds evidence for herding contagion – sharp, simultaneous increases in sovereign yields across countries – but shows that this contagion has been concentrated in time and among a few markets.

When financial crises happen in neighbouring countries in rapid succession, the notion that distress is capable of spreading like a contagious disease becomes popular. However, an important question that arises is: what makes these cross-country spill-overs become characterized as contagion? Karolyi (2003) surveys and synthesizes empirical evidence on international asset price co-movements, the volatility of cross-border capital flows, and the relationship between flows and asset prices and questions the existence of international financial contagion. He notes that observed co-movements during the 1990s might not have been excessively large given the global economic and capital market environment. He argues that the evidence of contagion effects is weak. While international flows have increased substantially, it is difficult to understand whether or how these flows affect asset prices. Karolyi (2003) gives an alternative explanation for these crises. He argues that crises that appear to be similar to contagion can actually be errors in domestic policy duplicated across nations in response to common economic shocks.

Financial crises that have possible contagion effects affect activity in the financial and real sector. Taking the debate on the presence of contagion forward, can we quantify the impact on economic variables? Fornari and Stracca (2013) evaluate the quantitative impact of financial shocks on key indicators of real activity and financial conditions. The authors find robust evidence that financial shocks exert a significant influence on key macroeconomic variables such as gross domestic product (GDP) and (particularly) investment. What remains unclear is whether these shocks are demand or supply shocks from the standpoint of their macroeconomic impact. Furthermore, the results also show that a country's financial development and structure does not have much effect on the intensity of the propagation of financial shocks. Financial shocks not only play a role in times of crisis, these results also hold under normal conditions.

Government debt defaults also have contagion effects and can endanger domestic bank stability. The recent Eurozone crisis has renewed interest in the desirability and design of public intervention in the banking sector. This is because the banking sector proved to be an important channel feeding negative spill-overs between banks' and a sovereign's stability (Leonello, 2018). Public insolvency caused great stress in the European banking sector, particularly banks in troubled countries that had high holdings of government bonds. As sovereign spreads rose, these banks increased their exposure to the bonds of their financially distressed governments in response to political pressure, thus leading to more fragility. Gennaioli, Martin, and Rossi (2014) investigate public default, bank bond holdings, and bank loans. They ask two questions. First, does bank exposure to sovereign risk affect lending? Second, why do banks buy public bonds, exposing themselves to default risk in the first place? Analysing sovereign bond holdings by 20,000 banks in 191 countries and 20 sovereign default episodes over the period 1998–2012, results show that banks have large holdings of government bonds in less financially developed countries. Second, during periods of default, banks without bond holdings have a higher rate of loan growth than those with average holdings of government bonds. These results indicate that the 'dangerous embrace' between banks and their national governments plays an important role during sovereign defaults and the strength of this effect is dependent on local conditions. Implicit in this analysis is that regulatory capture, moral hazard, and political leverage can contribute to instability even in otherwise well-designed institutional environments.

In addition to covering cross-country contagion and its potential impact on the real and financial sector, the volume also discusses contagion across investment categories such as hedge funds and other shadow banking institutions. Paying close attention to fundamentals affecting hedge fund performance can avert any potential shocks to fundamentals spiralling into crises and precipitating contagion. Boyson, Stahel, and Stulz (2010) study hedge funds and find strong evidence of contagion during the period 1990–2008. Large adverse shocks to asset and hedge fund liquidity strongly increase the probability of contagion. The authors find that commonly used models analysing hedge fund returns do not capture these shocks. Specifically, large adverse shocks to credit spreads, the T-bill and ED (TED) spread, prime broker and bank stock prices, stock market liquidity, and hedge fund flows are associated with a significant increase in the probability of hedge fund contagion. Overall, variables capturing hedge fund contagion point towards the role of liquidity risk being crucial for understanding crisis across countries and investment classes.

The role of liquidity is central not to specific investment classes but to the financial market as a whole. Brunnermeier and Pedersen (2009) model the link between an asset market's liquidity (i.e. the ease with which it is traded) and the traders' funding liquidity (i.e. the ease with which they can obtain funding). Both these types of liquidity exist in an interlocked relationship. Traders provide liquidity to the market and are able to do so because of the availability of funding. Tight funding liquidity conditions make traders reluctant to take 'capital intensive' positions in high-margin securities. This results in lower market liquidity and increasing margins. Based on these interconnections, the authors provide a unified explanation for market liquidity. The model shows that market liquidity can suddenly dry up, has commonality across securities, is related to volatility, is subject to 'flight to quality', and co-moves with the market. Their model provides new testable predictions, including that speculators' capital is a driver of market liquidity and risk premia.

Another key point illustrated in Brunnermeier and Pedersen's (2009) model linking asset market and traders' funding liquidity is that, amongst other things, investors' trading activity at a specific point in time depends on their expectations about illiquidity in the next period. Asset prices reflect market participants' expectations about the future (Söderlind & Svensson, 1997). An illustrative case is that of long-term interest rates. Long-term interest rates can be broken down into two parts; the expected path of short-term interest rates and a term premium or the compensation that risk-averse investors demand for holding long-term bonds (Cohen, Hördahl & Xia, 2018). Dell'Arricia, Schnabel, and Zettelmeyer (2006) study 'investor moral hazard' and investigate the effect of bailout expectations on sovereign bond spreads in emerging markets. Expectations of bailouts reduce investors' losses in case of a crisis. Changes in the likelihood of a bailout should translate into changes in emerging market spreads. Examining both the *levels* and cross-country *variance* of spreads, results indicate that the Russian sovereign debt default of 1998 was followed by a permanent, significant increase in the cross-sectional dispersion of spreads. This indicates that post-crisis, investors paid more attention to differences in country characteristics than they had done previously. The authors also show that there were significant increases in the levels of spreads in many countries, especially those with relatively weak fundamentals. The results imply that prior to the Russian sovereign debt default episode of 1998, lending must have mitigated the perceived risk of holding emerging market debt.

The volume ends with a fundamental question about the theory of sovereign debt. Given that there is no supranational institution for enforcing debt repayment, why do countries ever repay their debts? Pitchford and Wright (2013) consider this key question and review lessons from their application of the game-theoretical tools to the study of sovereign debt default. The authors find that the answer to this lies in the design of self-enforcing contracts and in the credibility of threats to punish defaulting countries. Furthermore, the authors also explore the reasons behind the inefficiency of sovereign debt restructuring, and in doing so advance a game-theoretical understanding of bargaining in environments where 'credible commitments' are absent. It is important to note that in a changing world, the concept of 'sovereign immunity' is being diluted. Defaulting governments are no longer immune from legal action by foreign creditors. Creditor lawsuits are an increasingly common feature of sovereign debt markets and sovereign debt is becoming more enforceable, as the recent cases involving Greek debt during the Eurozone debt crisis, the Argentinian debt default, and Iranian public debt have each contributed to an evolving legal landscape (Stolper & Dougherty, 2017; Grund, 2017; Buchheit & Gulati, 2019). More litigation is expected as China balances bilateral diplomacy with the possibilities of legal remedies in international courts for defaults arising from the 'Belt and Road Initiative'.

Changing norms in international law in turn affect debt management, government willingness to pay, and the resolution of debt crises (Schumacher, Trebesch & Enderlein, 2021), even as the global economic system enters uncharted waters amidst the COVID-19 pandemic. Widespread economic damage caused by the pandemic to many sectors of the economy and the subsequent contraction of tax revenues will make the balancing act ever more difficult to maintain: there will be understandable pressure on creditors to participate in sovereign debt restructurings that are sufficient to prevent serial defaults in order to avoid a lost decade or two of growth (Buchheit & Gulati, 2020). We can only hope that lessons have been learned from both the successes and the failures of the Washington Consensus.

References

Affinito, M., & Pozzolo, A. F. (2017). The interbank network across the global financial crisis: evidence from Italy. *Journal of Banking & Finance, 80*, 90–107.

Buchheit, L. C., & Gulati, G. M. (2019). Sovereign debt restructuring and US executive power. *Capital Markets Law Journal, 14*(1), 114–130.

Buchheit, L. C., & Gulati, M. (2020). Avoiding a lost decade—sovereign debt workouts in the post-Covid era. *Capital Markets Law Journal* (forthcoming, pre-print available at the SSRN Archive: https://papers.ssrn.com/sol3/papers.cfm?abstract_id=3704048).

Cohen, B. H., Hördahl, P., & Xia, F. D. (2018). Term premia: models and some stylised facts. *BIS Quarterly Review*, September, 79–90.

Grund, S. (2017). The legal consequences of sovereign insolvency – a review of creditor litigation in Germany following the Greek debt restructuring. *Maastricht Journal of European and Comparative Law*, *24*(3), 399–423.

Leonello, A. (2018). Government guarantees and the two-way feedback between banking and sovereign debt crises. *Journal of Financial Economics*, *130*(3), 592–619.

Shan, W., Zhang, S., & Su, J. (Eds.). (2020). *China and international dispute resolution in the context of the 'Belt and Road Initiative'*. Cambridge: Cambridge University Press.

Schumacher, J., Trebesch, C., & Enderlein, H. (2021). Sovereign defaults in court. *Journal of International Economics*, 131, 103388.

Söderlind, P., & Svensson, L. (1997). New techniques to extract market expectations from financial instruments. *Journal of Monetary Economics*, *40*(2), 383–429.

Stolper, A. E., & Dougherty, S. (2017). Collective action clauses: how the Argentina litigation changed the sovereign debt markets. *Capital Markets Law Journal*, *12*(2), 239–252.

47

FINANCIAL CONTAGION

Franklin Allen and Douglas Gale

Source: *Journal of Political Economy*, 108, 1, 2000, 1–33.

Financial contagion is modeled as an equilibrium phenomenon. Because liquidity preference shocks are imperfectly correlated across regions, banks hold interregional claims on other banks to provide insurance against liquidity preference shocks. When there is no aggregate uncertainty, the first-best allocation of risk sharing can be achieved. However, this arrangement is financially fragile. A small liquidity preference shock in one region can spread by contagion throughout the economy. The possibility of contagion depends strongly on the completeness of the structure of interregional claims. Complete claims structures are shown to be more robust than incomplete structures.

I. Introduction

There is a long tradition of regarding dislocation in the financial sector as a cause of economic fluctuations (Friedman and Schwartz 1963; Bernanke 1983; Bernanke and Gertler 1989). According to this view, financial crises are important because they raise the costs of intermediation and restrict credit, which in turn restrain the level of activity in the real sector and ultimately can lead to periods of low growth and recession.

The prevalence of financial crises has led many to conclude that the financial sector is unusually susceptible to shocks. One theory is that small shocks, which initially affect only a few institutions or a particular region of the economy, spread by contagion to the rest of the financial sector and then infect the larger economy. In this paper, we focus on one channel of contagion, the overlapping claims that different regions or sectors of the banking system have on one another. When one region suffers a bank crisis, the other regions suffer a loss because their claims on the troubled region fall in value. If this spillover effect is strong enough, it can cause a crisis in the adjacent regions. In extreme cases, the crisis passes from region to region and becomes a contagion.

In order to focus on the role of one particular channel for financial contagion, we exclude other propagation mechanisms that may be important for a fuller understanding of financial contagion. In particular, we assume that agents have complete information about their environment. Incomplete information may create another channel for contagion. If a shock in one region serves as a signal predicting a shock in another region, then a crisis in one region may create a self-fulfilling expectation of a crisis in another region.

We also exclude the effect of international currency markets in the propagation of financial crises from one country to another. Currency crises have been extensively studied, and Calvo (1995) and Chang and Velasco (1998), among others, have studied the interaction of the banking system and currency markets in a crisis; but the role of currency markets in financial contagion is left as a subject for future research.

The central aim of this paper is to provide some microeconomic foundations for financial contagion. Although the analysis may have some relevance to the recent Asian financial crisis, the model developed in this paper is not intended to be a description of any particular episode. If it does resemble any historical episode, it would be the banking crises in the United States in the late nineteenth and early twentieth centuries (Hicks 1989).

We take as our starting point the model presented in Allen and Gale (1998). The basic assumptions about technology and preferences have become the standard in the literature since the appearance of the Diamond and Dybvig (1983) model. There are three dates $t = 0, 1, 2$ and a large number of identical consumers, each of whom is endowed with one unit of a homogeneous consumption good. At date 1, the consumers learn whether they are early consumers, who value consumption only at date 1, or late consumers, who value consumption only at date 2. Uncertainty about their preferences creates a demand for liquidity.

Banks have a comparative advantage in providing liquidity. At the first date, consumers deposit their endowments in the banks, which invest them on behalf of the depositors. In exchange, depositors are promised a fixed amount of consumption at each subsequent date, depending on when they choose to withdraw. The bank can invest in two assets. There is a short-term asset that pays a return of one unit after one period and there is a long-term asset that pays a return $r < 1$ after one period or $R > 1$ after two periods. The long asset has a higher return if held to maturity, but liquidating it in the middle period is costly, so it is not very useful for providing consumption to early consumers. The banking sector is perfectly competitive, so banks offer risk-sharing contracts that maximize depositors' ex ante expected utility, subject to a zero-profit constraint.

Using this framework, we are interested in constructing a model in which small shocks lead to large effects by means of contagion, more precisely, in which a shock within a single sector can spread to other sectors and lead to an economy-wide financial crisis. One view is that financial crises are purely random events, unrelated to changes in the real economy (Kindleberger 1978). The modern version of this view, developed by Diamond and Dybvig (1983) and others, is that bank runs are self-fulfilling prophecies. An alternative view is that financial crises are an inherent part of the business cycle (Mitchell 1941; Gorton 1988; Allen and Gale 1998). The disadvantage of treating contagion as a "sunspot" phenomenon is that, without some real connection between different regions, any pattern of correlations is possible. So sunspot theories are equally consistent with contagion and the absence of contagion. We are interested in establishing a stronger result, that under certain circumstances every equilibrium of the model must be characterized by contagion. This form of contagion must be driven by real shocks and real linkages between regions.

The economy consists of a number of regions. The number of early and late consumers in each region fluctuates randomly, but the aggregate demand for liquidity is constant. This allows for interregional insurance as regions with liquidity surpluses provide liquidity for regions with liquidity shortages. The provision of insurance can be organized through an interbank market in deposits. Suppose that region A has a large number of early consumers when region B has a low number of early consumers, and vice versa. Since regions A and B are otherwise identical, their deposits are perfect substitutes. The banks exchange deposits at the first date before they observe the liquidity shocks. If region A has a higher than average number of early consumers at date 1, then banks in region A can meet their obligations by liquidating some of their deposits in the banks of region B. Region B is happy to oblige because it has an excess supply of liquidity in the form of the short asset. At the final date the process is reversed, as banks in region B liquidate the deposits they hold in region A to meet the above-average demand from late consumers in region B.

Interregional cross holdings of deposits work well as long as there is enough liquidity in the banking system as a whole. If there is an excess demand for liquidity, however, the financial linkages caused by these cross holdings can turn out to be a disaster. While cross holdings of deposits are useful for reallocating liquidity within the banking system, they cannot increase the total amount of liquidity. If the economywide demand from consumers is greater than the stock of the short asset, the only way to provide more consumption is to liquidate the long asset. This is very costly (see Shleifer and Vishny [1992] and Allen and Gale [1998] for a discussion of the costs of premature liquidation), so banks try to avoid liquidating the long asset whenever possible. In this case, they can avoid liquidating the long asset by liquidating their claims on other regions instead. This mutual liquidation of claims does not create any additional liquidity, however. It merely denies liquidity to the troubled region, and bank runs and bankruptcy may be the result. What begins as a financial crisis in one region can then spread by contagion to other regions because of the cross holdings of deposits.

The interbank market works quite differently from the retail market. In the latter, runs occur because deposit contracts commit banks to a fixed payment and banks must begin liquidating the long asset when they cannot meet liquidity demand from the short asset. In the interbank market the initial problem is caused by the fact that banks with an excess demand for liquidity cannot get anything from banks in other regions. This is the opposite of the problem in the retail market and, in contrast, cannot be solved by making the contracts discretionary or contingent since whatever their form they cancel each other out. Instead of being caused by the nature of interbank claims, spillovers and contagion result just from the fall in the value of bank assets in adjacent regions.

Whether the financial crisis does spread depends crucially on the pattern of interconnectedness generated by the cross holdings of deposits. If the interbank market is *complete* and each region is connected to all the other regions, the initial impact of a financial crisis in one region may be attenuated. On the other hand, if the interbank market is *incomplete*, each region is connected with a small number of other regions. The initial impact of the financial crisis may be felt very strongly in those neighboring regions, with the result that they too succumb to a crisis. As each region is affected by the crisis, it prompts premature liquidation of the long asset, with a consequent loss of value, so that previously unaffected regions find that they too are affected because their claims on the region in crisis have fallen in value.

It is important to note the role of the free-rider problem in explaining the difference between a complete and an incomplete interbank market. There is a natural pecking order among different sources for liquidity. A bank will meet withdrawals first from the short asset and then from holdings in other regions, and only in the last resort will it choose to liquidate the long asset. Cross holdings are useful for redistributing liquidity, but they do not create liquidity; so when there is a global shortage of liquidity (withdrawals exceed short assets), the only solution is to liquidate long assets. If every region takes a small hit (liquidates a small amount of the long asset), there may be no need for a global crisis. This is what happens with complete markets: banks in the troubled region have direct claims on banks in every other region, and there is no way to avoid paying one's share. With incomplete markets, banks in the troubled region have a direct claim only on the banks in adjacent regions. The banks in other regions pursue their own interests and refuse to liquidate the long asset until they find themselves on the front line of the contagion.

The notion of a region is intended as a metaphor for categories of banks that may differ along several dimensions. For example, some banks may be better at raising funds whereas other banks are better at lending them. Or it might be that banks focus on lending to different industries or in different regions and as a result have lending opportunities that are not perfectly correlated with their deposit base. In either case, an interbank market plays an important role in redistributing the funds efficiently. However, the existence of claims between different categories of banks opens up the possibility of contagion when one category is hit by a sudden demand for liquidity.

Our paper is related to a number of others. Perhaps the closest is that by Lagunoff and Schreft (1998), which studies the spread of crises in a probabilistic model. Financial linkages are modeled by assuming that each project requires two participants and each participant requires two projects. When the probability that

4

one's partner will withdraw becomes too large, all participants simultaneously withdraw; this is interpreted as a financial crisis. The banking system plays no role in Lagunoff and Schreft's analysis. Rochet and Tirole (1996) use monitoring as a means of triggering correlated crises: if one bank fails, it is assumed that other banks have not been properly monitored and a general collapse occurs. Financial multipliers are modeled by Kiyotaki and Moore (1998). In their model, the impact of illiquidity at one link in the credit chain travels down the chain. Models of crises based on multiple equilibria are contained in Cole and Kehoe (1996) and Cooper and Corbae (1997). For a survey of recent work on crises, see Calomiris (1995).

The rest of the paper is organized as follows. In Section II, we present a model of liquidity preference based on Diamond and Dybvig (1983) and Allen and Gale (1998). In Section III, we characterize optimal risk sharing in terms of a planning problem subject to incentive constraints and show that the incentive-efficient allocation is in fact the same as the first-best. Section IV shows how the first-best allocation can be decentralized through a competitive banking system with an interbank market in deposits. Several different market structures are described, and each turns out to be consistent with the first-best. The robustness of this schema is tested in the next three sections. We do this by perturbing the model to allow for an (aggregate) excess demand for liquidity in some states of nature. In Section V, it is shown that with an incomplete interbank market and a high degree of interconnectedness, a liquidity shock that causes a crisis in one region will spread by contagion to others. In Section VI, we consider a complete interbank market and an even higher degree of connectedness. It is shown that, with the same size shock and the same model parameters, there is no contagion. In Section VII, it is shown that with an incomplete interbank market and a low degree of connectedness, there is again no contagion. So the interaction of connectedness and incompleteness appears to be conducive to contagion. Section VIII considers alternatives to an interbank deposit market for sharing risk between regions. Finally, Section IX considers extensions of the basic framework.

II. Liquidity Preference

In this section we describe a simple model in which stochastic liquidity preference provides a motive for risk sharing. The framework is based on Diamond and Dybvig (1983) and Allen and Gale (1998), with some significant differences.

There are three dates, $t = 0, 1, 2$. There is a single consumption good that serves as the numeraire. This good can also be invested in assets to produce future consumption. There are two types of assets, a liquid asset and an illiquid asset. The liquid asset is represented by a storage technology. One unit of the consumption good invested in the storage technology at date t produces one unit of the consumption good at date $t + 1$. Because the returns to this asset are available one period later, we refer to it as the *short asset*. The illiquid asset has a higher return but requires more time to mature. For this reason we call it the *long asset.*

Investment in the long asset can take place only in the first period, and one unit of the consumption good invested in the long asset at the first date produces $R > 1$ units of output at the final date.

The long asset is not completely illiquid. Each unit of the long asset can be prematurely liquidated to produce $0 < r < 1$ units of the consumption good at the middle date. Here we assume that liquidation takes the form of physical depreciation of the asset, and the liquidation value is treated as a technological constant, the "scrap value." In practice, it is more likely that assets are liquidated by being sold, in which case the liquidation value is determined by the market price. Introducing a secondary market on which assets can be sold would complicate the analysis without changing the qualitative features of the model. Allen and Gale (1998) incorporate an asset market and endogenize the liquidation values of assets. Their analysis confirms that the liquidation value will be low for appropriate parameter values.

The economy is divided into four ex ante identical regions, labeled A, B, C, and D. The regional structure is a spatial metaphor that can be interpreted in a variety of ways. The important thing for the analysis is that different regions receive different liquidity shocks. Any story that motivates different shocks for different (groups of) banks is a possible interpretation of the regional structure. So a region can correspond to a single bank, a geographical region within a country, or an entire country; it can also correspond to a specialized sector within the banking industry.

Each region contains a continuum of ex ante identical consumers (depositors). A consumer has an endowment equal to one unit of the consumption good at date 0 and nothing at dates 1 and 2. Consumers are assumed to have the usual Diamond-Dybvig preferences: with probability ω they are early consumers and value consumption only at date 1; with probability $1 - \omega$ they are late consumers and value consumption only at date 2. Then the preferences of the individual consumer are given by

$$U(c_1, c_2) = \begin{cases} u(c_1) & \text{with probability } \omega \\ u(c_2) & \text{with probability } 1 - \omega, \end{cases}$$

where c_t denotes consumption at date $t = 1, 2$. The period utility functions $u(\cdot)$ are assumed to be twice continuously differentiable, increasing, and strictly concave.

The probability ω varies from region to region. Let ω_i denote the probability of being an early consumer in region i. There are two possible values of ω_i, a high value and a low value, denoted ω_H and ω_L, where $0 < \omega_L < \omega_H < 1$. The realization of these random variables depends on the state of nature. There are two equally likely states S_1 and S_2, and the corresponding realizations of the liquidity preference shocks are given in table 1. Note that, ex ante, each region has the same probability of having a high liquidity preference shock. Also, the aggregate demand for liquidity is the same in each state: half the regions have a high liquidity preference and half have a low liquidity preference.

6

Table 1 Regional Liquidity Shocks

	A	B	C	D
S_1	ω_H	ω_L	ω_H	ω_L
S_2	ω_L	ω_H	ω_L	ω_H

All uncertainty is resolved at date 1 when the state of nature S_1 or S_2 is revealed and each consumer learns whether he is an early or late consumer. A consumer's type is not observable, so late consumers can always imitate early consumers.

Before we introduce the banking sector into our story, it will be convenient to characterize the optimal allocation of risk.

III. Optimal Risk Sharing

In this section we characterize optimal risk sharing as the solution to a planning problem. Since consumers are ex ante identical, it is natural to treat consumers symmetrically. For this reason, the planner is assumed to make all the investment and consumption decisions to maximize the unweighted sum of consumers' expected utility.

We begin by describing the planner's problem under the assumption that the planner can identify early and late consumers. The symmetry and concavity of the objective function and the convexity of the constraints simplify the problem considerably. (1) Since there is no aggregate uncertainty, the optimal consumption allocation will be independent of the state. (2) Since the consumers in one region are ex ante identical to consumers in another region, all consumers will be treated alike. Without loss of generality, then, we can assume that every early consumer receives consumption c_1 and every late consumer receives c_2, independently of the region and state of nature. At the first date, the planner chooses a portfolio $(x, y) \geq 0$ subject to the feasibility constraint

$$x + y \leq 1, \tag{1}$$

where x and y are the per capita amounts invested in the long and short assets, respectively. (3) Since the total amount of consumption provided in each period is a constant, it is optimal to provide for consumption at date 1 by holding the short asset and to provide for consumption at date 2 by holding the long asset. Let the average fraction of early consumers be denoted by $\gamma = (\omega_H + \omega_L)/2$. Then the feasibility constraint at date 1 is

$$\gamma c_1 \leq y \tag{2}$$

and the feasibility constraint at date 2 is

$$(1-\gamma)c_2 \le Rx. \tag{3}$$

At date 0, each consumer has an equal probability of being an early or a late consumer, so the ex ante expected utility is

$$\gamma u(c_1) + (1-\gamma)u(c_2), \tag{4}$$

and this is what the planner seeks to maximize, subject to the constraints (1), (2), and (3). The unique solution to this unconstrained problem is called the *first-best allocation*.

The first-best allocation satisfies the first-order condition $u'(c_1) \ge u'(c_2)$. Otherwise, the objective function could be increased by using the short asset to shift some consumption from early to late consumers. Thus the first-best allocation automatically satisfies the *incentive constraint*

$$c_1 \le c_2, \tag{5}$$

which says that late consumers find it weakly optimal to reveal their true type rather than pretend to be early consumers. The *incentive-efficient allocation* maximizes the objective function (4) subject to the feasibility constraints (1), (2), and (3) and the incentive constraint (5). What we have shown is that the incentive-efficient allocation is the same as the first-best allocation.

PROPOSITION 1. The first-best allocation (x, y, c_1, c_2) is equivalent to the incentive-efficient allocation, so the first-best can be achieved even if the planner cannot observe the consumers' types.

In order to achieve the first-best, the planner has to transfer resources among the different regions. In state S_I for example, there are ω_H early consumers in regions A and C and ω_L early consumers in regions B and D. Each region has γc_1 units of the short asset, which provide γc_1 units of consumption. So regions A and C each have an excess demand for $(\omega_H - \gamma)c_1$ units of consumption and regions B and D each have an excess supply of $(\gamma - \omega_L)c_1 = (\omega_H - \gamma)c_2$ units of consumption. By reallocating this consumption, the planner can satisfy every region's needs. At date 2, the transfers flow in the opposite direction because regions B and D have an excess demand of $(\omega_H - \gamma)c_2$ units each and regions A and C have an excess supply of $(\omega_H - \gamma)c_2$ units each.

IV. Decentralization

In this section we describe how the first-best allocation can be decentralized by a competitive banking sector. There are two reasons for focusing on the first-best. One is technical: it turns out that it is much easier to characterize the equilibrium conditions when the allocation is the first-best. The second reason is that, as usual, we are interested in knowing under what conditions the market "works." For the moment, we are concerned only with the feasibility of decentralization. The optimality of the banks' behavior is discussed in Section IXA.

The role of banks is to make investments on behalf of consumers and to insure them against liquidity shocks. We assume that only banks invest in the long asset. This gives the bank two advantages over consumers. First, the banks can hold a portfolio consisting of both types of assets, which will typically be preferred to a portfolio consisting of the short asset alone. Second, by pooling the assets of a large number of consumers, the bank can offer insurance to consumers against their uncertain liquidity demands, giving the early consumers some of the benefits of the high-yielding long asset without subjecting them to the high costs of liquidating the long asset prematurely at the second date.

In each region there is a continuum of identical banks. We focus on a symmetric equilibrium in which all banks adopt the same behavior. Thus we can describe the decentralized allocation in terms of the behavior of a representative bank in each region.

Without loss of generality, we can assume that each consumer deposits his endowment of one unit of the consumption good in the representative bank in his region. The bank invests the deposit in a portfolio $(x^i, y^i) \geq 0$ and, in exchange, offers a deposit contract (c_1^i, c_2^i) that allows the depositor to withdraw either c_1^i units of consumption at date 1 or c_2^i units of consumption at date 2. Note that the deposit contract is not contingent on the liquidity shock in region i. In order to achieve the first-best through a decentralized banking sector, we need to put $(x^i, y^i) = (x, y)$ and $(c_1^i, c_2^i) = (c_1, c_2)$, where (x, y, c_1, c_2) is the first-best allocation.

The problem with this approach is that, while the investment portfolio satisfies the bank's budget constraint $x + y \leq 1$ at the first date, it will not satisfy the budget constraint at the second date. The planner can move consumption between regions, so he needs to satisfy only the average constraint $\gamma c_1 \leq y$. The representative bank, on the other hand, has to face the possibility that the fraction of early consumers in its region may be above average, $\omega_H > \gamma$, in which case it will need more than y to satisfy the demands of the early consumers. It can meet this excess demand by liquidating some of the long asset, but then it will not have enough consumption to meet the demands of the late consumers at date 2. In fact, if r is small enough, the bank may not be able to pay the late consumers even c_1. Then the late consumers will prefer to withdraw at date 1 and store the consumption good until date 2, thus causing a bank run.

There is no overall shortage of liquidity, it is just badly distributed. One way to allow the banks to overcome the maldistribution of the liquidity is to introduce an interbank market in deposits.

A. The Interbank Deposit Market

Suppose that banks are allowed to exchange deposits at the first date. This case of complete markets is illustrated in figure 1. Each region is negatively correlated

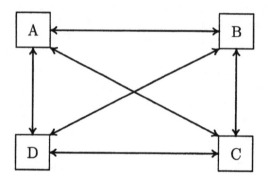

Figure 1 Complete market structure.

with two other regions. We therefore assume that every bank in region i holds $z^i = (\omega_H - \gamma)/2 > 0$ deposits in each of the regions $j \neq i$. Since bank deposits are identical and worth one unit each at the first date, the representative bank's budget constraint will still be satisfied at date 0. At the beginning of the second period the state of nature S is observed, and the banks have to adjust their portfolios to satisfy their budget constraints. If the region has a high demand for liquidity, $\omega^i = \omega_H$, it liquidates all its deposits in other regions. On the other hand, if it has a low demand for liquidity, $\omega^i = \omega_L$, it retains the deposits it holds in the other regions until the final date.

Consider the budget constraint of a bank in a region with a high demand for liquidity. It must pay c_1 to the fraction ω_H of early consumers in its own region and also redeem the $z^j = (\omega_H - \gamma)/2$ deposits of the other high-demand region. So the total demand for repayment is $\{\omega_H + [(\omega_H - \gamma)/2]\}_{c_1}$. On the other side of the ledger, it has y units of the short asset and claims to $3z^i = 3(\omega_H - \gamma)/2$ deposits in the other three regions. Thus the budget constraint that must be satisfied is

$$\left(\omega_H + \frac{\omega_H - \gamma}{2}\right) c_1 = y + \frac{3(\omega_H - \gamma)}{2},$$

which simplifies to the planner's constraint $\gamma c_1 = y$. A bank in a region with low liquidity demand must pay c_1 to a fraction ω_L of its own depositors and redeem $2z^i = \omega_H - \gamma$ deposits from the banks in the regions with high liquidity demand. It has y units of the short asset to meet these demands, so the budget constraint that must be satisfied is

$$\left[\omega_L + (\omega_H - \gamma)\right] c_1 = y.$$

Since $\omega_H - \gamma = \gamma - \omega_L$, this equation simplifies to the planner's constraint $\gamma c_1 = y$. In both cases, the cross holdings of deposits allow the banks to meet the demands of their depositors without liquidating the long asset.

At the last date, all the banks liquidate their remaining assets, and it is easy to show that if the budget constraints at the second date are satisfied, the budget constraints at the third date are automatically satisfied too. For example, the budget constraint at date 2 for a region that had high liquidity preference at date 1 will be

$$\left[(1-\omega_H)+(\omega_H-\gamma)\right]c_2 = Rx,$$

where the left-hand side is the demand for withdrawals, comprising the demand of the late consumers in the region $1-\omega_H$ plus the demand from the two regions with low liquidity preference, $2z^j = \omega_H - \gamma$. On the right-hand side, we have the liquidation value of the long asset Rx. This simplifies to the planner's constraint $(1-\gamma)c_2 = Rx$. The same is true of the budget constraint for the regions with a low liquidity shock:

$$\left[(1-\omega_i)+\frac{\omega_H-\gamma}{2}\right]c_2 = Rx + 3\left(\frac{\omega_H-\gamma}{2}\right)c_2.$$

Thus, by shuffling deposits among the different regions, banks are able to satisfy their budget constraints in each state S and at each date $t=0,1,2$ while providing their depositors with the first-best consumption allocation through a standard deposit contract.

B. Incompleteness in the Interbank Deposit Market

The interbank market in the preceding section is complete in the sense that a bank in region i can hold deposits in every other region $j \neq i$. In some cases, this may not be realistic. The banking sector is interconnected in a variety of ways, but transaction and information costs may prevent banks from acquiring claims on banks in remote regions. To the extent that banks specialize in particular areas of business or have closer connections with banks that operate in the same geographical or political unit, deposits may tend to be concentrated in "neighboring" banks. To capture this effect, which is crucial in the sequel, we introduce the notion of incompleteness in the interbank market by assuming that banks in region i are allowed to hold deposits in some but not all of the other regions. For concreteness we assume that banks in each region hold deposits only in one adjacent region, as shown in figure 2. It can be seen that banks in region A can hold deposits in region B, banks in region B can hold deposits in region C, and so on.

As before we suppose that the representative bank in region i holds an investment portfolio $(x^i, y^i) = (x, y)$ and offers a deposit contract $(c_1^i, c_2^i) = (c_1, c_2)$. We also assume that the bank holds $z^i = \omega_H - \gamma$ deposits in the adjacent region at the first date; that is, the bank in region A holds $\omega_H - \gamma$ deposits in region B, and so on. The first-period budget constraint is satisfied as before because the exchanges

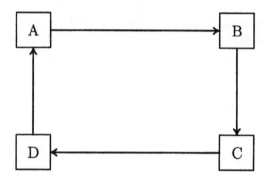

Figure 2 Incomplete market structure.

of deposits, having the same values, cancel out, leaving the budget constraint $x + y \leq 1$.

At date 1 the aggregate state is observed, and banks and consumers learn the liquidity shock in each region. As before, we need only to distinguish regions according to whether they have high or low demands for liquidity. Regions with the high liquidity shock ω_H liquidate their deposits in other banks at the second date whereas banks with the low liquidity shock ω_L do not. The market structure that is assumed here has the property that every region with a high liquidity shock has deposits in a region with a low liquidity shock, and vice versa. The budget constraint of a region with high liquidity shocks is

$$\omega_H c_1 = y + \left(\omega_H - \gamma\right)c_1,$$

and the budget constraint of a region with low liquidity shocks is

$$\left[\omega_L + \left(\omega_H - \gamma\right)\right]c_1 = y.$$

Substituting $\omega_H - \gamma = \gamma - \omega_L$ and simplifying, we see that both constraints are equivalent to the planner's constraint $\gamma c_1 = y$. Likewise, at the final date the budget constraints for the regions with high and low liquidity shocks are, respectively,

$$\left[\left(1 - \omega_H\right) + \left(\omega_H - \gamma\right)\right]c_2 = Rx$$

and

$$\left(1 - \omega_L\right)c_2 = Rx + \left(\omega_H - \gamma\right)c_2,$$

and both are equivalent to the planner's constraint $(1 - \gamma)c_2 = Rx$.

So even if the interbank deposit market is incomplete, it is possible to satisfy the budget constraints by shuffling deposits through the interbank market.

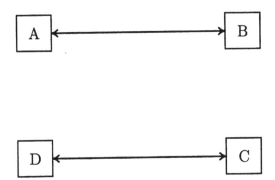

Figure 3 Disconnected incomplete market structure.

However, although it is possible to achieve the first-best with either complete or incomplete markets, we shall see that the implications for financial fragility are very different in the two cases.

One interesting feature of the market structure in figure 2 is that, although each region is relying on just its neighbor for liquidity, the entire economy is connected. Region A holds deposits in region *B*, which holds deposits in region *C*, and so on. In fact, this is unavoidable given the market structure assumed. Consider the alternative market structure shown in figure 3. Region A holds deposits in region B and region B holds deposits in region A. Likewise, region C holds one unit of deposits in region D and region D holds one unit of deposits in region C. This market structure is more incomplete than the one in figure 2, and the pattern of holdings in figure 2 is incompatible with it. However, it is possible to achieve the first-best through the pattern of holdings in figure 3. This is true even though the economy is disconnected, since regions A and B trade with each other but not with regions C and D and regions C and D trade with each other but not with regions A and B. Again, these patterns do not seem to have any significance as far as achieving the first-best is concerned; but they turn out to have striking differences for financial fragility.

V. Fragility

To illustrate the *financial fragility* of the optimal risk-sharing allocation, we use the decentralization results from Section IV. Then we perturb the model to allow for the occurrence of a state $\bar{S}$ in which the aggregate demand for liquidity is greater than the system's ability to supply liquidity and show that this can lead to an economywide crisis.

The market structure is assumed to be given by figure 2. The corresponding allocation requires each bank to hold an initial portfolio of investments (x,y) and offer a deposit contract (c_1, c_2), where (x, y, c_1, c_2) is the first-best allocation. In order to make this deposit contract feasible, the representative bank in each region holds $z = \omega_H - \gamma$ deposits in the adjacent region. Note that z is the minimal amount that is needed to satisfy the budget constraints. It will become apparent that larger cross holdings of deposits, while consistent with the first-best in Section IV, would make the contagion problem worse.

Now, let us take the allocation as given and consider what happens when we "perturb" the model. By a perturbation we mean the realization of a state $\bar{S}$ that was assigned zero probability at date 0 and has a demand for liquidity that is very close to that of the states that do occur with positive probability. Specifically, the liquidity shocks are given in table 2. In state $\bar{S}$, every region has the previous average demand for liquidity γ except for region A, where the demand for liquidity is somewhat higher at $\gamma = \epsilon$. The important fact is that the average demand for liquidity across all four regions is slightly higher than in the normal states S_1 and S_2. Since the abnormal state $\bar{S}$ occurs with zero probability, it will not change the allocation at date 0. In states S_1 and S_2 the continuation equilibrium will be the same as before at date 1; in state $\bar{S}$ the continuation equilibrium will be different.

In the continuation equilibrium beginning at date 1, consumers will optimally decide whether to withdraw their deposits at date 1 or date 2, and banks will liquidate their assets in an attempt to meet the demands of their depositors. Early consumers always withdraw at date 1; late consumers will withdraw at date 1 or date 2 depending on which gives them the larger amount of consumption. Because we want to focus on essential bank crises, we assume that late consumers will always withdraw their deposits at date 2 if it is (weakly) optimal for them to do so. Banks are required to meet their promise to pay c_1 units of consumption to each depositor who demands withdrawal at date 1. If they cannot do so, they must liquidate all their assets at date 1. As in Allen and Gale (1998), the proceeds of the liquidation are split pro rata among depositors (i.e., we do *not* assume first come, first served). If the bank can meet its obligations at date 1, then the remaining assets are liquidated at date 2 and given to the depositors who have waited until date 2 to withdraw. In the rest of this section, we describe the continuation equilibrium at date 1 in state $\bar{S}$, assuming the actions consistent with the first-best at date 0.

Table 2 Regional Liquidity Shocks with Perturbation

	A	B	C	D
S_1	ω_H	ω_L	ω_H	ω_L
S_2	ω_L	ω_H	ω_L	ω_H
$\bar{S}$	$\gamma + \epsilon$	γ	γ	γ

A. The Liquidation "Pecking Order"

At date 1 a bank can find itself in one of three conditions. A bank is said to be *solvent* if it can meet the demands of every depositor who wants to withdraw (including banks in other regions) by using only its liquid assets, that is, the short asset and the deposits in other regions. The bank is said to be *insolvent* if it can meet the demands of its deposits but only by liquidating some of the long asset. Finally, the bank is said to be *bankrupt* if it cannot meet the demands of its depositors by liquidating all its assets.

These definitions are motivated by the assumption that banks will always find it preferable to liquidate assets in a particular order at date 1. We call this the "pecking order" for liquidating assets, and it goes as follows: first, the bank liquidates the short asset, then it liquidates deposits, and finally it liquidates the long asset. To ensure that the long asset is liquidated last, we need an additional assumption,

$$\frac{R}{r} > \frac{c_2}{c_1}, \tag{6}$$

which is maintained in the sequel. Since the first-best consumption allocation (c_1, c_2) is independent of r (this variable does not appear in the first-best problem in Sec. III), we can always ensure that condition (6) is satisfied by choosing r sufficiently small.

Each of the three assets offers a different cost of obtaining current (date 1) consumption in terms of future (date 2) consumption. The cheapest is the short asset. One unit of the short asset is worth one unit of consumption today, and if reinvested in the short asset, it is worth one unit of consumption tomorrow. So the cost of obtaining liquidity by liquidating the short asset is one. Similarly, by liquidating one unit of deposits, the bank gives up c_2 units of future consumption and obtains c_1 units of present consumption. So the cost of obtaining liquidity by liquidating deposits is c_2/c_1. From the first-order condition $u'(c_1) = Ru'(c_2)$, we know that $c_2/c_1 > 1$. Finally, by liquidating one unit of the long asset, the bank gives up R units of future consumption and obtains r units of present consumption. So the cost of obtaining liquidity by liquidating the long asset is R/r. Thus we have derived the pecking order, short assets, deposits, long assets:

$$1 < \frac{c_2}{c_1} < \frac{R}{r}.$$

In order to maximize the interests of depositors, the bank must liquidate the short asset before it liquidates deposits in other regions before it liquidates the long asset.

The preceding argument assumes that the banks in other regions are not bankrupt. The bankruptcy rules require all assets to be liquidated immediately, so all deposit holders in a bankrupt institution will want to liquidate their deposits immediately regardless of their own condition.

B. Liquidation Values

The value of a deposit at date 1 is c_1 if the bank is not bankrupt, and it is equal to the liquidation value of all the bank's assets if the bank is bankrupt. Let q^i denote the value of the representative bank's deposits in region i at date 1. If $q^i < c_1$, then all the depositors will withdraw as much as they can at date 1. In particular, the banks in other regions will be seeking to withdraw their claims on the bank at the same time the bank is trying to redeem its claims on them. *All depositors must be treated equally*, that is, every depositor gets q^i from the bank for each unit invested at the first date, whether the depositor is a consumer or a bank from another region. Then the values of q^i must be determined simultaneously. Consider the representative bank in region A, for example. If all the depositors withdraw, the total demands will be $1+z$, since the banks in region D hold z deposits and the consumers in region A hold one deposit. The liabilities of the bank are valued at $(1+z)q^A$. The assets consist of y units of the short asset, x units of the long asset, and z deposits in region B. The assets are valued at $y + rx + zq^B$. The equilibrium values of q^A must equate the value of assets and liabilities:

$$q^A = \frac{y + rx + zq^B}{1+z}.$$

(7)

A similar equation must hold for any region i in which $q^i < c_1$.

If $q^B = c_1$, then we can use this equation to calculate the value of q^A; but if $q^B < c_1$ then we need another equation to determine q^B; this equation will include the value of q^C, and so on.

C. Buffers and Bank Runs

Suppose that a bank is insolvent and has to liquidate some of the long asset. For the moment, we assume that the late consumers wait until the last date, and we ignore the role of banks in other regions. How much can the bank afford to give the consumers at the first date? The bank must give the late consumers at least c_1 at date 2; otherwise they would be better off withdrawing at date 1. So a bank with a fraction ω of early consumers must keep at least $(1-\omega)c_1 / R$ units of the long asset to satisfy the late consumers at date 2. Then the amount of the long asset that can be liquidated at date 1 is $x - [(1-\omega)c_1 / R]$, and the amount of consumption that can be obtained by liquidating the long asset without causing a run is

$$b(\omega) \equiv r\left[x - \frac{(1-\omega)c_1}{R} \right].$$

We call $b(\omega)$ the bank's buffer.

In region A, the bank has $y = \gamma c_1$ units of the short asset. The fraction of early consumers is $\gamma + \epsilon$ in state $\bar{S}$, so in order to pay each early consumer c_1 units of consumption, the bank will have to get ϵc_1 units of consumption by liquidating the long asset. This is feasible, without any help from the banks in other regions, if and only if the increased demand for liquidity ϵc_1 is less than the buffer:

$$\epsilon c_1 \leq b(\gamma + \epsilon). \tag{8}$$

In most of what follows, we assume that condition (8) is violated. In other words, if region A had to remain self-sufficient, it would be bankrupt because there is no way it can feasibly offer its late consumers c_1 at date 2 (to prevent a run) and meet the demands of its early consumers for c_1 at date 1.

When $\epsilon > 0$ is small enough to satisfy the inequality (8), the banks in region A are insolvent, but there are no repercussions for the banks in other regions. The late consumers in region A are worse off because the premature liquidation of the long asset at date 1 prevents the bank from paying c_2 to depositors at date 2. (The pecking order implies that the banks in regions B, C, and D will liquidate their deposits in regions C, D, and A, respectively, rather than liquidate the long asset.)

When ϵ is large enough to violate condition (8), banks in region A will be bankrupt. Although they have deposits in region B, these deposits are of no use as long as the value of deposits in region A is $q^A = c_1$. Other regions will liquidate their deposits in order to avoid liquidating the long asset. As long as all the deposits have the same value, the mutual withdrawals simply cancel out. Once the banks in region A are bankrupt, there will be a spillover effect to region D. A deposit in region D is worth $q^D = c_1$ and a deposit in region A is worth $q^A < c_1$, so banks in region D suffer a loss when cross holdings of deposits are liquidated. If ϵ is not too large, this spillover effect will make region D banks insolvent but will not force them into bankruptcy.

Once bankruptcy has occurred in region A, all consumers are withdrawing at date 1 and the distinction between early and late consumers is immaterial. A further increase in ϵ will have no effect. The spillover effect to region D may be larger or smaller than region D's buffer. If the spillover is smaller than the buffer, the banks in region D will lose part of their buffer but the contagion will spread no further. If the spillover is larger than the buffer in region D, then region D banks will be bankrupt too.

The size of the spillover will depend on a number of parameters, especially the size of the liquidation value r. If r is small, then the loss of asset value in region A is large and the spillover effect is large. A small value of r also makes the buffer in each region smaller. Thus there are two ways in which a small liquidation value r makes it more likely that the spillover will exceed the buffer in region D.

The liquidation of region D's long assets will cause a loss to banks in region C, and this time the accumulated spillover effect is already large enough that region C too will be bankrupt. As we go from region to region the spillover gets larger and larger, because more regions are in bankruptcy and more losses have accumulated from liquidating the long asset. So once region D goes bankrupt, all the regions go bankrupt. This result is summarized in proposition 2 below.

As this informal discussion suggests, two conditions must be satisfied in order for the initial shock to region A to spread to all the other regions. First, the liquidity preference shock in region A must exceed the buffer in region A:

$$\epsilon c_1 > b(\gamma + \epsilon) \tag{9}$$

Second, the spillover effect to region D must exceed the buffer in region D. A lower bound for the spillover effect is $z(c_1 - \bar{q}^A)$, where z is the amount of deposits held and $\bar{q}^A$ is an upper bound on the value of the deposits in region A under bankruptcy. To derive the upper bound $\bar{q}^A$, we use equation (7) and assume that $q^B = c_1$:

$$q^A \le \bar{q}^A = \frac{y + rx + zc_1}{1 + z}. \tag{10}$$

Then a sufficient condition for the spillover to exceed the buffer in region D is

$$z(c_1 - \bar{q}^A) > b(\gamma). \tag{11}$$

The term zc_1 is the amount promised to the banks in region C, and $z\bar{q}^A$ is the upper bound on the value of deposits in region A. Hence the left-hand side of the condition is the difference between liabilities and the upper bound on assets in the interbank deposit market for region D. If this exceeds region D's buffer, the spillover will force region D banks into bankruptcy.

PROPOSITION 2. Consider the model with market structure described in figure 2 and perturb it by the addition of the zero probability state $\bar{S}$. Suppose that each bank chooses an investment portfolio (x, y, z) and offers a deposit contract (c_1, c_2), where (x, y) is the first-best investment portfolio, (c_1, c_2) is the first-best consumption allocation, and $z = \omega_H - \gamma$. Suppose that conditions (9) and (11) are satisfied. Then, in any continuation equilibrium, the banks in all regions must go bankrupt at date 1 in state $\bar{S}$.

Proof. The proof requires several steps.

Step 1.—We first suppose that there is a continuation equilibrium in which $q^i = c_1$ in every region i and show that this leads to a contradiction. The demand for deposits from early consumers is $\gamma + \epsilon$ in region A and γ in regions, C and D. The stock of the short asset is $y = \gamma c_1$, so there is an aggregate excess demand for liquidity that can be met only by liquidating the long asset in some region. To avoid liquidating the long asset, banks must redeem at least as many deposits as are withdrawn by banks from other regions. Since no bank wants to liquidate the long asset if it can be avoided, the only equilibrium is one in which all banks simultaneously withdraw their deposits in banks in other regions at date 1. These mutual withdrawals offset each other, so each region is forced to be self-sufficient; that is, no region is able to get extra liquidity from the other regions.

We have already seen that self-sufficiency implies that the banks in region A are bankrupt. Thus we have a contradiction that implies that the banks in some region must be bankrupt. In fact, the banks in region A must be bankrupt. By the earlier argument, $q^i < c_1$ for some i implies that all banks will withdraw their deposits in other regions. Then either $q^B = c_1$ and region A receives no net inflows from the interbank market or $q^B = c_1$ and the situation is even worse because region A loses money on its deposits in region B. In either case, $q^A = c_1$ is impossible because of condition (9).

Step 2.—Having established that banks in region A must be bankrupt, we next show that the financial crisis must extend to other regions. Consider region D first. For the reasons explained above, all banks will be liquidating their deposits in other regions in any continuation equilibrium in state $\bar{S}$. An upper bound on the liquidation value q^A of the deposits in region A is obtained by assuming that $q^B = c_1$, that is, $q^A \leq \bar{q}^A$. If banks in region D are not bankrupt, the liabilities of the banks in region D are $(\gamma + z)c_1$, because a fraction γ of consumers withdraw early, the banks in region C withdraw z deposits, and each deposit is worth c_1. The liquid assets of the bank are worth $y + zq^A$, and the buffer $b(\gamma)$ is the most that can be obtained from liquidating the long asset without violating the incentive constraint. So, to avoid bankruptcy, it must be the case that

$$\left(\gamma + z\right)c_1 \leq y + b\left(\gamma\right) + zq^A$$

$$\leq y + b\left(\gamma\right) + z\bar{q}^A.$$

Since $\gamma c_1 = y$, this inequality implies that $z(c_1 - \bar{q}^A) \leq b(\gamma)$, contradicting condition (11). Thus the banks in region D must be bankrupt also.

Step 3.—The argument from step 2 can be continued by induction. In fact, since we know that $\bar{q}^A < c_1$, we must have $q^D < \bar{q}^A$. Then it is easier to violate the nonbankruptcy condition in region C than it was in region D, and this shows that $q^C < \bar{q}^A$. Then using the same argument, we have $q^i < \bar{q}^A$ for every region i. All regions are in bankruptcy, and the only possible continuation equilibrium is one in which $q^i = y + rx < c_1$ for $i = $ A, B, C, D. Q.E.D.

VI. Robustness

The incompleteness of markets in figure 2 is essential to the contagion result in the following sense. There exist parameter values for which any equilibrium with incomplete markets involves runs in state $\bar{S}$ (this is the set of parameter values characterized in Sec. V). For the same parameter values, we can find an equilibrium with complete markets that does not involve runs in state $\bar{S}$.

To see this, we go back to the complete markets equilibrium in Section IV. The values of the investment portfolio (x, y) and the deposit contract (c_1, c_2) are the same; but to make the first-best allocation feasible at dates 1 and 2, the representative bank holds $z/2 = (\omega_H - \gamma)/2$ deposits in each of the other regions. The claim on any one region is smaller than in the equilibrium in Section V, but the total claim $3z/2$ is larger. Again, $z/2$ is the smallest amount of deposits consistent with feasibility.

Consider now what happens in a continuation equilibrium at date 1 when state $\bar{S}$ occurs, assuming that the actions at date 0 have not changed. We assume, of course, that the conditions of proposition 2 continue to hold. Using exactly the same argument as before, we can show that banks in region A are bankrupt: there is an aggregate excess demand for liquidity, the other regions will not provide liquidity, and because condition (8) is violated the banks in region A cannot meet their depositors' demands. The question is whether this requires that the other regions should also experience bankruptcy.

To address this question, we have to calculate the liquidation value of the deposits in region A. Assuming that none of the other regions is bankrupt, we observe that the assets are valued at $y + rx + 3(z/2)c_1$ and the liabilities are valued at $[1 + (3z/2)]q^A$, so

$$\bar{q}^{A*} = \frac{y + rx + 3(z/2)c_1}{1 + (3z/2)}. \tag{12}$$

The loss to each bank in regions $j \neq A$ because of the collapse of banks in region A is $(z/2)(c_1 - \bar{q}^{A*})$, and since the bank's holding of the short asset y is just enough to satisfy its own early consumers, the bank will be insolvent, but not bankrupt, if and only if this amount is less than or equal to the buffer:

$$\left(\frac{z}{2}\right)\left(c_1 - \bar{q}^{A*}\right) \leq b(\gamma). \tag{13}$$

Condition (13) can be satisfied even though conditions (8) and (11) are violated because the financial interdependence, measured by $z/2$, is smaller.

The special nature of the incompleteness of markets in figure 2 is discussed in the following section.

VII. Containment

The critical ingredient in the example of contagion analyzed in Section V is that any two regions are connected by a chain of overlapping bank liabilities. Banks in region A have claims on banks in region B, which in turn have claims on banks in region C, and so on. If we could cut this chain at some point, the contagion that begins with a small shock in region A would be contained in a subset of the set of regions.

Consider the incomplete market structure in figure 3 and the allocation that implements the first-best, which was described in Section IV. The allocation requires banks in regions A and B to have claims on each other and banks in regions C and D to have claims on each other, but there is no connection between the region {A, B} and the region {C, D}. If state $\bar{S}$. occurs, the excess demand for liquidity will cause bankruptcies in region A, and they may under certain conditions spread to region B; but there is no reason why they should spread any further. Banks in regions C and D are simply not connected to the troubled banks in regions A and B.

Comparing the three market structures we have considered so far—complete markets in figure 1, incomplete markets in figure 2, and the disconnected market structure in figure 3—we can see that there is a nonmonotonic relationship between completeness or incompleteness of markets and the extent of the financial crisis in state $\bar{S}$. With the complete markets structure of figure 1 the crisis is restricted to region A, with the market structure in figure 2 the crisis extends to all regions, and with the market structure in figure 3 the crisis is restricted to regions A and B.

It could be argued that the market structures are not monotonically ordered: the complete markets network does contain the other two, but the paths in the network in figure 3 are not a subset of the network in figure 2. This could be changed by adding paths to figure 2, but then the equilibrium of figure 3 would also be an equilibrium of figure 2. This raises an obvious but important point: that contagion depends on the *endogenous* pattern of financial claims. An incomplete market structure like the one in figure 2 may preclude a complete pattern of financial connectedness and thus encourage financial contagion; but a complete market structure does not imply the opposite: even with complete markets, there may be an endogenous choice of overlapping claims that causes contagion. In fact, the three equilibria considered so far are all consistent with the complete market structure. There are additional equilibria for the economy with the complete market structure. Like the three considered so far, they achieve the first-best in states S_1 and S_2 but have different degrees of financial fragility in the unexpected state $\bar{S}$, depending on the patterns of interregional deposit holding.

What is important about the market structure in figure 2, then, is that the pattern of interregional cross holdings of deposits that promotes the possibility of contagion is the only one consistent with this market structure. Since we are interested in contagion as an essential phenomenon, this market structure has a special role. The complete markets economy, by contrast, has equilibria with and without contagion and provides a weaker case for the likelihood of contagion.

VIII. Alternative Interbank Markets

In our analysis of contagion, interbank deposits play an important role. Without the interlinkages they provide, the financial crisis would not spread between regions. An important issue is whether there exist alternatives to interbank deposits that achieve risk sharing in states S_1 and S_2 but avoid contagion in state $\bar{S}$. In the context of banks' interactions with ordinary depositors in the retail market, it is well known from the work of Diamond and Dybvig (1983) and before that the combination of liquid liabilities (in the form of demand deposits) and illiquid assets is essential to the theory of bank runs. Runs can be prevented by making the amount paid out contingent on asset returns or by "suspending convertibility." The rationale for standard deposit contracts is not entirely clear, though some attempts have been made (see, e.g., Calomiris and Kahn 1991); but at least there is clear empirical evidence that deposit contracts are used. However, in the context of interbank markets, where deposit contracts are not as widely used, it is natural to ask whether there are feasible alternatives that would prevent runs.

Once we accept that consumers hold demand deposits, it is inevitable that banks in region A will come under pressure in state $\bar{S}$. What leads to contagion is the fact that (a) banks have an incentive to hoard liquidity when there is an excess demand for it and that (b) once bankruptcies have occurred in one or more regions, spillovers result from the ex ante claims that banks hold on each other. The crucial property of the claims traded on the interbank market is not that they are noncontingent. Rather, it is the fact that banks, by simultaneously liquidating their claims on each other, can effectively cancel them until at least one region goes bankrupt. Once banks in one region are bankrupt, the claims on that region have lower value and a spillover to its creditors follows.

Making the interbank claims contingent would not change the operation of the contagion. A similar result holds if the security traded on the interbank market is contingent on the state or on the level of demand for liquidity. As long as the holdings are symmetric across regions and the liquidation of cross holdings nets out to zero, so that region A has to find additional liquidity on its own, there will be contagion when the shock in region A is sufficiently large and the conditions of proposition 2 are satisfied.

This argument shows us that the use of demand deposits in the interbank market is not analogous to the use of demand deposits in the retail market. The two markets operate in very different ways. In the retail market, it is generally accepted that suspension of convertibility would prevent a bank run. The opposite is true in the interbank market. To illustrate this idea, suppose that interbank deposits are not payable on demand. Instead, banks can refuse payment at their own discretion. This kind of contract in the interbank market will support the first-best allocation (when the probability of $\bar{S}$ is zero), but it clearly will not prevent contagion in state $\bar{S}$. The reason is that banks will invoke their right to delay payment whenever they would otherwise have to liquidate the long asset. The option to delay payment is no different from using claims on other regions to cancel out the claims of those regions in the earlier analysis. The result in both cases is that banks in region A will have to satisfy the extra demand ϵ from ordinary depositors in state S from their own resources. This entails liquidating the long asset, and when their buffer is exhausted, it entails bankruptcy.

This argument shows that provided that there are ex ante contracts between banks that are signed at date 0, a contagion will occur even if contracts are not demand deposits. However, if liquidity was provided on an ex post basis, there would be no possibility of contagion. Suppose, for example, that instead of an interbank market for deposits at the first date, there is an interbank market for one-period loans at the second date. Then a bank that finds it has an excess demand for liquidity at date 1 has no preexisting claim on banks in other regions, but it can borrow from banks in regions with an excess supply of liquidity. In states like S_1 and S_2, this mechanism will be enough to achieve the first-best. If the lending rate is ρ, then the markets will clear if $1 + \rho = c_2/c_1$. In state $\bar{S}$, however, there will be an economywide shortage of liquidity. The fraction of early consumers is $\gamma + \epsilon$ in region A and γ in the other regions; but there is only enough of the short asset in the economy to provide for a fraction γ of early consumers. The only way in which more liquidity can be provided to the banks in region A is for the long asset to be liquidated. The other regions will be willing to do this only if the rate of interest on loans compensates for the cost of liquidation: $1 + \rho = R/r$. At this rate, the cost of borrowing is too high to be of any help to the banks in region A. It is just like liquidating more of the long asset, and we have already assumed that the bank is liquidating as much as it can, subject to the incentive constraint.

So the interbank loan market turns out to be of no use in state $\bar{S}$, where there is an economywide shortage of liquidity. It protects other regions from contagion but does nothing to stop the crisis in the affected region.

Although ex post markets allow banks to meet their liquidity needs at date 1, given the first-best choices at date 0, this arrangement is not an equilibrium. If banks expect to be able to borrow and lend at the rate ρ, they will not make the first-best choices at date 0. Thus, if the probability of contagion is very small, there will be a welfare loss associated with ex post markets. In richer models, ex post markets to provide liquidity will have problems associated with them. In particular, there can be a *lemons* problem if banks that have low asset values are more likely to use the ex post loan market than banks that have high asset values. Then it will be difficult for lenders to distinguish between banks that are in trouble because of poor loan performance and banks whose depositors have higher than average liquidity needs. The lemons problem may lead to extremely high interest rates on the ex post interbank market or even to a breakdown of the ex post interbank market. An alternative would be to negotiate a risk-sharing arrangement ex ante, when information is symmetric, and thus avoid the lemons problem altogether.

Another problem with ex post interbank markets arises when lenders have some *monopoly* power. Banks with excess liquidity can exploit banks with insufficient liquidity. Anticipating the possibility of a "holdup," banks will prefer to enter into an ex ante risk-sharing arrangement that fixes the price of liquidity at the risk of contagion.

We have argued that ex post markets can provide liquidity, without risk of contagion, when the uncertainty arises only from liquidity shocks. When

23

uncertainty arises from other sources, however, ex post markets may not be feasible. Consider, for example, the case in which the liquidity shock ω_i is non-stochastic but the return to the long asset in region i is a random variable R_i. If the returns are not perfectly correlated across regions, there will be gains from sharing risks, and this will lead banks to hold claims on each other. For appropriately specified contracts, the first-best can be achieved through an ex ante interbank market. Ex post, however, there will be no possibility of risk sharing once the values of the random variables $\{R_i\}$ are known. We chose not to examine this case formally here because of the complexity of the analysis and because the specification of the bankruptcy rules becomes somewhat arbitrary, but it is clear that ex post arrangements will not work in this case. The implications of asset risk are discussed further in Section IXD.

An interesting question is what kinds of arrangements banks will choose to set up, given the trade-off between the individual benefits of access to liquidity and the social costs of contagion. This is an important topic for further study.

IX. Discussion

A. Equilibrium

In the preceding sections we have discussed the continuation equilibrium at dates 1 and 2 but not said anything about the equilibrium behavior at date 0. It is clear that it is optimal for consumers at date 0 to deposit their endowment with the banks because they could not achieve the same level of expected utility in autarky, even if they were able to invest in both the short and the long assets. What is less obvious is whether the behavior of the banks is optimal in some sense.

The bank has to choose an investment portfolio, a deposit contract, and a position in the interbank deposit market to maximize the consumers' expected utility at date 0. The tricky part is choosing how much to trade on the interbank market. In order to finance deposits in other regions, it will have to sell its own deposits to other banks. But the value of its deposits will depend on the choice of the investment portfolio and the deposit contract and the withdrawal decisions made by depositors at the second and third dates. We can finesse the complex calculation of the banks' optimal behavior by noting that since all trade is voluntary, anything the bank does to make its own consumers better off cannot make anyone else worse off (since a single bank is negligible, the rest of the economy gets zero surplus from trading with it). Then the fact that the allocation at the second and third dates is first-best optimal implies that there is no deviation that the bank would prefer.

When the probability of a bank crisis is positive, things become much more complicated. The absence of aggregate uncertainty is necessary for the achievement of the first-best. When the probability of a crisis is positive, the first-best is no longer achieved at date 0, and as a result, markets for individual risk sharing are incomplete. As is well known, when markets are incomplete the valuation of assets may vary from individual to individual, there may be a lack of unanimity about the proper objective function for a bank, and the feasible actions for a bank are difficult to characterize.

However, although we have not extended the theory to the more general case, we do not believe that our results are dependent on the assumption that the probability of a crisis is exactly zero. As an illustration, consider the model described in Section V, but make it symmetric by assuming that each of the four regions has an equal probability of being the one with an excess demand for liquidity. The shocks are described in table 3, where each of the special states $S_A, \ldots, S_D$ occurs with probability $\delta > 0$ and states S_1 and S_2 occur with probabilities $\frac{1}{2} - 2\delta$. At date 0 each of the regions is ex ante identical.

Now suppose that risk sharing is to be achieved through a decentralized banking system of the kind described in Section V, but assume that all decisions at date 0 are made by a central planner. The planner will seek to maximize the ex ante expected utility of the representative agent at date 0. He can make any feasible decisions he likes at date 0, but he is constrained to work through the decentralized banking system at dates 1 and 2. In particular, he must use demand deposits to provide risk sharing for individuals and banks. Considerations of continuity imply that when δ is small, he must be able to get close to the first-best for the limiting economy with $\delta = 0$. If (c_1^δ, c_2^δ) is the optimal demand deposit and (x^δ, y^δ) is the optimal portfolio for $\delta > 0$, then $(c_1^\delta, c_2^\delta) \to (c_1, c_2)$ and $(x^\delta, y^\delta) \to (x, y)$ as $\delta \to 0$, where (c_1, c_2) is the optimal allocation and (x, y) the optimal portfolio from the planner's problem in Section III. This follows from continuity and the uniqueness of the planner's optimum. But then the arguments that we have used in Section V imply that in states $S_A, \ldots, S_D$ there must be contagion under the conditions given in Section V when δ is sufficiently small. So even if a planner were coordinating the choices made at date 0, there will still be contagion at date 1 in a decentralized banking system.

The reason for this can readily be seen. The way to prevent contagion is to hold a discrete amount more of the liquid asset to meet the extra liquidity demand in states $S_A, \ldots, S_D$. However, holding more of the liquid asset means that less of the illiquid asset is held and output is lower at date 2 in states S_1 and S_2. When δ is

Table 3 Regional Liquidity Shocks with Symmetric Perturbation

	A	B	C	D
S_1	ω_H	ω_L	ω_H	ω_L
S_2	ω_L	ω_H	ω_L	ω_H
S_A	$\gamma + \epsilon$	γ	γ	γ
S_B	γ	$\gamma + \epsilon$	γ	γ
S_C	γ	γ	$\gamma + \epsilon$	γ
S_D	γ	γ	γ	$+\epsilon$

25

sufficiently small, this trade-off is not worthwhile. It is better to simply allow the possibility of contagion.

The fact that the allocation at the second and third dates is constrained efficient rather than first-best efficient for $\delta > 0$ means that decentralized banks may not make even approximately the same choices as the planner at date 0. Such behavior would yield an ϵ-Nash equilibrium, but the action profile of an ϵ-Nash equilibrium does not have to be close in any sense to the action profile of a Nash equilibrium, however small ϵ becomes. Even though everyone would be better off if every bank made the same choices as a planner, they may all find it in their interests (in equilibrium) to behave in a very different way. It may even be true that this date 0 behavior is inconsistent with contagion at date 1; but although this is a theoretical possibility, we cannot think of any reason why it should occur and in fact are quite dubious that it would occur. This is an important topic for future research, but it lies outside the scope of this paper.

B. Many States and Regions

The arguments developed in this paper extend easily to the case of many regions and many states of nature. Suppose that there are n regions and suppose that the liquidity shocks ω^i are finite-valued and exchangeable. If the economywide fraction of early consumers is a constant, then the first-best allocation (x, y, c_1, c_2) is nonstochastic and independent of the consumer's region.

A market structure is characterized by a family of neighborhoods: for each region i the neighborhood N^i is the set of regions in which a bank in region i can hold deposits. The market structure is *connected* if for any regions i and j there is a finite chain of regions, beginning with i and ending with j such that, for each adjacent pair, banks in the first region can hold deposits in the second. As long as the market structure is connected and the maintained assumptions hold, the first-best can be decentralized by a competitive banking sector using standard deposit contracts.

A market structure is complete if banks in region i can hold deposits in every other region $j \neq i$; otherwise it is incomplete. The degree of completeness and connectedness is crucial for determining the inevitability of contagion. When markets are complete, increasing the number of regions eventually eliminates the necessity of contagion for any fixed set of parameter values. The reason is that the initial impact of a liquidity shortage in a single region becomes negligible as the number of regions becomes unboundedly large. In this sense, the banking system is robust against any shock to a single region when the economy is sufficiently large and markets are complete.

On the other hand, when markets are incomplete and the economy is large, small shocks can have extremely large effects. In the example of Section V, a liquidity shortage in one region can lead to crises in all four regions. The same argument works with any number of regions. In fact, as contagion "spreads" from one region to another, the spillovers become larger and it is easier to keep the contagion going. In the general case, contagion can spread from a single region to an arbitrarily large number n of regions.

In this sense, the results for the example of Section V are quite strong and are easily extended to large, complex economies.

C. Sunspot Equilibria

This paper focuses on financial contagion as an essential feature of equilibrium. We do not rely on arguments involving multiple equilibria. The aim is instead to show that under certain conditions every continuation equilibrium at date 1 exhibits financial contagion. Nonetheless, there are multiple equilibria in the model, and if one is so disposed one can use the multiplicity of equilibria to tell a story about financial contagion as a sunspot phenomenon.

To illustrate the multiplicity as simply as possible, suppose that markets are complete and the fraction of early consumers in each region is nonstochastic and equal to γ. There are no interregional cross holdings of deposits at date 0. If every consumer in every bank chooses to withdraw his deposit at date 1, regardless of the size of the liquidity shock, then the banks will all be bankrupt because $c_1 > y + rx$. This outcome is an equilibrium because it is optimal for each individual depositor to withdraw assuming that all other depositors withdraw. Of course, there also exists an equilibrium in which late consumers choose not to withdraw until date 2 and the bank's portfolio (x, y) allows the first-best to be achieved.

The low-probability event $\bar{S}$ is now a "sunspot." It represents extraneous uncertainty that does not change the demand for liquidity but simply triggers the self-fulfilling prophecy that a bank run will occur. The outcome in terms of the pattern of bank runs in state $\bar{S}$ is the same as in Section V. Whether one wants to call this a contagion is a matter of taste.

D. Risky Assets

For simplicity, we have assumed that the long asset has a nonstochastic return, but it would be more realistic to assume that the long asset is risky. In Allen and Gale (1998), the long asset is risky and bank runs are triggered by negative information about future asset returns. In the present framework, uncertainty about long asset returns could be used both to motivate interregional cross holdings of deposits and to provoke insolvency or bankruptcy. The results should be similar. What is crucial for the results is that the financial interconnectedness between the regions takes the form of claims held by banks in one region on banks in another region.

If, instead of holding claims on banks in other regions, banks were to invest directly in the long assets of that region, there would be a spillover effect, but it would be much weaker. To see this, suppose that banks in region A hold some of the long asset in region B. If asset returns are low in region B, then the depositors in region A must accept a reduction in consumption, but that is all. As long as the banks in region A are not bankrupt, they can afford to wait until date 2 to get the higher return $R>r$. Banks in region B, which hold a large proportion of their assets in region B, are forced to liquidate their assets at date 1 and therefore suffer a much greater loss because $r<R$.

On the other hand, if the banks in region A had invested in the banks in region B, then they would suffer a larger loss when the banks in region B liquidate their assets.

Another way in which banks can invest indirectly in risky assets is to lend to investors. If banks cannot observe the investment portfolio chosen by the investors, the investors will engage in risk shifting. Allen and Gale (2000) show that this kind of behavior can lead to bubbles in asset prices and increase the probability of a banking crisis (general default).

E. Alternative Market Structures

Figures 1–3 do not exhaust the possible range of market structures that could exist given the four regions A, B, C, and D. There are two more structures that are substantively different (we ignore the switching of identical regions, such as A for C or B for D). The first alternative is like figure 2, but with regions B and C interchanged. In this case, region A's and region B's deposits are made with positively correlated regions rather than with negatively correlated regions as in figure 2. This does not prevent the achievement of the first-best. However, the size of deposits banks must hold in the first-best allocation is doubled. Depending on the state and date, regions will be required to satisfy not only their own liquidity needs but that of the region next to them. In order to do this they must hold twice the deposits they did with figure 2's market structure, where they had to satisfy only their own region's shortfall. The higher the level of deposits, the higher the amount of the spillover and hence the more likely there is contagion.

The second remaining market structure is like that in figure 1 but without any deposits in positively correlated regions (i.e., there are no cross links between regions A and C or regions B and D). The first-best can again be achieved. The difference is that in state S the amount of spillover and hence contagion is different. The amount of A's deposits spread between other regions is smaller than in figure 1 but larger than in figure 2. As a result, the spillover is larger and the contagion more likely than in figure 1; the reverse is true compared to figure 2.

So far we have not mentioned the central bank. The analysis of contagion suggests that one way of thinking about the role of a central bank is to complete markets. In the market structure with a central bank, all banks have a link to it. By intervening appropriately, the central bank can ensure that the inefficient liquidation associated with contagion can be avoided.

Earlier versions of this paper were presented in seminars at Boston College, the Federal Reserve Bank of Minneapolis, the International Monetary Fund, Juan Carlos III University, the National Bureau of Economic Research Summer Institute Workshop on Macroeconomic Complementarities, New York University, Pompeu Fabra University, Queen's University in Kingston, and the University of Pittsburgh. We thank the participants for their helpful comments, especially Russell Cooper, Dean Corbae, Pat Kehoe, Garey Ramey, and Andres Velasco. We are particularly grateful to Lars Hansen (the editor) and an anonymous referee for their suggestions, which have significantly improved the paper. The financial support of the National Science Foundation, the C. V. Starr Center for Applied Economics at New York University, and the Wharton Financial Institutions Center is gratefully acknowledged.

References

Allen, Franklin, and Gale, Douglas. "Optimal Financial Crises." *J. Finance* 53 (August 1998): 1245–84.

———. "Bubbles and Crises." *Econ. J.* 110 (January 2000): 1–20.

Bernanke, Ben S. "Nonmonetary Effects of the Financial Crisis in Propagation of the Great Depression." *A.E.R.* 73 (June 1983): 257–76.

Bernanke, Ben S., and Gertler, Mark. "Agency Costs, Net Worth, and Business Fluctuations." *A.E.R.* 79 (March 1989): 14–31.

Calomiris, Charles W. "Financial Fragility: Issues and Policy Implications." *J. Financial Services Res.* 9 (December 1995): 241–57.

Calomiris, Charles W., and Kahn, Charles M. "The Role of Demandable Debt in Structuring Optimal Banking Arrangements." *A.E.R.* 81 (June 1991): 497–513.

Calvo, Guillermo. "Varieties of Capital Market Crises." Manuscript. College Park: Univ. Maryland, Center Internat. Econ., 1995.

Chang, Roberto, and Velasco, Andres. "Financial Fragility and the Exchange Rate Regime." Manuscript. New York: New York Univ., Dept. Econ., 1998.

Cole, Harold, and Kehoe, Timothy. "Self-Fulfilling Debt Crises." Manuscript. Minneapolis: Fed. Reserve Bank, Res. Dept., 1996.

Cooper, Russell, and Corbae, Dean. "Financial Fragility and the Great Depression." Manuscript. Cambridge, Mass.: NBER, 1997.

Diamond, Douglas W., and Dybvig, Philip H. "Bank Runs, Deposit Insurance, and Liquidity." *J.P.E.* 91 (June 1983): 401–19.

Friedman, Milton, and Schwartz, Anna Jacobson. *A Monetary History of the United States, 1867–1960.* Princeton, N.J.: Princeton Univ. Press (for NBER), 1963.

Gorton, Gary. "Banking Panics and Business Cycles." *Oxford Econ. Papers* 40 (December 1988): 751–81.

Hicks, John R. *A Market Theory of Money.* Oxford: Clarendon, 1989.

Kindleberger, Charles P. *Manias, Panics, and Crashes: A History of Financial Crises.* New York: Basic Books, 1978.

Kiyotaki, Nobuhiro, and Moore, John. "Credit Chains." Manuscript. London: London School Econ., Dept. Econ., 1998.

Lagunoff, Roger, and Schreft, Stacy. "A Model of Financial Fragility." Manuscript. Washington: Georgetown Univ., Dept. Econ., 1998.

Mitchell, Wesley Clair. *Business Cycles and Their Causes.* Berkeley: Univ. California Press, 1941.

Rochet, Jean-Charles, and Tirole, Jean. "Interbank Lending and Systemic Risk." *J. Money, Credit and Banking* 28, no. 4, pt. 2 (November 1996): 733–62.

Shleifer, Andrei, and Vishny, Robert W. "Liquidation Values and Debt Capacity: A Market Equilibrium Approach." *J. Finance* 47 (September 1992): 1343–66.

RISK AVERSION AND RISK PREMIA IN THE CDS MARKET[1]

Jeffery D. Amato

Source: *BIS Quarterly Review* Part 5, December, 2005, 55–68.

Credit default swap (CDS) spreads compensate investors for expected loss, but they also contain risk premia because of investors' aversion to default risk. We estimate CDS risk premia and default risk aversion to have been highly volatile during 2002–2005. Both measures appear to be related to fundamental macro-economic factors, such as the stance of monetary policy, and technical market factors, such as issuance of collateralised debt obligations.

One of the more difficult tasks in the analysis of financial markets is sorting out what portion of changes in asset prices are due to changes in economic factors affecting payoffs versus changes in risk premia. Credit markets are no exception. Was the large widening of credit spreads in the summer of 2002 the result of the rapid deterioration in the outlook or did investors suddenly become more risk-averse? Has the narrowing of corporate spreads to historically low levels since then been driven mainly by improving corporate balance sheets or a steady increase in risk appetite? And what of the spike in spreads in the spring of 2005 after downgrades in the US auto sector? The answers to these questions have implications for the signals policymakers take from credit markets, both during normal periods and in times of market stress. The answers should also interest academics for what they tell us about asset pricing models, as well as market participants searching for relative value opportunities across credit instruments and asset classes.

This article constructs measures of risk premia and risk aversion in credit markets using data from the fast growing credit default swap (CDS) market covering the period 2002–05. Spreads on default swaps should reflect expected losses from default and risk premia as compensation for bearing default risk. We find estimated premia to be highly volatile over time, consistent with the view of many market practitioners that changing attitudes towards risk can explain a good deal of the movements in asset prices. We also seek to identify the main determinants of risk premia in credit markets. Our findings suggest that default risk premia and risk aversion are strongly related to fundamental factors, such as indicators of real economic activity and the stance of monetary policy, and technical market factors, such as issuance of collateralised debt obligations (CDOs).

Our study begins by providing background on the CDS and CDS index markets that are the core of the empirical investigation. We then briefly discuss related literature and the data used in the analysis before turning to the construction of measures of CDS risk premia and default risk aversion. After analysing the determinants of these measures, we conclude with a summary and suggestions for future work.

The CDS market

Our study focuses on the CDS market, one of the fastest growing segments of the global financial system in recent years. A CDS is an insurance contract that protects the buyer against losses from a credit event associated with an underlying reference entity. In exchange for credit protection, the buyer of a default swap pays a regular premium to the seller of protection ("investor") for the duration of the contract.[2] Most of the initial development in the CDS market was in single-name contracts. However, since late 2003 there has also been increasing activity in contracts related to CDS indices, which are the main objects of our analysis. BIS statistics indicate that the total notional amount outstanding of single- and multi-name default swaps was $10.2 trillion as of June 2005.[3]

There are several reasons to focus on the CDS market instead of the cash market. One is that default swaps now play a central role in credit markets: a broad range of investors use default swaps to express credit views; banks use them for hedging purposes; and default swaps are a basic building block in synthetic credit structures. Another is that the relatively high liquidity in the default swap market means that CDS spreads are presumably a fairly clean measure of default and recovery risk compared to spreads on most corporate bonds. This facilitates the identification of credit risk premia.[4]

There are also benefits to be gained by focusing on CDS indices. Swap contracts and notes based on CDS indices are traded in the market, unlike in the case of corporate bonds, and so our results could be used directly to analyse market index spreads. Our findings may also be useful in studies of derivatives based on the indices, such as index tranches or default swaptions. Index tranches, which give investors the opportunity to take on exposures to specific segments of the CDS index default loss distribution, are priced and hedged partly based on the behaviour of index spreads.[5] Similarly, the valuation of options on the index depends upon the dynamics of index spreads.

Related literature

The results in this article add to a small but growing literature on the empirical properties of CDS spreads and the risk aversion of credit investors. The most closely related study is the paper by Berndt et al (2005), who estimate risk premia using CDS data on a set of 67 US firms in three industries and Moody's KMV's Expected Default Frequencies (EDFs™) as measures of default probabilities. They identify default risk premia by estimating fully specified dynamic credit risk models for each entity. We adopt a simpler approach to measuring risk premia, though we consider a broader set of firms – the constituents in the main US investment grade CDS index – and we analyse the relationships of these measures with macroeconomic and credit market activity variables.

Given the relatively short life of the CDS market, most research on spreads has been conducted using bond data. Elton et al (2001) examine how much of the variation over time in spreads (less expected loss and taxes) can be explained by the Fama-French factors, and then calculate a risk premium based on these contributions. Driessen (2005) estimates a dynamic term structure model by dividing spreads into several components. He finds evidence of large and time-varying default risk premia, as well as liquidity premia. Amato and Luisi (2005) estimate risk premia in a model that includes macroeconomic variables as determinants of the term structure of corporate bond spreads.

Data

Given our methodology for estimating risk premia (see next section), we require data on CDS index spreads and default probabilities on the index constituents. We construct a historical synthetic time series of spreads for a fixed set of firms using data from Markit. This is done for two reasons. First, we focus on a fixed group of firms to achieve consistency in the series across time. The composition of the leading market indices has changed over time due to mergers and rolls in the indices every six months.[6] Second, we wish to analyse data over the longest period possible. Daily time series can be constructed for most of the firms in our sample beginning in May 2002. Since index contracts started trading in mid-2003, we could, in principle, use market quotes at the index level; but this would leave us with a short sample and a non-homogeneous set of firms due to changes in the "on-the-run" index.

The group of firms we consider are the members of the DJ CDX North America investment grade series 4 index (CDX.NA.IG.4).[7] Contracts on this version of the index were on-the-run from 21 March to 20 September 2005. There are 125 entities in the index; most have a credit rating in the range A+/A1 to BBB–/Baa3. We are mainly interested in the aggregate index, though we also analyse five sectors to determine to what extent sector patterns match up to aggregate behaviour. The sectors considered are: consumer, energy, financial, industrial and TMT. Synthetic series of index and sector spreads are constructed as equal-weighted averages of spreads on single-name contracts.

The synthetic series we construct may differ from market quotes on the index for at least two reasons.[8] First, while in principle the mark to market index spread should equal the average of spreads on the 125 reference entities, in practice there have been discrepancies (a non-zero "basis"). This is probably due, in part, to the convenience of using index contracts for hedging macroeconomic risk. As such, caution should be exercised when interpreting our results directly in the context of market index spreads. Second, index contracts restrict the eligible types of credit event to bankruptcy or failure to pay. This corresponds to the no-restructuring documentation clause in single-name CDS contracts.[9] However, most single-name contracts in the United States are traded with a modified restructuring clause. To maximise the sample size, for each day and each firm we construct a weighted average, expressed on a no-restructuring basis, of the quotes available across clauses in the Markit database. It is probable that the value of the cheapest-to-deliver option on contracts allowing restructuring varies systematically with the credit cycle. Any such variation would introduce an error in our (fixed) weighting scheme, but it is likely to be small.[10]

Daily time series of CDS spreads for the aggregate index at maturities of one, five and 10 years are plotted in Graph 1. A few features of the series are worth noting. First, the term structure of spreads is upward sloping at lower spread levels; in particular, there have been large differences over the past couple of years between one-year and five-year CDS rates. This means that care must be taken in choosing the maturity in our subsequent analysis. Second, spreads are highly persistent and much of their variation occurs over lower frequencies, such as a month or more. Thus, even though we must aggregate CDS rates on a monthly basis for most of our analysis (to accord with the availability of other data series), there is a good deal of variation in spreads at this frequency.

To proxy for default probabilities, we use one-year EDFs™ as in the study by Berndt et al (2005). EDFs™ are constructed using balance sheet and equity price data under the principles of a Merton-type model for gauging the likelihood of

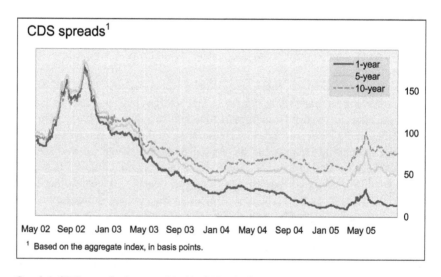

Graph 1 CDS spreads. Sources: Markit; BIS calculations.

default.[11] Our data on EDFs™ are available at a monthly frequency for all but two firms in the CDX.NA.IG.4 index. Aggregate and sector EDFs™ are constructed as simple arithmetic averages of existing data on the constituents.

Measuring default risk premia

In this section, we provide estimates of CDS risk premia and default risk aversion using the synthetic CDS index data introduced above.

In order to see how we obtain measures of risk premia and risk aversion, note that CDS spreads can be roughly decomposed as follows:

$$\text{CDS spread} \cong \text{expected loss} + \text{risk premium}$$

$$= \text{expected loss} \times \text{risk adjustment}$$

where

$$\text{risk adjustment} = 1 + \text{price of default risk}$$

The first equation above says that the CDS spread is approximately equal to expected loss plus a risk premium, where the latter is compensation paid to investors for enduring exposure to default risk. In the second equation, the spread is re-expressed in terms of risk-adjusted expected loss, where the risk adjustment varies proportionally with the price of default risk. The price of default risk has the interpretation as the compensation per unit of expected loss. It is an indicator of investors' aversion to default risk: a positive price of risk means that investors demand that they be paid more than actuarial losses. Hereafter, we will use the terms "price of default risk" and "indicator of default risk aversion" interchangeably.

While the formulations of spreads above isolate a "risk premium" and a "price of risk", in principle there are two distinct types of default risk that may command a premium. One is cyclical variation in expected loss, which usually rises during economic downturns, when overall income growth is low. The other is the actual default of an entity and its impact on investors' wealth due to an inability to perfectly diversify credit portfolios. In the literature, these are generally referred to as systematic and jump-at-default risk, respectively.[12] In the following, we will construct measures of CDS risk premia and the price of default risk that implicitly incorporate both of these types of risk.[13] See the box for a more precise description of CDS pricing and the components of spreads.

Our method for estimating risk premia and risk aversion is straightforward. First, we construct a measure of the risk premium by subtracting an estimate of expected loss from CDS spreads. Expected loss is estimated using observable EDF™ data as a proxy for the probability of default and assuming that loss-given-default is constant and equal to 60%. This figure is based on historical loss rates

35

on US senior unsecured bonds using data from Moody's.[14] Since our EDF™ data attempt to measure default probabilities over a one-year horizon, we mainly concentrate on the risk premium in one-year CDS rates. Second, the price of default risk is estimated as the ratio of CDS spread to expected loss.

Table 1 reports summary statistics on monthly time series of the main variables of interest for the aggregate index.[15] As shown in the table, CDS rates are higher than EDFs™ on average and more volatile; they are also more skewed. The one-year risk premium is positive on average, and its distribution (over time) is positively skewed and has fat tails. The average one-year price of default risk is 1.42. Under the assumption that loss-given-default is constant, this means that risk-adjusted default probabilities have been roughly 140% higher than actual default probabilities. The price of default risk also varies significantly, reaching a minimum of 0.31 and a maximum of 2.92.

Graph 2 shows the time variation in the variables. The left-hand panel plots time series of CDS spreads with a one-year maturity against EDFs™, and the right-hand panel shows estimates of the risk premium and price of default risk. The graph illustrates four key features of the series. First, it is evident that the largest changes in CDS spreads occurred in 2002.[16] This is true both on the upside, when one-year CDS rates widened by over 10 basis points in each of three weeks in July of that year, and on the downside, when spreads sharply narrowed in November. It was in July 2002 that WorldCom filed for bankruptcy with assets of $107 billion, and this appears to have had a market-wide contagion effect on CDS spreads. Default probabilities on the aggregate index also rose during this period, but by much less, indicating that WorldCom's default mainly affected market risk premia. Second, starting in early 2003, both spreads and expected default frequencies declined and have since remained relatively stable, with spreads widening only briefly in the spring of 2005 around the events related to General Motors and Ford. Third, risk premia have largely followed the same path as spreads. Fourth, the price of default risk has experienced more ups and downs than risk premia,

Table 1 Summary statistics[1]

	One-year CDS	Five-year CDS	EDF™	Risk premium[2]	Price of default risk[2]
Mean	55.33	75.07	35.40	34.09	1.42
Median	33.82	56.20	22.84	21.11	1.30
Standard deviation	44.62	37.01	22.88	31.95	0.66
Skewness	1.00	1.21	0.70	1.24	0.26
Kurtosis	2.81	3.35	2.01	3.57	2.51
Minimum	11.15	37.31	9.09	2.64	0.31
Maximum	167.81	175.70	81.43	121.95	2.92

[1] Based on the aggregate index, in basis points (except price of default risk).
[2] Based on a one-year horizon.
Sources: Markit; Moody's KMV; BIS calculations.

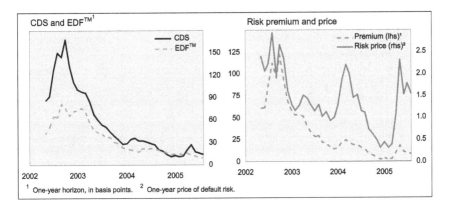

Graph 2 CDS risk premium and price of default risk. Sources: Markit; Moody's KMV; BIS calculations.

reaching its maximum value in mid-2002, but also rising to high levels in early 2004 when the slope of the Treasury curve steepened significantly, and again in May 2005 during the turbulence surrounding the auto sector downgrades.

THE COMPONENTS OF CDS SPREADS

This box illustrates how to obtain the (approximate) decomposition of CDS spreads used in this article as a basis for constructing measures of risk premia and the price of default risk. For concreteness, we model credit events ("default") using an intensity-based framework.[17] This model assumes that defaults occur randomly, where the probability of default over a short time interval (eg a day or a month) is equal to the intensity, denoted by h^P. In principle, h^P may be a stochastic variable that varies in accordance with macroeconomic, sector-specific or firm-specific conditions. Other key inputs to the model include: loss-given-default (L); risk-free interest rates for discounting cash flows (r); and the prices of systematic risk and jump-at-default risk (Γ). Each of these elements may also vary with economic conditions.

In general, the risk-adjusted intensity (denoted h^Q) that is relevant for pricing CDS contracts will differ from the actual intensity h^P. This adjustment depends upon the price of jump-at-default risk, namely $h^Q = h^P(1+\Gamma)$. If investors do not demand a premium for jump-at-default risk, then risk-adjusted and actual intensities are equal; otherwise, we would generally expect that $\Gamma > 0$, so that $h^Q > h^P$.

The spread on a CDS contract is obtained by solving for the quarterly premium that equates the expected present value of payments made by the protection buyer ("premium leg") to the expected present value of default costs to be borne by the protection seller ("protection leg"). CDS contracts specify M quarterly payment dates, $t = t_1, t_2, \ldots, t_M$, on which the premium is to be paid.[18] At origination of a contract at time t, the expected present value of the premium leg is equal to the expected sum of discounted premium payments, where the *effective* discount rate, $r+h$, is the risk-free rate adjusted for the possibility of default:

$$V_{prem}(t) = E_t^Q \left[\sum_{i=1}^{M} \exp\left(-\int_t^{t_i} \left[r(s) + h^Q(s) \right] ds \right) \cdot CDS(t) \right]$$

$CDS(t)$ is the quarterly premium and $E_t^Q(\cdot)$ denotes expectations adjusted for systematic risk.

The expected present value of the protection leg is the discounted value of the expected loss at possible default dates:[19]

$$V_{prot}(t) = E_t^Q \left[\sum_{i=1}^{M} h^Q(t_i) \cdot L(t_i) \cdot \exp\left(-\int_t^{t_i} \left[r(s) + h^Q(s) \right] ds \right) \right]$$

The premium is found by setting $V_{prem} = V_{prot}$ and solving for $CDS(t)$:

$$CDS(t) = \frac{\sum_{i=1}^{M} E_t^Q \left[h^Q(t_r) \cdot L(t_i) \cdot \exp\left(-\int_t^{t_i} \left[r(s) + h^Q(s) \right] ds \right) \right]}{\sum_{i=1}^{M} E_t^Q \left[\exp\left(-\int_t^{t_i} \left[r(s) + h^Q(s) \right] ds \right) \right]}$$

The above equation implies that CDS spreads are weighted averages of risk-adjusted expected losses, $E_t^Q(h^Q L)$; in other words, $CDS(t) \cong E_t^Q(h^Q L)$.

There are potentially two differences between $E_t^Q(h^Q L)$ and actual expected loss, $E_t^P(h^P L)$, where $E_t(\cdot)$ denotes expectations based on actual real-world probabilities. First, as noted above, h^Q may differ from h^P if investors demand compensation for jump-at-default risk ($\Gamma > 0$). Second, expectations of $h^Q L$ are evaluated using probabilities adjusted to take account of investors' aversion to systematic risk. This implies that CDS spreads are approximately equal to the sum of actual expected loss ($h^P L$), a jump-at-default risk premium ($h^P L \Gamma$) and a systematic risk premium.

Turning to data at the sector level, Graph 3 plots one-year CDS rates and EDFs™ against the implied estimates of the price of default risk for two sectors.[20] Trend movements in both CDS spreads and EDFs™ are similar across sectors, and hence with the aggregate index. Nonetheless, the implied level and volatility of the price of default risk have varied significantly across these two sectors. For example, the level averaged 2.18 for industrial firms but only 0.62 for financial

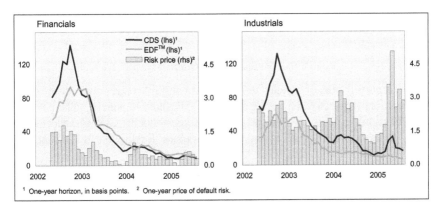

Graph 3 Selected CDS index sectors. Sources: Markit; Moody's KMV; BIS calculations.

firms. Moreover, it rose precipitously on industrial firms in April-May 2005, whereas it hardly changed on financial firms during this tumultuous period.[21]

What drives CDS risk premia?

Which variables are the main drivers of movements in CDS risk premia and our indicators of default risk aversion? Earlier we identified a few key episodes when these measures were at elevated levels. In this section, we use regression analysis to estimate possible relationships with macroeconomic and credit market activity variables. Due to space considerations, we focus solely on the aggregate index.[22]

Choice of variables

To the extent that the state of the macroeconomy affects the risk preferences of investors in the CDS market, we would expect to find statistically significant relationships between macroeconomic variables and CDS risk premia measures.[23] In our analysis we consider several series, including measures of inflation, real economic activity, consumer confidence, risk-free interest rates and the stance of monetary policy.

We also include measures of credit market activity in the regressions. The high-yield default rate is used as a monthly indicator for a host of other fundamental variables that would be expected to affect default risk premia. In addition, we consider the impact of straight bond and note issuance by US non-financial corporations, and global funded and unfunded issuance of synthetic CDOs. This latter variable is especially relevant for the CDS market, as CDO arrangers typically hedge deals by selling protection on single-name or index default swap contracts. There has been considerable speculation among market participants that this type of activity, known as the "structured credit bid", has had a dampening effect on CDS spreads over the past two years.

Regression results

Table 2 reports results of selected univariate and multiple regressions for the CDS risk premium (top panel) and price of default risk (bottom panel).[24] The univariate regressions (columns 1–5 in each panel) indicate that the CDS measures have strong links to macroeconomic and credit variables. First, it is evident that real

Table 2 Regressions of CDS risk premium and price of default risk[1]

Dependent variable: Risk premium

Variable[2]	1	2	3	4	5	6	7
HS	-0.140*					-0.096*	-0.102*
	(0.023)					(0.030)	(0.029)
NP		-0.120*				-0.015	-0.019
		(0.036)				(0.035)	(0.034)
RG			0.276*			0.162*	0.155*
			(0.071)			(0.059)	(0.059)
DEF				0.629*		0.184	
				(0.198)		(0.168)	
CDO					-0.911*		-0.355
					(0.439)		(0.312)
R-squared	0.51	0.24	0.30	0.22	0.11	0.62	0.62

Dependent variable: Price of default risk

Variable[2]	1	2	3	4	5	6	7
HS	-0.002*					-0.002*	-0.002*
	(0.001)					(0.001)	(0.001)
NP		-0.001				0.001	0.001
		(0.001)				(0.001)	(0.001)
RG			0.006*			0.004*	0.004*
			(0.001)			(0.001)	(0.001)
DEF				0.009*		0.004	
				(0.004)		(0.004)	
CDO					-0.025*		-0.018*
					(0.009)		(0.007)
R-squared	0.24	0.04	0.32	0.11	0.20	0.44	0.51

[1] Based on aggregate index measures at one-year horizon, in basis points. * indicates significance at 5% level. Standard errors are in parentheses. [2] HS: housing starts (in thousands); NP: non-farm payrolls (change, in thousands); RG: real policy rate gap (in basis points); DEF: high-yield default rate (in basis points); CDO: global funded and unfunded synthetic CDO issuance (in billions of US dollars). RG is defined as the real federal funds rate less the natural rate of interest, where the real rate is the nominal rate adjusted for four-quarter consumer price inflation and the natural rate is defined as the average real rate (1985–2003) plus four-quarter growth in potential output less its long-term average. Monthly values are linearly interpolated from quarterly averages. See BIS (2004, Chapter IV).
Sources: Bloomberg; JPMorgan Chase; Markit; Moody's; Moody's KMV; BIS calculations.

activity, as captured by housing starts or the change in non-farm payrolls, has a negative and statistically significant relationship with the risk premium and, to a lesser extent, the indicator of default risk aversion. This is consistent with results in Amato and Luisi (2005), who find that real activity has a large impact on risk premia in corporate bonds over a longer sample period.

Second, there is a strong relationship between the real interest rate gap and default risk aversion, as illustrated in Graph 4 (left-hand panel). The real interest rate gap is an indicator of economy-wide demand conditions, but even more directly it is a measure of the stance of monetary policy. The real rate gap is constructed as the difference between estimates of the real federal funds rate and the natural rate of interest, where the latter is a proxy for the equilibrium real interest rate consistent with stable consumer price inflation (see Table 2 footnotes for more details). During the period under review, monetary policy was highly accommodative by this measure, and our results suggest that default risk aversion declined as the real federal funds rate fell further below the natural rate. As an inverse indicator of aggregate output, it is perhaps not surprising that the real rate gap varies positively with the price of default risk, since aversion to risk tends to decline during good times. Alternatively, the regression evidence is consistent with easy monetary policy having facilitated greater risk-taking, as investors took more highly leveraged positions that could be financed (relatively) cheaply.[25]

To be sure, a word of caution is in order when interpreting these results. The estimates imply that when the real rate gap was below its *sample* mean, risk appetite was abnormally high. Yet the real interest rate gap was *negative* during our entire sample period. By contrast, from a longer-term perspective, default risk aversion was relatively high in mid-2002 and again in May 2005. Thus, whether

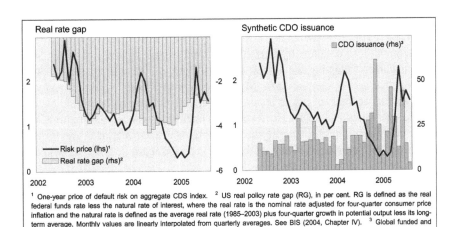

[1] One-year price of default risk on aggregate CDS index. [2] US real policy rate gap (RG), in per cent. RG is defined as the real federal funds rate less the natural rate of interest, where the real rate is the nominal rate adjusted for four-quarter consumer price inflation and the natural rate is defined as the average real rate (1985–2003) plus four-quarter growth in potential output less its long-term average. Monthly values are linearly interpolated from quarterly averages. See BIS (2004, Chapter IV). [3] Global funded and unfunded synthetic CDO issuance, in billions of US dollars.

Graph 4 Macro liquidity, CDO issuance and default risk aversion. Sources: JPMorgan Chase; Markit; Moody's KMV; BIS calculations.

or not the estimated relationships with the real rate gap hold over a full business cycle has not yet been tested and is open to debate.

A third striking result is that months of relatively high synthetic CDO issuance coincide with a lower price of default risk (Graph 4, right-hand panel). This suggests that greater demand to sell protection in the single-name CDS market due to increased CDO issuance has a negative impact on measured risk aversion. However, these results might also be influenced by reverse causation; namely, that greater appetite for risk might lead to increased demand for, and hence greater issuance of, exotic credit products such as synthetic CDOs.

The statistical significance of default rates and synthetic CDO issuance in the univariate regressions may reflect correlations of these series with more fundamental macroeconomic variables. To control for this possibility, in Table 2 we also report results from multiple regressions that include the macroeconomic variables along with the default rate or CDO issuance. These regressions have much higher explanatory power as indicated by higher R^2 statistics. In the case of the risk premium, housing starts and the real interest rate gap appear to be the most significant variables, while the coefficients on the high-yield default rate and CDO issuance are no longer significant. By contrast, CDO issuance remains statistically significant in the equation for the price of default risk, though its marginal impact is somewhat weaker when variables proxying for the state of the economy are included. This is further evidence that the degree of activity in the structured credit market – the so-called "structured credit bid" – may have lowered the effective degree of risk aversion in recent years.

Summary and future work

This article has provided estimates of CDS risk premia and default risk aversion over the period 2002–05. Both measures have been very volatile, implying that investor risk aversion changes frequently. Our measures are similar to and complement those obtained by Berndt et al (2005). Large spikes in the estimated series occurred following the default of WorldCom in 2002 and the turmoil surrounding the auto sector in April–May 2005. Furthermore, regression analysis indicates that changes in risk aversion are related to both macroeconomic factors and technical market factors. However, our conclusions should be qualified. We have made several strong simplifying assumptions to construct measures of risk premia and risk aversion. Moreover, the sample period spans just over three years, which does not cover a full credit cycle.

There are several avenues to explore in future research. First, a more careful analysis would require building a model along the lines of Berndt et al (2005). Estimates obtained in this way would need to be tested for robustness to model specification. Recent work by Pan and Singleton (2005) on sovereign CDS spreads, for instance, indicates that estimates of risk aversion can be sensitive to the form of the model. Second, it would be desirable to relate measures of risk aversion and risk premia estimated using CDS data to those obtained from other credit instruments or asset classes, such as equities and government bonds. This would help further our understanding of the extent to which prices on assets in different markets are driven by common forces.

Notes

1 The author thanks JPMorgan Chase for providing data on synthetic CDO issuance, Claudio Borio, Frank Packer and Philip Wooldridge for helpful comments, and Jhuvesh Sobrun for research assistance. The views expressed in this article are those of the author and do not necessarily reflect those of the BIS.

2 Several sources contain descriptions of CDS contracts and their features (eg O'Kane, Naldi et al (2003)). Most contracts cover four types of credit event: bankruptcy, failure to pay, repudiation and material restructuring of debt (including acceleration). Hereafter, the term default will be synonymous with credit event.

3 While the net value of exposures is much smaller ($267 billion as of June 2005), trading volumes are estimated to be significantly greater than in the underlying bond markets.

4 CDS contracts may be more liquid than bonds for several reasons. For instance, most default swaps benefit from having standardised contracts, where the credit events that trigger payment to the protection buyer are defined in the ISDA credit derivatives definitions (ISDA (2003)). Default swaps also allow market participants to short credit risk with less difficulty and at lower cost than with corporate bonds. See Longstaff et al (2005) for further discussion.

5 See Amato and Gyntelberg (2005) for a general discussion of CDS indices and index tranches, and of some of the issues involved in pricing these instruments.

6 The index market began with a set of competing indices, which then merged in the spring of 2004 to form the CDX and iTraxx families. The constituents in these indices are chosen every six months based on a dealer poll.

7 The constituents of this index can be found on Markit's website at http://www.markit .com.

8 We can compare our synthetic series to official index spreads from Markit. For the difference in daily five-year spreads over the period 21 March to 31 August 2005, the mean is 0.6 basis points, the mean absolute value is 1.9 basis points and the standard deviation is 2.6 basis points.

9 See ISDA (2003) for a description of documentation clauses.

10 The weights reflect observed patterns in spreads across clauses in a sample where quotes for more than one type of contract exist for an entity on a given day. See also O'Kane, Pedersen and Turnbull (2003) and Packer and Zhu (2005) for analysis of restructuring clauses.

11 See Kealhofer (2003) for further details.

12 This terminology is somewhat misleading, for the inability to perfectly diversify against single-name defaults is a "systematic" risk as well.

13 Our formulation of the price of default risk is also non-standard. More specifically, in the literature, the price(s) of systematic risk is (are) typically identified as the compensation per unit of *volatility* of the risk factor(s); the price of jump-at-default risk is the compensation per unit of expected loss.

14 Thus, we do not allow loss rates to vary systematically across the credit cycle. A growing body of evidence suggests that loss rates covary positively with default probabilities (eg Altman et al (2004)); however, the strength of the relationship depends on whether losses are measured by market prices shortly after default or by ultimate recovery rates.

15 Monthly CDS spreads are constructed as averages of daily values.
16 This is also evident at a higher frequency in Graph 1. For instance, nine of the 10 largest weekly changes in one-year CDS rates (in absolute value, measured on a Friday-to-Friday basis) occurred in 2002.
17 Previous studies of CDS spreads using intensity models include Berndt et al (2005), Longstaff et al (2005) and Pan and Singleton (2005).
18 Payment is made only as long as the reference entity has not already defaulted.
19 For simplicity, this assumes that default can only occur on premium payment dates. In practice, when default occurs between premium payment dates, sellers of protection receive an accrual payment.
20 The other sectors are not shown to conserve space. Broadly put, the trends in CDS spreads and estimates of default risk aversion are similar across sectors. The estimated level of default risk aversion in the consumer sector is similar to industrials, whereas it has been much lower in the TMT sector since the beginning of 2003.
21 Amato and Remolona (2005) find that the price of default risk is higher for firms with higher credit ratings. In the CDX index, however, financial firms have higher ratings on average than those in other sectors. This suggests that a different explanation, other than credit quality, is needed to explain sector differences in our estimates. Further examination of sector differences is a subject for future research.
22 Regressions were also computed for each of the sectors and the estimates are broadly similar to those for the aggregate index. These and other unreported results discussed below are available from the author upon request.
23 Similarly, measures of economic activity should account for systematic movements in the probability of default (EDFs™ in our study). Indeed, in results not reported, we find that EDFs™ have a negative and statistically significant relationship with several real activity variables. In addition, EDFs™ are positively related to default rates.
24 We also found evidence of economically and statistically significant relationships with several other real economic activity indicators. In most cases, inflation measures and bond issuance generally have statistically insignificant coefficients.
25 See BIS (2005, Chapter VI) for further discussion.

References

Altman, E I, B Brady, A Resti and A Sironi (2004): "The link between default and recovery rates: theory, empirical evidence and implications", *Journal of Business,* forthcoming.

Amato, J and J Gyntelberg (2005): "CDS index tranches and the pricing of credit risk correlations", *BIS Quarterly Review,* March, pp 73–87.

Amato, J and M Luisi (2005): "Macro factors in the term structure of credit spreads", *BIS Working Papers,* forthcoming.

Amato, J and E Remolona (2005): "The pricing of unexpected credit losses", *BIS Working Papers,* no 190.

Bank for International Settlements (2004): *74th Annual Report.*

_____ (2005): *75th Annual Report.*

Berndt, A, R Douglas, D Duffie, M Ferguson and D Schranz (2005): "Measuring default risk premia from default swap rates and EDFs", *BIS Working Papers,* no 173.

Driessen, J (2005): "Is default event risk priced in corporate bonds?", *Review of Financial Studies,* 18, pp 165–95.

Elton, E J, M J Gruber, D Agrawal and C Mann (2001): "Explaining the rate spread on corporate bonds", *Journal of Finance,* 56, pp 247–77.

International Swaps and Derivatives Association (2003): *ISDA Credit Derivatives Definitions, Supplements and Commentaries.*

Kealhofer, S (2003): "Quantifying credit risk I: default prediction", *Financial Analysts Journal,* January/February, pp 30–44.

Longstaff, F, S Mithal and E Neis (2005): "Corporate yield spreads: default risk or liquidity? New evidence from the credit default swap market", *Journal of Finance,* 60, pp 2213–53.

O'Kane, D, M Naldi, S Ganapati, A Berd, C Pedersen, L Schloegl and R Mashal (2003): *The Lehman Brothers guide to exotic credit derivatives,* supplement, *Risk* magazine, November.

O'Kane, D, C Pedersen and S Turnbull (2003): "The restructuring clause in credit default swap contracts", *Fixed Income Quantitative Credit Research,* Lehman Brothers, April.

Packer, F and H Zhu (2005): "Contractual terms and CDS pricing", *BIS Quarterly Review,* March, pp 89–100.

Pan, J and K Singleton (2005): *Default and recovery implicit in the term structure of sovereign CDS spreads,* Stanford University, mimeo.

49

THE GREEK DEBT CRISIS

Likely Causes, Mechanics and Outcomes

Michael G. Arghyrou and John D. Tsoukalas

Source: *World Economy* 34, 2011, 173–191.

1. INTRODUCTION

The ongoing crisis in the market for Greek government bonds is the first major test of the eurozone area. As such, it is certain to attract, in due course, considerable academic attention shedding light to its origins, mechanics and lessons. But with events still unfolding, time is of the essence: any insights to the likely causes of the crisis, mechanics and outcomes, however imperfect, are bound to be useful.

When in unchartered territory, academics' typical initial response is a first-pass assessment using tools available at hand. This article provides such an attempt. More specifically, we offer an initial exploration of the Greek crisis up to the date of writing (April 2010) using insights drawn from the literature on currency crises. We argue that insights from this literature explain surprisingly well the recent turmoil in the behaviour of prices and yields for Greek debt and can provide valuable lessons for EU policymakers. In particular, the steep ascending path of yields on Greek government bonds in the last months and the ensuing loss of confidence in the country's ability to service its debt can be explained by a simple model using ingredients from Obstfeld's (1996) framework of self-fulfilling currency crises and Krugman's (1998) treatment of the 1998 Asian crisis.

In a nutshell, the simple model we propose in this paper combines three factors. First, deteriorating macroeconomic fundamentals over the period 2001–09, mirrored in an external competitiveness deficit coupled with an unsustainable path for fiscal finances. Second, a shift in market expectations pricing a possible exit of Greece from the EMU, mainly due to the lack of commitment of Greek authorities to undertake unpopular structural reforms. Third, the pricing by markets of a (previously non-existent) default risk that follows the withdrawal of an implicit guarantee on Greek debt by other EMU countries (mainly Germany). Interestingly, our account of the factors sparking and escalating the crisis also helps explain why prices on Greek government bonds have not recovered but continued to plummet following the announcement of the EU/IMF rescue plan.

Our analysis suggests the involvement of an external institution like the IMF in EU affairs will in all likelihood widen market uncertainty over possible coordination failures between the EU and IMF policymakers and fail to stabilise market expectations on a credible resolution of the Greek crisis.

The rest of the paper is structured as follows. Section 2 provides a brief description of events surrounding the crisis. Section 3 brings together elements from the currency crises literature to explain the onset and intensification of the Greek crisis. Section 4 discusses future outcomes, and Section 5 concludes.

2. THE FACTS

We provide a description of the events that a theory of the Greek debt crisis should be able to explain. Up to the point of writing (end April 2010), the crisis has evolved in five distinct stages. Its starting point can be traced at the onset of the USA sub-prime crisis in the summer of 2007 (see Figure 1). Starting from a value of 25 basis points (b.p.), the spread of the 10-year Greek government bond yield against the German bund entered a moderately ascending path reaching 65 b.p. in August 2008. A second, much more intense, phase followed between September 2008 and March 2009. This marked the peak of the global credit crunch crisis, by the end of which the Greek spread had reached 285 b.p. Similar developments were observed in the rest of the EMU periphery countries; it was clear, however, that markets were distinguishing against Greek and Irish bonds. A brief period of de-escalation, between April and August 2009, coinciding with the partial easing of the global crisis, followed. Nevertheless, although in August 2009 the Greek

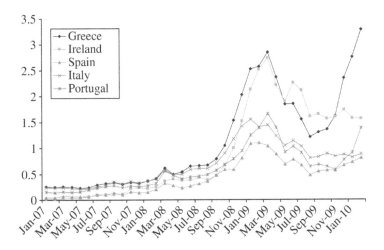

Figure 1 Spread of Ten-year Government Bond Yields against Germany (Monthly average). Note: Values reported for April 2010 are those recorded on 22 April 2010, the eve of the Greek request for the activation of the IMF/EMU support mechanism. Source: Eurostat.

spread declined to 121 b.p., it was clear that, relative to other periphery EMU countries, markets continued to have Greek and Irish bonds on their bad books.

The fourth stage of the crisis covers the period between September 2009 and mid-November 2010. During this period, the Greek spread increased only marginally, remaining in the range of 120–130 b.p. However, we classify this as a separate period because it includes three key events. First, the run-up to a snap election called for 4 October 2009. This produced a landslide government change. Second, the new government's announcement in mid-October 2009 of a substantial overshooting in the previous government's projection for the value of Greece's 2009 budget deficit, from 6 to 12.7 per cent of GDP. Third, the submission by the new government to the European Commission, in mid-November 2010, of Greece's proposed public budget for 2010. This event defines the beginning of the fifth and most intense phase, with spreads increasing from 135 b.p. in mid-November 2009, and a rapid acceleration after February 2010, to 586 b.p. on 22 April 2010. Similar trends were observed in Portugal and, to a lesser extent, Spain, involving, however, significantly lower spread levels.

Negotiations among EMU member states in the first quarter of 2010 regarding actions to contain the crisis revealed a clear split. A number of countries, most prominently Germany, opposed a Greek bailout, whereas others, including France, appeared more favourable. Eventually, on 25 March 2010, EU leaders agreed on a compromise, involving a mechanism of bilateral loans to Greece from other EU members, as well as IMF loans at rates lower than the market rate. The announced plan involved a total sum of approximately 45 billion euros, with two-thirds coming from bilateral EU loans and one-third from the IMF. The plan's announcement failed to calm markets, which put Greek bonds under further intense pressure. Finally, and following another upward revision of the 2009 Greek budget deficit to 13.6 per cent of GDP, on 23 April 2010 Greek authorities formally requested the activation of the EU/IMF rescue mechanism.

3. LIKELY CAUSES AND MECHANICS

a. The Background: Deteriorating Greek Fundamentals

So how can the literature on currency crises help us explain the Greek debt crisis and what does it predict, if anything, regarding its eventual outcome? In the first-generation crisis model proposed by Krugman (1979), the speculative attack against a currency peg is the deterministic outcome of an unsustainable fiscal expansion pursued by a myopic government and financed by excessive money creation depleting foreign currency reserves. When reserves fall below a critical threshold, rational agents, in anticipation of the peg's future collapse, buy the government's remaining reserves forcing an immediate devaluation. This restores the exchange rate to a value consistent with purchasing power parity (PPP).

This story's basic premise, i.e. unsustainable fiscal policy, is clearly present in the case of Greece. Also, since EMU accession in 2001, the country has experienced consistently higher inflation than the EMU average, resulting in substantial deviation from PPP, pronounced competitiveness losses and record current account deficits (see Arghyrou and Chortareas, 2008). Overall, there is little doubt that Greek fundamentals have deteriorated enough to justify a first-generation attack had Greece run a currency of its own.

But can the model explain the escalating nature of the crisis? It is rather difficult to suggest so. In Krugman's model, the speculative attack is caused by the full predictability of the peg's ultimate collapse, prompting agents to buy all remaining reserves to avoid the capital losses associated with holding the domestic currency after its certain forthcoming devaluation. For this argument to apply in the bonds market, we have to assume a fully predictable, or at least a highly likely, default on public debt. That is an assumption too heroic to accept for Greece at the beginning of the crisis. When compared with the collapse of a conventional peg, debt default is a much rarer and therefore much less likely event, particularly for a eurozone member with additional access to IMF emergency cash. So, although the deterioration of Greek fundamentals plays a key role in current events, the escalation of the crisis in November 2009 is unlikely to have been caused by market fears of an imminent Greek debt default.

b. Shift in Market Expectations about Greek EMU Membership

The second-generation currency crisis model by Obstfeld (1996) offers some further insights. In this model, honouring or abandoning an exchange-rate peg commitment is the outcome of a loss minimisation problem solved by a fully rational government. To decide its optimal course of action, the government balances the credibility cost incurring by defaulting on the peg against the macroeconomic cost arising from deviating from the equilibrium (PPP-consistent) exchange rate implied by the peg's maintenance. The cost of honouring the peg is a positive, quadratic function of the size of the peg's misalignment relative to PPP. In case of an overvaluation, this may take the form of negative output gap/increasing unemployment and/or higher interest on public debt. Below a critical overvaluation threshold, abandoning the peg is costlier than maintaining it, so the government finds it optimal to honour it; above this critical threshold, the opposite holds. Therefore, as in the first-generation model, excessive deterioration in fundamentals will result in the peg's unambiguous collapse.

Crucially, however, in the second-generation model, the peg's cost is endogenous to the private sector's expectations. For every level of overvaluation, defending the peg is less costly under credible commitment.[1] This gives rise to two rather than one government loss functions: a relatively flat one, applying under credible peg commitment, and a relatively steep one, applying under non-credible peg commitment (see Figure 2). This feature gives rise to two key characteristics. First, assuming for simplicity a constant cost of abandoning the peg equal to C, a zone of multiple equilibria: the same level of overvaluation (Q) corresponds to

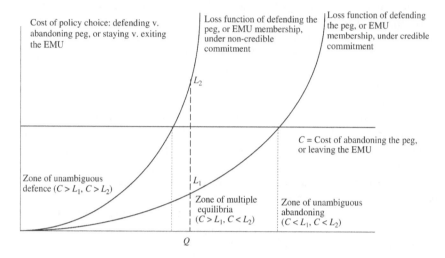

Figure 2 The Second-generation Crisis Model.

two rather than one potential exchange rate outcomes: maintaining the peg under credible commitment (L_1 on the flat loss function); and abandoning it under non-credible commitment (L_2 on the steep loss function). Second, self-fulfilling crises: within the multiple-equilibria zone, a shift in expectations from credible to non-credible commitment tilts the government's optimal response from maintaining to abandoning the peg. In that case, the peg collapses simply because the markets expect it to.

We now interpret commitment to an exchange rate peg as commitment to future EMU participation, indeed the ultimate form of a fixed exchange rate regime. A possible interpretation of events surrounding the Greek crisis is then as follows: in the wake of the global credit crunch in late 2008/early 2009, Greek fundamentals were correctly judged by markets to have deteriorated enough to be inconsistent with long-run euro participation. To convey this message to Greek authorities, markets sold a substantial, yet still not critical, volume of Greek bonds, prompting the government to take corrective action. At that stage, Greek commitment to the EMU was not questioned and the authorities operated under the flat loss function (i.e. L_1). The Greek government, however, perhaps with an eye to the forthcoming election, failed to recognise the message and no corrective action was taken. The subsequent easing of the global credit crunch took some pressure off Greek bonds. Greece, however, along with Ireland remained under market scrutiny, as their spreads remained at levels considerably higher than those of Italy, Portugal and Spain.

Following the election of October 2009, the markets gave the new government a window of opportunity to signal its policy intentions. But like its predecessor, the new government did not interpret correctly the markets' signals. During a few crucial initial weeks in office, it appeared divided over its priorities and sent mixed signals regarding its policy intentions by charging (wrongly) the markets with putting Greek bonds under unjustified speculative pressure. This lack of urgency/direction was confirmed by the exceedingly cautious, under the circumstances, proposed 2010 budget submitted to the European Commission in mid-November 2010. This proved to be a pivotal point, as markets interpreted the revealed unwillingness, or inability, of two successive Greek governments from both sides of the political spectrum to address unsustainable fundamentals as new information regarding the arithmetic of Greece's loss function. In response, for the first time in the crisis, they started questioning Greece's commitment to the euro.

Therefore, the proposed budget submitted to the EU in mid-November 2010 was a game changer; it shifted the balance of expectations from credible to non-credible commitment, putting Greece from the flat to the steep loss function (L_2). This explains the steep increase in Greek bond spreads observed in mid-November/December 2009 in the absence of further negative news on fundamentals. Events gathered momentum in the first quarter of 2010, with the release of data suggesting a deepening economic recession and increasing unemployment. In the markets' eyes, this restricts the already questionable government's ability to pursue reforms and reinforces the perceived temptation for Greece to leave the euro. This causes further negative shifts in expectations, further widening of spreads and an increasing cost of public debt which, in a circular process, causes further deterioration in expectations.

If the analysis above is correct, what we have observed in November 2009 was the mutation of a challenging crisis of deteriorating fundamentals into a full-blown crisis of confidence in the Greek monetary regime. This explains the failure of the announced EU/IMF rescue plan to relieve the pressure on Greek spreads. It failed to do so because the Greek spread was not only driven by an increasing risk of default (to be fully explained below) but also increasingly strong expectations that Greece cannot bear, or is not willing to bear, the cost of reforms necessary to stay in the euro. In other words, the markets worry that Greece will eventually opt for a voluntary exit from the EMU causing Greek bond holders capital losses through currency devaluation. This also explains the post-November 2009 Greek 'de-coupling' from Ireland, a country whose spread Greece was following closely up to that point. The difference between the two countries is that following the peak of the global credit crunch crisis in March 2009, Ireland announced bold, corrective measures convincing markets about its long-term commitment to the euro.

c. A New Element: Withdrawal of Implicit Fiscal Guarantees

Finally, the third-generation crisis model, initially proposed by Krugman (1998), allows us to introduce a third decisive factor, default risk. The model's main assumptions are high international liquidity and government guarantees to the liabilities of insufficiently regulated financial intermediaries. In this model, the currency crisis is just one aspect of a wider financial crisis caused by the distorting effects of guarantees on investment incentives. Under guarantees and lax supervision, intermediaries have both the incentive and ability to borrow short-term funds at low interest rates from international money markets. These are used to finance highly speculative domestic investment projects with fat right-hand-side tails, i.e. projects of low expected return but involving a small probability of very large gains. These guarantees imply investors bear no downside risk, as they offer a 'heads-you-win, tails-you-do-not-lose' deal. Investors demand stakes in these projects in high quantities, driving up their prices and the value of the intermediaries that finance them. This increases confidence in the projects' success, leading to more short-term loans to intermediaries, further increases in demand for projects and further accelerating prices, significantly above fair value.

Then, returns on the projects are gradually revealed. Unavoidably, these will on average be lower than the best-case scenario investors had over-optimistically paid for. Less-than-maximum returns reduce asset prices and the market value of their managing intermediaries. Some over-leveraged intermediaries are refused finance to cover their liabilities and are driven out of business. Investors receive the government bailout, but receding confidence in intermediaries, accompanied by more revelations of less than maximum returns reduces asset prices further. The circular process described above now works in reverse, causing more bailouts. At some point, the cost of bailout reaches a critical level, prompting investors to realise that the government cannot afford them any further. This has a magnifying effect on capital losses, as asset prices adjust not only to the less-than-maximum current returns but also to the withdrawal of future guarantees. In one discrete drop, asset prices shift from being the sum of current disappointing returns plus the discounted value of all future best possible outcomes, to the sum of the current disappointing returns plus all future expected outcomes. This causes extensive capital losses, resulting in more intermediaries' closures, capital flight, forced currency devaluation and a credit crunch spreading the crisis to the economy's real sector.

What is the relevance of this analysis to the Greek debt crisis? Consider a scenario applying to the best part of the past decade with international investors having access to ample liquidity. Investors assess Greek bonds as a stake into a risky project, namely the restructuring of a relatively low-income, under-competitive and highly indebted economy, with two possible scenarios. First, an optimistic one, in which Greece would promote competitiveness-boosting reforms. In that case, starting from a low-income base, Greece would become a fast-growing economy whose bond prices would appreciate generating large gains for investors who took the bet. Second a pessimistic one, in which Greece would not promote reforms. In that case, Greek bond prices would depreciate and possibly involve losses for investors. In an undistorted environment, like the one prevailing before Greece's accession to the EMU, markets would price Greek bonds by assessing the probability of reform, i.e. future expected Greek fundamentals. In that case, Greek bonds would be priced at their fair value.

We now introduce Greece's 2001 EMU accession into the analysis and draw the analogy with Krugman's model. With Greece becoming a member of the single currency, considerably European (largely German) funds flow into the country. Markets perceived that the rest of the EMU countries had a vested interest in Greek reforms and Greece's continued participation in the EMU. This sentiment was further reinforced by Germany's long-term political commitment to the European integration project. Therefore, Greek accession was perceived to convey an implicit bailout guarantee to holders of Greek bonds, with Germany in the role of the guarantor played by the government in Krugman's model. As a result, markets stopped pricing Greek bonds on the basis of expected fundamentals and started pricing them exclusively on the basis of the best-case scenario, i.e. achievement of full real convergence to German fundamentals. This is consistent with the downward structural break Arghyrou et al. (2009) have found to occur in real Greek interest rates in 2000:Q3 not reversed in subsequent years.

Events then moved as follows: in the absence of an effective EU-sponsored mechanism of fiscal monitoring and imposed reform, Greek governments over 2001–09 did not implement sound economic policies, thus allowing further deterioration of fundamentals. Therefore, the project of Greek restructuring did not achieve the best-case scenario of real convergence envisaged by investors: indeed, in previous research, we have found that due to the lack of reforms, EMU accession caused net costs rather than net benefits in a number of areas (see Arghyrou, 2006, 2009). As a result, starting in the summer of 2007, lower than anticipated returns on the Greek project gradually reduced the prices of Greek bonds, with losses accelerating significantly in the wake of the global credit crunch in 2009:Q1.

At that point, with the Greek bond market coming under intense pressure, investors in the Greek project looked to Greece's main guarantor, Germany, to back the Greek economy. Germany, however, refused to do so: it initially responded with a policy officially described as 'constructive ambiguity' and then, to the markets' great surprise, in February/March 2010, made it clear that it was not prepared to help Greece unconditionally. The German stance was interpreted by markets as withdrawal of the fiscal guarantee for Greece. Therefore, the price of Greek bonds promptly plummeted, as the latter reverted to the value implied by the now significantly worse, compared with their 2001 level, Greek fundamentals. Without the fiscal guarantee, the EU/IMF rescue plan was judged as too small to cope with the ballooning Greek budget deficit and public debt. Overall, Germany's choice not to bail out Greece introduced a previously non-existent default risk, causing the decline in Greek bond prices to accelerate in March–April 2010.

In all fairness, we have to note that successive German governments of all persuasions had been consistently stating over the years that if the circumstances ever arise, they will uphold the no-bailout clause. Therefore, the policy of 'constructive ambiguity' was justified on the grounds that a bailout would be seen as a shift in long-standing German policy, causing moral hazard discouraging Greece and other countries from pursuing reforms, thereby intensifying the present crisis and making future crises more likely. This was a fully plausible analysis which, however, now seems to have been wrong. It turns out that markets had never believed the no-bailout clause and had been pricing, even well into the crisis, Greek and other EMU bonds assuming a bailout. Hence, from the markets' point of view, a bailout would not be news and thus would not destabilise the eurozone further; instead the news was that there was to be no bailout. All in all, the German-led policy of 'constructive ambiguity' seems to have backfired: the withdrawal of the fiscal guarantee not only contributed to the collapse of the Greek bonds market, thus escalating the crisis it was meant to contain, but may have also sown the seed of contagion to the markets for other EMU periphery bonds, also operating hitherto under the assumption of a German fiscal guarantee.

Are markets responsible in any way for the escalation of the Greek crisis? The answer is probably yes for misjudging the credibility of Germany's commitment to the no-bailout clause. Perhaps, they ought to know better. The closest available historical analogy is the ERM crisis of 1992–93. At the time Germany was called to make a choice between two conflicting objectives: on the one hand, maintaining internal price stability and economic restructuring following German re-unification. These goals called for higher German interest rates. On the other, maintaining momentum for European monetary integration by helping its ERM partners to cope with an economic recession. This called for lower German interest rates. Germany opted for the former, causing the ERM's demise and putting in jeopardy the whole EMU project just one year after the signing of the Maastricht Treaty. This event, combined with the consistent post-war nature of German economic policy confirmed that the latter's Holy Grail is low internal inflation and external currency stability. To this objective, everything else, including Germany's commitment to European monetary integration, comes second. With this experience available and with German policy announcements traditionally regarded among the most credible in the world, why markets chose to doubt Germany's commitment to the no-bailout clause is, to say the least, surprising.

d. Putting Everything Together: A Summary of the Greek Debt Crisis

We now have a full set of ingredients offering a first analytically tractable explanation of the causes, mechanics and timing of events of the Greek debt crisis. Our analysis suggest that the crisis and its escalating nature are due to deteriorating fundamentals over the period 2001–09 and a double regime shift in market expectations, from a regime of credible EMU commitment under guaranteed fiscal liabilities, to one of non-credible commitment under no guarantees. This transformed a challenging crisis of fundamentals, first to a crisis of confidence in Greece's monetary regime, and then to a crisis of confidence both in the Greek monetary regime and in Greece's ability to service its public debt.

These events can be explained within a framework extending the second-generation crisis model into one accounting for fiscal guarantees. We present such a model in Appendix A and Figure A1. This involves three rather than two loss functions associated with continued EMU participation. The first applies to credible EMU commitment with fiscal guarantees. The second to non-credible EMU commitment under fiscal guarantees and the third applies to non-credible EMU commitment without fiscal guarantees. The model predicts that under the third scenario, the cost of maintaining EMU participation rises to levels rendering continued participation almost impossible without non-market public debt financing.

Before concluding this section, it is worth noting that further factors may be relevant. Their role, however, is unlikely to be decisive. For example, Greek spreads may involve an increasing liquidity premium. As, however, this is present in the market for the bonds of other periphery EMU countries, its disproportionate increase in Greece is almost certainly due to the collapse of the Greek bonds caused by the factors explained above. In other words, any liquidity premium is most likely endogenous to the exchange rate and default premium. It is also possible that Greek spreads include overshooting effects caused either by real rigidities or by increasing market risk aversion. However, as the length of the crisis has given markets enough time to correct any initial over-pessimistic assessments, it is unlikely that over-reaction is a major factor.

4. LIKELY OUTCOMES

a. Greece

Having analysed the likely causes of the crisis, we now turn to likely outcomes. Assuming that the withdrawal of the EMU/German fiscal guarantee is permanent, for Greek spreads to fall it is vital that Greece return to a regime of credible EMU commitment. To achieve this, Greece must be seen to have the willingness and ability to implement the reforms necessary to improve its fundamentals. Given the loss of credibility Greece sustained after November 2009, the country would be highly unlikely to achieve a credible EMU commitment on its own. Therefore, activating the EU/IMF rescue mechanism was the only option available. By undertaking the unpopular decision of delegating its economic policy discretion to EU/IMF officials, Greece has sent the signal that it wants to maintain its EMU membership. This is an important step, but, on its own, not enough. Greece must now convince markets not only that she wants to but can also implement required reforms. This creates a clear binary path for future events.

The first, optimistic scenario is that Greek authorities will show determination in implementing reforms and Greek citizens will accept them without major opposition causing social upheaval. In that case, as markets will be observing reforms' progress, confidence in the ability of Greece to implement them will gradually be built. With emergency EU/IMF funds offering a temporary fiscal guarantee, spreads will gradually subside, gaining momentum as Greek fundamentals are seen to be improving. In time, reforms will be seen to have progressed enough to establish full confidence in EMU participation, allowing withdrawal of the emergency EU/IMF fiscal guarantee and a gradual return to a regime of credible commitment and fiscal sustainability. Greece will have returned to a path of sustainable growth and its economy will emerge restructured and stronger. This will be a positive outcome, but there should be no illusions: progress will only be gradual and not easy: there will initially be significant short-run welfare losses through higher unemployment and reduced output. There are also external risks: the optimistic scenario assumes no further global economic shocks, no crisis's contagion to the bond markets of other EMU countries and the availability of further EU/IMF funds if the necessity arises. Success through this path will certainly be difficult; but it is equally certainly possible; and even more certainly Greece's best, indeed only, hope to stay in the EMU.

The second, pessimistic scenario is that reforms will be strongly resisted and Greek authorities will shy away from pushing them through. In that case, markets will refuse to lend Greece funds and the EU/IMF rescue mechanism, which will involve conditionality clauses, will be discontinued. To stave-off an imminent social/economic breakdown Greece will then have no option other than to leave the EMU. This will eliminate the risk premium currently associated with the possible exit, but will almost certainly replace it by a premium associated with uncertainty surrounding the now independent Greek monetary policy. Furthermore, the devaluation of the new drachma against the euro will also devalue the assets of Greek banks, spreading the crisis into the real economy through liquidity shortages and high lending interest rates. Overall, an EMU-exit may provide some temporary breathing space, but even that is not guaranteed, and will not address the causes of deteriorating Greek fundamentals. Greece will still have to undertake the same painful reforms, this time, however, outside the EMU, and without any financial support its EMU partners may be willing to provide her economy.

Therefore, it all comes down to a straightforward question of public choice, ultimately to be decided by Greek citizens. Greek authorities must communicate the dilemma the country faces in clear, unambiguous terms, spelling out the full implications of both possible choices. They must also convince citizens that it is in the country's best interest to implement the reforms necessary to remain in the eurozone. Authorities should also convey to citizens the message that the country needs to make a rapid decision: if markets do not observe substantial progress within the next few months, they will infer Greece has chosen not to stay in the euro and will force her out.

b. Other Periphery EMU Countries

This brings us to the last, but by no means least, aspect of the Greek crisis, the possibility of contagion. Like Greece, since the euro's introduction in 1999, the remaining club-med countries (Italy, Spain and Portugal) and Ireland have all experienced significant deterioration in the value of fundamentals crucial for ensuring long-term EMU membership (see Figure 3). These include competitiveness losses leading to substantial current account deficits, particularly in Portugal

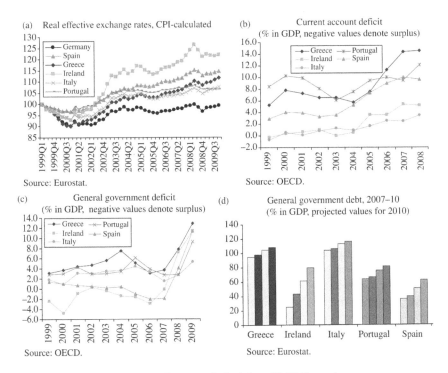

Figure 3 Macroeconomic Developments in Periphery EMU Countries.

and Spain (see also Arghyrou and Chortareas, 2008), and with the possible exception of Italy, a major fiscal deterioration in 2008–09. However, despite its relative stability, the Italian public debt to GDP ratio in 2010 is projected to be above the 100 per cent threshold. At the same time, and compared with its 2007 value, public debt will have almost doubled in Spain and more than trebled in Ireland.

Based on the above, we conclude that although none of the other periphery EMU countries tick, as Greece does, all boxes in the explosive triplet of budget deficit, current account deficit and debt to GDP ratio, they are either close to doing so or they converge fast towards that point. The deterioration observed in the fundamentals of these countries may well have set them on a path where markets will soon question their commitment to future EMU participation, particularly in view of increasing unemployment rates. Furthermore, like Greece, all four countries now operate without the implicit EMU/German fiscal guarantee markets had perceived until very recently. As a result, any further increases in their public debt to GDP ratio may introduce a default premium into the interest rate of their government bonds.

Recent trends in the movements of spreads suggest that the country regarded by markets as most vulnerable is Portugal, followed by Spain. Despite the strong positive signals it has sent to markets in recent months, Ireland also remains vulnerable, as markets appear doubtful about their eventual success. Italy appears the most stable of all five periphery EMU countries. However, with a public debt to GDP ratio in excess of 100 per cent and structural weaknesses deeply entrenched, she can by no means take markets' confidence for granted. Albeit at different degrees, all four countries are vulnerable to the risk of contagion. To avoid this, it is essential for these countries to ensure that they continue operating under a regime of credible EMU participation and perceived fiscal solvency. Therefore, they must also introduce, without delay, fiscal consolidation and extensive structural reforms addressing their competitiveness deficit. These will undoubtedly cause short-term welfare losses, raising the prospect of internal opposition. Therefore, the need to communicate clearly to their citizens the implications of hesitating to introduce reform is as important and urgent as in Greece.

5. SUMMARY AND CONCLUDING REMARKS

This paper has used insights from the literature on currency crises to offer an analytical treatment of the crisis unfolding in the market for Greek government bonds. We conclude that the crisis and its escalating nature are the result of (i) steadily deteriorating macroeconomic fundamentals over the period 2001–09 to levels inconsistent with long-term EMU participation, and (ii) a double shift in markets' expectations, from a regime of credible commitment to future EMU participation under an implicit EMU/German guarantee of Greek fiscal liabilities, to a regime of non-credible EMU commitment without fiscal guarantees, respectively taking place in November 2009 and February/March 2010. Following this shift, resorting to the EU/IMF mechanism of emergency financing on 23 April 2010 was the only option available for Greece to avert an imminent EMU exit.

There is now a clear binary path regarding the outcome of the crisis. Either Greece will introduce the reforms necessary to address the initial source of the crisis, i.e. deteriorating fundamentals, in which case and, assuming a favourable external environment, her economy will gradually regain the markets' confidence and the country will stay in the EMU, or Greece will not promote any reforms, in which case she will have no option than to leave the euro.

Regarding the possibility of contagion, all other periphery EMU countries, Ireland, Italy, Portugal and Spain, appear (at varying degrees) vulnerable, as since their euro accession in 1999 they have also experienced significant deterioration in key fundamentals. Furthermore, the withdrawal of the implicit EMU/German fiscal guarantee applies to these countries too. To avoid the adverse shift in markets' expectations Greece has experienced, these countries must also pursue, without delay, fiscal consolidation and extensive structural reforms.

What are the institutional lessons drawn from the Greek crisis so far? To minimise the risk of contagion of the present crisis and to avert future ones, it is important for the EMU to undertake institutional reforms in two directions. First, to prevent future crises, improve the effectiveness of fiscal supervision applied to individual EMU member states. Second, for handling this crisis and future ones, minimise the risk of default risk. To achieve this, the EMU must develop a mechanism of emergency financing, with clear and transparent rules. The EU/ IMF mechanism put in place for Greece is helpful but unlikely to avert crises in other countries, as it is an *ad hoc* arrangement involving an external institution, the IMF, to EMU affairs. This is a disadvantage for the following reason. The prospect of IMF involvement into handling future EMU crises may fail to reduce market uncertainty, as no effective *ex ante* guarantee can be given for the possibility of coordination failure between the EMU and the IMF. Therefore, without an exclusively EMU-run mechanism of crisis management, the EMU may find it difficult to stabilise market expectations at the crucial initial stages of a crisis. Defining the rules of a European Monetary Fund will be a challenging task, as these should be able to reassure investors without causing moral hazard leading to excessive deficits and lack of reform. This is a topic calling for significant attention from academics and policymakers alike.

But when all is said and done, ending the current EMU crisis and averting future ones ultimately depends on one single factor: the willingness of societies in the EMU periphery to take the significant short-run welfare cost that will accompany reforms. It is therefore vital for governments to communicate clearly to their citizens what the stakes are in not promoting reforms now, and convince them that since the latter will have to take place anyway, it will be preferable for their own long-run welfare to undertake them within the euro rather than outside it.

There is one final risk: over the past decade, EMU periphery economies have diverged so much from those of core EMU countries that either they cannot sustain or markets regard them as not being able to sustain, the cost of reforms necessary to stay in the eurozone. At this stage, it is impossible to know whether this is true; but if it is, it will be extremely challenging for European governments to sustain the euro. We believe that European governments must have a plan to face such a scenario. Allowing individual economies to exit the euro on a unilateral basis is an easy, yet inappropriate response, as one country's exit will very likely cause a domino effect, with markets eventually forcing all struggling economies out. From an EMU perspective, such a development will obviously be catastrophic, but is there any alternative?

We believe there is: in a recent paper (Arghyrou and Tsoukalas, 2010), we have spelled out a plan of last resort to resolve the present crisis, to be used only if everything else fails. The key ingredients involve a temporary split of the euro into two currencies both run by the ECB. The hard euro will be maintained by the core EMU members, whereas the periphery EMU countries will adopt the weak euro for a suitable period of time. All existing debts will continue to be denominated in strong euro terms. The plan involves a one-off devaluation of the weak euro versus the strong one simultaneously with the introduction of far-reaching reforms and rapid fiscal consolidation in the periphery EMU countries. We argue that due to enhanced market credibility, the plan will have a realistic chance of success, maintaining the project of European monetary integration and leaving the door open to the periphery countries for a return to the strong euro.

APPENDIX A: A MODEL OF EMU-EXIT UNDER SHIFTING MEMBERSHIP EXPECTATIONS AND WITHDRAWAL OF FISCAL GUARANTEES

Assume a country joins the EMU at an exchange rate against the euro given (in logs) by $\bar{s}$. Every period following accession, the government decides whether to stay in or exit the euro. To do so, the government balances the cost of exiting versus the cost of continued EMU participation. The former is assumed to be given by a fixed constant C. The latter is a positive quadratic function of the over-valuation of $\bar{s}$ relative to the country's equilibrium (PPP-consistent) exchange rate against the euro, denoted by s^*. Overvaluation of $\bar{s}$ relative to s^* is costly as it reduces external competitiveness. This leads to negative economic outcomes, including lower output, increased unemployment, higher budget deficits implying higher borrowing requirements and a higher interest rate on government bonds, and higher current account deficit, increasing the stock of external debt and future interest payments to foreign creditors.

The government's optimisation problem is solved conditional upon private sector expectations, which may fall in three regimes. In the first, markets perceive the country's future EMU participation as fully credible and outstanding government bonds to be fully guaranteed by the country's EMU partners. In that case, the loss of staying in the euro is given by L_1:

$$L_1 = \left[\gamma_1 \left(s^* - \bar{s} \right) \right]^2, \quad \gamma_1 > 0. \tag{A1}$$

The second possibility is that markets perceive future EMU participation as non-credible, in which case the interest rate of government bonds incorporates an exchange rate premium compensating for the risk of capital losses to follow reversion to the old national currency. Fiscal liabilities continue to be perceived as guaranteed by the country's EMU partners. For every level of overvaluation, the exchange rate risk premium increases the cost of staying in the EMU, giving rise to the loss function described by the following equation:

$$L_2 = \left[\left(\gamma_1 + \gamma_2 \right) \left(s^* - \bar{s} \right) \right]^2, \quad \gamma_1, \gamma_2 > 0. \tag{A2}$$

Finally, in the third regime, markets do not regard commitment to future par-ticipation to the EMU as credible and do not perceive repayments of govern-ment liabilities to be guaranteed.[2] In that case, interest rates on government bonds include not only an exchange rate premium but also a default premium. For every level of overvaluation, the cost of continued EMU participation increases further and is now given by:

$$L_3 = \left[\left(\gamma_1 + \gamma_2 + \gamma_3 \right) \left(s^* - \bar{s} \right) \right]^2, \quad \gamma_1, \gamma_2, \gamma_3 > 0. \tag{A3}$$

Under all regimes, the government will choose to stay in the EMU if the cost of continued EMU participation is lower than the cost of euro exit.

$$L_i < C, \quad i = 1, 2, 3. \tag{A4}$$

Normalising without loss of generality $\bar{s}$ equal to zero, the condition for staying in the euro is as follows:

Under credible EMU commitment and guaranteed fiscal liabilities:

$$s^* < \frac{\sqrt{C}}{\gamma_1}. \tag{A5}$$

Under non-credible EMU commitment and guaranteed fiscal liabilities:

$$s^* < \frac{\sqrt{C}}{\gamma_1 + \gamma_2}. \tag{A6}$$

Under non-credible EMU and non-guaranteed fiscal liabilities:

$$s^* < \frac{\sqrt{C}}{\gamma_1 + \gamma_2 + \gamma_3}. \tag{A7}$$

Given $\gamma_2, \gamma_3 > 0$, we obtain:

$$\frac{\sqrt{C}}{\gamma_1 + \gamma_2 + \gamma_3} < \frac{\sqrt{C}}{\gamma_1 + \gamma_2} < \frac{\sqrt{C}}{\gamma_1}. \tag{A8}$$

Conditions (A5), (A6) and (A7) state that for every expectations' scenario, there exist a critical threshold of overvaluation above which continued EMU member-ship is suboptimal. Condition (A8) implies that this threshold reduces with nega-tive shifts in expectations regarding the country's commitment to future EMU participation and the extent of fiscal guarantees. The model is presented dia-grammatically in Figure A1. Compared with the second-generation crisis model discussed in Figure 2, the model now allows for two rather than one zone of multiple equilibria: the possibility of withdrawing fiscal guarantees increases the cost of defending EMU participation under non-credible EMU commitment, thus restricting further the range of successful EMU participation defence.

Figure A1 can be used to explain the escalating nature of the Greek bonds cri-sis. The deterioration of Greek fundamentals occurring during 2001–09 caused an overvaluation of the Greek exchange rate given by Q. This increased the cost of EMU participation by increasing interest rates on government bond yields, without, however, initially affecting market expectations. Interest rates on Greek government bonds subsequently increased along the predictions of loss function

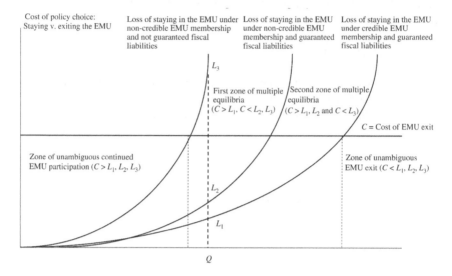

Figure A1 A Model of EMU Exit under Shifting Membership Expectations and Withdrawal of Fiscal Guarantees Macroeconomic Developments in Periphery EMU Countries.

L_1. The unwillingness subsequently shown by Greek authorities to commit to the necessary reforms, as confirmed by the proposed 2010 budget submitted to the European Commission in November 2010, put Greece's long-term commitment to the EMU into doubt. With expectations shifting from credible to non-credible commitment, interest rates on Greek government bonds increased to the level predicted by the loss function L_2, tilting the trade-off analysis against EMU participation. Finally, the revelation in February/March 2010 that the implicit fiscal guarantee perceived to have been given by the other EMU countries to Greece was not in place shifted Greece to loss function L_3 increasing the cost of servicing public debt to levels inconsistent with continued EMU participation. The realisation of this fact prompted Greece to look for non-market financing of its public debt, thereby asking for the activation of the EU/IMF rescue plan on 23 April 2010.

Notes

1 In this case, from uncovered interest parity static exchange rate expectations imply a lower interest rate on government bonds.
2 There is a fourth regime, in which the private sector views future EMU participation as credible without fiscal guarantees of government bonds from EMU partners. In this case, however, the country's commitment to EMU participation implies a strong incentive for sound fiscal finances. We therefore view this case as isomorphic to the first regime, namely credible EMU participation and guaranteed fiscal liabilities.

REFERENCES

Arghyrou, M. G. (2006), *The Effects of the Accession of Greece to the EMU: Initial Estimates* (Athens: Centre of Planning and Economic Research (KEPE)), Study No. 64.

Arghyrou, M. G. (2009), 'Monetary Policy Before and After the Euro: Evidence from Greece', *Empirical Economics,* **36**, 621–43.

Arghyrou, M. G. and G. Chortareas (2008), 'Current Account Imbalances and Real Exchange Rates in the Euro Area', *Review of International Economics,* **16**, 747–64.

Arghyrou, M. G. and J. Tsoukalas (2010), 'The Option of Last Resort: A Two-currency EMU', published on 7 February 2010 at http://www.roubini.com. Available at: http://www.roubini.com/euromonitor/258379/the_option_of_last_resort_a_two-currency_emu (accessed 18 January 2011).

Arghyrou, M. G., A. Gregoriou and A. Kontonikas (2009), 'Do Real Interest Rates Converge? Evidence from the European Union', *Journal of International Financial Markets, Institutions and Money,* **19**, 447–60.

Krugman, P. R. (1979), 'A Model of Balance of Payments Crises', *Journal of Money, Credit and Banking,* **11**, 311–25.

Krugman, P. R. (1998), 'What Happened to Asia?'. Available at: http://web.mit.edu/krugman/www/disinter.html (accessed 18 January 2011).

Obstfeld, M. (1996), 'Models of Currency Crises with Self-fulfilling Features', *European Economic Review,* **40**, 1037–48.

THE PRICING OF SOVEREIGN RISK AND CONTAGION DURING THE EUROPEAN SOVEREIGN DEBT CRISIS

John Beirne and Marcel Fratzscher

Source: *Journal of International Money and Finance* 34, 2013, 60–82.

ABSTRACT

The paper analyses the drivers of sovereign risk for 31 advanced and emerging economies during the European sovereign debt crisis. It shows that a deterioration in countries' fundamentals and fundamentals contagion – a sharp rise in the sensitivity of financial markets to fundamentals – are the main explanations for the rise in sovereign yield spreads and CDS spreads during the crisis, not only for euro area countries but globally. By contrast, regional spillovers and contagion have been less important, including for euro area countries. The paper also finds evidence for herding contagion – sharp, simultaneous increases in sovereign yields across countries – but this contagion has been concentrated in time and among a few markets. Finally, empirical models with economic fundamentals generally do a poor job in explaining sovereign risk in the pre-crisis period for European economies, suggesting that the market pricing of sovereign risk may not have been fully reflecting fundamentals prior to the crisis.

1. Introduction

The European sovereign debt crisis initially came as a surprise to most observers and policy-makers. Economic growth was generally strong, fiscal deficits limited and public debt levels were rising only modestly in most of Europe prior to the 2007–2008 global financial crisis, in particular among those euro area countries that are now engulfed most intensely in the subsequent debt crisis. This has spurred some observers and policy-makers to argue that financial markets have been overreacting and overpricing sovereign risk since the 2007–2008 crisis, and that this overreaction is due to contagion, in particular from the most affected countries, such as Greece, to other more innocent or prudent bystanders.

The question about the drivers of sovereign risk is important also from a longer-term policy perspective in order to understand how policy can react to the challenges of the sovereign debt crisis and the great global recession in the next decade. As Reinhart and Rogoff (2011, p. 3) argue: "The combination of high and climbing public debts (a rising share of which is held by major central banks) and the protracted process of private deleveraging makes it likely that the ten years from 2008 to 2017 will be aptly described as a decade of debt."

To what extent have financial markets been overpricing sovereign risk in the euro area during the European sovereign debt? And what has been the role of contagion for sovereign risk? The paper critically examines these questions for a broad set of 31 advanced economies (AEs) and emerging market economies (EMEs) by empirically modeling the link between three measures of sovereign risk (long-term government spreads, CDS spreads and ratings of sovereigns) and economic fundamentals over the period 2000–2011. As is common in the literature, contagion is defined as the *change* in the way countries' own fundamentals or other factors are priced during a crisis period, i.e. a change in the reaction of financial markets either in response to observable factors, such as changes in sovereign risk among neighboring countries, or due to unobservables, such as herding behavior of market participants.

We motivate the empirical analysis for the determinants of sovereign yields through a standard definition of sovereign risk as reflecting credit risk, liquidity risk and risk appetite. Based on this conceptual framework, the first part of the analysis highlights that if one takes the relationship between fundamentals and sovereign risk during the pre-crisis period 2000–2007 as the true relationship, then sovereign risk is indeed substantially overpriced in many Europeans economies, and in particular among the euro area periphery (Greece, Ireland, Portugal, Spain and Italy – GIPSI), but not for many EMEs, especially outside Europe. However, it is striking that those fundamentals that one would expect to be the most important determinants for the price of sovereign risk – the public debt level, fiscal deficit, growth and the current account – explain very little of the pricing of risk in GIPSI countries before the crisis, but have much more explanatory power for sovereign risk in other AEs and EMEs. In fact, the most important determinant for the price of sovereign debt in GIPSI countries in the pre-crisis period was the price of public debt among other European countries, such as that of Germany. And indeed, the small spreads and very high comovements of sovereign yields within the euro area suggest that other factors than fundamentals may have been the prime determinants of sovereign debt in Europe before the crisis.[1]

This finding thus suggests that country-specific fundamentals had less importance for the pricing of sovereign risk in the euro area during the pre-crisis period compared to other economies. The empirical analysis of the paper shows that the price of sovereign risk has been much more sensitive to fundamentals and that fundamentals explain a substantially higher share of the movements and cross-country differences in sovereign risk during the 2008–2011 crisis than in the pre-crisis period. Applying this counterfactual analysis for the crisis period shows

65

that sovereign yields and CDS spreads would have been much more dispersed before 2007, in particular among euro area countries, if markets had priced fundamentals in the pre-crisis period in the same way that they did in 2008–2011. In fact, there is a negative correlation between the "mispricing" of sovereign risk – i.e. the deviation of actual market prices of risk from those implied by empirical models based on fundamentals – during the crisis and in the pre-crisis period. In other words, those countries for which sovereign risk was "underpriced" in the pre-crisis period were also those that became "overpriced" relative to economic fundamentals during the crisis.

The findings raise the question of what constitutes a "fair" pricing of sovereign risk and an over-pricing or under-pricing of such risk.[2] A basic intertemporal budget constraint for a government highlights the importance of expectations for determining the sensitivity of the pricing of sovereign risk – market expectations about the future primary balance, debt level, inflation, as well as about a government's willingness and ability to serve debt all influence how markets price existing fundamentals that are relevant for the sustainability of public debt. As such, the empirical findings of the paper suggest that there may be multiple equilibria between the market price of sovereign risk and underlying fundamentals, which depend on existing market expectations.

What explains these disparities and shift in the pricing of sovereign debt during the 2008–2011 period? There are three different conceptual reasons for such a change. First, market participants may come to price the same fundamentals in a different way over time. While they may have ignored cross-country differences or changes in country-specific fundamentals during some periods, they may react a lot more strongly during a crisis period. This is what the literature has referred to as "wake-up call" contagion or fundamentals contagion (Goldstein, 1998; Bekaert et al., 2010). In fact, the findings indicate that for some countries, such as the GIPSI countries, there is strong evidence in favor of this "wake-up call" contagion, though for other countries there is much less of such evidence.

Second, the pricing of sovereign risk may have been affected by cross-country contagion, i.e. the transmission of a negative sovereign shock in countries such as Greece may have raised the price of sovereign risk in other, related countries. We refer to this as "regional contagion" following the argument of some that such a transmission across countries was particularly important within the euro area in 2008–2011. The third conceptual reason for changes in the pricing of sovereign risk relates to herding behavior or panic among investors. The literature refers to this type of contagion often as "pure contagion" or herding contagion. It is the most difficult type of contagion to measure empirically, as it at least partly reflects factors that are unobservable to the economic modeler. Yet it may also be the most difficult one to address for policy-makers as using firewalls, financial support and improving fundamentals may be insufficient to fully address it.

We find evidence that regional contagion has not been important during the 2008–2011 sovereign debt crisis in Europe. Interestingly, the estimates indicate that the cross-country spillovers of sovereign risk were stronger prior to the crisis than during the crisis. In other words, while financial markets tended to price sovereign risk within a region, in particular within the euro area, in a similar way, irrespective of differences across countries' fundamentals, they started to discriminate on the basis of fundamentals more strongly during the crisis. Moreover, even after accounting for "fundamentals contagion" and "regional contagion", there is a substantial part of the increase in the price of sovereign risk in 2008–2011 that remains unexplained and that points to the importance of "pure contagion".

To get at the role of pure contagion, we analyze the comovements of that part of the price of sovereign risk that cannot be explained by either changes in fundamentals, by fundamentals contagion or by regional contagion. Following the approach of Boyson et al. (2010), we analyze the clustering in time of large unexplained changes in the pricing of sovereign risk. We find that there is indeed some evidence of such clustering among euro area countries, but that this occurred at the height of the global financial crisis in 2008 and mostly not during 2010 and 2011 with the exception of July–September 2011 when 70% of euro area countries experienced sharp increases in the pricing of their sovereign risk. However, this period was very short, indicating that herding contagion can help explain the overall dynamics of sovereign risk to a very limited extent.

For the last part of the analysis, we try to quantify the importance of each of the three types of contagion for the pricing of sovereign risk during the 2008–2011 sovereign debt crisis. A first important finding in this regard is that most of the increase in the price of sovereign risk during the 2008–2011 sovereign debt crisis among GIPSI and other euro area countries was due to a deterioration in countries' fundamentals and fundamentals contagion. By contrast, regional contagion and spillovers were relatively unimportant overall while also pure contagion played a small, but limited role. In fact, we find strong evidence for a decoupling among European sovereign debt markets during the crisis, with changes in one country's sovereign debt being transmitted to neighboring countries much less intensely during the crisis than compared to before the crisis. Overall, therefore, the findings suggest that the deterioration of fundamentals and fundamentals contagion are the prime explanations for the sharp rise in sovereign risk during the European sovereign debt crisis.

The paper is organized as follows. Section 2 discusses the related academic literature on modeling the pricing of sovereign risk. Section 3 describes the methodology to measure the impact of fundamentals, regional risk and contagion on the price of sovereign risk, while Section 4 describes the data and presents a number of stylized facts about the evolution of sovereign risk during the crisis. Section 5 outlines the main empirical results and various extensions. Finally, Section 6 summarizes the findings and discusses implications for the policy discussion.

2. Related literature

A range of previous papers has analyzed the determinants of the pricing of sovereign risk. Early studies tended to focus on government bond yield spreads as the reference measure for sovereign risk, and also on explaining sovereign risk in emerging economies, e.g. Ferrucci (2003). More recent work also included examining sovereign CDS spreads and sovereign ratings. An early study of the factors driving government bond spreads was carried out by Edwards (1984), who found that domestic macroeconomic fundamentals were important determinants, including factors such as the public debt, foreign reserves, the current account balance and inflation. More recently, Aizenman et al. (2011), focusing on pricing sovereign risk for 60 economies based on CDS spreads, find evidence of mis-pricing in the euro area periphery relative to a set of macroeconomic fundamentals comprised of public debt, fiscal balance, trade openness, external debt, inflation and the TED spread (see also Amato, 2005; Packer and Zhu, 2005; Cecchetti et al., 2010).

One of the first empirical studies on the determinants of sovereign credit ratings was carried out by Cantor and Pecker (1996), who focused on an examination of both the criteria underlying ratings and their impact on sovereign borrowing costs. They found that ratings can be explained by per capita income, GDP growth, inflation, external debt, the level of economic development, and the default history. Amadou (2001) focused on bond spreads and sovereign credit ratings in emerging economies, highlighting differences between the market and rating agency perception of the price of sovereign risk. Afonso et al. (2007) assess the determinants of sovereign debt credit ratings using a panel estimation and probit model over the period 1995–2005. They find that the sovereign credit rating is a function of GDP per capita, GDP growth, government debt, government effectiveness indicators, external debt, external reserves, and default history.[3] Doetz and Fischer (2010) focus on euro area countries, explaining how the volatility in sovereign bond spreads is indicative of a rise in market perception of default probability. Manganelli and Wolswijk (2007) assess the determinants of euro area sovereign spreads after the introduction of the euro. The paper was written in the context of historically low spreads in the euro area since 1999 despite adverse fiscal situations and developments in many countries. The underlying market perception was that financial integration in the euro area eliminated markets' willingness/ability to discriminate between the creditworthiness of different national fiscal policies. A particular focus is on whether market discipline is advanced or obstructed by financial integration and by fiscal rules such as those contained in the Stability and Growth Pact. Using a fixed-effects panel model, these authors also provide strong empirical evidence that spreads depend on the ratings of the underlying bond and to a large extent are driven by the level of short-term interest rates. Attinasi and Nickel (2009) use a dynamic panel approach to explain the determinants of widening sovereign spreads in the euro area over the period 2007–2009, finding an important role played by budget deficits and government debt ratios relative to Germany.

As well as understanding the drivers of the price of sovereign risk, some more recent papers have examined the issue of capital flows into government bond markets. For example, in recent years the bond market has experienced much greater inflows of capital, notably from emerging to advanced economies, which has helped to suppress US bond yields (e.g. Hauner and Kumar, 2009). In addition, Baldacci and Kumar (2010) make the point that the greater integration of government bond markets globally has enabled a more efficient pricing of sovereign risk and better facilitated price discovery. A further strand of the literature examines whether the sovereign risk of particular economic regions is perceived differently by the market. Hauner et al. (2010) assess whether rating agencies and investors perceived the sovereign risk of the new EU Member States to be different to that of other emerging markets. They found that higher policy credibility owing to EU membership helped led to a lower perceived sovereign risk of the new EU Member States compared to other emerging economies. As regards the issue of the crisis, there is an emerging academic literature. For example, Schuknecht et al. (2010) make the interesting point that while bond yield spreads in the euro area before and during the crisis can be largely explained by fundamentals, the market has penalized fiscal imbalances much more harshly in the period after the collapse of Lehman Brothers.

The European sovereign debt crisis that began to intensify during 2010 has called into question the extent to which the price of sovereign risk reflects macroeconomic fundamentals. Where the price of sovereign risk cannot be explained by fundamentals, this would suggest that the risk is driven by other factors, such as financial market sentiment or contagion. Our analysis builds on the previous literature by providing an assessment of the extent to which sovereign risk may be mis-priced, looking in particular at emerging and advanced economies in both non-crisis and crisis regimes. In addition, we assess whether sovereign risk mis-pricing spills over to other regions in crisis compared to non-crisis times.

3. Methodology

The starting point to motivate the empirical analysis for the determinants of sovereign yields is a standard definition of sovereign risk as reflecting credit risk, liquidity risk and risk appetite:

$$r_t = \left(1 - P\left(X_t\right)\right)\left(1 - \mu_t\right) + \Omega_t + \Phi_t \tag{1}$$

where r_t is the sovereign yield of a particular country relative to a risk-free asset, $1 - P(X_t)$ the probability of default, $(1 - \mu_t)$ the loss given default, Ω_t a risk premium and Φ_t the liquidity premium. This raises the question about which fundamentals determine these three terms, and thus influence the price of sovereign risk. To gauge this, it is useful to think of a basic intertemporal budget constraint for a government:

$$\sum_{j=0}^{\infty} E_t \left[\frac{\tau_{t+j} - g_{t+j} + s_{t+j} + T_{t+j}}{(1+r)^j} \right] \geq \frac{M_{t-1} + D_{t-1}}{P_t} \tag{2}$$

where the numerator on the left-hand-side is the primary government balance (τ tax revenue, s seignorage, T transfers, g primary expenditures), M the money stock, D the public debt level, and P the price level. The important point here, to which we will return further below, is that expectations may play a central role in determining fiscal sustainability, thus giving rise to multiple equilibria in the relationship between fundamentals and the price of sovereign risk r.

Based on this conceptual framework, we examine the determinants of the pricing of sovereign risk both in non-crisis and crisis states for a range of advanced and emerging economies, using a standard panel model with country fixed effects (building on a common approach in the literature, e.g. Edwards, 1984; Hauner et al., 2010). In its most simple form, the approach is based on the following models:

$$s_{i,t} = \alpha_0 + \alpha_i + \beta_1 X_{i,t} + \gamma_1 S_{j,t} + \varepsilon_{i,t} \tag{3}$$

We extend this benchmark specification to allow for a shift in the parameters over time, and in particular during crisis times, in the following way:

$$s_{i,t} = \alpha_0 + \alpha_i + \beta_1 X_{i,t} + \gamma_1 S_{j,t} + \left(\delta_0 + \delta_i + \beta_2 X_{i,t} + \gamma_2 S_{j,t}\right) D_t^C + \varepsilon_{i,t} \tag{4}$$

where $s_{i,t}$ represents the price of sovereign risk (which can either be government bond spreads relative to a benchmark rate, CDS spreads relative to a benchmark, or sovereign credit risk ratings), $X_{i,t}$ represents a set of economic fundamentals, and D^C is a crisis dummy taking the value of one in the period after the collapse of Lehman Brothers in September 2008.[4] $S_{j,t}$ is the regional price of sovereign risk for the region in which country i is located and excludes country i itself. In the benchmark specification, this regional risk is simply an unweighted average of the price of sovereign risk in other regional economies, while in the extensions the model also allows for a transmission across different prices of sovereign risk (e.g. from ratings to bond yields), either domestically or regionally.

α_i and δ_i are country-specific fixed effects, and as common intercepts are included as well, these are country-specific deviations from the common intercepts. Note that equation (3) is a representation of sovereign risk for a particular time period, while equation (4) extends this framework to allow for a change in the pricing of fundamentals and of regional risk during the crisis period. The estimation is done via OLS with robust standard errors, and at monthly data frequency.

As is common in the literature, contagion is defined as the *change* in the way countries' own fundamentals or regional risk are priced during a particular period, i.e. a change in the reaction of financial markets either in response to observable factors, such as changes in sovereign risk among neighboring countries, or due to unobservables, such as herding behavior of market participants.

Conceptually, there are five sources for changes in the pricing of sovereign risk. The first one is a change in fundamentals $X_{i,t}$ or a change in the regional risk

$S_{j,t}$, e.g. with a deterioration of the quality of fundamentals or a rise in regional risk driving up the price of sovereign risk. In our terminology, none of these two factors is referred to as contagion as the pricing of the factors is unchanged from the pre-crisis period.

A second source is a change in the way financial markets price a particular fundamental during the crisis, as markets may, for example, become more sensitive to the same fundamental during the crisis (as measured by parameters β_2). This is what the literature has referred to as "wake-up call" contagion or fundamentals contagion. A third source is related to the pricing of regional risk $S_{j,t}$ (indicated by parameters γ_2), with a change in this pricing what we refer to as "regional contagion", i.e. an intensification in the cross-country transmission of sovereign risk.

A fourth reason for changes in the pricing of sovereign risk is the country-specific fixed effects during the crisis δ_i. It is hard to gauge what these country-specific effects measure. It may be that they reflect a change in unobservable fundamentals during the crisis, or alternatively a change in the sensitivity with which unobservable factors are priced. In the former case, we would not refer to this phenomenon as contagion, while the latter would indeed imply contagion. Nevertheless, since these terms are constant over time (allowing for a discrete change during the crisis) none of these two descriptions may be entirely plausible, and a better way to describe them is merely as country risk premia.

The fifth source for changes in the pricing of sovereign risk is a shift in the residual $\varepsilon_{i,t}$. While the residuals in equations (3) and (4) are unsystematic components of the pricing of risk, they may nevertheless provide an indication of herding contagion across countries at certain points in time. Following the approach of Boyson et al. (2010), we analyze the clustering across countries of large unexplained changes in the pricing of sovereign risk. Herding contagion is present if there are large positive residuals simultaneously, at the same point in time, in several countries. More precisely, we look at the distribution of the residuals of equation (4), and extract those that lie in the top 10th percentile of each country's distribution. If the residuals were uncorrelated across countries, then in each period t about 10% of the residuals of all countries should be in their respective top decile. However, if we find a substantial clustering in the number of countries with large unexplained increases in the pricing of sovereign risk, it is indicative of what we refer to as "pure contagion" or herding contagion.

There are a number of points that need emphasizing. A first one is that the choice of the empirical model for the pricing of sovereign risk is far from uncontroversial as there is a multitude of potential fundamentals that may influence the sustainability of debt and thus the price of sovereign risk. As we will explain in the next section, our aim is to stay as close as possible to the literature in the specification of the empirical model, though we conduct a number of robustness tests with additional determinants.

A second point relates to the spillover of changes in prices of sovereign risk. The framework of equations (3) and (4) allows only for the transmission within the same region and within the same asset class (e.g. within the government bond market, or within the CDS market), while a transmission may also occur across market segments and across regions. In extensions to the benchmark specification below, we are particularly interested in cross-market spillovers, such as, for example, whether changes in sovereign ratings are particularly important in driving bond yield spreads or CDS prices, both within countries and across countries.

A third point refers to the question of whether the price of sovereign risk is truly exogenous to the fundamentals included in the model. In particular during the European sovereign debt crisis, it has been obvious that a rise in sovereign spreads has adversely affected confidence and thus may have also exerted an effect on fundamentals. While it is likely that such a transmission has been present, it does not seem plausible that such effects materialise immediately, within the same month.

Finally, it is likely that there is heterogeneity in the way financial markets price fundamentals across countries. To test for such heterogeneity, after estimating the benchmark models (3) and (4), we also provide estimates for various country groups and subsamples in order to gauge the extent and potential pattern of such heterogeneity.

4. Data and stylized facts

This section discusses the choice of data and presents some stylized facts on the evolution of sovereign risk over the past decade.

A first crucial issue is the definition of sovereign risk. Our approach is to take a financial market perspective and analyze how financial markets price sovereign risk. More specifically, we analyze three separate financial prices of sovereign risk – the government bond yield spreads (relative to 3-month money market rates), sovereign CDS spreads, and Standard & Poors sovereign credit ratings. As is common in the literature, sovereign ratings are transformed linearly into a numerical format, ranging from 1 (AAA) to 20 (default). All of these series are obtained from Bloomberg. Each of the three measures of sovereign risk has its shortcomings. For instance, sovereign yield and CDS spreads may be influenced by risk premia and liquidity premia,[5] while ratings have a discrete nature, and rating changes may frequently be anticipated by market participants. While we mostly focus on sovereign yield spreads as our preferred measure, we also check for robustness of the findings using the other two measures.

In line with the literature on the determinants of sovereign spreads and ratings (see also discussion above), the country-specific macroeconomic variables are the public debt/GDP ratio, fiscal balance/GDP ratio, real GDP growth, and the current account balance/GDP ratio, while we also include the VIX index to reflect a common global risk factor (as in Hauner et al., 2010). Given the lack of availability of some of these variables at a monthly frequency, we follow the literature in this regard using standard interpolation (e.g. Hauner et al., 2010; Dell'Ariccia et al., 2006; Ferrucci, 2003). Data for country-specific fundamentals stems from the

IMF's IFS, while the VIX series is taken from Bloomberg. Tables 1 and 2 provide summary statistics for the countries covered, and for the variables of the empirical analysis.

A crucial choice is the country sample. Our approach is to include as many financially open countries as possible, based on data availability, including emerging markets. Our benchmark sample is for 31 advanced and emerging economies for the period from 1999 to 2011. In order to check for heterogeneity across countries, all of our estimations are conducted both for the whole country sample as well as for sub-samples, distinguishing in particular between euro area countries, EMEs, and other advanced economies (AEs). EMEs in our analysis include Brazil, Bulgaria, Chile, China, Colombia, Hungary, Malaysia, Mexico, Peru, Philippines, Poland, Russia, South Africa, and Turkey. The advanced economies are comprised of the following euro area advanced economies: Belgium, Finland, France, Germany, Netherlands, Greece, Italy, Portugal, Spain, and Ireland; and the following non-euro area advanced economies: Australia, Denmark, New Zealand, Sweden, Switzerland, the United Kingdom, and the United States.

Turning to some key stylized facts, Fig. 1 and Table 3 show how the sovereign debt crisis has impacted upon the price of sovereign risk across a range of advanced and emerging economies. The largest rise in the price of sovereign risk is evident in the case of the euro area programme countries, i.e. Greece, Ireland and Portugal. The impact of the sovereign debt crisis appears to have had a much more muted effect in Latin America and Asia, with the price of sovereign risk in fact declining in some countries. Emerging European countries, on the other hand, have experienced some negative reactions, notably in the cases of Hungary and Poland. The other advanced euro area countries have also experienced a rise in the price of sovereign risk as measured by bond spreads and CDS spreads.

Changes in the price of sovereign risk mask the fact that levels of risk may remain fundamentally different across countries. Fig. 2 plot the *levels* in sovereign

Table 1 List of countries/regions.

Euro area economies	Other advanced economies	Emerging market economies	
		Latin America	Other EMEs
Belgium	Australia	Brazil	Bulgaria
Finland	Denmark	Chile	Hungary
France	New Zealand	Colombia	Poland
Germany	Sweden	Mexico	Russia
Netherlands	Switzerland	Peru	South Africa
Greece	United Kingdom		Turkey
Italy	United States		China
Portugal			Malaysia
Spain			Philippines
Ireland			

Table 2 Descriptive statistics.

	Pre-crisis				Crisis			
	Avg	*Max*	*Min*	*Std dev*	*Avg*	*Max*	*Min*	*Std dev*
Bond spreads								
Euro area	71.92	243.80	-137.70	83.05	3186.60	-148.00	330.33	3186.60
Other Aes	-0.58	353.70	-295.70	122.34	143.01	345.10	-267.20	117.03
EMEs	201.38	984.34	41.85	147.37	263.23	1366.32	37.21	159.26
CDS spreads								
Euro area	7.91	84.56	1.00	9.71	187.77	2989.93	7.50	299.27
Other Aes	9.32	88.12	1.43	11.85	57.06	206.28	10.00	30.67
EMEs	119.53	838.90	4.50	129.99	191.41	783.38	53.00	117.06
Sovereign ratings								
Euro area	2.63	7.00	1.00	1.82	3.96	20.00	1.00	3.43
Other Aes	1.14	2.00	1.00	0.35	1.15	3.00	1.00	0.37
EMEs	9.39	14.00	5.00	2.49	8.80	13.00	4.00	2.33
Public debt/GDP								
Euro area	65.30	111.70	21.75	25.75	85.27	170.97	34.81	28.22
Other Aes	41.66	73.40	9.36	19.12	49.81	103.70	12.40	23.42
EMEs	37.76	73.08	4.01	18.26	38.02	80.74	5.40	20.24
Real GDP growth								
Euro area	2.68	6.57	-3.87	1.62	-0.91	5.55	-9.14	3.32
Other Aes	2.70	4.73	-1.50	1.22	0.49	7.16	-6.30	3.23
EMEs	6.02	14.64	0.12	2.43	2.92	10.62	-8.83	4.67
Δ Current account/GDP								
Euro area	-0.70	4.42	-6.93	1.90	0.64	6.91	-8.25	2.44
Other AEs	-0.42	3.85	-17.92	2.34	1.02	16.87	-15.42	3.44
EMEs	-0.31	6.79	-12.25	2.68	0.56	21.18	-11.77	4.13
Δ Budget balance/GDP								
Euro area	-0.07	3.00	-7.65	1.77	-1.36	30.14	-20.53	5.56
Other AEs	0.27	4.09	-4.24	1.54	-1.38	3.51	-7.23	2.61
EMEs	0.75	6.30	-4.58	1.54	-0.86	7.54	-12.08	3.09

Δ VIX index	0.41	13.94	-15.57	5.96	-0.07	39.37	-41.86	18.08
Regional bond spreads								
Euro area	71.92	234.05	-106.20	82.52	355.27	1422.73	-119.03	253.18
Other AEs	-0.58	196.84	-198.47	80.14	143.01	255.35	-192.60	89.36
EMEs	201.81	338.25	122.77	55.02	267.28	517.30	157.26	75.64
Regional CDS spreads								
Euro area	7.91	45.80	1.58	8.27	187.77	1296.39	9.26	227.61
Other AEs	9.32	35.68	1.93	5.77	57.06	164.00	15.55	25.91
EMEs	120.09	301.39	35.82	56.78	196.34	607.90	112.72	93.24
Regional ratings								
Euro area	2.63	5.00	1.25	1.18	3.96	11.50	1.25	2.71
Other AEs	1.15	1.17	1.00	0.06	1.15	1.33	1.00	0.07
EMEs	9.40	10.67	8.38	0.46	8.80	9.23	8.38	0.19

Source: Bloomberg

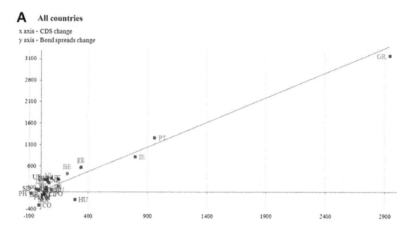

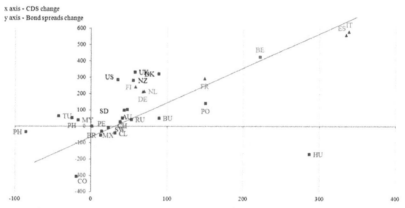

Notes: The figures shows the change in sovereign bond spreads and CDS spreads – in basis points –
between September 2008 and September 2011. Figure 1.B excludes the programme countries Greece,
Ireland and Portugal in order to better show the differences among other countries.

Figure 1 Changes in sovereign bond spreads and CDS spreads during the crisis.

yield spreads against sovereign ratings (Fig. 2A–B) and of CDS spreads against
sovereign ratings (Fig. 2C–D) before the crisis (in September 2008) and at the
end of the sample period in September 2011. Recall that a higher number for
sovereign ratings indicates higher risk, i.e. a worse rating. There are two points to
note. First, there is a clear relationship between the rating and the market price of
sovereign risk, whether measured by government bond yields or by CDS spreads.

A second, and highly intriguing finding is that the pricing of risk for euro
area/EMU countries seems to be very different to that of non-EMU countries.
In essence, there is no systematic difference in the pricing-rating relationship

Table 3 Changes in the price of sovereign risk during the crisis.

	Bond spreads			CDS			Ratings		
	Sep '08	Sep '11	bpsΔ	Sep '08	Sep '11	bpsΔ	Sep '08	Sep '11	NotchΔ
Brazil	332.6	277.3	-55.3	129.9	142.3	12.4	10.0	9.0	-1.0
Chile	223.2	181.0	-42.1	61.5	92.6	31.1	5.0	5.0	0.0
Colombia	497.6	191.0	-306.6	160.1	141.1	-19.0	10.0	10.0	0.0
Mexico	274.8	266.8	-8.0	117.8	140.5	22.7	8.0	9.0	1.0
Peru	309.9	279.4	-30.5	133.5	147.2	13.7	10.0	10.0	0.0
Bulgaria	301.5	351.5	50.0	185.0	274.0	89.0	9.0	9.0	0.0
Hungary	725.3	555.4	-169.8	124.3	411.0	286.7	9.0	11.0	2.0
Poland	168.8	309.0	140.2	68.0	217.8	149.8	6.0	6.0	0.0
Russia	299.1	340.4	41.3	133.0	185.8	52.8	8.0	8.0	0.0
South Africa	197.4	248.7	51.3	173.5	148.5	-25.0	8.0	8.0	0.0
Turkey	290.4	354.1	63.7	266.2	223.6	-42.6	13.0	12.0	-1.0
China	227.8	277.8	50.0	66.0	107.0	41.0	5.0	4.0	-1.0
Malaysia	194.2	233.1	38.9	132.3	115.7	-16.6	8.0	9.0	1.0
Philippines	324.0	288.9	-35.1	243.8	158.1	-85.7	13.0	12.0	-1.0
Greece	11.4	3186.6	3175.2	50.7	2989.9	2939.2	7.0	20.0	13.0
Ireland	-59.3	760.0	819.3	29.8	822.5	792.7	2.0	8.0	6.0
Italy	-26.1	551.8	577.9	40.1	378.7	338.6	5.0	6.0	1.0
Portugal	-70.3	1192.5	1262.8	37.7	994.4	956.7	5.0	12.0	7.0
Spain	-83.1	475.1	558.2	37.5	372.1	334.6	3.0	4.0	1.0
Belgium	-73.3	350.5	423.8	20.5	242.5	222.0	3.0	3.0	0.0
Finland	-111.6	129.0	240.6	9.3	67.5	58.3	1.0	1.0	0.0
France	-111.2	181.2	292.4	11.1	160.0	148.9	2.0	2.0	0.0
Germany	-148.0	65.3	213.3	7.5	75.3	67.8	1.0	1.0	0.0
Netherlands	-105.3	108.2	213.5	9.2	78.9	69.7	1.0	1.0	0.0
Australia	-161.5	-57.3	104.2	19.5	66.8	47.3	1.0	1.0	0.0
Denmark	-256.8	64.0	320.7	10.3	98.8	88.5	1.0	1.0	0.0
New Zealand	-221.6	59.9	281.5	22.7	78.0	55.3	2.0	3.0	1.0
Sweden	-184.5	-84.9	99.6	10.0	53.2	43.2	1.0	1.0	0.0
Switzerland	-13.1	14.6	27.7	19.5	57.6	38.1	1.0	1.0	0.0
UK	-202.7	130.3	333.0	17.7	75.3	57.6	1.0	1.0	0.0
US	-128.5	157.8	286.3	16.3	51.3	35.0	1.0	1.0	0.0

Notes: The table shows the level of the three proxies of sovereign risk immediately before and at the end of the crisis, as well as the total change over the crisis period.

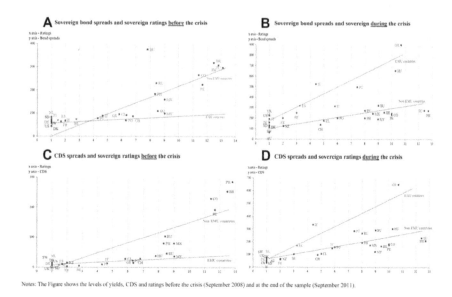

Notes: The Figure shows the levels of yields, CDS and ratings before the crisis (September 2008) and at the end of the sample (September 2011).

Figure 2 Market pricing of sovereign risk versus sovereign ratings in EMU and non-EMU countries.

between EMU countries and non-EMU countries for those with low sovereign risk. However, there is a substantial difference between those EMU countries and non-EMU countries (the latter being EMEs) with high sovereign risk. Before the crisis, differences in yields and CDS spreads across EMU countries were very small, while differences in sovereign ratings were larger – resulting in relatively flat regression lines in Fig. 2A and C for EMU countries. By contrast, during the sovereign debt crisis this relationship shifted substantially. Most importantly, the link between the market price of sovereign risk and ratings became much steeper for EMU countries during the crisis.

How should one interpret this shift in the link between the market price of sovereign risk and sovereign ratings during the crisis? It is hard to provide a definite answer to this question. In principle, there should, at all times, be a fairly close link between the market price of risk and the rating. Of course the two do not proxy the same thing. For instance, yield spreads and CDS spreads are subject to risk and liquidity premia, and may also be affected by adverse market contagion from other countries, factors which presumably do not affect the ratings of sovereigns. However, if the ratings correctly reflect a country's fundamentals, then the steeper sovereign price-rating link for EMU countries compared to non-EMU countries suggests that markets "overprice" the sovereign risk of EMU countries. By contrast, if market prices are "correct" in pricing fundamentals, then this steeper relationship implies that sovereign ratings tend to be too favorable during the crisis for EMU countries relative to non-EMU countries. Such an implication stands in sharp contrast to the widely heard allegations by some policy-makers that rating agencies have exacerbated the European sovereign debt crisis, as the latter interpretation would imply that rating agencies have been too timid in downgrading some EMU countries during the crisis.

The analysis of the pricing of sovereign risk, and the drivers of this pricing and the potential role of contagion is the objective of the remainder of the paper.

5. Empirical results

This section presents and discusses the empirical results. It starts by outlining the empirical results of the benchmark model for the pricing of sovereign risks, then turns to different proxies for the "mis-pricing" of sovereign risk, and concludes by analyzing various potential sources of contagion.

5.1. The benchmark model

As a starting point, we derive a comprehensive yet simple model for the pricing of sovereign risk, which follows standard approaches in the literature, and includes five fundamental determinants of sovereign risk: public debt to GDP ratio, fiscal balance to GDP ratio, real GDP growth, the current account balance relative to GDP, and finally, as a common determinant, the degree of risk in global financial markets, as proxied by the VIX index. Using this benchmark specification, we estimate model (4) in order to gauge how well this model explains sovereign risk, and equally importantly, whether there is evidence for fundamentals contagion or regional contagion. Tables 4 and 5 provide the estimates for equation (4), showing β_1 and γ_1 for the pre-crisis period and the total effects $(\beta_2 + \gamma_2)$ for the crisis period, as well as splitting the sample for various country groups.[6]

The tables yield, overall, a plausible and intuitive link between fundamentals and sovereign risk – with higher public debt, lower growth, a worsening in the fiscal balance and the current account in previous years all being associated with higher sovereign risk in financial markets. Moreover, there are plausible cross-country differences in this link between fundamentals and sovereign risk. For instance, when focusing on yield spreads, EMEs are much more sensitive to public debt, growth and fiscal balances in the relatively more tranquil pre-crisis period than other country groups. This is consistent with the argument that EMEs in the past were forced to run tighter (and often highly pro-cyclical) fiscal policies because of the much higher sensitivity of financial markets to changes in fiscal conditions in EMEs than in advanced economies.

A second compelling finding relates to changes over time in the relationship between fundamentals and the price of sovereign risk. It is the pricing of sovereign risk of the GIPSI countries which has been most sensitive to fundamentals during the sovereign debt crisis, while for EMEs there has generally been little change in this relationship. This evidence indicates the presence of "wake-up

Table 4 Determinants of bond yield spreads.

	All	All EA	GIPSI	Other EA	Other AE	EME
Pre-crisis						
Public debt/GDP	3.03***	0.28***	0.08	0.39***	1.39***	8.24***
Real GDP growth	-1.24**	0.34	0.25	-0.19	8.45***	-3.92***
Δ Current account/GDP	0.24	0.25	0.44	-0.24	-0.22	1.92
Δ Fiscal balance/GDP	-0.02	-2.20***	-0.63*	-0.36	12.31	-46.08**
ΔVIX	-0.00	-0.01	0.04	-0.01	-0.25	0.19
Regional bond spreads ($i \neq j$)	0.81***	0.98***	1.01***	0.99***	0.81***	0.58***
Crisis						
Public debt/GDP	5.62***	13.01***	17.84***	0.45	7.24***	7.25***
Real GDP growth	-5.16***	-17.51***	-28.38***	-1.74***	5.24***	-1.67***
Δ Current account/GDP	-0.75	-6.02	-7.75	-3.78**	-3.61**	-4.01**
Δ Fiscal balance/GDP	-2.48*	1.71	-5.78	-3.90	-12.96**	0.17
ΔVIX	-0.00	-2.49***	-1.72	-0.13	-1.11	1.96**
Regional bond spreads ($i \neq j$)	0.65***	0.31***	0.20	0.99***	0.77***	0.77
Adjusted R-squared	0.86	0.93	0.91	0.99	0.83	0.76
No. of countries	31	10	5	5	7	14
No. of observations	4278	1490	690	745	966	2086

Notes: Table 4 shows the estimates from equation (4). $s_{i,t} = \alpha_0 + \alpha_i + \beta_1 X_{i,t} + \gamma_1 S_{j,t} + (\delta_0 + \delta_i + \beta_2 X_{i,t} + \gamma_2 S_{j,t})D_t^C + \varepsilon_{i,t}$ (4) where $s_{i,t}$ represents government bond spreads, $X_{i,t}$ represents a set of macroeconomic fundamentals, D^C is a crisis dummy taking the value of one in the period after the collapse of Lehman Brothers in September 2008, and $S_{j,t}$ is the regional price of sovereign risk for the region in which country i is located and excludes country i itself. α_i and δ_i are country-specific fixed effects, and as common intercepts are included as well, these are country-specific deviations from the common intercepts. Note that the table shows β_1 and γ_1 for the pre-crisis period and the total effects $(\beta_2 + \gamma_2)$ for the crisis period. ***, **, * indicate statistical significance at the 99%, 95% and 90% levels, respectively.

Table 5 Determinants of CDS spreads.

	All	All EA	GIPSI	Other EA	Other AE	EME
Pre-crisis						
Public debt/GDP	0.82***	-0.04	0.02	-0.15*	-0.03	9.25***
Real GDP growth	-0.91**	-0.83**	0.44	-0.45**	-1.07**	-6.58***
Δ Current account/GDP	-0.22	4.02	0.77	0.06	-0.27**	-6.05***
Δ Fiscal balance/GDP	0.36	0.55	0.20	-0.08	-0.49	-25.46**
Δ VIX	-0.00	-0.00	0.03	-0.00	-0.00	0.00
Regional CDS spreads ($i \neq j$)	0.51***	0.70***	0.94***	0.31**	0.26**	0.34***
Crisis						
Public debt/GDP	1.95***	6.67***	10.42***	0.48**	0.73**	2.29**
Real GDP growth	-2.83***	-7.33***	-38.34***	-1.33***	-1.06	-2.36***
Δ Current account/GDP	-0.42	-0.65	6.65	-4.54	0.03	-0.53
Δ Fiscal balance/GDP	-2.58	-4.33	-0.74	-1.66	0.92	4.57
Δ VIX	-0.10	-0.00	-0.38	0.00	-0.00	0.00
Regional CDS spreads ($i \neq j$)	0.76***	0.44***	0.33***	0.65***	0.96***	0.88***
Adjusted R-squared	0.87	0.82	0.88	0.87	0.89	0.85
No. of countries	31	10	5	5	7	14
No. of observations	2852	920	460	460	644	1288

Notes: Table 5 shows the estimates from equation (4). $s_{i,t} = \alpha_0 + \alpha_i + \beta_1 X_{i,t} + \gamma_1 S_{j,t} + (\delta_0 + \delta_i + \beta_2 X_{i,t} + \gamma_2 S_{j,t}) D_t^C + \varepsilon_{i,t}$ (4) where $s_{i,t}$ represents CDS spreads, $X_{i,t}$ represents a set of macroeconomic fundamentals, D^C is a crisis dummy taking the value of one in the period after the collapse of Lehman Brothers in September 2008, and $S_{j,t}$ is the regional price of sovereign risk for the region in which country i is located and excludes country i itself. α_i and δ_i are country-specific fixed effects, and as common intercepts are included as well, these are country-specific deviations from the common intercepts. Note that the table shows β_1 and γ_1 for the pre-crisis period and the total effects $(\beta_2 + \gamma_2)$ for the crisis period. ***, **, * indicate statistical significance at the 99%, 95% and 90% levels, respectively.

call" or fundamentals contagion during the crisis, in particular for the GIPSI countries. Note that although most of the coefficients have the expected signs, they are sometimes not statistically significant, in part due to the relatively small number of countries.

A third key finding is that regional contagion during the crisis has been unimportant, in particular for European countries. The estimates show that the cross-country transmission of sovereign risk within the euro area has decreased significantly during the crisis (implying a negative γ_2). Note that this does not imply that there has been no regional spillovers of sovereign risk during the crisis – in fact there has been as indicated by the positive sum of coefficients $(\gamma_1 + \gamma_2)$ – but the sensitivity of domestic sovereign debt markets to foreign markets has decreased.

Another interesting finding relates to the pricing of regional risk prior to the crisis. This has nowhere been as high as in the euro area – with a coefficient of close to 1 indicating that changes in sovereign risk in the region was transmitted one-for-one to domestic markets. Looking at the GIPSI countries during the pre-crisis period indicates that what has been driving the pricing of sovereign risk in these economies prior to 2008 was primarily the sovereign risk elsewhere in the region, while domestic fundamentals played little or no role. This may indeed be suggestive of an underpricing of fundamentals in sovereign debt markets, an issue which we address in more detail in the next section.

Fourth, comparing the empirical estimates across the three types of sovereign risk – bond spreads, CDS spreads and sovereign ratings – yields qualitatively very similar results. We noted above the shortcomings of the analysis for ratings, given the discrete nature of the ratings as well as the few changes in ratings, in particular for other advanced economies, and hence that these findings needs to be interpreted cautiously. It is important to stress, nonetheless, that across the three types of sovereign debt markets, a similar story prevails as regards the determinants of the price of sovereign risk prior and during the crisis.

Finally, we extend model (4) to allow for spillovers and contagion not only within the same region but also specifically from the GIPSI countries, and we also allow for spillovers and contagion across market segments. For instance, some observers have argued that the rating downgrades of some European countries have been important in driving up sovereign yield spreads and CDS spreads.

Table 6 shows the estimates for this extended model for sovereign bond yield spreads, highlighting two main points. The first point is that there seems to have been little cross-market spillovers or contagion. In particular ratings downgrades (indicated by a rise in the rating scale in the data for the estimates) are not associated with a rise in yield spreads, thus not lending support to the claim that ratings changes systematically triggered a rise in yield spreads. The second point is that there does not seem to have been any spillover or contagion from changes in sovereign risk in GIPSI countries to other regions. None of the GIPSI contagion coefficients for the crisis period is statistically significant in the estimation.

Table 6 Determinants of bond yield spreads – with own-contagion and cross-contagion.

	All	All EA	GIPSI	Other EA	Other AE	EME
Pre-crisis						
Public debt/GDP	2.15***	-0.02	0.57***	-0.26	3.00***	4.39***
Real GDP growth	-0.32	1.43**	0.16	0.02	18.31***	-15.59***
Δ Current account/GDP	0.02	-0.25	0.12	-0.73	-3.68**	1.01
Δ Fiscal balance/GDP	0.16	-2.13***	0.57	-0.74	-1.37	-23.45
ΔVIX	-0.34	0.05	-0.02	0.03	0.14	0.94
Regional CDS spreads ($i \neq j$)	-0.22***	-0.16**	-0.12*	0.02	-0.48*	0.14*
Regional bond spreads ($i \neq j$)	0.85***	1.01***	1.01***	0.87***	-0.16	0.18**
Regional ratings ($i \neq j$)	-3.26	2.68	0.20	-1.84	10.59	1.48
GIPSI bond spreads				0.13*	0.97***	0.06
GIPSI CDS spreads				0.01	0.34	0.48
GIPSI ratings				-1.28	18.00	41.62***
Crisis						
Public debt/GDP	6.46***	12.96***	18.66***	0.24	9.52***	6.25***
Real GDP growth	-5.58***	-16.34***	-29.88***	-0.63	6.21***	0.03
Δ Current account/GDP	-1.89**	-5.73	-10.16	-2.57***	-3.27**	-6.03***
Δ Fiscal balance/GDP	-3.84	0.85	-6.45	-0.56	-9.23**	1.70
ΔVIX	-0.29	-1.41**	-1.62	-0.07	-0.59	2.15***
Regional CDS spreads ($i \neq j$)	-0.00	-0.04	0.07	-0.24**	0.36*	0.22***
Regional bond spreads ($i \neq j$)	0.80***	0.49***	0.21*	1.00***	0.75***	0.47***
Regional ratings ($i \neq j$)	-61.68***	-24.61***	-11.42	-354.09	202.67**	47.99
GIPSI bond spreads				0.03	0.01	-0.05
GIPSI CDS spreads				0.01	-0.08	0.00
GIPSI ratings				-3.57	-10.65	5.99
Adjusted *R*-squared	0.88	0.93	0.90	0.98	0.91	0.77
No. of countries	31	10	5	5	7	14
No. of observations	2852	920	460	460	644	1288

Notes: The table shows the estimates for an extended version of equation (4) for bond spreads. $s_{i,t} = \alpha_0 + \alpha_i + \beta_i D^C + \beta_1 X_{i,t} + \gamma_1 \sum_k S_{j,k,t} + (\delta_0 + \delta_i + \beta_2 X_{i,t} + \gamma_2 \sum_k S_{j,k,t}) D^C_t + \varepsilon_{i,t}$ (4) where $S_{i,k,t}$ represents government bond spreads, $X_{i,t}$ represents a set of macroeconomic fundamentals, D^C is a crisis dummy taking the value of one in the period after the collapse of Lehman Brothers in September 2008. α_i and δ_i are country-specific fixed effects, and as common intercepts are included as well, these are country-specific deviations from the common intercepts. Note that the table shows β_1 and γ_1 for the pre-crisis period and the total effects ($\beta_1 + \gamma_2$) for the crisis period. ***, **, * indicate statistical significance at the 99%, 95% and 90% levels, respectively. The estimation where $S_{j,k,t}$ represents, in turn, CDS spreads and sovereign credit ratings are qualitatively very similar and are available from the authors upon request.

5.2. Detecting potential mis-pricing of sovereign risk

We now turn to the question to what extent one can derive normative implications from the empirical estimates presented above. It is important to note that the presence of contagion, as identified in the previous sub-section, does not necessarily imply a mis-pricing or over-pricing of sovereign risk for GIPSI (or any other) countries. It merely indicates that there has been a shift in the pricing of fundamentals or regional risk between the pre-crisis period and the crisis period. It might well be that sovereign risk was under-priced prior to the crisis. If one takes the entire country sample as the benchmark to which to compare the pricing of sovereign risk, Tables 4 and 5 suggest that during the pre-crisis period sovereign risk in GIPSI countries may indeed have been under-priced because financial markets did not seem to consider any of the fundamentals, bar the fiscal balance, for the pricing of sovereign risk in GIPSI countries. By contrast, markets priced fundamentals more strongly for GIPSI countries than this benchmark during the crisis.

In order to get at a normative notion of the pricing of sovereign risk, it is useful to conduct a counterfactual analysis and ask how sovereign risk would have been priced during the crisis if the pre-crisis model was the correct one, i.e. the one that reflects an accurate relationship between fundamentals and sovereign risk. We then compare this prediction with one that takes the crisis model as the true one to see what it would have implied for the pricing of sovereign risk in the pre-crisis period for different countries.

Fig. 3 shows the estimates from this counterfactual exercise for bond yield spreads.[7] From the pre-crisis estimation of equation (3) for the all-country sample and including own fundamentals only, we extract the predicted values for the crisis period based on the pre-crisis parameters. Similarly, from the crisis estimation of equation (3), we take the predicted values for the pre-crisis period. The figures plot against both the actual price of sovereign risk for pre-crisis and crisis periods.

Two main findings stand out. First, when using the pre-crisis model as benchmark, then the actual price of sovereign risk of GIPSI countries is substantially over-priced, i.e. actual yields in GIPSI countries are much higher than those implied by the pre-crisis relationship between fundamentals and risk. This is consistent with the findings of the previous section, which showed that markets became much more sensitive to fundamentals. By contrast, for the core euro area countries, such as Germany, France and the Netherlands, sovereign risk according to this benchmark has been under-priced significantly during the crisis, i.e. actual yields have remained substantially below those implied by the pre-crisis model. This is not, or much less often the case for countries outside the euro area, for most of which actual spreads and predicted spreads are quite close also during the crisis.

The second finding is that the picture reverses if one takes the crisis model of equation (3) and derives implied spreads for the pre-crisis period. This analysis shows that spreads would have been higher, in particular for Greece and to some extent for other euro area countries such as Italy and Belgium, in the pre-crisis period than they actually were.[8] By contrast, those of the core euro area

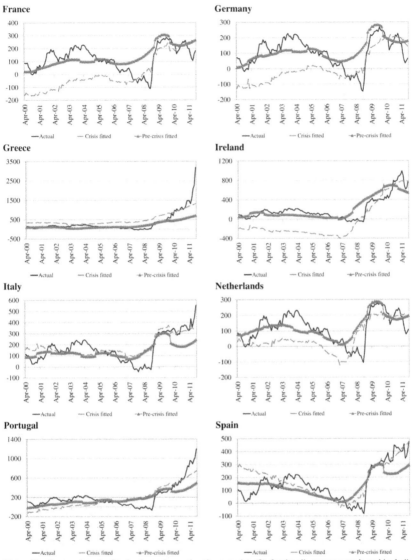

Notes: The figures show the fitted values when estimating equation (3), for the all-country sample and including own fundamentals only, for the crisis period based on the pre-crisis parameters, and similarly for the pre-crisis period based on the crisis model. For space reasons, we present the results only for the GIPSI countries plus a selection of non-GIPSI euro area countries.

Figure 3 Counterfactual analysis – sovereign bond spreads.

countries would have been much lower. It is worth noting that there exists some heterogeneity across the GIPSI countries as regards the predicted spreads based on the pre-crisis and crisis models, which may be related to whether crises were driven by government budget deficits or the private sector (Stein, 2011). While the pattern is very similar for Greece, Portugal and to a lesser extent Italy (i.e. negative prediction errors in the pre-crisis period and positive prediction errors in the crisis period), the pattern is somewhat different for Spain and very different in the case of Ireland.[9] As regards Ireland, counterfactual spreads would have actually been lower before the crisis, given that the country actually had low levels of public debt and high growth rates. Moreover, large liabilities due to the financial sector in Ireland have been an important factor during the crisis. There is one *additional* element that may be important for explaining the *levels* of sovereign risk, and this is the country-specific premia as measured by the country-fixed effects α_i for the pre-crisis period and δ_i for the crisis period. As these are constants they cannot account for any of the time variations within each sub-period, but they may explain, for example why a country has a relatively high price of its sovereign debt while its observable fundamentals may be comparatively strong, and vice versa. As discussed in detail above, it is hard to give an economic interpretation to these fixed effects, and they likely, at least in part, reflect country-specific risk premia that financial markets demand to hold a particular country's public debt.

Understanding how these country-specific premia have evolved during the crisis may thus provide important information about cross-country changes in the pricing of sovereign risk. Fig. 4 plot the pre-crisis premia α_i against the crisis premia δ_i from the estimation of the full model (4) for all countries for bond spreads and CDS spreads. Our prior is that there should be a positive relationship between pre-crisis fixed effects and crisis fixed effects if the evolution of the price of sovereign risk in the empirical model is primarily explained by fundamentals and regional spillovers.

Fig. 4 shows that there is no such systematic relationship for EMU countries.[10] In fact, all EMU countries, including the GIPSI countries, had very similar country fixed effects during the pre-crisis period, but very different premia during the crisis, suggesting that markets did not discriminate much across euro area countries. What is striking is that the country fixed effects are much more negative for GIPSI countries, which implies that the observable fundamentals of the GIPSI countries in the model during the crisis indicate that sovereign spreads should have been even higher for these countries (if markets had priced fundamentals in the same way across all countries). It is consistent with the finding of the previous section that in fact the sensitivity of financial markets to fundamentals in GIPSI countries became particularly high during the crisis.[11]

Focusing on the pre-crisis period, conducting a counter-factual analysis only for the pre-crisis period, estimating (3) for the pre-crisis period over the entire country sample and including only fundamentals into the model, is informative about the premia during the pre-crisis period. Our analysis shows that the highest

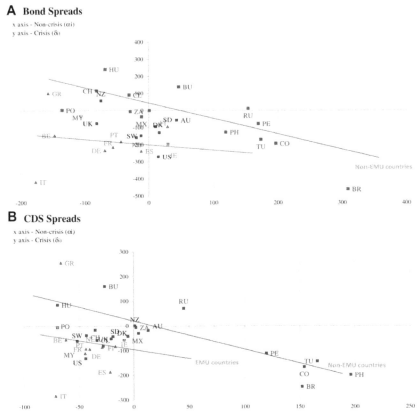

Note: Figures 4A-4B plot the pre-crisis premia ᵢ against the crisis premia ᵢ from the estimation of the full model (4) for all countries for bond spreads and CDS spreads.

Figure 4 Fixed effects in the pre-crisis (α_i) and crisis (δ_i).

negative country premia during the pre-crisis period existed for countries, such as Italy and Greece. This means that these countries should have had much higher sovereign spreads before the crisis, based on their fundamentals alone, than they actually did. And this premium is substantial at above 400 basis points, which would have brought spreads for these two countries to similar levels as in the pre-EMU period of the 1990s. By contrast, fixed effects for most EMEs were positive and substantial, implying that those governments had to pay positive premia to investors for purchasing their sovereign debt.

5.3 *Herding contagion*

One of the potential shortcomings of models, such as equation (4), for identifying contagion is that they assume that contagion is present persistently over the crisis period, i.e. parameters are allowed to change with the crisis, but not in individual periods within the crisis episode. However, there may be contagion during individual weeks or months of a crisis, but not necessarily during the entire crisis period. As such, equation (4) measures an average form of contagion during the crisis period.

A second potential shortcoming of such models is that contagion is defined on the basis of changing relationships of *observable* fundamentals. The advantage of such an approach is that one can actually give contagion a meaningful interpretation, and in turn derive policy recommendations. However, any empirical model may exclude relevant variables. In fact, behavioral explanations of financial market reactions, such as those often linked to herding behavior, is difficult to capture with observable fundamentals.

A complementary approach to equations (3) and (4) to address both caveats and to get at the role of herding contagion during the European sovereign debt crisis is to look at the cross-country correlation of the unexplained components of sovereign risk. More precisely, we employ the approach of Boyson et al. (2010) and examine the distribution of the residuals from equation (4) across countries at each point in time. In particular, we investigate the presence of tail clustering at the tenth percentile of the distribution, focusing on differences between the non-crisis and crisis periods, and between the euro area and other regions.

Fig. 5 below presents the results of this analysis for the tenth percentile of the residual distribution for all 31 countries, for the euro area, and for emerging economies. The figures plot the percentage share of countries for which the model indicates that the residual is in its top 10th percentile in a particular month. If residuals were uncorrelated across countries, then there should be no systematic clustering and about 10% of all countries should have residuals in their top 10th percentile every month. By contrast, a large share of countries experiencing such a sharp increase in sovereign risk that cannot be explained by the model's fundamentals and regional spillovers, indicates the presence of what we refer to as herding or pure contagion. As we noted before, the caveat of such an exercise is that we don't precisely know what the underlying factor is that explains such clustering and simultaneously sharp increase in sovereign risk.

Fig. 5 provides compelling evidence in favor of herding contagion, but that it played at most a minor role during the European sovereign debt crisis. In particular, such herding contagion is concentrated in time – for euro area countries it rises sharply in 2008, for a number of months, i.e. well before the start of the European debt crisis, and again in July–September 2011. The latter is a period when Italy was under substantial pressure by financial markets. In each of these episodes, the clustering rises sharply for a few months, but then again falls significantly. Moreover, we find a similar rise across EME yield spreads, though the clustering for these occurred mainly in 2009. Hence, although this evidence

A All countries

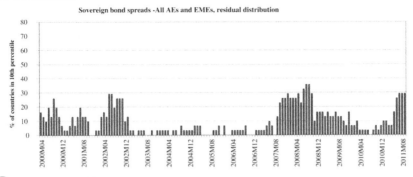

B Euro area countries

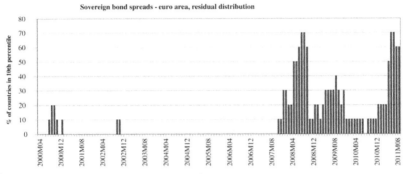

C EMEs

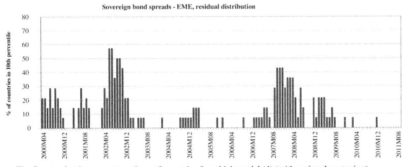

Notes: The figures plot the percentage share of countries for which model (4) (with regional contagion) indicates that the residual is in its top 10th percentile in a particular month. If residuals were uncorrelated across countries, then there should be no systematic clustering and about 10% of all countries should have residuals in their top 10th percentile every month.

Figure 5 Herding contagion – residual distribution for bond spreads.

suggests the presence of herding contagion, it also stresses clearly that such contagion has been temporary and relatively short-lived and did not dominate the European crisis period.

5.4 Economic significance

We have shown so far that fundamentals contagion, regional contagion as well as herding contagion have all played a role during the European sovereign debt crisis, and in particular for euro area countries. But how important have these different elements been? Are GIPSI countries, or at least some of them, innocent bystanders who mostly suffered from adverse contagion from other euro area countries, while fundamentals contagion played only a minor role? Or is it the reverse, in that a deterioration in fundamentals and a higher sensitivity of markets to such a deterioration explains the largest share of the sharp increase in the price of sovereign risk in the euro area?

To get at these questions, we estimate equation (4) and then extract the different elements of equation (4) for the last month before the crisis (September 2008, indicated by a superscript 08) and the last month of the crisis in the sample (September 2011, indicated by a superscript 11). We then derive the total *change* in sovereign risk over the entire crisis period as:

$$\Delta s_i^{crisis} = \left(s_i^{11} - s_i^{08}\right) = \hat{\delta}_i + \hat{\beta}_1 \Delta X_i + \hat{\gamma}_1 \Delta S_j + \hat{\beta}_2 X_i^{11} + \hat{\gamma}_2 S_j^{11} + \hat{\eta}_i$$

$$= \hat{\delta}_i + \hat{\beta}_1 \Delta X_i + \hat{\gamma}_1 \Delta S_j + \hat{\beta}_2 \Delta X_i + \hat{\beta}_E X_i^{08} + \hat{\gamma}_2 \Delta S_j + \hat{\gamma}_2 S_j^{08} + \hat{\eta}_i$$

with the terms being defined as follows:

$\hat{\delta}_i$ the country-fixed effect

$\hat{\beta}_1 \Delta X_i$ the change in a country's fundamentals at pre-crisis pricing

$\hat{\beta}_2 \Delta X_i$ fundamentals contagion: the change in a country's fundamentals with change of pricing in crisis

$\hat{\beta}_2 X_i^{08}$ fundamentals contagion: the level of a country's pre-crisis fundamentals with change of pricing in crisis

$\hat{\gamma}_1 \Delta S_j$ the change in regional sovereign risk at pre-crisis pricing

$\hat{\gamma}_2 \Delta S_j$ regional contagion: the change in regional sovereign risk with change of pricing in crisis

$\hat{\gamma}_2 S_j^{08}$ regional contagion: the level of regional sovereign risk with change of pricing in crisis

$\hat{\eta}_i$ unexplained change in price of sovereign risk during crisis

The added advantage of looking at the changes is that it allows for gauging whether it is the change in fundamentals or regional risk over the crisis period and to what extent it is the pricing of these two types of risk that influences sovereign risk. Fig. 6 show the different components for the September 2011 levels of sovereign yield spreads, as well as for the different contributions to the changes over the crisis period.[12]

Focusing first on the GIPSI countries shows that most of the spreads are explained by fundamentals, and not by regional spillovers or regional contagion. The dominance of fundamentals for the explanation of sovereign yield spreads is strongest for Greece, but it also holds for all of the GIPSI countries. Moreover, an important finding is that regional contagion during the crisis has been relatively unimportant. The negative coefficient for γ_2 implies that there has only been a modest adverse total spillover of regional risk during the crisis ($\gamma_1 + \gamma_2$), generally about 100–200 basis points for the GIPSI countries. Looking at the changes in spreads leads to the same conclusions, given that, as we have seen above, macroeconomic fundamentals explained very little of the price of sovereign risk in GIPSI countries prior to the crisis. The main point of the estimates for the changes in spreads is that the rise in sovereign spreads in GIPSI economies has been due to two factors: (i) a higher sensitivity of financial markets to existing fundamentals (β_2), and (ii) a deterioration in fundamentals (ΔX_i).

Turning to other, non-GIPSI countries yields the same conclusions: it is mainly the strength of countries' fundamentals that explain the level of spreads at the end of 2011 as well as the change in overall spreads during the crisis. An important finding is that for all regions, markets have become more sensitive to existing fundamentals, and as fundamentals have deteriorated in almost all economies globally during the crisis, fundamentals have worked to push up sovereign yields everywhere, not just in GIPSI economies. Hence fundamentals contagion has played a role, and an economically meaningful one, for most countries, not just for GIPSI countries.

By contrast, regional contagion through the spillover of sovereign risk in the region has not played a significant role during the crisis. In fact, the strength of the spillover of sovereign risk has mostly weakened somewhat during the crisis, as indicated by a negative γ_2 coefficient. Nevertheless, total regional spillovers during the crisis ($[\gamma_1 + \gamma_2]*S_j$) has not been negligible, accounting for an increase in spreads of about 100 basis points for most EMEs, of about 50 basis points for core euro area countries, and 20–30 basis points for other AEs.

A final point relates to the country fixed effects. Although α_i and δ_i are individually mostly quite sizeable, they in many cases partly offset each other with the sum of both for the crisis ($\alpha_i + \delta_i$) being more modest in magnitude. Interestingly, the crisis-specific fixed effects are mostly negative for AEs, and are especially large for the US and Germany while fundamentals alone for these two countries would indicate that sovereign yields should have risen much more during the crisis than they actually did. This is consistent with a flight-to-safety explanation, in which in particular sovereign bonds of the US and Germany benefit from safe haven flows.

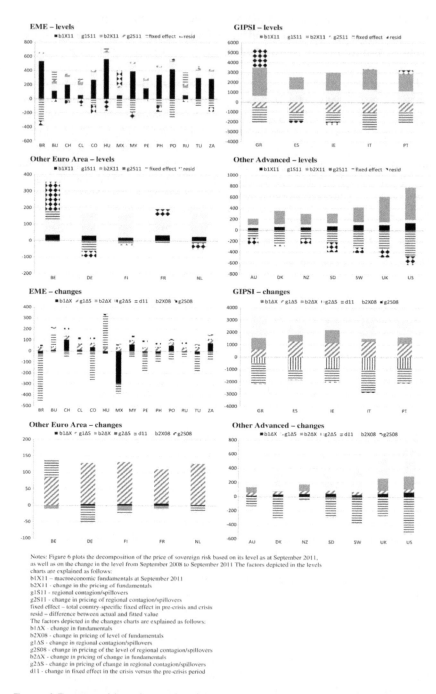

Notes: Figure 6 plots the decomposition of the price of sovereign risk based on its level as at September 2011, as well as on the change in the level from September 2008 to September 2011 The factors depicted in the levels charts are explained as follows:
b1X11 – macroeconomic fundamentals at September 2011
b2X11 - change in the pricing of fundamentals
g1S11 - regional contagion/spillovers
g2S11 - change in pricing of regional contagion/spillovers
fixed effect – total country-specific fixed effect in pre-crisis and crisis
resid – difference between actual and fitted value
The factors depicted in the changes charts are explained as follows:
b1ΔX - change in fundamentals
b2X08 - change in pricing of level of fundamentals
g1ΔS - change in regional contagion/spillovers
g2S08 - change in pricing of the level of regional contagion/spillovers
b2ΔX - change in pricing of change in fundamentals
g2ΔS - change in pricing of change in regional contagion/spillovers
d11 - change in fixed effect in the crisis versus the pre-crisis period

Figure 6 Decomposition of sovereign risk – bond spreads.

6. Conclusions

Europe's ongoing sovereign debt crisis has raised calls for more global and con-certed policy intervention to stop, in particular, the crisis from spreading conta-giously across countries and regions. The paper has analyzed whether contagion has indeed been present during the crisis, distinguishing between three types of contagion – fundamentals contagion due to a higher sensitivity of financial markets to existing fundamentals, regional contagion from an intensification of spillovers of sovereign risk across countries, and herding contagion due to a temporary overreaction of financial markets that is clustered across countries. The focus of the analysis has been not only on euro area countries, but also on other advanced and emerging economies globally, covering 31 countries in total over the period 1999–2011, in order to have alternative benchmarks for comparison.

A key finding of the analysis is that there has indeed been fundamentals con-tagion, or "wake-up call" contagion, as financial markets have become more sensitive to countries' economic fundamentals during the crisis compared to the pre-crisis period. And this increase in sensitivity has been particularly pronounced for the GIPSI economies in the European periphery. By contrast, regional spillo-vers of sovereign risk has not increased systematically during the crisis, but in fact decreased in particular in the euro area. This does not mean that there has been no cross-country spillovers of sovereign risk during the crisis – in fact regional spillovers may explain as much as 100–200 basis points of the rise in sovereign yield spreads among GIPSI countries – but it implies that markets have started to discriminate more on the basis of countries' fundamentals during the crisis than before, in particular within the euro area.

In terms of overall economic significance, the analysis of the paper shows that most of the level of sovereign risk and the rise during the crisis period is explained by countries' own economic fundamentals, and its underlying fundamentals con-tagion, while regional contagion explains a much more modest magnitude of sov-ereign risk. This applies equally to all regions, including for the euro area.

The analysis of the paper also detects evidence that is consistent with the pres-ence of herding contagion in sovereign debt markets during the crisis. However, we find that such herding contagion is concentrated in time and geographically. For EMEs, simultaneous sharp rises in sovereign risk were concentrated in 2009. For euro area countries, sharp increases in sovereign risk occurred in 2008 and in August–September 2011, though these periods were short-lived and can account for only a small extent of the dynamics of sovereign debt prices during the European crisis.

There has been the notion among some observers and policy-makers that finan-cial markets have overreacted during the crisis and that sovereign risk is mis-priced or has become "over-priced", especially for the GIPSI economies. It is very hard to evaluate such a normative claim as any statement about a mispricing requires having a precise definition of what an adequate, equilibrium pricing of risk should imply. In fact, the empirical findings suggest that there have been substantial and sustained differences in the pricing of fundamentals for sovereign risk among euro area countries before and during the crisis, suggesting the presence of multiple equilibria in this relationship.

At the same time, the question which of these equilibria are sustainable ones and ones that are attainable by policy is a crucial issue from a policy perspective as it determines what policy could or should do to deal with financial markets' pricing of countries' sovereign risk. While we are very cautious in stressing the limits of any normative interpretation, using different benchmarks our analysis suggests that financial markets may not have fully priced in countries' fundamentals and thus may have under-priced sovereign risk in the euro area during the pre-crisis period.

Acknowledgments

We would like to thank the participants at the Danmarks Nationalbank-Journal of International Money and Finance conference on "The European Sovereign Debt Crisis: Background and Perspectives", and in particular our discussant Jim Lothian, for comments and discussion. The views expressed in this paper are those of the authors and do not necessarily reflect those of the European Central Bank or the Eurosystem.

Notes

1 Some have speculated that a market perception of an implicit bail-out guarantee, or simply ignorance among financial market participants to country-specific fundamentals may be the main explanations for this comovement. We stress that the paper cannot provide an answer to the precise reasons for this high comovements in the pre-crisis period.

2 We stress that the terms "overpricing" and "underpricing" as used throughout the paper with regard to sovereign risk should not necessarily be interpreted in a normative sense, because such a normative interpretation would require making a statement about what the "true" pricing of risk should be.

3 Afonso et al. (2007) also highlight the difficulty in modeling sovereign spreads. Firstly, as the ratings are ordinal qualitative measures, a linearity is assumed between rating levels. While a probit modeling technique would appear to be the most appropriate model given the nature of the rating measure, a very large sample would be needed for asymptotic robustness. To attain sufficient power, they argue that a panel model with country-specific effects is the best approach.

4 We choose this starting date for the crisis, though one could also take a later date, such at the end of 2009 when tensions in European sovereign debt markets intensified. In the empirical analysis, however, it turns out that the empirical estimates are quite robust to changing the precise starting point.

5 Moreover, sovereign CDS data for a broad cross-section of countries is available only from 2004 onwards.

6 For brevity reasons, we report the results for bond spreads and CDS spreads. The results for ratings, which are qualitatively very similar to those of the other two measures of sovereign risk, are available from the authors upon request.

7 Corresponding figures for CDS spreads and ratings are not shown for brevity reasons. They yield qualitatively very similar findings, and are available upon request. Also for reasons relating to space, we have shown only the results for the GIPSI countries plus a selection of non-GIPSI euro area countries. The results for all other countries in the sample are available from the authors upon request.

8 The findings in relation to Greece are consistent with those of Gibson et al. (2012), who make the point that before the crisis, interest rate spreads were much lower than justified by fundamentals owing to the role played by Greece's euro area membership on biasing investor expectations. After the crisis, interest rate spreads have been higher than those predicted by fundamentals due to a lack of belief by the market that sustainable fiscal consolidations measures and structural reforms had been implemented.

9 In Greece, Italy, and Portugal, structural government balances were around twice as high as the euro area average in the period 1998–2007, while they were notably lower in Ireland and Spain. Thus the cross-country heterogeneity observed in the evolution of the predicted spreads based on the pre-crisis and crisis models may be related to the origin of the crisis. While government budgetary policy and large structural deficits were underlying factors for Greece, Italy and Portugal, the crisis in Ireland and Spain was closely linked to the private banking sector.

10 This is consistent with the results based on sovereign credit ratings, which are not shown for space reasons.

11 Of course, there may be complementary interpretations of these country fixed effects, especially for euro area countries. The negative effects for GIPSI countries may have partly resulted also from financial support through EU-IMF programmes.

12 We present for brevity reasons the results only for sovereign bonds spreads. The results for the CDS spreads and sovereign credit ratings yield qualitatively similar results and are available from the authors upon request.

References

Afonso, A., Gomes, P., Rother, P., 2007. What Hides behind Sovereign Debt Ratings?. ECB Working Paper No. 711.

Aizenman, J., Hutchinson, M., Jinjarak, Y., 2011. What Is the Risk of European Sovereign Debt Defaults? Fiscal Space, CDS Spreads and Market Pricing of Risk. NBER Working Paper No. 17407.

Amadou, S., 2001. Emerging Market Bond Spreads and Sovereign Credit Ratings: Reconciling Market View with Fundamentals. IMF Working Paper 01/165.

Amato, J.D., 2005. Risk aversion and risk premia in the CDS market. BIS Quarterly Review, 55–68. Part 5 (December).

Attinasi, C., Nickel, C., 2009. What Explains the Surge in Euro Area Sovereign Spreads during the Financial Crisis of 2007–09. ECB Working Paper No. 1131.

Baldacci, E., Kumar, M.S., 2010. Fiscal Deficits, Public Debt, and Sovereign Bond Yields. IMF Working Paper 10/184.

Bekaert, B., Ehrmann, M., Fratzscher, M., Mehl, A., 2010. Global Crises and Equity Market Contagion. NBER Working Paper No. 17121.

Boyson, N.M., Stahel, C.W., Stulz, R., 2010. Hedge fund contagion and liquidity shocks. Journal of Finance 65 (5), 1789–1816.

Cantor, R., Pecker, F., 1996. Determinants and impact of sovereign credit ratings. Federal Reserve Bank of New York Economic Policy Review, 37–54. October.

Cecchetti, S., Mohanty, M.S., Zampolli, F., 2010. s. The Future of Public Debt: Prospects and Implication. BIS Working Paper No. 300.

Dell'Ariccia, G., Schnabel, I., Zettelmeyer, J., 2006. How do official bailouts affect the risk of investing in emerging markets? Journal of Money, Credit and Banking 38, 1689–1714.

Doetz, N., Fischer, C., 2010. What Can EMU Countries' Sovereign Bond Spreads Tell Us about Market Perceptions of Default Probabilities during the Recent Financial Crisis?. Deutsche Bundesbank Discussion Paper No. 11/2010.

Edwards, S., 1984. LDC foreign borrowing and default risk: an empirical investigation, 1976–80. American Economic Review 74 (4), 726–734.

Ferrucci, G., 2003. Empirical Determinants of Emerging Market Economies' Sovereign Bond Spreads. Working Paper No. 205. Bank of England, London.

Gibson, H.D., Hall, S.G., Tavlas, G.S., 2012. The Greek financial crisis: growing imbalances and sovereign spreads. Journal of International Money and Finance 31, 498–516.

Goldstein, M., 1998. The Asian Financial Crisis Causes, Cures, and Systematic Implications. June 1998. Institute for International Economics, Washington D.C.

Hauner, D., Kumar, M.S., 2009. Fiscal Policy and Interest Rates: How Sustainable Is the New Economy?. IMF Working Paper 06/112.

Hauner, D., Jonas, J., Kumar, M.S., 2010. Sovereign risk: are the EU's new Member states different? Oxford Bulletin of Economics and Statistics 72 (4), 411–427.

Manganelli, S., Wolswijk, G., 2007. Market Discipline, Financial Integration, and Fiscal Rules. ECB Working Paper No. 745.

Packer, F., Zhu, H., 2005. Contractual terms and CDS pricing. BIS Quarterly Review, 89–100. Part 8 (March).

Reinhart, C.M., Rogoff, K.S., 2011. A Decade of Debt. NBER Working Paper 16827, February 2011.

Schuknecht, L., Von Hagen, J., Wolswijk, G., 2010. Government Bond Risk Premiums in the EU Revisited – The Impact of the Financial Crisis. ECB Working Paper No. 1152.

Stein, J.L., 2011. The diversity of debt crises in Europe. Cato Journal 31 (2), 199–215.

51

DOES INTERNATIONAL FINANCIAL CONTAGION REALLY EXIST?

G. Andrew Karolyi

Source: *International Finance* 6, 2, 2003, 179–199.

Abstract

This article surveys the various definitions and taxonomies of international financial contagion in the academic literature and popular press and relates it to the existing evidence on co-movements in international asset prices, on the growth and volatility of international capital flows and on the relationship between flows and asset prices. The central argument of the article is that the empirical evidence is not as obviously consistent with the existence of market contagion as many researchers, the press, or market regulators believe. Policy implications of this alternative viewpoint are presented.

I. Financial Crises and Contagion

The financially turbulent decade of the 1990s is a challenge for market-oriented economists to explain. Conservative economists since Adam Smith have promoted the idea that a free-market economy that is light on government regulation of the forces of supply and demand is the most efficient and reliable economic system. Yet, in the 1990s, exchange rate crises followed stock market crashes which, in turn, followed economic contractions, and these events devastated countries around the world. The frequency and extent of these events led many policy makers, regulators, journalists and many participants in the markets to declare a 'crisis in global capitalism' and to call for reforms in the form of a new 'international financial architecture'.[1]

The exact sequence of events is not difficult to trace. Things began to go wrong at the beginning of the decade in Asia with the sudden decline of Japan's Nikkei 225 in 1989 and the subsequent near-insolvency in the Japanese real estate and banking sectors. Two currency crises in September 1992 and August 1993 in Europe reflected uncertainty about the new Exchange Rate Mechanism (ERM) and the imminent launch of the euro in 1999. Mexico experienced a currency crisis just after the inauguration of President Ernesto Zedillo in December 1994. The fixed exchange rate regime for the peso broke into a gradual controlled devaluation which led to significant declines in the stock and sovereign bond markets of other Latin American countries and emergency financial assistance from the International Monetary Fund. The Asian financial crisis of 1997 occurred in two rounds. The first round was ignited by the forced devaluation of the Thai baht on 2 July and led to a chain of devaluations and stock market declines in neighbouring Philippines, Malaysia and Indonesia. The second round occurred in October 1997 when rumours circulated that Hong Kong might abandon its fixed rate regime. Within two months, South Korea experienced a stock market decline, bank panic and devaluation and received a sizeable relief package from the IMF. In August 1998, Russia simultaneously defaulted on its treasury debt and devalued the rouble. This led to defaults by Russian banks on rouble-based forward foreign exchange contracts with North American counterparties and waves of stock and bond market declines around the world. In January 1999, Brazil suffered a depreciation of its currency after one of its states refused to make scheduled payments to the national government. Ecuador, only months later, became the first nation to default on a Brady bond issue. Argentina's markets declined in November 2001 after eliminating its US dollar exchange-rate peg.

These are the highlights of the low points of the 1990s. Europe, Asia, Russia and Latin America experienced currency crises, stock market crashes, deflation, recession, sovereign insolvency and political instability. That financial distress struck neighbouring countries in rapid succession led to the acceptance of a notion that financial trouble is capable of spreading like a contagious disease. 'Contagion' is a term that derives from the field of epidemiology. It is a mathematical theory that helps epidemiologists to predict the course of infection and mortality of a virulent disease or illness, such as influenza. For some, the metaphor with epidemiology fits the economics of crises. Stanley Fischer, former deputy manager of the International Monetary Fund, in his David Finch Lecture at the IMF in 1998, pointed out that the turbulence in capital markets in the 1990s stemmed from two sources:

1   The volatility of international capital flows, especially to emerging markets, and the limited ability of countries to deal with this volatility.
2   The susceptibility of international capital markets to 'financial contagion' – a phenomenon which he associated with dependencies among countries that allow market shocks to an individual country to affect other countries, often on a regional basis.[2]

Many writers in the financial press have also come to accept that financial contagion exists. An on-line search on Lexis-Nexis yielded 2,083 'hits' on the key words 'financial AND contagion' between 1994 through April 2002. Figure 1 provides a time series of these media hits by year. Interestingly, the distribution of hits across time is not uniform. The peak number occurs in 1998 (768 hits), but before

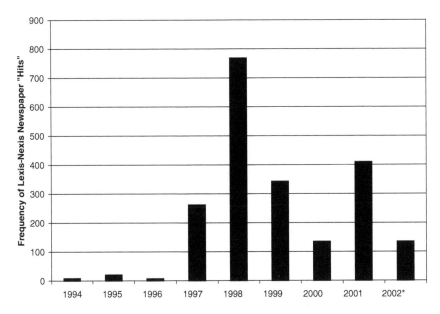

Figure 1 Nexis-Lexis media hits on 'Financial Contagion'1994–2002. *Notes:* For each year, I count the number of newspaper, magazine, journal, wire or transcript stories that include references to "financial contagion" using the on-line Nexis-Lexis Business News search engine (http://www.lexis-nexis.com/).

1997, there were very few. The hits dissipate for a few years until a second surge in 2001 (409 hits). The media sources are also distributed unequally with dispro-portionately large numbers of hits in *Latin Finance, Business Times* (Malaysia), *Emerging Markets On-line* and fewer among *Financial Times* (London) and *New York Times*. An independent search on the *New York Times* web site actually revealed 398 hits since 1994, still a healthy contribution.

Academics have also devoted substantial effort towards the study of contagion in the past several years. Their primary focus is to measure the spread of market disturbances (especially on the downside and especially around crises) from one country to the other in the form of co-movements in exchange rates, stock prices, sovereign spreads and capital flows. They also study the 'channels of contagion', or the means by which these disturbances spread, including international trade and capital flows, and actions of banks and other creditors, including global port-folio managers. There are now dozens of published and working papers on the topic, including a book edited by Claessens and Forbes (2001) based on a World Bank conference on contagion in 2000. This surge of interest has inspired – or was, in turn, inspired by – policy makers who have been debating new regula-tions on foreign ownership restrictions, exchange rate convertibility, hedge fund disclosure and the free flow of global capital in general.

The key objective of this article is to question the existence of international financial contagion. To this end, I survey and synthesize the empirical evidence on international asset price co-movements, on the volatility of cross-border capital flows and the relationship between flows and asset prices. My thesis is that these observed co-movements during the 1990s might not have been excessively large given the global economic and capital market environment. It is a fact that markets, in and of themselves, do go to extremes and that these extreme movements have occurred often in quick succession or in clusters across time and by region. It is also a fact that large amounts of capital flowed into afflicted nations in the years before their collapse. What is *not* a fact is that the magnitude and the volatility of the flows can be directly and causally linked with financial instability in those countries and regions. Proponents of the financial contagion metaphor see traders of 'hot money' as the carriers of the virulent diseases. This, in the purest sense, is what popular psychology calls the 'herd mentality'.[3] The bottom line is that we cannot yet prove whether contagion exists or not, and so policy prescriptions that call for a major overhaul of the 'international financial architecture' may be premature, at best, and even more disruptive, at worst.

I build my case in four steps. First, I critique of the most popular definition of financial contagion and its associated taxonomy of the contagion channels. Second, I sketch the evidence on the dynamics of co-movements in financial asset prices. This is an important discussion because in order to determine the existence of 'excessive' co-movements, we need to establish what 'normal' co-movements are. Third, I confirm the growth in cross-border capital flows, particularly to emerging markets. Since flows connect markets, it is logical to associate the growth and volatility of flows with heightened co-movements of asset prices. To this end, I discuss the evidence on the joint dynamics of flows and returns and argue, in fact, that the relationship is not as strong as contagion advocates think. Finally, I discuss some new line of research based on extreme-value theory that provides a useful perspective.

II. The Taxonomy of Financial Contagion

Contagion, in general, is used to refer to the spread of market shocks – mostly, on the downside – from one country to another, a process observed through co-movements in exchange rates, stock prices, sovereign spreads and capital flows.[4] Contagion can occur for different reasons and is often conceptually divided into two categories.

The first category emphasizes co-movements in financial asset prices that result from the normal interdependence among market economies due to real and financial linkages. Often, this is referred to as 'fundamentals-based contagion'. Most empirical studies seek to explain the degree of co-movements and mechanisms for transmitting them. The fundamental factors that drive co-movements are of several types. One type is a common global factor, such as a major economic shift in industrial countries or a shock to commodity prices, which can trigger crises or large capital flows into or out of markets. US interest rate policy shifts have been identified with movements in capital flows to Latin America and the strengthening of the US dollar against the yen has been shown to weaken exports of East Asian countries (Calvo and Reinhart 1996). Another fundamental factor is a local economic shock that is transmitted across borders by means of a trade link.[5] Any major trade partner of a country where a financial crisis has led to a currency depreciation could experience declines in asset prices, capital outflows or become the target of a speculative attack. A game of competitive devaluation could also cause greater currency depreciation than that required by any initial deterioration in fundamentals (Eichengreen et al. 1996). Finally, financial links related to trade and investment, such as extensions of trade credit, foreign direct investment and other capital flows, can facilitate local economic shocks and can affect co-movements in asset prices (Schinasi and Smith 2001). If a country is integrated in global financial markets, then financial markets are the mechanisms that make asset prices in those markets and other variables move together.

The second category of contagion involves financial crises that cannot necessarily be linked to changes in macroeconomic or other fundamentals but that arise as a result of the behaviour of investors or other financial agents. Such co-movements cannot be explained by fundamentals, such as global shocks, trade or financial linkages that integrate economies and markets. Researchers often refer to this as 'irrational contagion' and associate it with financial panic, herd behaviour, loss of confidence and increases in risk aversion.

This dichotomy is too simple on several dimensions. First, trade linkages and financial markets may facilitate the transmission of real or common global shocks, but they do not cause them. Second, it is not obvious that the actions of investors in facilitating how shocks spill over from one country to another – even in the absence of real and financial linkages – are necessarily irrational. One can imagine situations in which these actions are individually rational and even collectively rational. One form of individual rational behaviour relates to liquidity and other constraints on lenders or investors. If banks from a common creditor country experience a marked deterioration in the quality of its loans to one country, they may attempt to reduce the overall risk of the loan portfolio by reducing exposures in other higher risk investments elsewhere.[6] Worse, the liquidity problems and the incidence of financial contagion might afflict most severely those countries whose financial assets are widely traded in global markets and whose markets are more liquid.

Another form of rational investor behaviour relates to imperfect information and differences in investor expectations. A crisis in one country may lead to an attack on the currency of another country which has conditions similar to those of the country where the crisis began. This can reflect rational as well as irrational behaviour. If the crisis reveals weak fundamentals, investors may rationally conclude similar countries have similar problems. Investors simply do not have a full picture of the condition of each and every country as it affects returns, which can simply reflect the cost of processing information. Moreover, less well-informed investors will tend to seek new information from those who have acted earlier in adjusting their portfolios, a kind of 'information cascade'. Herd behaviour may not be irrational as it reflects the fixed cost of gathering and processing information for an investor base that is diversified across many markets (Bikhchandani et al. 1992).

A final form of rational investor behaviour is related to changes in expectations that are self-fulfilling in markets with multiple equilibria. Consider simple bank-run models with both bad and good equilibria (Diamond and Dybvig 1983). It is rational for individuals either to retain their funds in the bank or withdraw funds depending on perceived actions of other depositors. Investors could just as easily suddenly withdraw investments from an emerging market if they fear that, if they do not, they will be too late to have a claim on a limited pool. Barberis et al. (2002) identify similar trading patterns among investors to rationalize the existence of what they call 'category-based' and 'habitat-based' co-movements in the structure of domestic asset returns.

I propose a new taxonomy system for regional crises in financial markets. It is one that dispenses with the word 'contagion' for all but the third of three categories, as it establishes that the coincidence of crises can occur for a number of reasons beyond irrationality of market agents. We need to recognize that co-movements in international financial asset prices are a natural outcome of real and financial linkages ('fundamentals-based co-movements') and of rational investment decision making by financial agents in the absence of such strong linkages ('rational investor-based co-movements'). For now, I will allow for the existence of a residual category: 'irrational co-movements' or 'contagion'. It is important to establish their tougher hurdle in the search for the existence of financial contagion in the empirical literature that follows.

III. Searching for Financial Contagion

Empirical examination of the evidence for contagion has largely focused on co-movements in asset prices and much less on 'excessive' co-movements in prices given capital flows, market volatility or disturbances in real markets. Studies have concentrated on changes in asset-price co-movements around crises which are typically associated with volatility in net capital flows. Finding this association between returns and flows is key to uncovering the existence of contagion. I will discuss the evidence in three stages. The first stage presents the evidence on flows, its growth in magnitude and volatility over time. The second stage describes the association between flows and returns. The third and final stage will discuss what we know about comovements in financial asset prices over time.

A. Capital Flows

Cross-border capital flows have grown dramatically in the past three decades, especially to developing countries. In 1975, gross cross-border transactions between US residents and foreign residents were the equivalent of 4% of US Gross Domestic Product (GDP). By 1991, these transactions exceeded GDP and, by 2000, they had grown to 245% of GDP.[7] More interestingly, net portfolio flows, especially in equities, have become an economically significant component of total capital flows. Figure 2 shows the net purchases by US residents of Latin American and Asian equities. In both cases, the net equity inflows have grown from very little in 1990 to almost $1 billion per month with Latin America and over $2 billion per month with Asia in the late 1990s. Over the decade, US investors accumulated $70 billion and $170 billion positions in these emerging market equities, respectively. Another striking feature of the figure, however, is that the amplitude of the monthly fluctuations in net flows has also increased. One can observe large positive and negative spikes, such as the $4 billion outflow from Latin America in January 1995, but, more often than not, the volatility of net flows is clustered in time. It is through this accelerated growth and increased volatility in net flows that researchers have sought a link to asset price co-movements.[8]

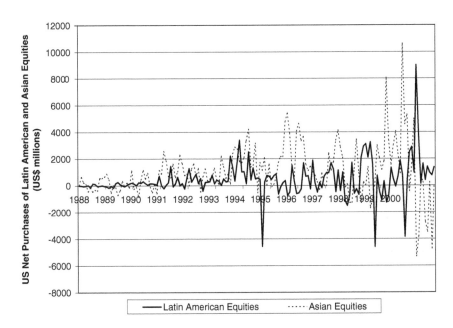

Figure 2 Net equity flows to Latin America and Asia from USA, 1988–2001. *Notes:* Using the Treasury International Capital (TIC) database from the US Treasury department, I compute monthly purchases of Asian and Latin American equities by US residents from foreigners net of monthly sales of Asian and Latin American equities of US residents to foreigners. See www.treasury.gov.

B. Net Capital Flows and Asset Returns

With free capital flows, markets are more closely connected. Investors who think that one market will have higher expected returns can move their investments to that market and this connection implies that markets move together more than they would if they were segmented with large barriers to flows. But can changes in equity valuations be traced directly to capital flows? If so, does the impact of capital flows reflect the information that foreign investors have that is not yet incorporated into prices or just the destabilizing by-product of the large and volatile flows? Early evidence by Tesar and Werner (1994) found strong, positive, contemporaneous correlations between US portfolio flows to developed and emerging markets and market index returns. They used quarterly data from the US Treasury Bulletin. Brennan and Cao (1997) rationalized this evidence in a Bayesian model that relates international flows to differences in information between foreign and domestic investors. The foreign investors update their forecasts of future market returns with greater frequency than local investors in response to public information, as their priors are more diffuse and reflect a 'cumulative informational disadvantage'. Their empirical evidence corroborated their theory and confirmed that of Tesar and Werner but for more countries.

One possible explanation for these findings was that the coarseness of low-frequency data masked the true dynamics of flows and returns. Indeed, Bohn and Tesar (1996) extended the analysis to monthly data. They were the first to find evidence of a delayed response of US net flows to returns in which foreign investors are 'positive feedback' traders: buying following positive returns and selling following negative returns. They interpreted this finding as evidence that foreign investors have less information than local investors about local equities. This positive-feedback pattern has been verified further by even more recent studies with even higher-frequency data, such as Choe et al. (1999), Froot et al. (2001), Karolyi (2002) and Griffin et al. (2002). Froot et al. used proprietary data from State Street Bank and Trust on daily reporting of trades from their institutional investors in 44 different countries to find the most dramatic evidence yet. They compute a covariance ratio statistic (CVR), or standardized cross-covariance between current returns and current, past and future net flows spanning 180 days. Positive-feedback trading was strong, comprising 80% of the CVR, and the reaction of returns to current and past flows was proportionately small (4% and 16% of the CVR, respectively). It implies that positive-feedback trading, while possibly profitable for foreign investors, is not destabilizing for the underlying markets. More importantly, it calls into question whether the actions of institutional investors represent an important channel for the transmission of shocks across markets. It is more likely, in fact, that these investors are simply reacting on a delayed basis to public information news from those markets.

C. Co-movements in Asset Returns

Even if changes in equity valuations cannot be traced directly to net flows, stronger asset price co-movements around the world could still be a by-product of the long-term growth in capital flows. Much of our understanding of asset price co-movements focuses on one measure: correlation. Typically, studies have shown that correlations of stock or bond index returns across international markets – especially, with emerging markets – are low. But, with increased market liberalization and stronger real and financial linkages, it has been hypothesized that correlations have trended upward over time. Actually, the evidence is remarkably weak. Figure 3 shows how difficult it is to perceive a trend in the rolling, 12-month correlations between the Morgan Stanley Capital International US and Asia and Europe indexes, respectively. Longin and Solnik (1995) tested the equality of return covariances for seven developed markets across sixteen different five-year periods through 1990 and rejected equality in slightly better than half of those comparisons. Bekaert and Harvey (1995) apply a multivariate time-series model with time-varying volatility and correlations and with regime-switching features to test for shifts in correlations to over 30 countries. They find that there is little evidence of regime shifting. In a follow-on study, Bekaert and Harvey (2000) focus on liberalization dates per se and show that correlations were measurably higher in only nine of 17 emerging markets they study.[9]

While there is no clear evidence that correlations are increasing over time, there is substantial evidence that correlations vary over time. King et al. (1994),

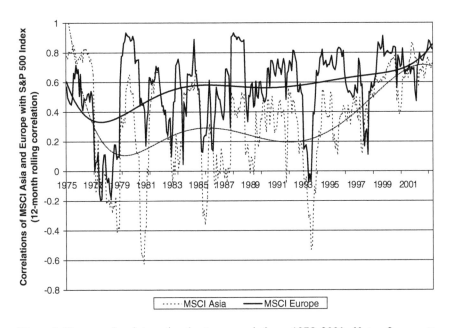

Figure 3 Time-varying international return correlations, 1975–2001. *Notes:* I compute correlations over rolling 12-month periods of monthly returns of Morgan Stanley Capital International's Asia and Europe index returns with the US S&P 500 monthly returns. A polynomial trend line smoothed over 6 months is displayed for each of the correlation series.

Longin and Solnik (1995) and Karolyi and Stulz (1996) examine monthly and intradaily stock return correlations using a similar multivariate time-series model to Bekaert and Harvey (1995). They allow these conditional correlations to vary with market returns, dividend yields, interest rates, trading volume and even macroeconomic news. Interestingly, the only instrument with reliable predictive power is the magnitude and direction of market returns themselves, especially so for negative market returns. Some have pointed at this asymmetry effect in correlations – higher correlations when markets decline – as evidence of contagion.

A possible explanation for the weak association of time-varying correlations and economic fundamentals is poor measurement. There have, after all, been a host of studies of statistically strong leading and lagging relationships among national index returns and volatilities. These studies have often been classified as 'spillover' studies. Among the earlier studies, Eun and Shim (1989) examined the joint dynamics of daily returns across national markets using a vector autoregression (VAR) model and showed that the US market returns systematically led and captured a significant fraction of the total predictable variation in other developed market returns. Hamao et al. (1990), Bae and Karolyi (1994), Lin et al. (1994) and, most recently, Connolly and Wang (2003) focused on spillovers of volatility rather than returns and found more symmetric relationship across markets.

The problem with this evidence on co-movements and spillovers is that it is difficult to separate two competing hypotheses. On the one hand, the comovements could simply reflect innovations in common, unobservable global factors. On the other hand, the increases in correlations, especially around stressful, bear market periods, represent the work of uninformed investors who overreact to news in one market relative to another or who respond to shifts in sentiments regardless of fundamentals in those markets. This drew many researchers in the latest wave of contagion studies to examine changes in correlations around the crisis periods of the 1990s. Each of Calvo and Reinhart (1996), Frankel and Schmukler (1998) and Bailey et al. (2000) have suggested that the aftermath of the Mexican peso crisis in 1995 revealed 'contagion' in unusually high correlations of weekly or intradaily returns on equities and Brady bonds. Forbes and Rigobon (2002) show that, in the presence of greater volatility around crises, an increase in correlation could simply be a continuation of the same transmission mechanism that exists in more tranquil periods, and thus not at all evidence of contagion. Bekaert et al. (2003) offer the best attempt yet to separate the two competing hypotheses by working with a multifactor model of time-varying expected returns and beta risks to accommodate various degrees of market integration between markets. They show that increased raw returns correlation during the Mexican peso and Asian crises are not revealed in the correlations of residuals from their model and, thus, may not be evidence of contagion but of the consequence of different market exposures to a common global factor.

IV. Measuring Contagion a Better Way

One of the limitations of the existing literature on contagion has been its focus on correlations of asset prices. Few of the concerns expressed about contagion seem to be based on linear measures of association. Rather, the concerns seem to be founded on some presumption that there is something different about extremely bad events that might lead to irrational outcomes, excess volatility and panic that grip investors. The problem with correlations is that they give equal consideration to small and large price changes which precludes an evaluation of the special impact of large changes.

There have been numerous studies of extreme asset price changes (Mandelbrot 1963; Fama 1963; Longin 1996), but only a few recent ones have looked at the coincidence of extreme price changes across different markets. Longin and Solnik (2001) applied multivariate extreme value analysis, a nonparametric to the joint distribution of monthly returns on stock indexes of the G-5 countries between 1959 and 1996. They found that the correlation of large negative returns, or 'co-crashes' is much higher than that expected from a multivariate normal distribution. Hartmann et al. (2001) employ a similar non-parametric measure for stock and bond markets in the G-5 and show that, while single bond or stock market crashes are rare, the conditional probabilities of having a crash in one market, given one occurred in another market, are considerably higher, thus implying the existence of contagion.

An important limitation of these statistical approaches for modelling financial contagion, however, is that, though they do focus on extreme asset returns, they do not control for economic fundamentals. Bae et al. (2003) develop a way to meet both of these challenges and thus a better way to understand and measure financial contagion. Their contribution is threefold. First, they focus on extreme outcomes in terms of exchange rates, stock returns or interest rates, which are defined as the bottom or top 5% tail of the distribution ('exceedances'). They specifically consider days in which more than one market synchronously experiences such tail events, which are referred to as 'co-exceedances'. Second, they dispense with study of correlations and focus on the conditional probabilities of co-exceedances. Third, they adopt a statistical methodology commonly used in epidemiology for research on contagious diseases to measure the likelihood of co-exceedances. Specifically, they use multinomial logistic regression models to model occurrences of co-exceedances. The advantage of such a model is that it, as in epidemiology, allows for covariates that characterize the 'health profile' of the market, such as exchange rate changes, interest rate changes and prevailing volatility of the markets.

Figure 4 plots the co-exceedances of daily stock returns in ten Asian and seven Latin American emerging markets that Bae et al. (2003) seek to model. The co-exceedance time series represent the daily count of the number of countries of each region in which their national index returns fall into the top or bottom 5% tail. I only show the co-exceedances of two or more countries in each region in

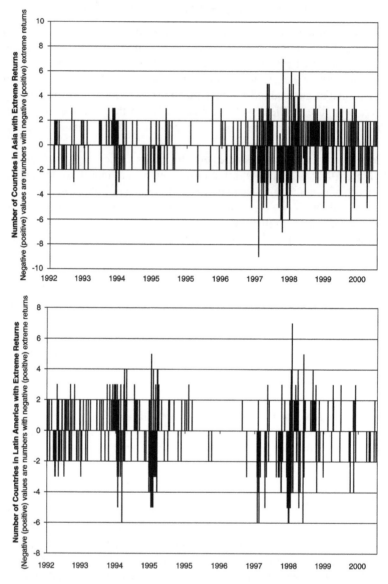

Figure 4 Frequency of daily stock return co-exceedances within Asian and Latin American emerging markets,1992–2001. *Notes*: I compute daily national stock index returns of the International Financial Corporation (IFC) Emerging Markets Database for ten countries in Asia (China, Korea, Philippines, Taiwan, India, Indonesia, Malaysia, Pakistan, Sri Lanka and Thailand) and for seven countries in Latin America (Argentina, Brazil, Chile, Colombia, Mexico, Peru and Venezuela). Each day, I count the number of countries in each region that have returns below the lowest 5% quantile or above the highest 5% quantile of their returns distribution.

the figures. There are clusters of co-exceedances around certain episodes, such as the Mexican peso crisis in December of 1994 for Latin American markets (left plot) and, interestingly, around the Russian crisis in August 1998 for those same markets. For Asian markets (right plot), the magnitude of the clusters is greatest in mid-1997, the onset of the Asian financial crisis, and also just prior to the Russian crisis in 1998. While the frequency of exceedances in the top or bottom tails is constrained to be 5% of the sample, there appear to be more joint occurrences of bottom tail events than top tail events around these special periods.[10]

The daily co-exceedances of positive and negative extreme returns within a particular region are categorized as a polychotomous variable and modelled using a multinomial logistic regression model. These models compute the probability, P_i, associated with a likelihood that category i occurs out of m possible categories. For example, Bae et al. (2003) define a category as the event that at least four of the seven Latin American stock markets experience a negative extreme return on a given day. The models are applied separately for negative and positive extremes in Asian and Latin American markets and for co-exceedance categories of one, two, three or four or more countries in a region. The multinomial distribution is defined as,

$$P_i = \exp\left(\beta_i' x\right) / 1 + \sum_{j=1}^{m-1} \exp\left(\beta_j' x\right) \qquad (1)$$

where x is the vector of covariates and β_i is the coefficients associated with the covariates. The covariates include the level of local market interest rates, exchange rates and an estimate of the conditional stock market volatility. Goodness of fit is measured using a pseudo-R^2 measure that compares the log-likelihood function values for the restricted (constants only as covariates) and unrestricted (all covariates) models. This is important for their statistical measure of contagion. The full model for a particular region captures the benchmark level of intra-regional co-exceedance activity and then evaluates 'contagion effects' in which some portion of the unexplained co-exceedance activity in one region can be explained or even predicted by co-exceedance activity in another region. The marginal effects revealed in the coefficients on the other region's co-exceedances, the associated chi-squared statistics for zero-exclusion tests and the incremental pseudo-R^2 are all employed to measure the statistical and economic significance of the interregional contagion effects.

Bae et al. (2003) show that these multinomial logit models perform quite well in explaining these co-exceedance events for positive and negative extreme returns. The basic models for Asia have pseudo-R^2 that reach as high as 11% for Asia and 12% for Latin America. They also implement a base model for the USA and Europe to evaluate whether the co-exceedances in one region can help to explain and even predict the likelihood of co-exceedances in another region, even after controlling for fundamental factors. These effects are precisely measured:

the chi-squared zero-exclusion tests of these inter-regional effects easily reject that they are negligible. The economic importance of these effects, however, is very small. The marginal effects on those inter-regional covariates are small and the increase in pseudo-R^2 is typically less than 1%. Little contagion is detectable. For example, during the period of the Asian financial crisis, the incremental explanatory power of Asian co-exceedance events increased the goodness-of-fit in Latin America from 7.84% to 8.89% and that in the USA from 6.16% to 6.57%.

V. An Alternative View

Is there really such a thing as financial contagion? When financial crises occur in neighbouring countries in rapid succession, the notion can gain acceptance that this distress is capable of spreading like a contagious disease. Moreover, it is logical to look for potential carriers of such a disease in the actions of market participants, like commercial banks, international mutual funds and global investors, in general.

The problem is that the evidence of contagion effects is weak. While we do know that international capital flows have increased significantly as markets around the world have liberalized, it is difficult to perceive whether or how these flows affect asset prices. Of course, it may be that the mechanisms through which these shocks are transmitted across markets, while difficult to measure, still exist and lead to co-movements in asset prices that are exacerbated around crisis periods. Unfortunately, the evidence that international stock return correlations have increased over time is also weak. While it is true that time-varying correlations are difficult to reconcile with real and financial factors, this does not automatically give us carte blanche to declare the existence of contagion. It also does not help the case for contagion that experts continue to struggle with a formal definition and a taxonomy that is flawed, or, at the very least, inadequate.

What kind of new international financial architecture should be built to prevent and manage the inevitable market crises of the future? The solutions are not obvious, because the problem is not clearly understood. The various reform proposals to date have been pitched at three levels: the national level, the international level and the supra-national level (Sell 2001). In my opinion, much more energy has been devoted to study of the reforms at the international level, such as choosing the appropriate exchange rate and international financial market regimes, and at the supra-national level, such as how to organize the IMF and the World Bank group of the future. Reforms at the national level have been given too little attention. After all, as the arguments in this article suggest, the appearance of what some have called financial contagion could be ascribed to errors in domestic financial policy that have simply been duplicated across affected countries in response to common economic shocks. I think harder questions should be directed at fiscal and monetary policy makers about how best to regulate the access to the domestic financial sector, how best to improve the supervision of markets by the central bank or qualified agencies and how best to introduce and maintain supervisory and prudential standards to improve risk management for the financial services sector.

This article is based on speech given at a conference of the Administrative Sciences Association of Canada on 'Rethinking Globalization: Critical Perspectives' in Winnipeg, Manitoba, 28 May 2002. I am grateful for the comments of two anonymous referees, the editor, Benn Steil, and for many discussions on this topic with my colleague, René Stulz. All remaining errors and misstatements are my own. I thank the Dice Centre for Financial Economics at the Ohio State University for financial support.

Notes

1   German Chancellor Gerhard Schröder said 'Japan, Europe and the United States agree on this: we are on the eve of a new financial architecture' (Bloomberg News, 20 January 1999) and President Bill Clinton proposed that '... it is now time for the world to take the next steps of implementing a new financial architecture and long-term reform of the global financial system. This should include steps to reduce the entire financial system's vulnerability to rapid capital flows.' (Market News International, 20 April 1999).
2   Fischer had used the term two years earlier in rationalizing the IMF bailout of Mexico in 1995: 'Of course, there was another justification: contagion effects. They were there and they were substantial.' See his speech in Calvo et al. (1996).
3   Good references include Chapter 8 ('Herd Behavior and Epidemics') of Shiller (1999) and Friedman (1999), which explicitly features the importance of the 'electronic herd' of global investors.
4   This definition is from Dornbusch et al. (2001). Other conceptual contributions are due to Masson (1999), Kodres and Pritsker (2002) and Forbes and Rigobon (2002).
5   An important example is provided in Eichengreen and Rose (1997).
6   This argument is not original; see Kodres and Pritsker (2002).
7   See Figure 2 in Karolyi and Stulz (2003) which uses data from the US Treasury's TIC (Treasury International Capital) reporting system available online at www.treasury.gov.
8   Bekaert and Harvey (2003) review all the empirical evidence on emerging financial markets and feature the link uncovered in studies between the higher volatility of net capital flows following market liberalization events.
9   Erb et al. (1994) show that the forecast power for cross-market correlations stem from the coincidence of business cycles across countries, but there is little, if any, secular trend. Goetzmann et al. (2003) argue that the perceived increase in global market correlations during the past 20 years stems from the expanded opportunities in emerging markets and not from any changes in institutional arrangements or international market integration.
10   Kaminsky and Schmukler (1999) examine similarly constructed stock return co-exceedances, or 'market jitters', around the Asian crisis of 1997–1998 and search for news on agreements with international organization, credit ratings agencies, national economic or political stories on Bloomberg related to these events. They find that these large stock price changes cannot be explained by any substantial news and suggest instead that they are triggered by herd instincts of the markets, which they associate with the 'root of financial contagion'.

References

Bae, K.-H., and G. A. Karolyi (1994), 'Good News, Bad News and International Spillovers of Stock Return Volatility between Japan and the US', *Pacific-Basin Finance Journal*, 2, 405–38.

Bae, K.-H., G. A. Karolyi, and R. Stulz (2003), 'A New Approach to Measuring Financial Contagion', *Review of Financial Studies*, 16(3), 87–133.

Bailey, W., K. Chan and Y. P. Chung (2000), 'Depositary Receipts, Country Funds and the Peso Crash: The Intraday Evidence', *Journal of Finance*, 55, 2693–717.

Barberis, N., A. Shleifer and J. Wurgler (2002), *'Co-movements'*, Harvard University Working Paper.

Bekaert, G., and C. Harvey (1995), 'Time-varying World Market Integration', *Journal of Finance*, 50, 403–44.

Bekaert, G., and C. Harvey (2000), 'Foreign Speculators and Emerging Equity Markets', *Journal of Finance*, 55, 565–613.

Bekaert, G., and C. Harvey (2003), 'Emerging Market Finance', *Journal of Empirical Finance*, 10, 3–55.

Bekaert, G., C. Harvey and A. Ng (2003), 'Market Integration and Contagion', *Journal of Business*, forthcoming.

Bikhchandani, S., D. Hirshleifer and I. Welch (1992), 'A Theory of Fads, Fashion, Custom and Cultural Changes as Information Cascades', *Journal of Political Economy*, 100, 992–1020.

Bohn, H., and L. Tesar (1996), 'U.S. Equity Investment in Foreign Markets: Portfolio Rebalancing or Return Chasing?', *American Economic Review*, 86, 77–81.

Brennan, M., and H. Cao (1997), 'International Portfolio Investment Flows', *Journal of Finance*, 52, 1851–80.

Calvo, G., M. Goldstein and E. Hochreiter (1996), *Private Capital Flows to Emerging Markets after the Mexican Crisis.* Washington, DC: Institute for International Economics.

Calvo, G., and C. Reinhart (1996), 'Capital Flows to Latin America: Is There Evidence of Contagion Effects?', in G. Calvo, M. Goldstein and E. Hochreiter (eds), *Private Capital Flows to Emerging Markets after the Mexican Crisis*, Washington, DC: Institute for International Economics.

Choe, H., B.-C. Kho and R. Stulz (1999), 'Do Foreign Investors Destabilize Stock Markets? The Korean Experience in 1997', *Journal of Financial Economics*, 54, 227–64.

Claessens, S., and K. Forbes (2001), *International Financial Contagion*, New York: Kluwer Academic Publishers.

Connolly, R., and A. Wang (2003), 'International Equity Market Co-movements: Economic Fundamentals or Contagion', *Pacific Basin Finance Journal*, 11, 23–44.

Diamond, D., and P. Dybvig (1983), 'Bank Runs, Deposit Insurance and Liquidity', *Journal of Political Economy*, 91, 401–19.

Dornbusch, R., Y.-C. Park and S. Claessens (2001), 'Contagion: How It Spreads and How It Can Be Stopped', in S. Claessens and K. Forbes (eds), *International Financial Contagion*, New York: Kluwer Academic Publishers.

Eichengreen, B., and A. Rose (1997), 'Contagious Currency Crises: Channels of Conveyance', in T. Ito and A. Krueger (eds), *Changes in Exchange Rates in Rapidly Developing Countries: Theory, Practice and Policy Issues*, Chicago, IL: University of Chicago Press.

Eichengreen, B., A. Rose and C. Wyplosz (1996), 'Contagious Currency Crises: First Tests', *Scandinavian Journal of Economics*, 98, 463–84.

Erb, C., C. Harvey and T. Viskanta (1994), 'Forecasting International Equity Correlations', *Financial Analysts Journal*, 4, 32–45.

Eun, C., and S. Shim (1989), 'International Transmission of Stock Market Movements', *Journal of Financial and Quantitative Analysis*, 24, 241–56.

Fama, E. (1963), 'Mandelbrot and the Stable Paretian Hypothesis', *Journal of Business*, 36, 420–29.

Forbes, K., and R. Rigobon (2002), 'No Contagion, Only Interdependence: Measuring Stock Market Co-movements', *Journal of Finance*, 57, 2223–62.

Frankel, J., and S. Schmukler (1998), 'Crises, Contagion, and Country Funds: Effects on East Asia and Latin America', in R. Glick (ed.), *Management of Capital Flows and Exchange Rates: Lessons from the Pacific Rim*, Cambridge: Cambridge University Press.

Friedman, T. (1999), *The Lexus and the Olive Tree*. New York: Farrar, Straus and Giroux.

Froot, K., P. O'Connell and M. Seasholes (2001), 'The Portfolio Flows of International Investors', *Journal of Financial Economics*, 59, 151–93.

Goetzmann, W., L. Li and G. Rouwenhorst (2003), 'Long-term Global Market Correlations', Yale University Working Paper.

Griffin, J., F. Nardari and R. Stulz (2002), 'Daily Cross-border Portfolio Equity Flows: Pushed or Pulled?', Ohio State University Working Paper.

Hamao, Y., R. W. Masulis and Victor Ng (1990), 'Correlations in Price Changes and Volatility Across International Stock Markets', *Review of Financial Studies*, 3, 281–308.

Hartmann, P., S. Straetmans and C. de Vries (2001), 'Asset Market Linkages in Crisis Periods', Universiteit Maastricht Working Paper.

Kaminsky, G. L., and S. L. Schmukler (1999), 'What Triggers Market Jitters?', *Journal of International Money and Finance*, 18, 537–60.

Karolyi, G. A. (2002), 'Did the Asian Financial Crisis Scare Foreign Investors Out of Japan?', *Pacific Basin Finance Journal*, 10, 411–42.

Karolyi, G. A., and R. M. Stulz (1996), 'Why Do Markets Move Together? An Investigation of U.S.–Japan Stock Return Co-movements', *Journal of Finance*, 51, 951–86.

Karolyi, G. A., and R. M. Stulz (2003), 'Are Assets Priced Locally or Globally?', in G. Constantinides, M. Harris and R. M. Stulz (eds), *The Handbook of the Economics of Finance*, New York: North-Holland Publishers.

King, M. A., E. Sentana and S. Wadhwani (1994), 'Volatility and Links Between National Stock Markets', *Econometrica*, 62, 901–33.

Kodres, L., and M. Pritsker (2002), 'A Rational Expectations Model of Financial Contagion', *Journal of Finance*, 57, 769–99.

Lin, W., R. Engle and T. Ito (1994), 'Do Bulls and Bears Move Across Borders? Transmission of International Stock Returns and Volatility', *Review of Financial Studies*, 7, 507–38.

Longin, F. M. (1996), 'The Asymptotic Distribution of Extreme Stock Market Returns', *Journal of Business*, 59, 383–408.

Longin, F. M., and B. Solnik (1995), 'Is the Correlation in International Equity Returns Constant: 1970–1990?', *Journal of International Money and Finance*, 14, 3–26.

Longin, F. M., and B. Solnik (2001), 'Extreme Correlations of International Equity Markets During Extremely Volatile Periods', *Journal of Finance*, 56, 649–76.

Mandelbrot, B. (1963), 'The Variation of Certain Speculative Prices', *Journal of Business*, 36, 394–419.

Masson, P. (1999), 'Contagion', *Journal of International Money and Finance,* 18, 587–602.

Schinasi, G., and T. Smith (2001), 'Portfolio Diversification, Leverage and Financial Contagion', in S. Claessens and K. Forbes (eds), *International Financial Contagion*, New York: Kluwer Academic Publishers.

Sell, F. (2001), *Contagion in Financial Markets.* Cheltenham, UK: Edward Elgar.

Shiller, R. (1999), *Irrational Exuberance.* Princeton, NJ: Princeton University Press.

Tesar, L., and I. Werner (1994), 'International Equity Transactions and US Portfolio Choice', in J. Frankel (ed.), *The Internationalization of Equity Markets*, Chicago, IL: University of Chicago Press.

52

WHAT DOES A FINANCIAL SHOCK DO?

First International Evidence

Fabio Fornari and Livio Stracca

Source: Working Paper Series No 1522, European Central Bank, March 2013.

Abstract

In this paper we attempt to evaluate the quantitative impact of financial shocks on key indicators of real activity and financial conditions. We focus on financial shocks as they have received wide attention in the recent literature and in the policy debate after the global financial crisis. We estimate a panel VAR for 21 advanced economies based on quarterly data between 1985 and 2011, where financial shocks are identified through sign restrictions. Overall, we find robust evidence that financial shocks can be separately identified from other shock types and that they exert a significant influence on key macroeconomic variables such as GDP and (particularly) investment, but it is unclear whether these shocks are demand or supply shocks from the standpoint of their macroeconomic impact. The financial development and the financial structure of a given country are found not to matter much for the intensity of the propagation of financial shocks. Moreover, we generally find that these shocks play a role not only in crisis times, but also in normal conditions. Finally, we discuss the implications of our findings for monetary policy.

Non-technical summary

In this paper we attempt to provide international evidence on the impact of financial shocks on key indicators of real activity and financial conditions. We estimate a panel Vector Autoregression (VAR) model for 21 advanced countries based on quarterly data between 1985 and 2011, where financial shocks are identified through sign restrictions derived partly from intuition and partly from dynamic stochastic general equilibrium (DSGE) models with financial frictions (Gilchrist et al. 2009, Hirakata et al. 2010, Nolan and Thoenissen 2009, Meh and Moran 2010). In particular, financial shocks are identified as those structural shocks having a positive impact on both the absolute share price of the financial sector as well as the share price relative to remaining sectors, a positive impact on credit to the private sector and on investment, and do not lead to a fall in the short term interest rate (in order to distinguish it from a monetary policy shock). In order to support the choice of the identification scheme, in the paper we also show evidence suggesting that the relative share price of the financial sector is highly correlated with the "health" of this sector and more generally of the financial intermediation process.

The VAR model is estimated and sign restrictions are imposed in each country individually. Cross country results are aggregated using a Bayesian stochastic pooling approach as in Canova and Pappa (2007).

The main results of the analysis are as follows:

- Overall, we find robust evidence that financial shocks can be separately identified from other shock types and that they exert a significant influence on key macroeconomic variables such as GDP and (particularly) investment.
- At the same time, it is not clear whether these shocks are demand or supply shocks from the standpoint of their macroeconomic impact. Hence, our empirical work does not dispel the existing uncertainty about the nature of this shock which prevails across different DSGE models.
- Surprisingly, financial development and structure of a given country are found not to matter much for the intensity of the propagation of financial shocks. Moreover, we generally find that these shocks play a role not only in crisis times, but also in normal conditions. In particular, we test whether results are different when excluding developments through the 2007–09 global financial crisis, or periods of credit booms and busts or with very low nominal and real interest rates.
- Finally, we discuss the implications of our findings for monetary policy. One important policy implication of this study is that monetary policy is rather well placed to fight financial shocks, as its effects are found to be to a large extent the mirror image of these shocks. Indeed, we find that a contractionary monetary policy shock reduces GDP, investment and credit; it is therefore largely (though not completely) a 'financial shock in the reverse'. A crucial question mark that our work still leaves open, however, is whether financial shocks are ultimately mainly demand shocks – in which case the role for monetary policy is well established – or rather supply shocks, in which case the optimal response of the monetary authority is in principle far less straight-forward, although this may also be model-dependent.

1 Introduction

The global financial crisis 2007–09 has shaken the previous consensus, widespread amongst policy makers and academics, that 'leaning against the wind' policies are undesirable or impractical, both in the regulatory and macro-prudential sphere as well as a strategy of monetary policy for central banks (Bernanke and Gertler 2001). In the regulatory field, initiatives to strengthen the 'leaning against the wind' orientation of policies are well under way in a global context under the aegis of the G20, while in the monetary policy field we are still at a relatively early stage of the debate.

It is important to be clear, however, against what type of underlying phenomena and shocks the policies (including monetary policy) should lean. In the paper we focus in particular on credit creation and conditions in the financial sector and we aim to understand whether they are autonomous sources of shock against which policies need to take steps or just a side-show or a second order phenomenon which can be accounted for by more traditional and better understood macroeconomic shocks. Indeed, many of the shocks that have been considered in the academic literature as well as in the practice of policy for decades (such as demand, supply and cost push shocks) can and should as well lead to fluctuations in credit, asset prices and financial market conditions. Therefore, what are the features of the winds that one should lean against?

There is already a large literature analysing the role of the financial sector as an amplifier of other types of shock. Credit cycles may result from collateral constraints and financial frictions, as emphasised by Kiyotaki and Moore (1997). Monetary policy and technology shocks may be propagated differently in an environment in which agents have collateral constraints. However, this amplification mechanism is already quite well understood, and thus taking this possible amplification better into account could lead at most to a refinement, rather than to a radical change, in the policy conduct after the crisis. In addition, the literature has emphasised that the degree of amplification stemming from credit constraints is empirically very limited outside crisis periods (Kocherlakota 2000; Cordoba and Ripoll 2004).[1]

In this paper, therefore, we do not focus on the amplification role of a given shock that financial intermediation could exert on real activity. Rather, we are closer to another, now almost mainstream narrative of the 2007–09 global financial crisis, which interprets it as resulting from shocks originating endogenously within the financial sector. Some of these contributions emphasise how changes in asset prices may be driven by non-fundamental or 'inefficient' shocks. Gilchrist and Leahy (2002), for example, identify asset price bubbles as resulting from favourable news about future productivity that eventually fail to materialise. A small but growing literature examines the relevance of 'news' and 'confidence' shocks, as in Blanchard et al. (2009), Barsky and Sims (2008), and Beaudry and Portier (2006). Farmer (2009) proposes a model in which confidence is an independent driver of economic activity. In this literature, confidence may be driven, in particular, by 'noise shocks', i.e. news items which are wrongly interpreted as anticipators of gains in productivity and which therefore lead to a later reversal in confidence and in real activity (see also Gilchrist and Leahy, 2002). Lorenzoni (2009) uses a very similar concept in order to build a theory of aggregate demand shocks. Geanakoplos (2009) relates variations in leverage to fluctuations in asset prices and concludes that the leverage cycle is potentially harmful and should be regulated. In his work, leverage cycles are primarily caused by lenders' perception of (default) risk, which is time-varying. A small but burgeoning literature (Jermann and Quadrini 2009; Gilchrist et al. 2009; Nolan and Thoenissen 2009; Meh and Moran 2010; Hirakata et al. 2010) propose Dynamic Stochastic General Equilibrium (DSGE) models with 'financial shocks', which are either i) shocks affecting the degree to which collateral can be used in financial intermediation or ii) shocks to the financial friction in a Bernanke-Gertler-Gilchrist financial accelerator model. In this way, these shocks can directly affect the extent in which borrowers are constrained and as such they also directly influence leverage. For example, exogenous changes in the loan to value ratio of a mortgage contract, due to a more optimistic view about future developments in credit risk, could be characterised as a financial shock. Adrian et al. (2010) also posit that changes in the risk appetite of financial intermediaries, induced by the time variation in a Value-at-Risk type constraint on their portfolios, influence the growth of the balance sheets of these intermediaries and hence their leverage.

Against this background, this paper represents a first attempt at a systematic *quantification* of the real and financial effects associated to financial shocks based on a panel of 21 advanced economies. One of the greatest challenges for the identification of leverage cycles lies in the data availability, since consistent time series of leverage and credit spreads simply do not exist in most countries, let alone the problem of cross country comparability. For this reason we take a more indirect route, estimating VAR models at a country level for each of the 21 countries to then aggregate the cross sectional results via the 'stochastic pooling' approach of Canova and Pappa (2007). In this way, the weight of a single country in the aggregate is inversely proportional to the precision of the estimates of the country-specific VAR. Based on the impulse responses of the VAR models we seek to identify three different types of shocks: (non-financial) aggregate demand, monetary policy and financial. We identify the structural shocks through sign restrictions. In particular, we impose that the financial shock has an impact on the *relative share price of the financial sector vs. the non-financial sectors,* given that this sector (i) is at the heart of the financial intermediation process that is subject to the disturbance and (ii) is itself significantly more leveraged than the rest of the economy.[2] The intuition behind this choice is that a shock that is accompanied by rising leverage and less stringent credit constraints has a larger impact on the return on equity (and hence the share price) of those sectors that are more highly exposed to the external finance premium and therefore benefit more than others from more favourable financing conditions. For example, a shift to a more optimistic assessment of credit risk should affect much more the equity of a firm that is heavily dependent on external finance, say a high tech firm, and much less a firm that is typically largely financed out of its own means, say a large energy company.

Overall, the key objective of this paper is to empirically identify financial shocks based on a wide database covering all main industrial countries, in order to evaluate their impact on standard macro variables, also relative to other types of shocks, and to assess their domestic and global relevance. We also address the question of whether the strength and propagation of financial shocks depends on the structural characteristics of the individual countries, such as the degree of financial development and openness. Is it the case, for instance, that a country with a particularly large financial sector, such as Iceland or Ireland, is more exposed to financial shocks? Finally, we touch upon the potential role of monetary policy in offsetting the effect of financial shocks which is relevant in the 'leaning against the wind' debate, similar to Assenmacher-Wesche and Gerlach (2010).

Being severely constrained in the set of variables that have sufficiently harmonised data at an international level, our approach should be considered as a first attempt to collect international evidence and is possibly not the ideal way to identify financial shocks from a methodological standpoint. In particular, the identification of financial shocks could be corroborated and improved when looking at a more restricted set of countries for which more data are available, such as credit spreads and balance sheets of financial intermediaries.

It should also be noted that the financial shocks that we seek to identify in this paper are different from the credit demand and supply shocks that have been typically dealt with in the literature. Credit demand and supply shocks can have their roots in developments recorded both within and outside the financial sector, which in turn may be largely unrelated to the financial shocks examined in this paper. For example, a positive technology shock can increase both credit demand (by increasing borrowers' permanent income) and credit supply (by increasing borrowers' net worth). By contrast, financial shocks (since they have a direct connection to leverage and credit creation) should be correlated primarily with those shocks that drive asset prices *and credit,* the shocks which – according to many observers – are most dangerous from a financial stability perspective (Blinder 2008; Schularick and Taylor 2009). This can be illustrated by looking at the data reported in *Figure 1*, which shows the share price of the financial sector in the United States relative to a composite stock market index of that country that includes all non-financial firms (henceforth named *relative share price*). The collapse of the dot-com bubble in the early 2000s has had little impact on the relative share price (while the financial distress of 1998–99 is clearly visible in the data), especially when compared to its large and abrupt fall observed during the 2007–09 global financial crisis. We now know the different macroeconomic implications of the two episodes.

Our study reaches four main conclusions. First, we find evidence that a financial shock – at least the kind of financial shock we identify – exerts a non-negligible influence on key macroeconomic variables such as output, investment and the price level. Second, we find that it is generally not clear whether the financial shock is mainly an aggregate demand shock or a supply shock, since the impact of this shock on the CPI (which would tell apart one interpretation from the other) is not estimated very precisely. Third, we find that our results are not driven in particular by crisis times, including the 2007–09 global financial crisis.

119

Figure 1 Relative share price of the financial sector vs. non-financial sector in the United States, in logs. Note: Sectoral stock price data are from Datastream. See *Table 2* for the sources of the data.

This suggests that financial shocks affect the economy also in normal times and not only in turbulent periods, as could have been surmised. We also find that results are generally robust when taking out periods of credit booms and busts as well as those characterised by very low nominal and real interest rates. Finally, we find that the propagation of the financial shocks does not depend much on the financial and economic structures of the countries, nor do financial development and structure generally matter for the transmission of the other identified shocks (demand and monetary policy) within a given country.

The paper is structured as follows. Section 2 presents the econometric approach and the strategy underlying the identification of the shocks. Section 3 describes the data and presents some preliminary analysis. Section 4 presents the results. Section 5 draws the implications of our results for monetary policy and Section 6 concludes.

2 Specification and identification of the financial shock

For each country *i* (see *Table 1* for the country list) we estimate a VAR model and apply sign restrictions as in Rubio-Ramirez, Waggoner and Zha (2010) to identify structural shocks. In each domestic VAR foreign variables are included in order to control for international interdependence and to better identify domestic, as opposed to global or foreign, structural shocks. The estimated VAR is therefore,

Table 1 List of countries

United States	Sweden
United Kingdom	Switzerland
Austria	Canada
Belgium	Japan
Denmark	Finland
France	Ireland
Germany	Portugal
Italy	Spain
Luxembourg	Australia
Netherlands	New Zealand
Norway	

$$A_{i0}x_{it} = A_i(L)x_{i,t-1} + C_i(L)x_{it}^* + B_i\varepsilon_{it} \tag{1}$$

where x is a $k \times 1$ vector,

$$x_{it} = \left[p_{it}, y_{it}, inv_{it}, R_{it}, \tilde{q}_{it}, q_{it}^{NONFIN}, b_{it} \right] \tag{2}$$

$$\tilde{q}_{it} = \frac{q_{it}^{FIN}}{q_{it}^{NONFIN}} \tag{3}$$

with R the short-term interest rate, p the log of the CPI, y log real GDP, inv log investment, q^{NONFIN} is the composite share price index of non-financial sectors ($\tilde{q}$ is the relative share price of the financial sector compared with the rest of the stock market), b is credit to the private sector, and A_{i0} is a non-singular $k \times k$ matrix. All variables in the VAR except the nominal rate R are in logs and standardised, in order to ensure comparability across countries. We allow for 2 quarterly lags for all countries (1 lag for the variables in the x^* vector).

The x^* vector

$$x_{it}^* = \left[p_{it}^*, y_{it}^*, R_{it}^*, b_{it}^* \right] \tag{4}$$

contains country-specific "external" variables included as exogenous variables in the VAR for each country i. The "external" variables for each country are computed by aggregating those variables over the remaining countries using their relative real GDP weight at Purchasing Power Parity (PPP), hence excluding country i itself. The data are quarterly and the sample starts in 1985 so that data come from a relatively homogeneous period in terms of macroeconomic volatility and monetary policy regime.

A crucial step in our analysis is the identification of the financial shock and of the other structural shocks. We rely as much as possible on existing DSGE models to figure out what the implications of these shocks on the variables of interest should be. In particular, we interpret the financial shock primarily as a *shock to the financial sector,* i.e. as a sectoral shock, in line with the interpretation of Hirakata et al. (2010): a positive financial shock is a transfer of net worth from the non-financial to the financial sector. Hirakata et al. (2009) show that the distribution of net worth between the financial and non-financial sector matters for investment. This concept is closely related to the definition of financial shock given by Hall (2010): a positive financial shock is akin to a selective fall in taxation of financial intermediation, which makes financial intermediation less costly and more efficient. As a consequence of this supply-like shock, firms offering financial intermediation services – the financial intermediaries – become more profitable, and more credit is extended. Nolan and Thoenissen (2009) also have a similar definition where "financial frictions shocks" are shocks to the efficiency of contractual relationships between borrowers and lenders. After such a shock, it becomes more (or less) difficult and costly to write debt contracts. Gilchrist et al. (2009) define the financial shock as an additive shock to the external finance premium. Meh and Moran (2010) identify the financial shock as an exogenous change in bank net worth (such as a tax on bank capital). Since bank capital is a key tool of financial intermediaries' debt production capacity, the shock may have wider consequences for financing conditions and the real economy.

Against this background, this paper uses the stock price of the financial sector as the key variable for the identification of the financial shock. If the financial shock is akin to a *sectoral tax on financial intermediation,* then it should further compress profits in the financial intermediation sector relative to the broader economy, especially relative to sectors that are more distant from financial intermediation and debt. Therefore, we postulate that a positive (negative) financial shock has a positive (negative) impact on the ratio between the share price of the financial sector and the composite stock market index, under the assumption that share prices correctly discount current and expected profits.[3] In addition, as the financial sector is also typically more leveraged than most other sectors, it is bound to be affected more strongly than less leveraged sectors by a disturbance to intermediaries' debt production capacity and a corresponding rise in the external finance premium. Indeed, in several DSGE models with financial frictions, the impact of financing conditions on entrepreneurial net worth is larger for highly leveraged entrepreneurs (see e.g. Christensen and Dib 2008, eq. (15), p. 160; Gilchrist et al. 2009, eq. (25), page 18). For *both* these reasons, we expect a financial shock to influence the share price index of the financial sector more than the broad index. Note that in the remainder of this paper, unlike in the mentioned DSGE models, and mainly for illustration purposes, a financial shock has a positive connotation, i.e. it is a situation where debt accumulation is made easier and financial intermediation is more profitable.

In addition to its effect on the financial stock price index, we expect a positive financial shock to lead to higher credit to the private sector and to higher private investment, on account of the fact that external finance is an important element in the production of capital goods, more so than for consumption goods (Hall 2010).[4] This also helps distinguish this shock from a *credit demand* shock, which should push the quantity of credit and its price in the same direction. A rise in the price of credit (for which international data of sufficiently harmonised nature are unfortunately not available) should arguably have a negative, not a positive effect on investment. Note that we are instead open as to whether the financial shock is mainly a demand or a supply shock in terms of overall economic activity, and therefore do not constrain the reaction of the price level to this shock. Theoretically, one could expect either effect to prevail depending on whether credit availability matters more for the expenditure or the production side of the economy (e.g. whether the credit shock is more concentrated in the household or the corporate sector). In some recent DSGE models like Meh and Moran (2010) and Gerali et al. (2010), the financial shock is mainly a supply shock because it influences firms' marginal costs. In other models, however, a credit supply shock has the effect of an aggregate demand shock (e.g. Curdia and Woodford 2010).[5]

Another important element for the identification of the financial shock is the need to ensure that it is not contaminated by other shocks and that shocks are identified in a mutually exclusive way so that they do not fully overlap. In this respect, a particular concern could be that the financial shock is actually capturing an expansionary monetary policy shock. A tightening of monetary policy conditions might indeed have effects (fall in investment and credit, stronger contraction of profits in the financial sector) that are similar to those generated by a negative financial shock. We therefore impose that, after a positive financial shock (i.e. when credit conditions improve), the reaction of the short term interest rate is *not negative.* We also include non-financial, non-monetary demand shocks in the identification, in order again not to confound them with the financial shock. Specifically, a demand shock is a shock leading to a rise in the price level, output as well as to a higher interest rate, conditions which keep it distinct from a monetary policy shock. The non-financial demand shock is also assumed to lead to a rise in the share price of non-financial firms, but not to a larger rise in the stock price of financial firms, in contrast with the financial shock; this latter condition ensures that all the shocks we identify are mutually exclusive. We identify the three structural shocks simultaneously, since this should produce more reliable results (see Paustian 2007), although this is computationally challenging in our multi-country analysis. Overall, these considerations lead to the following matrix of sign restrictions:

Table – Sign restrictions applied

	Non financial demand shock	Monetary policy shock	Financial shock
p_t	> 0 (a)	> 0 ($t+8$)	
y_t	> 0 (a)	> 0 (a)	
inv_t		> 0 (a)	> 0
R_t	≥ 0	< 0	≥ 0
$\dfrac{q_t^{FIN}}{q_t^{NONFIN}}$	≤ 0		> 0 (and $q_t^{FIN} > 0$)
q_t^{NONFIN}	> 0	> 0	
b_t			> 0

Note: Sign restrictions are imposed using the approach of Rubio-Ramirez, Waggoner and Zha (2010). They are imposed on impact unless otherwise stated.

(a) Restriction also imposed on the accumulated impulse response after one year.

We estimate the VAR models country-by-country and therefore need a metric to standardise the size of the structural shocks. To ensure comparability across countries, as noted, we standardise all variables with the exception of the short term interest rate, and assume that (i) the size of the demand shock is determined by its impact on real GDP, (ii) the size of the monetary policy shock by its impact on the short term rate, and (iii) the size of the financial shock by its impact on the relative share price of the financial sector. The size of the monetary policy shock, in particular, is equal to a rise of the short term rate by 100 basis points. Finally, we follow Fry and Pagan (2010) and select a single model among the many which are found to satisfy the sign restrictions. This is chosen as the model which generates impulse responses having the minimum distance from the median impulse response computed across all models which satisfy the restrictions. Although it is more common to report the median impulse response across all models satisfying the restrictions, selecting a single model has the advantage that structural shocks are orthogonal, which allows the computation of the variance decomposition, i.e. the contribution of the different shocks to the expected movements in selected variables of the VAR.

Country-level impulse responses and the associated standard errors are aggregated with a stochastic pooling approach as proposed by Canova and Pappa (2007) and in particular as applied in Calza et al. (2011). In this (Bayesian) stochastic pooling approach, described formally in the Annex, each country receives a weight which is inversely proportional to the precision of the associated impulse responses. In other words, a country whose impulse response is characterised by very large standard errors will receive a smaller weight than a country with smaller standard errors. Since this may imply that some countries receive a tiny weight, we also look at simple averages of the impulse responses across countries (where standard errors are obtained assuming no cross sectional dependence) as a robustness check.

3. Data and preliminary analysis

The empirical analysis is conducted on data from 21 advanced countries (see *Table 1*), sampled quarterly between 1985:1 and 2011:2 (or longest available sample). In addition to the variables included in the VAR (see the beginning of Section 2) we also use Moody's data on Expected Default Frequencies (henceforth EDF) computed across financial and non-financial firms separately, considering the median EDF across these firms as well as their 90th percentile, although these data do not enter the VAR in direct way. *Table 2* reports information on the sources and characteristics of the data that we use. *Table 3* reports the summary statistics for all variables. Note that the EDF data are available for a smaller sample (since 1992) and also for fewer countries than the 21 considered in the VAR estimation. For this reason we keep them out of the baseline analysis, for which over 2,000 quarterly observations are available as a whole.

We also collect annual data on selected structural characteristics of the countries (not reported in *Table 3*) which may be behind the origination and/or the propagation of financial shocks. In particular, we look at three measures of financial development compiled by the World Bank, namely stock market capitalisation over GDP, private credit over GDP, and liquid liabilities over GDP. We also look at four measures of openness, namely financial openness (sum of external financial assets and liabilities over GDP), the ratio of foreign loans and international debt to GDP, and trade openness (sum of imports and exports over GDP). These data are helpful to test the robustness of our results, i.e. their stability across different country groups.

Because the relative share price of the financial sector vs. the non-financial sectors plays a key role for the identification of the financial shocks, it is important to first devote some time to the analysis of its properties. As noted in the previous section, ideally we would like this measure to reflect both the relative health of the financial sector (compared to the rest of the economy) and the relative performance of the more leveraged sectors, i.e. the sectors that are more exposed to external finance. On the first question, we need to evaluate, in particular, whether the fluctuations in the relative share price of the financial sector just reflect the business cycle as such, or they really capture the larger degree of distress prevailing in the financial sector. In order to test for this conjecture, we estimate the following panel regression,

$$\tilde{q}_{it} = \alpha_i + \gamma_t + \beta \tilde{q}_{i,t-1} + \delta\, ygap_{it} + \zeta\, Bankcrisis_{it}$$
$$+ \theta EDF\_FIN_{it} + \phi EDF\_NONFIN_{it} + u_{it}$$

(5)

where *ygap* is the output gap (obtained by detrending real GDP using the HP filter), *Bankcrisis* is a dummy variable taking values 1 if the country is experiencing a banking crisis and zero otherwise (with baking crisis data taken from Laeven and Valencia, 2008), *EDF_FIN* and *EDF_NONFIN* are the Moody's measures

Table 2 Sources of the data

Variable	Source	Notes
Real GDP, GDP deflator, CPI, non-residential investment, trade openness, 3-month interest rate	OECD Economic Outlook database	Trade openness is the sum of imports and exports over GDP
Credit to the private sector	ECB for EU countries, IMF (International Financial Statistics), Flow of Funds statistics for the United States	The IMF IFS data are subject to infrequent jumps apparently caused by structural breaks in the data. The data have therefore been corrected for these breaks.
Expected Default Frequency (EDF) at 1-year horizon: financial and non-financial sector, median and 90th percentile	Moody's	The data are provided by KMV and refer to an horizon of one year. They are initially computed at the firm level, based on balance sheet data, and then aggregated across sector or countries as a whole. They are computed according to the KMV model which is in turn based on Merton's (1974) model.
Relative share price of financial sector; share price of non-financial sectors	Datastream.	
Real effective exchange rate (CPI based)	Bank for International Settlements database	Data are based on a narrow index of 27 trading partners.
Banking crisis dummy	Laeven and Valencia (2008)	Original data are annual and are interpolated to a quarterly frequency by linear smoothing
Stock market capitalisation over GDP, private credit to GDP, credit to deposits ratio, liquid liabilities to GDP, foreign loans to GDP, international debt to GDP	World Bank Database of Financial Development and Structure	Annual frequency
Financial openness	IMF International Financial Statistics	Sum of external financial assets and liabilities over GDP; annual frequency

Note: Data, unless otherwise specified, are available at a quarterly frequency from 1985:1 to 2011:2; they refer to the countries listed in *Table 1*.

Table 3 Summary statistics

Variable	Obs	Mean	Std. Dev.	Min	Max
Log CPI	2174	0.00	1.00	-2.89	1.66
Log real GDP	2248	0.00	1.00	-2.67	1.85
Log investment	2248	0.00	1.00	-2.85	1.94
Short term rate	2244	5.72	4.09	0.03	25.78
Log relative share price of fin. sector	2162	0.00	0.66	-3.63	5.01
Credit growth	2172	0.03	0.04	-0.34	0.34
Log real effective exch. rate	2246	4.59	0.10	4.24	5.05
EDF fin. Sector	1349	0.37	0.69	0.01	8.48
EDF non-fin. Sector	1274	0.55	0.50	0.02	3.23
EDF fin. Sector, 90th percentile	1349	3.98	5.17	0.06	35.00
EDF non.fin sector, 90th percentile	1274	7.56	7.24	0.15	35.00
Output gap	2248	0.00	0.08	-0.49	0.34
Real GDP growth	2227	0.03	0.05	-0.40	0.33
Banking crisis dummy	2268	0.17	0.37	0.00	1.00

Note: The sample period is 1980:1 to 2011:2 (or longest available period), quarterly data. See *Table 2* for the sources of the data. Note that data for the CPI have been seasonally adjusted using the X12 ARIMA approach. For the country list and the sources of the data see *Tables 1–2*.

of distance to default in the financial and non-financial sectors respectively. *Table 4* reports results from a pooled OLS regression where we first include only the output gap, then the banking crisis dummy, then the EDF measures, and finally all variables together (which however significantly reduces the sample size). The relative share price is not correlated with the business cycle and with real GDP growth, while the bank crisis dummy has a strong and statistically significant downward impact. When putting all variables together, the only significant variables are the bank crisis dummy and the EDF *of the financial sector only,* while the output gap and the EDF of the non-financial sector are insignificant.[6] Note that this regression does not intend to establish causal interpretations; we are simply suggesting that the relative share price of the financial sector is a good indicator of the 'state of health' of that sector and does not just reflect pro-cyclicality alone.

Another piece of evidence indirectly suggesting that the variable that we use is a good indicator of financial health or distress could be gathered by looking at its behaviour across countries. In *Figure 2* we report the indicator for two countries, Ireland and Finland, which are known to be polar cases as far as the effect of the 2007–09 global financial crisis is concerned. Indeed, the relative share price of the Irish financial sector plummets in 2008–09, while it stays afloat in Finland, where instead it fell sharply in the mid-1990s, owing to the Nordic financial crisis.

Turning to the second question, namely whether the relative share price of the financial sector really mirrors the worsening conditions for the more levered firms at times of turbulence, we compute (for the US only, due to data availability) the returns of two stock indices: the former refers to firms which are highly levered, the second to firms which have low leverage. In this exercise, leverage

Table 4 Panel regression, log relative share price of financial sector vs. non-financial sector

	(1)	(2)	(3)	(4)	(5)	(6)
Log relative share price of fin. sector, t-1	0.9135***	0.9137***	0.9134***	0.9311***	0.9400***	0.9355***
	(0.0188)	(0.0190)	(0.0189)	(0.0190)	(0.0162)	(0.0194)
Output gap	0.0282		0.0213	-0.0458	-0.0320	-0.0745
	(0.0825)		(0.0790)	(0.0762)	(0.0988)	(0.0963)
Real GDP growth		0.0267				
		(0.2422)				
Banking crisis dummy			-0.0781**			-0.1185**
			(0.0314)			(0.0436)
EDF of financial sector				-0.0195		-0.0291**
				(0.0198)		(0.0120)
EDF of non-financial sector					-0.0292	-0.0040
					(0.0182)	(0.0173)
Observations	2,122	2,121	2,122	1,347	1,272	1,272
Number of countries	21	21	21	18	17	17
R2 Within	0.869	0.869	0.869	0.903	0.915	0.916
R2 Between	0.658	0.667	0.632	0.974	0.971	0.972
R2 Overall	0.868	0.868	0.869	0.904	0.916	0.917
Adj. R2	0.862	0.862	0.862	0.897	0.909	0.910

Note: Pooled OLS. The sample period is 1985:1 to 2011:2. The model includes country fixed effects and time dummies. Robust standard errors in parentheses, */**/*** denotes significance at the 10%/5%/1% level. The output gap is obtained by applying the HP1600 filter to the log of real GDP. See *Table 2* on the sources and definitions of the variables.

128

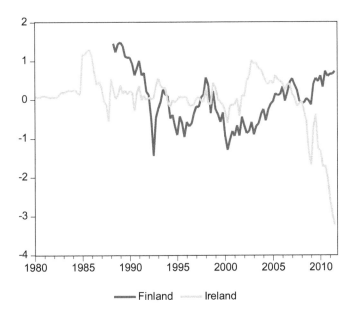

Figure 2 Relative share price of the financial sector vs. non-financial sector in Ireland and
Finland, in logs. Note: Sectoral stock price data are from Datastream. See *Table
2* for the sources of the data.

is measured through the Total Assets/Common Equity Ratio as reported at
year-end in the firms' balance sheet, which are collected and distributed by
Worldscope. To assign firms to the two groups we first i) compute, as of each
year-end (t) between 1984 and 2009, the 10% and 90% percentile of the distribution of the cross sectional Total Assets to Common Equity ratios and then
ii) assign to the first group, for all quarters in year t +1, the firms whose Total
Assets to Common Equity ratio is below the 10% percentile and to the second group those firms whose ratio exceeds the 90% percentile. We also compute the return indices via the 25% and 75% percentiles of the Total Assets to
Common Equity ratio, finding only minor differences on results. Overall, as of
December 2010 we look at around 1000 US firms, while back in 1985 the number of available firms drops to around 400. In principle, we could enlarge the
number of firms by considering as well those firms that ceased activity before
end-2010, but this would not necessarily lead to a better measure of the difference in returns between the two groups. When constructing the returns for the
two groups, we consider all sectors, although some more pronounced differences between the two groups could emerge if we were to keep financial and
non financial firms separated. Once identified the firms in the two groups, we
construct the respective indices by aggregating firm-level returns through their
market capitalization recorded in the preceding quarter.

In *Figure 3*, we report the relative share price of high-levered firms vs. low-levered firms constructed in this way. Indeed, there is a high positive correlation between this series and the relative share price of the financial sector relative to the composite index.

In order to further validate our choice of this relative share price index as our key indicator for the identification of the financial shock, we regress the monthly returns on ten US sectoral equity indices (Oil and Gas, Basic Materials, Industrials, Consumer Goods, Healthcare, Consumer Services, Telecom, Utilities, Financials, Technology) on the lagged return of the aggregate equity index, the change in the US credit spread and lagged US output gap. The credit spread (a proxy for the external finance premium) is the difference between the yield on 10-year Baa-rated US industrial bonds as computed by Moody's and on the 10-year US Government bonds. For this analysis, the output gap is computed applying the HP filter to the monthly US Industrial production index. The regressions for the ten sectors are run between January 1985 and September 2010 so to broadly match the sample for which the VAR is estimated and the regressors are lagged by between 1 and 4 quarters, so to allow a delayed response of stock returns to the emergence of tighter credit conditions or changes in economic activity.

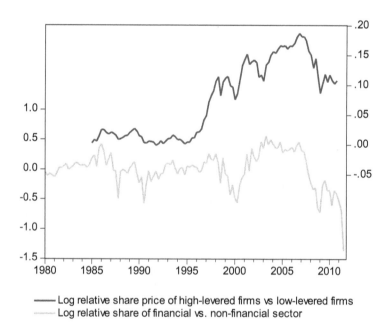

Log relative share price of high-levered firms vs low-levered firms
Log relative share of financial vs. non-financial sector

Figure 3 Log relative share price of the financial sector (black line) and log relative share price of the high-leverage firms vs. low-leverage firms (grey line). Note: The relative share price of the financial sector is reported on the right axis, the relative share price of high-leverage firms on the left axis.

Again, this analysis is carried out for the United States only, where better data and longer time series are available and results are briefly described here but not reported for brevity (but they are available from the authors upon request). The sensitivity of sectoral equity returns to credit conditions is computed summing the coefficients of the four lags of the Baa credit spread if they were individually significant. Overall, the Oil and Gas and the Industrial sector do not appear to be affected by developments in the credit spread, once one controls for the aggregate movement of the equity market as well as for the cyclical position of the US economy. At the other extreme, Consumer Services, Financials, Telecommunication and Utilities evidence a large negative exposure to the credit spread, i.e. the price indices of these sectors fall when credit spreads have been getting wider, possibly reflecting a higher dependence on external finance conditions.

4 Results

4.1 Baseline

Figure 4 reports the impulse responses of all the variables in the VAR to monetary policy, demand and financial shocks, after aggregating the impulse responses across countries using the stochastic pooling approach (see the Annex). Overall, the impulse responses agree with the conventional wisdom on the effect of monetary policy and demand shocks. For example, the effect of the expansionary monetary policy shock (middle column) reduces the interest rate on impact and leads to a temporary rise in real GDP, investment, the share price of non-financial sectors, and credit. Although the financial stock price also rises after a monetary policy shock, the relative share price actually falls, indicating that a monetary policy loosening does not favour the financial sector in a particularly strong way compared with other sectors. Unlike the typical result of identifications achieved through a Cholesky decomposition (although rather common when applying sign restrictions), there is no price puzzle as the log CPI rises on impact.

Turning to the aggregate demand shock, we find that this shock is particularly "non-financial": it leads to a statistically significant *fall* in the relative share price of the financial sector (note that our sign restrictions only imply that this variable *does not rise* in a statistically significant way) and the impact on credit to the private sector is not significant. It is likely that the latter result is due to the offsetting effects of, on the one hand, the rise in economic activity following the demand shock (which should support credit growth) and, on the other, of the rise in the interest rate and hence in lending rates, which has the opposite influence (see also Hristov et al. 2011 and Helbling et al. 2010).

Coming to the key shock for our analysis, i.e. the financial shock, we find that its impact is positive and statistically significant for both real GDP and investment; the impact on investment is much larger than for GDP (about 10 times), not only in absolute terms but also in relation to what we see for the monetary policy shock. Therefore, the relative reaction of investment as compared with

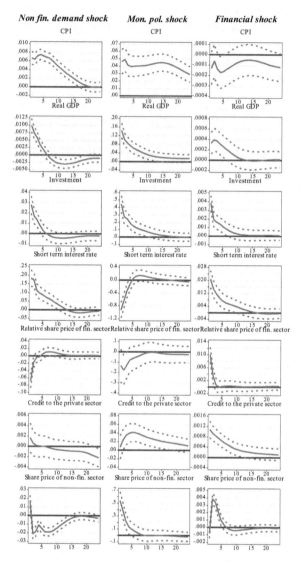

Figure 4 Impulse responses to structural shocks. Note: The chart reports impulse responses to structural shocks identified by applying sign restrictions as in Rubio-Ramirez, Waggoner and Zha (2010). The size of the shocks is 100 basis points of the interest rate for the monetary policy shock; a rise by 1% of the standardised level of real GDP for the demand shock; and a rise of 1% of the standardised level of the relative share price of the financial sector for the financial shock. The impulse responses are based on a VAR model estimated on quarterly data from 1985:1 to 2011:2 on 21 countries, and after aggregating cross country impulse responses by applying the stochastic pooling approach (see text and Annex for further explanation).

GDP may be a good way to identify a financial shock from other shocks such as aggregate demand and monetary policy. Overall, we find that the financial shock has expansionary features, as also visible in the sizeable and statistically significant upward impact on the share price of non-financial corporations. However, the impact on the CPI is not measured very precisely. As it tends to be negative, it would suggest that the shock has on balance the features of a supply shock, as also found for example in Gerali et al. (2010), although it is not statistically significant. Moreover, this result is not very robust across specifications (see further below). We also find a statistically significant and relatively large movement of the interest rate in response to a financial shock, suggesting that central banks have typically tended to react to such shocks or at least, indirectly, to their influence on key macro variables.

The stochastic pooling aggregation procedure may produce rather uneven weights across countries, depending on how precisely the respective impulse responses are estimated. This raises the question of whether results may be driven by a small subset of countries which happen to have very precise estimates. To test the robustness of the baseline results, *Figure 5* reports impulse responses based on the stochastic pooling approach (as in the baseline exercise in *Figure 4*) as well as on simple averages across countries, assuming that structural shocks are uncorrelated across countries. The results are overall the same in terms of sign and statistical significance; indeed for all variables the difference with the baseline estimation is not statistically significant.

How much can the financial shock account for the observed fluctuations in key macro variables? This is an important part of our analysis since we are not only interested in the statistical significance of this shock, but also – and even more – in judging its economic significance. *Table 5* reports the variance decomposition for the variables included in the VAR at an horizons of 24 quarters. The importance of the financial shock is non-negligible at that horizon (results for alternative horizons, not reported for brevity, led to similar results). Indeed, this shock is found to explain some 12% of real GDP variability, 16% of credit variability, and 15% of the variability of the share price of non-financial firms. These are values which are in the same ballpark of other key shocks (such as demand and monetary policy). Hence, the financial shock does play a role, although not a dominant one, in explaining business cycle fluctuations, at least according to the model and the identification scheme proposed here.

One caveat which applies to the results just presented is that we estimate a VAR for each country separately. In reality, there is a large degree of co-movement among macroeconomic and financial variables across countries and the inclusion of the foreign variables (the x^* vector in equation (1)) might be an insufficient or inefficient way to capture international interlinkages. Nonetheless, it is reassuring that we find structural shocks to be little correlated across countries, which suggests that a country-by-country estimation makes good sense from an econometric point of view. In *Table 6*, we report the average correlations and the average of the absolute values of the correlations across countries. The numbers

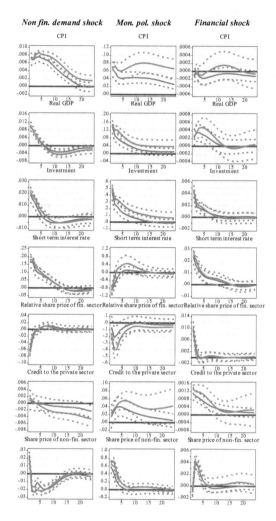

Figure 5 Impulse responses to structural shocks, stochastic pooling (thin lines) vs. simple average (thick line). Note: Thin lines are impulse responses to structural shocks identified by applying sign restrictions as in Rubio-Ramirez, Waggoner and Zha (2010) and aggregated across countries using the stochastic pooling approach. The size of the shocks is 100 basis points of the interest rate for the monetary policy shock; a rise by 1% of the standardised level of real GDP for the demand shock; and a rise of 1% of the standardised level of the relative share price of the financial sector for the financial shock. The impulse responses are based on a VAR model estimated on quarterly data from 1985:1 to 2011:2 on 21 countries, and after aggregating cross country impulse responses by applying the stochastic pooling approach (see text and Annex for further explanation). The thick lines report the same impulse responses which are aggregated across countries by taking the arithmetic average across them without any further adjustment, and assuming that countries are independent among each other.

Table 5 Variance decomposition of selected shocks

	Non-financial demand shock	Monetary policy shock	Financial shock	Other shocks
CPI	18.8	14.8	9.5	56.8
Real GDP	14.7	19.1	11.8	54.3
Investment	10.8	15.7	10.9	62.6
Short term rate	16.3	18.9	14.0	50.7
Relative share price of fin. sector	11.7	10.4	16.5	61.4
Credit to the private sector	14.7	16.7	16.4	52.2
Share price of non-fin. sector	13.0	11.7	14.8	60.6

Note: the table shows the variance decomposition at 24 quarters horizon. This is based on VAR models estimated on each country separately, and aggregated using the stochastic pooling approach (see Annex in the text). The variance decomposition is based on a single model per country, which ensures that the structural shocks are orthogonal among each other. The sample period is 1985:1 to 2011:2.

Table 6 Average cross-section correlation among estimated structural shocks

	Average corr.	Average absolute corr.
Non-fin. demand shock	0.04	0.12
Mon. pol. shock	0.06	0.14
Financial shock	0.07	0.15

Note: The table reports the average correlation among the estimated structural shocks, identified using the sign restrictions approach. See the notes to *Figure 5* for additional information. The sample period is 1985:1 to 2011:2.

reported in the table are relatively low and suggest that cross sectional dependence is unlikely to be a major factor undermining our results, although it may certainly affect results for individual countries.[7]

4.2 Do financial shocks matter also in normal times?

Another potential concern with the results of the VAR exercise is that they are based on a linear structure. It may be argued that financial shocks do matter in crisis times or when they are particularly large, but not otherwise (in normal times). We cannot address this question in full in the context of our linear framework, but it is still interesting to see how our results depend on crisis times as opposed to normal times. We therefore carry out two alternative exercises in this section. First, we re-estimate the VAR models excluding the periods which have been classified as "banking crisis" by Laeven and Valencia (2008). Second, we estimate the VARs until 2007:2, leaving out the period of the global financial crisis which could arguably disproportionately influence our results.[8] The first exercise (not reported for brevity) leads to impulse responses that are very similar to the baseline ones. The outcome for the second exercise is reported in *Figure 6*. Again, results are mostly the same (quantitatively and qualitatively) as in the baseline exercise, suggesting that the latter do not depend on the observations from the global financial crisis only.

Another question which may arise is whether results are disproportionately driven by possibly a few episodes of booms and busts in credit growth. To address this question, we identify credit boom and bust periods by looking at deviations of real credit to the private sector (for at least two consecutive quarters) from a recursively estimated linear trend and taking a threshold which takes out 10 percent of all observations. Moreover, in another variant of the baseline model we take out periods of very low interest rates (nominal short term rate below 2% or negative real interest rate) in order to check whether financial shocks arise in particular in periods of very low interest rates, as has been suggested by several observers. The results (not reported for brevity) are, overall, in line with the baseline results, again suggesting that non-linearities are possibly not very important qualitatively.

4.3 Dealing with euro area monetary policy

One important caveat to our results (and indeed to all similar empirical exercises including euro area countries after 1999) is the possible mis-specification arising from the fact that country-level monetary policy shocks do not make much sense after 1999 for euro area countries. Indeed, the behaviour of the short-term interest rate is largely exogenous for the small countries in the euro area, and only partially endogenous for the larger countries. In principle, monetary policy shocks should become perfectly correlated across euro area countries after 1999, and any model where this is not the case is likely to be misspecified (although the same consideration might be valid, at least to some extent, for countries pegging their exchange rate to a foreign currency). To understand whether this potential source of mis-specification matters a lot for our results, we re-estimated the VAR models excluding the observations for countries joining the euro area from the moment they give up their own currency. The exercise is reported in *Figure 7*: results are qualitatively the same as in the baseline exercise, although they are less precise for some variables on account of the smaller sample size. Moreover, it is interesting to note that the CPI falls after the financial shock in a statistically significant way, suggesting a supply shock interpretation of this shock in this alternative exercise.

4.4 Financial structure and the propagation of financial shocks

A further step in the analysis aims to test whether financial shocks are more important (in terms of their size and propagation) depending on the financial structure of the selected countries. Is it true, for example, that financial shocks are more important in countries that are more financially developed and have a bigger financial sector (say, Iceland or Ireland), as the experience of the global financial crisis of 2007–09 appears to suggest?

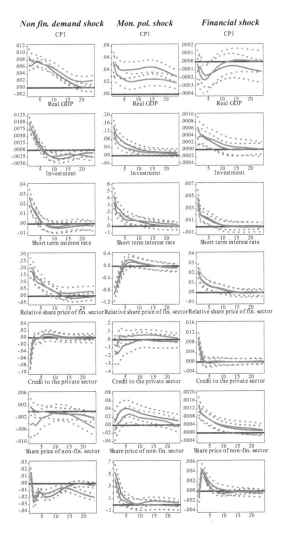

Figure 6 Impulse responses to structural shocks, <u>full sample</u> (thin lines) vs. <u>excluding the 2007–09 global financial crisis</u> (thick line). Note: <u>Thin lines</u> are impulse responses to structural shocks identified by applying sign restrictions as in Rubio-Ramirez, Waggoner and Zha (2010) and aggregated across countries using the stochastic pooling approach. The size of the shocks is 100 basis points of the interest rate for the monetary policy shock; a rise by 1% of the standardised level of real GDP for the demand shock; and a rise of 1% of the standardised level of the relative share price of the financial sector for the financial shock. The impulse responses are based on a VAR model estimated on quarterly data from 1985:1 to 2011:2 on 21 countries, and after aggregating cross country impulse responses by applying the stochastic pooling approach (see text and Annex for further explanation). The <u>thick lines</u> report the same impulse responses when the VAR models are estimated up to <u>2007:2</u>.

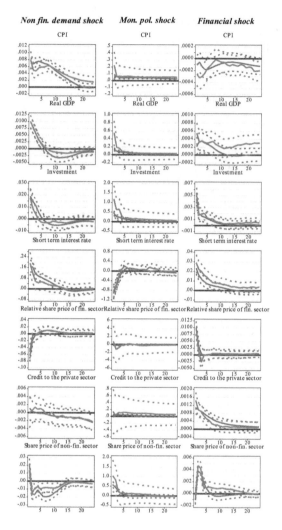

Figure 7 Impulse responses to structural shocks, basedline vs. <u>excluding euro area countries from 1999</u> (baseline in thin lines, excluding euro area countries in thick lines). Note: <u>Thin lines</u> are impulse responses to structural shocks identified by applying sign restrictions as in Rubio-Ramirez, Waggoner and Zha (2010) and aggregated across countries using the stochastic pooling approach. The size of the shocks is 100 basis points of the interest rate for the monetary policy shock; a rise by 1% of the standardised level of real GDP for the demand shock; and a rise of 1% of the standardised level of the relative share price of the financial sector for the financial shock. The impulse responses are based on a VAR model estimated on quarterly data from 1985:1 to 2011:2 on 21 countries, and after aggregating cross country impulse responses by applying the stochastic pooling approach (see text and Annex for further explanation). The <u>thick lines</u> report the same impulse responses when the VAR models are estimated after <u>excluding</u> observations for euro area countries after 1999.

There are two equally plausible conjectures that one can make as to the role of financial structure in influencing the size and the transmission of financial shocks. On the one hand, a more developed financial system may lead to a better resilience in the face of unfavourable shocks, by providing a better diversification of the sources of funds. For example, if the market for a particular source of financing seizes up, firms and households can more easily tap alternative sources of funds. Regulation may also be better in more financially developed countries. Finally, in countries with lower financial development a larger share of households and firms may be financially constrained, suggesting that they are more exposed to shocks in the external finance conditions. In fact, before the 2007–09 financial crisis it was common wisdom that banking and financial crises and financial headwinds were more likely in emerging countries, characterised by a significantly lower degree of financial development (see Dorrucci et al. 2009). On the other hand, it can also be argued that financial shocks may have a bigger impact in countries with a higher degree of financial development, since this implies that more economic actors take, and depend, on debt. In these countries economic agents may be better insulated from local shocks due to the possibility of diversification, but they may be actually more vulnerable to global financial shocks. This may be particularly true for households and small firms, which do not have access to international capital markets.

In order to tackle this question, we classify our 21 countries as having 'low' or 'high' financial development and openness according to the chosen indicators (see *Table 7*). Among these variables, three pertain to financial developments (stock market capitalisation to GDP, private credit to GDP, and liquid liabilities to GDP) and four to openness (financial openness, foreign loans and international debt to GDP, and trade openness). Countries are classified as low or high if the corresponding values of these variables are above or below the cross country average. If financial development matters for the transmission of financial shocks, then we should observe that these shocks have a larger impact in countries

Table 7 Structural indicators

	Low	countries	High	countries
Private credit / GDP	0.73	11	1.15	10
Financial openness	1.39	11	5.45	10
Foreign loans / GDP	0.19	11	0.72	10
International debt / GDP	0.20	11	0.41	10
Liquid liabilities / GDP	0.56	11	0.95	10
Trade openness	0.48	11	0.95	10
Stock mkt. cap. / GDP	0.41	10	1.00	10

Note: The table reports sample averages of the chosen structural indicators. 'Low' is the average of the countries which are below the median, and 'High' the number of countries which are above the median. The median values are computed on the longest available sample for each country. Computing averages over the longest joint sample leads to very similar results.

with comparatively higher readings for the proxies for development and openness. Within the subgroups of 'high' and 'low' openness/development countries, we apply the same procedure described for the baseline exercise, aggregating country-level impulse responses through the stochastic pooling approach of Canova and Pappa (2007).

Overall, we find that the short answer to the question posed above is that the degree of financial development does not matter much, at least amongst the advanced countries considered in our sample, in influencing the propagation of financial shocks. As an illustration, in *Figure 8* we classify countries according to their credit to GDP ratio, in *Figure 9* according to their financial openness and in *Figure 10* according to their stock market capitalisation to GDP ratio. The thin grey lines represent the countries with lower financial development or openness, and the thicker grey lines the countries with higher development or openness. The analysis of these results (as well as the others for the alternative indicators in *Table 7*, not reported for brevity) reveals that the fundamental characteristics and quantitative impact of the financial shock do not change much, or at least not in a statistically significant way, depending on countries' financial and economic structure.[9] On the positive side, this also suggests that the baseline results (*Figure 4*) are remarkably robust, as they tend to prevail in all of the country groups that we look at. Again, an exception to this general robustness finding is the reaction of the price level to the financial shock, which is statistically significant in some country groups but not in others.

Finally, it could be that financial and economic structure matters not for the propagation of shocks, but for their size, for which we need to look at a variance decomposition analysis. We therefore analyse the variance decomposition, and in particular the share of the variance explained by the financial shock, in the country groups depending on whether they are 'high' or 'low' countries. This analysis – not reported for brevity – again does not reveal economically significant differences between the two groups, according to most of the considered variables.

A caveat surrounding this analysis is that we are looking at a sample of advanced countries, whose financial and economic structure may be relatively similar (and also be endogenous). It would be interesting to repeat the analysis for emerging countries, which would represent a better test for whether the financial structure is an important factor in the transmission of financial (and non-financial) shocks.

5 Implications for monetary policy

What do our results suggest for the optimal reaction of monetary policy to financial shocks, which – as argued in the Introduction – should be a material element of the discussion on the 'leaning against the wind' approach of monetary policy? To some extent, monetary policy shocks are the mirror image of financial shocks: based on our results, a contractionary monetary policy leads to a fall in investment, GDP and credit, thus potentially countering the effect of a financial shock.

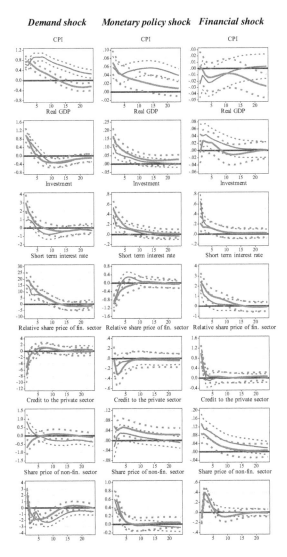

Figure 8 Impulse responses to structural shocks, including foreign variables in the VAR, depending on countries' <u>private credit to GDP ratio</u> ('high' countries in thick grey lines, 'low' countries in thin grey). Note: See notes to *Figure 5* on how impulse responses are computed. In this Figure, we divide countries in two groups according to whether they are above or below the median in terms of private credit to GDP ratio. Within each sub-group, countries are aggregated using the stochastic pooling approach. Impulse responses are shown in <u>thin, grey</u> lines for countries with a low reading of this structural indicator, and <u>thick grey</u> lines for high readings.

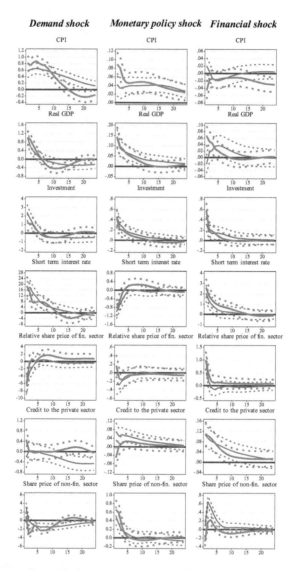

Figure 9 Impulse responses to structural shocks, including foreign variables in the VAR, depending on countries' <u>financial openness</u> ('high' countries in thick grey lines, 'low' countries in thin grey). Note: See notes to *Figure 5* on how impulse responses are computed. In this Figure, we divide countries in two groups according to whether they are above or below the median in terms of financial openness (sum of cross border financial assets and liabilities over GDP). Within each sub-group, countries are aggregated using the stochastic pooling approach. Impulse responses are shown in <u>thin, grey</u> lines for countries with a low reading of this structural indicator, and <u>thick grey</u> lines for high readings.

142

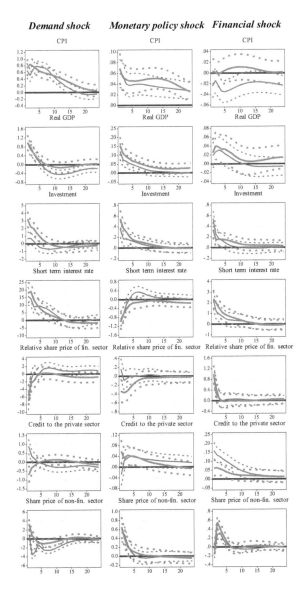

Figure 10 Impulse responses to structural shocks, depending on countries' stock market capitalisation to GDP ratio ('high' countries in thick grey lines, 'low' countries in thin grey). Note: See notes to *Figure 5* on how impulse responses are computed. In this Figure, we divide countries in two groups according to whether they are above or below the median in terms of stock market capitalisation to GDP ratio. Within each sub-group, countries are aggregated using the stochastic pooling approach. Impulse responses are shown in thin, grey lines for countries with a low reading of this structural indicator, and thick grey lines for high readings.

In this section, we deal with two questions, namely (i) if it is desirable for monetary policy to lean against financial shocks and (ii) if leaning against the wind is a feasible strategy when such shocks are large, on account of the zero bound for the nominal interest rate. It should be clarified that the question we address here departs from the standpoint taken in Assenmacher-Wesche and Gerlach (2010). There, the question is whether monetary policy is well placed to stabilise both asset prices and economic activity (as measured by GDP growth and consumer price inflation, with their answer being essentially that it is not. Our analysis is *conditional on the occurrence of financial shocks*: given that a financial shock takes place, how should monetary policy react and in particular can monetary policy withstand the impact of the shock on the variables it traditionally cares about, such as economic activity and inflation?

On the first question (the *should*) the fundamental matter is whether the financial shock acts, in terms of its effects, like a demand shock (the reaction to which is straightforward) or a supply shock like an oil shock, the reaction to which depends on central bank preferences for output and inflation stabilisation, or finally it produces effects which are in between those generated by the two shocks. As mentioned, the question is unresolved in the existing DSGE literature. For example, in models like Gilchrist et al. (2009) the financial shock is mainly a supply shock similar to an oil shock: like oil, financial intermediation is a necessary intermediate input in the production process.[10] In Curdia and Woodford (2010), credit is an important determinant of aggregate demand, and shocks to credit spreads affect the IS curve and are thus akin to demand shocks. Our international evidence is also inconclusive in this regard.

If a financial shock is ultimately a linear combination of demand and supply shocks in terms of its effects on the macro-economy, it is evident that some reaction from the monetary authority may be warranted, though not as forceful as it would be if this shock were an aggregate demand shock. Another element that our analysis brings to the policy debate is that the impact of financial shocks appears to be pretty much linear, i.e. not very dependent on whether turbulent periods are included or not. This is a further element suggesting that monetary policy may be an adequate tool to withstand these shocks, at least partially. Clearly, the question of whether monetary policy should react to a financial shock is best addressed with a full-fledged DSGE model, but the empirical analysis is useful in order to give a direction and some stylised facts that a good DSGE model should be able to reproduce. We conclude that more research is needed on this important question.

Turning now to the second question (*can* central banks withstand financial shocks), how much leeway does monetary policy have in order to go against 'large' financial shocks? Based on the results of the baseline exercise reported in *Figure 4*, a 100 basis points increase in the short term rate leads to a peak contraction of about 5 percent in the CPI, 14 percent of real GDP and 45 percent in investment (note that these numbers should not be taken at face value since variables are standardised and computed as simple averages across countries, in order to ensure comparability across countries). How much of an effect would a large financial shock have? Although it is not easy to answer this question, as we don't have a clear idea of what a sensible order of magnitude for a financial shock should be, let us consider one example here. We assume a shock driving the relative share price of the financial sector down one standard deviation; as is evident from *Figure 1*, this is more or less the order of magnitude that we see in the US data in the aftermath of the default of Lehman Brothers (note that data in *Figure 1* are standardised). Assuming that monetary policy would want to fully compensate for this shock, how large would the interest rate intervention have to be?

Rescaling the size of the impulse responses in *Figure 4*, we obtain that the large negative financial shock would lead to a decline in real GDP as of around 3 percent, and investment by around 35 percent. Hence, taking our estimates at face value, the same effect could be compensated (taking real GDP as the key variable) by a decline in the nominal interest rate by little more than 20 basis points; the decline in the interest rate would however have to be much larger to offset the impact on investment. This evidence indicates that, unless the interest rate is already very low, even a Lehman-type shock does not necessarily push the central bank dangerously close to the zero bound. Nevertheless, this conclusion is surrounded by a number of caveats. The first is the mechanical nature of the exercise in a backward looking model like a VAR, which should really be tested in general equilibrium and under rational expectations. Second, even though hitting the zero bound is not a major concern for even very large financial shocks *in a given quarter,* the risk is still present when negative financial shocks hit *in sequence,* as was arguably the case in the 2007–09 global financial crisis. Finally, the construction of the VAR and the identification of the structural shocks requires the shocks to be orthogonal. In reality, however, a banking and financial crisis is often accompanied by sharp declines in confidence which suggest that the central bank will have to deal with the additional impact of a negative aggregate demand shock. This could further complicate the task for monetary policy and bring the interest rate closer to the zero bound.

6 Conclusions and policy implications

In this paper, we have used data from 21 advanced countries to shed some light on the existence, impact and importance of financial shocks, which we identify using a sign restrictions approach guided by some recent contributions in the DSGE literature (Gilchrist et al. 2009, Hirakata et al. 2010, Nolan and Thoenissen 2009, Meh and Moran 2010). A key variable for the identification of the financial shock in this paper is the relative share price of the financial sector; we show evidence suggesting that this indicator is highly correlated with the health of the financial sector and more generally of the financial intermediation process.

We estimate a VAR model over 21 countries on a sample period of quarterly data going from 1985 to 2011 and aggregate country-level impulse responses across countries using the stochastic pooling approach proposed by Canova and Pappa (2007). We find that financial shocks have a noticeable influence on key macroeconomic variables such as output, investment and the consumer price index. We also find that the financial shock is neither an aggregate demand shock or a supply shock, and our analysis does not dispel the uncertainty about the nature of this shock which exists across different DSGE models. An important finding of our analysis is that investment reacts much more than overall GDP to the financial shock, significantly more so than for demand and monetary policy shocks. This feature may help to identify financial shocks in real time.

In addition, we find that our key results are not driven by crisis periods only, nor by developments through the 2007–09 global financial crisis, as could have been suspected, nor by periods of credit booms and busts or of very low nominal and real interest rates. This in turn suggests that the effects of the financial shock prevail also in normal times and it is therefore a force to be reckoned with also in normal circumstances. Finally, we find that our results (with the exception of the effect on the price level and hence the connotation of the shock as a demand or supply shock) are broadly unaffected by the financial and economic structure of the countries.

One important policy implication of this study is that monetary policy is rather well placed to fight financial shocks, as its effects are found to be to a large extent the mirror image of these shocks. Indeed, we find that a contractionary monetary policy shock reduces GDP, investment and credit; it is therefore largely (though not completely) a 'financial shock in the reverse'. A crucial question mark that our work still leaves open, however, is whether financial shocks are ultimately mainly demand shocks (in which case the role for monetary policy is well established) or rather supply shocks (in which case the optimal response of the monetary authority is far less straightforward). Be it what it may, if central banks want to be able to control financial shocks more effectively, either by using monetary policy or – in collaboration with other authorities – macro-prudential tools, they will need to invest more in collecting direct and reliable data on leverage and credit risk, a point also emphasised by Geanakoplos (2009).

This conclusion, and indeed the whole of our analysis, is subject to two important caveats. Our empirical approach is linear, and implies that the effect of financial shocks can be studies using linear models. If there are important non-linearities (say, a financial shock is either too small to matter in normal times or devastating when large, in crisis times; or its effects accumulate slowly over time and subsequently crash abruptly) then the role of monetary policy to withstand these shocks is much less straightforward. To some extent we have tried to address this question by looking at results based on including or not including crisis times, but this is only a first step. Second, our analysis has been heavily constrained by data availability at an international level and there is ample scope to improve our identification when studying an individual country (such as the US) or a very restricted set of countries where more pertinent data may be available. There is still a lot to be done in understanding the nature of financial shocks, and the optimal policy response to them.

Notes

1 See however recent attempt by Liu et al. (2010). An important, more recent twist to this literature, based on the role of banks' risk limits (such as Value at Risk) and their amplification role, has been proposed by Adrian and Shin (2008).

2 The way in which we identify higher or lower exposure to financial leverage is inspired by the classic paper of Rajan and Zingales (1998).

3 Indeed, in the DSGE model of Meh and Moran (2010) a negative financial shock (negative shock to bank capital in their terminology) leads to a fall in investment and in bank net worth, the latter bigger than the fall in entrepreneurial net worth. If the stock market is rational, this should translate into a fall in the *relative* share price of the financial intermediation (banking) sector.

4 Indeed, as pointed out by Hall (2010), the Great Recession of 2008–09 is almost entirely concentrated in investment (including consumer durables).

5 For an overview, see Table 2 in Hristov et al. (2011).

6 In interpreting the size of the coefficients, note that the relative share price of the financial sector used in Table 4 is standardised.

7 Correlations are indeed higher for specific country pairs. They are however almost never above 0.5.

8 As a caveat, note that we do not change the identification of the shocks when removing observations from the sample to ensure comparability. This is based on the assumption that, when removing only a few observations, the structural shocks continue to be (at least approximately) orthogonal.

9 Although we do not have the space to discuss this in detail here, we also find this to be the case for other key shocks, such as demand shocks and monetary policy shocks. This is also surprising since it may have been expected that financial structure would matter for these shocks too, even though the precise direction in which it would matter is not clear ex ante.

10 The question is not discussed explicitly but is evident from Meh and Moran (2010), Fig. 5 on page 571; and from Gilchrist et al. (2009), Fig. 4–5 on pages 40–41.

11 We refer in particular to their procedure for US states. Note that we specify our prior on the impulse response functions directly, rather than on the coefficients of the structural MA representation as in Canova and Pappa (2007). Since shocks are of unitary size there is a direct linear mapping between the two concepts, and the two approaches are therefore equivalent.

12 In Canova and Pappa $\gamma_x = 1$ while we set $\gamma_x = 0.25$ in order to allow for a slower decay in the cross-country differentiation with respect to the horizon, which appears to be more realistic. We calibrate τ_x (i.e., the degree of heterogeneity after 1 period) to be of the same order of magnitude as the average impulse response for each variable *on impact,* thereby allowing for a significant degree of cross-country heterogeneity.

References

[1] Adrian, T. and H. S. Shin (2008): "Financial intermediaries, financial stability and monetary policy", paper presented at the Federal Reserve Bank of Kansas City Symposium at Jackson Hole, August 2008.

[2] Adrian, T., Moench, E. and H. S. Shin (2010): "Macro risk premium and intermediary balance sheet quantities", Federal Reserve Bank of New York Staff Reports, N. 428.

[3] Assenmacher-Wesche, K. and S. Gerlach (2010): "Monetary policy, credit and asset prices: facts and fiction", Economic Policy, 25, 63, pp. 437–482.

[4] Barsky, R. B. and E. R. Sims (2008): "Information, animal spirits, and the meaning of innovations in consumer confidence", NBER Working Paper No. 15049.

[5] Beaudry, P. and F. Portier (2006): "Stock prices, news, and economic fluctuations", American Economic Review, pp. 1293–1307.

[6] Bernanke, B. and M. Gertler (2001): "Should central banks respond to movements in asset prices?", American Economic Review, 91, 2, pp. 253–257.

[7] Blanchard, O. J., L'Huillier, J.-P. and G. Lorenzoni 2009): "News, noise, and fluctuations: an empirical exploration", NBER Working Paper No. 15015.

[8] Blinder, A. (2008): "Two bubbles, two paths", The New York Times, 15 June.

[9] Calza, A., Monacelli, T. and L. Stracca (2011): "Housing finance and monetary policy", Journal of the European Economic Association, forthcoming.

[10] Canova F. and E. Pappa (2007): "Price Differentials in Monetary Unions: The Role of Fiscal Shocks", Economic Journal, 117, 520, pp. 713–737.

[11] Canova F. and M. Paustian (2011), "Business cycle measurement with some theory ", Journal of Monetary Economics, 58, pp. 345–61.

[12] Christensen, I. and A. Dib (2008): "The financial accelerator in an estimated New Keynesian model", Review of Economic Dynamics, 11, pp. 155–178.

[13] Cordoba, J. C. and M. Ripoll (2004): "Credit cycles redux", International Economic Review, 45, 4, pp. 1011–1046.

[14] Curdia, V. and M. Woodford (2010): "Credit spreads and monetary policy", Journal of Money, Credit and Banking, 42, 6, pp. 3–35.

[15] Dorrucci, E., Meyer-Cirkel, A. and D. Santabarbara (2009): "Domestic financial development in emerging economies: evidence and implications", ECB Occasional Paper No. 123.

[16] Farmer, R. E. A. (2009): "Confidence, crashes and animal spirits", NBER Working Paper No. 14846.

[17] Fry, R. and A. Pagan (2010), "Sign Restrictions in Structural Vector Autoregressions: A Critical Review", NCER Working Paper Series 57, National Centre for Econometric Research.

[18] Geanakoplos, J. (2009): "The leverage cycle", Cowles Foundation Discussion Paper No. 1715.

[19] Gerali, A., Neri, S., Sessa, L. and F. M. Signoretti (2010): "Credit and banking in a DSGE model of the euro area", Journal of Money, Credit and Banking, 42, 6, pp. 108–141.

[20] Gilchrist, S. and J. Leahy (2002), "Monetary Policy and Asset Prices", Journal of Monetary Economics, 49, 75–97.

[21] Gilchrist, S., Ortiz, A. and E. Zakrajsek (2009): "Credit risk and the macroeconomy: evidence from an estimated DSGE model", mimeo.

[22] Hall, R. E. (2010): "Why does the economy fall to pieces after a financial crisis?", Journal of Economic Perspectives, 24, 4, pp. 3–20.

[23] Helbling, T., Huidrom, R., Kose, M. A. and C. Otrok (2010): "Do credit shocks matter? A global perspective", IMF Working Paper No. 10/261.

[24] Hirakata, N., Sudo, N. and K. Ueda (2009): "Chained credit contracts and financial accelerators", IMES Discussion Paper Series No 2009-E-30.

[25] Hristov, N., Hulsewig, O. and T. Wollmershauser (2011): "Loan supply shocks during the financial crisis: evidence from the euro area from a panel VAR with sign restrictions", mimeo.

[26] Jermann, U. and V. Quadrini (2009): "Macroeconomic effects of financial shocks", American Economic Review, forthcoming.

[27] Kiyotaki, N. and J. Moore (1997): "Credit cycles", Journal of Political Economy, 105, 2, pp. 211–248.

[28] Kocherlakota, N. (2000): "Creating business cycles through credit constraints", Federal Reserve Bank of Minneapolis Quarterly Review, 24, 3, pp. 2–10.

[29] Laeven, L. A. and F. V. Valencia (2008): "Systemic Banking Crises: A New Database", IMF Working Papers 224/08.

[30] Liu, Z., Wang, P. and T. Zha (2010): "Do credit constraints amplify macroeconomic fluctuations?", Federal Reserve Bank of Atlanta Nr. 2010–01.

[31] Lorenzoni, G. (2009): "A theory of demand shocks", American Economic Review, 99, 5, pp. 2050–2084.

[32] Meh, C. and K. Moran (2010): "The role of bank capital in the propagation of shocks", Journal of Economic Dynamics and Control, 34.

[33] Nolan, C. and C. Thoenissen (2009): "Financial shocks and the US business cycle," Journal of Monetary Economics, vol. 56, 4, pages 596–604.

[34] Paustian, M. (2007): "Assessing sign restrictions", The B. E. Journal of Macroeconomics, Topics, Vol. 7, Issue 1, Article 23.

[35] Rajan, R. and L. Zingales (1998): "Financial Dependence and Growth", American Economic Review, vol. 88(3), pages 559–86.

[36] Rubio-Ramirez, J. F., Waggoner, D. F. and T. Zha (2010): "Structural vector autoregressions: theory or identification and algorithms for inference", Review of Economic Studies, 2010, 77, 2, pp. 665–696.

[37] Schularick, M. and A. M. Taylor (2009): "Credit booms gone bust: monetary policy, leverage cycles and financial crises, 1870–2008", NBER Working Paper No. 15512.

Annex – Description of the stochastic pooling approach

We aggregate the cross-sectional information based on the "stochastic pooling" Bayesian approach proposed by Canova and Pappa (2007). Let $dX^i(k)$ be the estimated impulse response (say to a unit size financial shock) of variable X at horizon k for country i. Similar to Canova and Pappa (2007)[11], we assume that the prior distribution is

$$dX^i(k) = \mu_k + v_k^i,\tag{6}$$

where μ_k is the cross-country average and

$$v_k^i = N\left(0, \frac{\tau_x^2}{k^{\gamma_x}}\right),\tag{7}$$

where $\tau_x > 0$ represents the assumed degree of dispersion across countries of the response of each variable X. We choose τ_x so as to allow for a significant degree of dispersion across units. The dispersion across countries decays over time at a rate dictated by the parameter γ_x.[12] We choose a very diffuse prior for μ_k, so that the average impulse responses are practically entirely driven by the data. As shown by Canova and Pappa (2007), the posterior mean for μ_k (the variable of interest in our analysis) is a weighted average of the OLS estimates across countries, with weights given by the precision of the estimates, i.e., the inverse of their variances; the posterior precision is also a linear combination of the τ_x parameters as well as the weighted precision of the OLS estimates.

53

BANKS, GOVERNMENT BONDS, AND DEFAULT

What do the Data Say?

Nicola Gennaioli, Alberto Martin, and Stefano Rossi

Source: *IMF Working Paper* 14/120.

Abstract

We analyze holdings of public bonds by over 20,000 banks in 191 countries, and the role of these bonds in 20 sovereign defaults over 1998-2012. Banks hold many public bonds (on average 9% of their assets), particularly in less financially-developed countries. During sovereign defaults, banks increase their exposure to public bonds, especially large banks and when expected bond returns are high. At the bank level, bondholdings correlate negatively with subsequent lending during sovereign defaults. This correlation is mostly due to bonds acquired in pre-default years. These findings shed light on alternative theories of the sovereign default-banking crisis nexus.

1. Introduction

Recent events in Europe have illustrated how government defaults can jeopardize domestic bank stability. Growing concerns of public insolvency since 2010 caused great stress in the European banking sector, which was loaded with Euro-area debt (Andritzky (2012)). Problems were particularly severe for banks in troubled countries, which entered the crisis holding a sizeable share of their assets in their governments' bonds: roughly 5% in Portugal and Spain, 7% in Italy and 16% in Greece (2010 EU Stress Test, authors' calculations). As sovereign spreads rose, moreover, these banks greatly increased their exposure to the bonds of their financially distressed governments (2011 EU Stress Test, authors' calculations; see also Brutti and Sauré (2013)), leading to even greater fragility. As *The Economist* put it, "Europe's troubled banks and broke governments are in a dangerous embrace."[1] These events are not unique to Europe: a similar relationship between sovereign defaults and the banking system has been at play also in earlier sovereign crises (IMF (2002)).

Despite the relevance of these phenomena, there is little systematic evidence on them. This paper fills this gap by documenting the link between public default, bank bondholdings, and bank loans. We use the BANKSCOPE dataset, which provides us with information on the bondholdings and characteristics of over 20,000 banks in 191 countries and 20 sovereign default episodes between 1998 and 2012. We address two broad questions:

1. Does banks' exposure to sovereign risk affect lending? In particular, do the banks that hold more public bonds exhibit a larger fall in loans when their government defaults?
2. Why do banks buy public bonds, becoming exposed to default risk in the first place?

The goal of our analysis is to document robust stylized facts regarding these questions, not to identify causal patterns, which our data does not allow us to do. These stylized facts can shed light on the presumption that sovereign defaults damage banks, and thus the real economy, through their bondholdings. Moreover, our analysis allows us to assess whether the dangerous embrace between banks and sovereigns comes about because banks buy and hold public bonds well before sovereign default materializes, or because banks buy many public bonds during the default event itself. Our main findings are:

- Holdings of public bonds are large in normal times, particularly for banks that make fewer loans and are located in financially less developed countries. In non-defaulting countries, banks hold on average 9% of their assets in public bonds. Among countries that default at least once (which are financially less developed), average bank bondholdings in non-default years are 13.5%. In both groups of countries, bondholdings in non-default years are decreasing in bonds' expected return.
- During default years, average bondholdings increase from 13.5% to 14.5% of bank assets. Critically, this increase is concentrated in large banks. Moreover, during default years, bondholdings are increasing in bonds' expected return.
- During sovereign defaults, there is a large, negative and statistically significant correlation between banks' bondholdings and subsequent lending activity. A one dollar increase in bonds is associated with a 0.60 dollar decrease in bank loans during defaults. Strikingly, about 90% of this decline is accounted for by the average bonds held by banks before the default takes place; only 10% of this decline is explained by the additional bonds bought in the run-up to and during default.

These results are very robust to alternative specifications and controls. In particular, results on within country, cross-bank variation are robust to adjusting for *any* time-varying country-wide shocks. Within *the same* defaulting country and default year, it is the banks most loaded with government bonds that subsequently cut their lending the most.

Our results support the notion that banks' holdings of public bonds are an important transmission mechanism of sovereign defaults to bank lending. As we discuss in Section 5, these findings are broadly consistent with the following narrative. Public bonds are very liquid assets (e.g., Holmström and Tirole (1998)) that play a crucial role in banks' everyday activities, like storing funds, posting collateral, or maintaining a cushion of safe assets (Bolton and Jeanne (2012), Gennaioli, Martin, and Rossi (2014)). Because of this, banks hold a sizeable amount of government bonds in the course of their regular business activity, especially in less financially developed countries where alternatives are fewer. When default strikes, banks experience losses on their public bonds and subsequently decrease their lending. During default episodes, moreover, some banks deliberately hold on to their risky public bonds while others accumulate even more bonds. This behavior could reflect banks' reaching for yield (Acharya and Steffen (2013)), or it could be their response to government moral suasion or bailout guarantees (Livshits and Schoors (2009), Broner et al. (2013)). Whatever its origin, this behavior is largely concentrated in a set of large banks and is associated with a further decrease in bank lending.

Our data suggests that all bondholdings, regardless of whether they are accumulated before or during sovereign default events, contribute to transmitting the effects of defaults to private loans. Critically, though, our analysis also shows the bulk of the drop in lending that takes place during defaults is associated with bond purchases that take place well before the defaults themselves. In Section 5 we discuss the broad implications of these results for recent research on the European crisis and for the design of policy.

Our paper is related to the literature studying the costs of sovereign defaults. Quantitative models like Arellano (2008) typically find that, when calibrated to match the data, exclusion from financial markets is too short to account for the observed low frequency of defaults. In line with her findings, recent work posits that sovereign default is costly because it inflicts a "collateral damage" to the domestic economy. This damage arises because default is assumed to be nondiscriminatory, so that it hurts domestic bondholders as well as foreign ones and this has consequences for domestic financial markets. Some examples of this work are Broner and Ventura (2011), where nondiscriminatory default destroys domestic risk sharing, and Brutti (2011), where it reduces entrepreneurial wealth and investment.

In Gennaioli, Martin, and Rossi (2014), we built a model where nondiscriminatory defaults reduce the net worth of banks holding public bonds and hamper financial intermediation.[2] We also provided cross-country evidence that, following a public default, the decline in private credit is larger in those countries where the banking system holds more public bonds.[3] In this paper, we substantially extend the evidence by using bank-level data, which enables us to take a granular look at bondholdings and their effect on lending during defaults.

Our paper is also related to a recent strand of work that, largely motivated by the European crisis, has studied the two-way link between banking sector fragility and public defaults. Acharya, Drechsler, and Schnabl (2013) study "Irish-style" crises, in which banking sector bailouts raise the likelihood of public defaults. They show that bailouts are associated with subsequent spikes in sovereign spreads and with declines in banks' stock returns. Other work focuses on how bank bondholdings may expose the financial system to public defaults. Acharya and Steffen (2013) examine holdings of troubled bonds by Eurozone banks in recent years, finding evidence that banks have engaged in 'carry trade' by borrowing short-term to invest in risky bonds. Brutti and Sauré (2013) study holdings of European bonds by Eurozone banks during the recent sovereign debt crisis, and document that the share of troubled bonds held by domestic banks has been increasing in the bonds' risk. Battistini, Pagano, and Simonelli (2013) also study Eurozone banks and obtain similar results. Finally, Reinhart and Sbrancia (2011) study the increase in aggregate bondholdings around defaults and attribute it to financial repression. All of these papers focus on specific crisis episodes and find support for the view that banks have incentives to accumulate bonds precisely when they are risky.[4]

Our paper contributes to these works by providing a panoramic view of bank-level bondholdings around the world, both during normal times and during default episodes. Moreover, while these works focus on the behavior of bank bondholdings in periods of high risk, we are also interested in the implications of these bondholdings for lending once a sovereign default takes place.

The paper proceeds as follows. Section 2 describes the data. Section 3 analyzes the patterns of bondholdings and Section 4 studies the relationship between bondholdings and lending during sovereign defaults. Section 5 discusses our findings in light of alternative hypotheses and concludes.

2. Data

We build a dataset that includes bondholdings and lending activity at the bank level, as well as a large set of bank-level characteristics and macroeconomic indicators that are meant to capture the state of a country's economy. We explain each of our data sources below.

We obtain bank-level data from the BANKSCOPE dataset, which contains information on the holdings of public bonds for 20,337 banks in 191 countries over the period 1998-2012 (99,328 bank-year observations). This dataset, which is provided by Bureau van Dijk Electronic Publishing (BvD), provides balance sheet information on a broad range of bank characteristics: bondholdings, size, leverage, risk taking, profitability, amount of loans outstanding, balances with the Central Bank and other interbank balances. The nationality of the bonds is not reported. We shall return to this last issue later on. The information in BANKSCOPE is suitable for international comparisons because BvD harmonizes the data.

All items are reported at book value, including bonds.[5] This implies that variations in the bonds-to-assets ratio, both within and across countries, to a large extent capture variations in the relative quantity of public bonds held by banks, particularly in country-years away from sovereign crises. During sovereign crises, however, large declines in the prices of bonds and of other bank assets can contaminate the bonds-to-assets ratio that we use as a measure of bondholdings. For instance, if the price of bonds drops more (less) than the price of other bank assets, book value reporting may overstate (understate) the market value of the bonds-to-assets ratio. This aspect should be borne in mind when interpreting our results. It should be noted, though, that book value estimates significantly shape the actions and beliefs of regulators, markets, and bank managers, so they provide a good measure of bondholdings for our purposes.[6]

We start with the full sample of banks in BANKSCOPE and examine their unconsolidated accounts. We construct our dataset by assembling the annual updates of BANKSCOPE.[7] We filter out duplicate records, banks with negative values of all types of assets, banks with total assets smaller than $100,000, and years prior to 1997 when coverage is less systematic.[8] This procedure results in 99,328 observations of the bondholdings variable at the bank-year level over 1998-2012. For our regression analysis, we impose two additional requirements on the remaining banks: first, that we observe at least two consecutive years of data, so that we can examine the banks' changes in lending activity; and second, that data is available on all of the other main variables such as leverage, profitability, cash and short term securities, exposure to Central Banks, and interbank balances. Our constant-continuing sample for the regression analysis then consists of 7,391 banks in 160 countries for a total 36,449 bank-year observations. We take the location of banks to be the one reported in Bankscope, which coincides with the location of the bank's headquarters. Commercial banks account for 33.2% of our sample; cooperative banks for 38.2%; savings banks for 20.6%; investment banks for 1.6%; the rest includes holdings, real estate banks, and other credit institutions.

Data on the macroeconomic conditions of the different countries is obtained from the IMF's International Financial Statistics (IFS) and the World Bank's World Development Indicators (WDI). Table AI in the Appendix describes these variables. To measure the size of financial markets we use the ratio of private credit provided by money deposit banks and other financial institutions to GDP, which is drawn from Beck et al. (2000). This widely used measure is an objective, continuous proxy for the size of the domestic credit markets.

We follow the existing literature and proxy for sovereign default with a dummy variable based on Standard & Poor's, which defines default as the failure of a debtor (government) to meet a principal or interest payment on the due date (or within the specified grace period) contained in the original terms of the debt issue. According to this definition, a debt restructuring under which the new debt contains less favorable terms to the creditors is coded as a default. The Greek bond swap that was launched in February of 2012, for instance, is identified as a default by Standard & Poor's because the retroactive insertion of collective action clauses was deemed to materially change the original contract terms. According to this definition, our sample contains 20 sovereign defaults of different duration in 17 countries, which are listed in Table AI of the Appendix.[9]

In our robustness tests, we complement our analysis by using two alternative measures of sovereign default, namely, i) a monetary measure of creditors' losses given default, i.e., "haircuts", from the work of Cruces and Trebesch (2013) and Zettelmeyer, Trebesch, and Gulati (2012) and; (ii) a market-based measure, whereby a country is defined to be in default if it is in default according to S&P, or if its sovereign bond spreads relative to the U.S. or German bonds exceed a given threshold (using extreme value theory, Pescatori and Sy (2007) identify such a threshold to be approximately 1000 basis points). These measures cover dimensions of sovereign risk that are not captured by the S&P default dummy, such as spikes in credit spreads and the economic magnitude of creditors' losses. As we show in Section 4, our results are robust to these alternative measures. In our main analysis, however, we stick to the S&P default dummy because these measures have problems of their own. In particular, measures of haircuts depend heavily on the assumptions one makes about counterfactuals (e.g., Sturzenegger and Zettelmeyer (2008)), and measures based on sovereign bond spreads require observing reliable data on secondary market trading, which limits our sample size.

Table AI shows that the default episodes included in our sample contain large variations both in the size of defaulting countries and in the extent of bank coverage. A few countries such as Argentina, Russia, Nigeria, Kenya and Honduras have the lion's share of banks; at the other end of the spectrum, there are eight defaulting countries in which our data covers five banks or less. One concern is that countries that are small and have few banks might drive our results. In our robustness tests we re-estimate our regressions focusing on large defaulting countries and discarding countries with fewer than five (or ten, or fifteen) banks during a default episode, respectively, and we show that our results are unaffected.

Before concluding, we comment on two other important data series that we use, those measuring the realized and the expected returns of sovereign bonds. Realized bond returns in emerging countries are obtained from the J.P. Morgan's Emerging Market Bond Index Plus file (EMBIG+). For developed countries, we use the J.P. Morgan's Global Bond Index (GBI) file (see Kim (2010) for a detailed description; see also Levy-Yeyati, Martinez-Peria, and Schmukler (2010)). These indices aggregate the realized returns of sovereign bonds of different maturities and denominations in each country. Returns are expressed in dollars. The index takes into account the change in the price of the bonds and it assumes that any cash received from coupons or pay downs is reinvested in the bond. This data on returns is available for 68 countries in our sample and it covers 7 default episodes in 6 countries (Argentina, Russia, Greece, Cote d'Ivoire, Ecuador, and Nigeria), so that any exercise involving bond returns reduces sample size.

Obtaining data for expected returns is more problematic, because this variable is not directly observable, and standard proxies such as yield-to-maturity are clearly not appropriate for studying default episodes. We construct our series of expected returns using a two-step process. In the first step, we regress returns on a set of country-specific economic, financial, and political risk factors:

$$R_{c,t} = \gamma_t + \beta_0 + \beta_1 Z_{c,t-1} + u_{i,c,t}, \qquad (1)$$

where $R_{c,t}$ is the realized return of public bonds in country c at time t, γ_t are time dummies, which capture variations in the global risk-free rate, and $Z_{c,t-1}$ is a vector of political, economic and financial risk ratings compiled by the International Country Risk Guide. These ratings provide a comparable measure of political stability and of economic and financial strengths in many countries, and they have been shown to be strong predictors of bond returns (see e.g. Comelli (2012)). In the second stage, we define expected returns as the fitted values of this first-stage regression. We describe this data, as well as all variables used in the analysis, in Table AII in the Appendix.[10]

2.1 Bondholdings and Returns Data

The BANKSCOPE dataset is widely used and has an established track record, but there is one important dimension along which its reliability has not been scrutinized: its measure of government bondholdings.[11] To check the quality of this measure, we compare it to other data sources on bondholdings: the country-level measure of "banks' net claims on the government" from the IMF, and the bank-level data from the recent European Stress Test.

Table I compares the BANKSCOPE data on bondholdings with the IMF measure. Panel A contains the mean, the median, and the standard deviation of bondholdings (as a share of total assets) in the full BANKSCOPE sample. Mean bondholdings are at 9.3% of assets, while median bondholdings are approximately half as high. The standard deviation of bondholdings in the sample is also high.[12] Panel B reports somewhat lower figures for the constant-continuing sample, where we observe also the covariates and that we use in our regression analysis. Panel C reports the same information, but only for the subset of countries for which the IMF also reports banks' bondholdings. Panel D reports the IMF measure of "financial institutions' net claims to the government," computed as a share of total assets.[13] Mean, median and standard deviation of the IMF measure are close to the BANKSCOPE data. The IMF data gives a slightly higher mean bondholdings, but measurement in the two datasets converges towards the end of the sample, particularly when examining the subsample of banks in countries covered by IMF. Any discrepancy between IMF and BANKSCOPE data is likely due to the fact that the former also captures non-bond finance and to the fact that the banks used to compute the IMF measure may differ from those in BANKSCOPE.

The IMF data cannot address the quality of the BANKSCOPE data on a bank-by-bank basis. We thus compare our measure of bondholdings to the one reported by the European stress test of 2010. This also allows us to evaluate

Table 1 Bank's Holdings of Government Bonds in Bankscope and IMF data, by year

Year	1997	1998	1999	2000	2001	2002	2003	2004	2005	2006	2007	2008	2009	2010	2011	2012	Overall
Panel A – Bankscope data by bank																	
Mean	8.63	7.14	7.39	7.06	7.08	7.93	8.33	8.24	8.50	8.11	7.69	7.86	8.42	11.13	11.31	11.45	9.28
Median	5.40	4.08	4.02	3.34	3.15	3.13	3.54	3.83	4.13	3.96	3.58	3.62	4.40	7.54	7.68	7.75	5.15
Std Dev	9.81	9.05	9.52	9.94	10.59	11.73	12.38	11.40	11.34	10.93	10.37	10.33	10.67	11.63	11.73	11.86	11.24
No banks	3,610	4,306	4,412	4,258	4,043	3,821	3,753	4,015	5,111	5,202	5,141	5,337	5,822	13,706	12,144	14,647	20,337
No countries	114	111	118	122	127	130	133	136	141	147	157	165	158	171	159	176	191
Panel B – Bankscope data by bank, Constant-Continuing Sample																	
Mean		6.74	6.24	5.79	5.49	6.21	6.94	6.39	6.48	6.06	5.57	5.65	6.82	6.39	7.79	8.59	6.67
Median		4.25	3.63	2.69	2.04	1.95	1.83	1.96	2.15	2.11	1.90	1.64	2.36	2.37	4.33	4.93	2.81
Std Dev		7.55	7.47	8.35	8.96	10.11	11.39	9.92	9.71	9.09	8.52	8.74	9.93	9.27	9.49	10.06	9.37
No banks		2,005	2,109	2,071	1,998	1,875	1,841	1,783	1,914	2,421	2,442	2,341	2,332	2,592	4,344	4,381	36,449
No countries		55	57	59	70	73	73	84	103	116	118	123	137	131	115	120	160
Panel C – Bankscope data by bank, countries covered by IMF																	
Mean		7.75	6.94	6.54	6.61	7.37	7.87	7.85	8.29	7.84	7.44	7.37					7.44
Median		4.35	3.93	3.19	3.01	2.93	3.26	3.72	4.04	3.82	3.41	3.31					3.51
Std Dev		9.65	8.95	9.35	10.07	11.24	12.05	11.10	11.21	10.74	10.23	10.00					10.48
No banks		1,544	4,092	3,962	3,782	3,535	3,457	3,662	4,663	4,739	4,653	4,683					42,772
No countries		53	64	65	65	118	118	120	120	121	121	120					128
Panel D – IMF data, by country																	
Mean		8.53	10.79	11.42	11.53	10.85	10.78	9.67	8.12	7.31	6.69	5.71	.	.	.		9.06
Median		7.05	8.17	8.38	8.44	7.37	7.90	7.15	6.16	5.10	4.51	3.78	.	.	.		6.22
Std Dev		11.63	14.16	14.56	15.44	15.79	14.86	14.11	14.02	12.51	11.50	11.51	.	.	.		13.85
No countries		53	64	65	65	116	118	118	120	121	121	120	.	.	.		128

The table reports summary statistics of bank bondholdings as a percentage of total assets for various samples over 1998-2012. Panel A reports statistics on the full Bankscope universe; Panel B reports statistics on the constant-continuing sample from Bankscope, defined as the sample for which data on other bank characteristics is available; Panel C reports bank-level statistics for the countries covered by the IMF; Panel D reports aggregate country-level statistics from the IMF.

the mismeasurement that may arise because, differently from the stress test, BANKSCOPE does not break down bonds by nationality.

Table II reports bondholdings from the European stress tests of 2010 and 2011. Panel A of the table reports bondholdings for the full sample contained in the stress test, whereas Panel B reports bondholdings for the subset of the banks in the stress test sample that is contained in BANKSCOPE. The bondholdings reported by BANKSCOPE are shown in Panel C. The data from both sources are highly comparable. The bank-by-bank correlation between the bondholdings reported by BANKSCOPE and by the stress test is 80%. The small discrepancies between our measure and the stress test measure are thus most likely due to differences in the time at which the measurement itself took place.[14]

The evidence is reassuring. Even in highly integrated European markets, where domestic and foreign bonds are in many cases treated symmetrically by the regulatory framework, more than 75% of bank bondholdings correspond to domestic bonds. This share is in all likelihood much larger in the subset of developing countries that provide most of our observations on sovereign defaults. In sum, the BANKSCOPE measure is a good proxy for the domestic public bonds held by banks around the world, and we use it as such in the rest of the paper.

Table III reports descriptive statistics on these bondholdings around the world. Panel A shows that in the full sample, in non-defaulting countries banks hold on average 9% of their assets in public bonds. Among countries that default at least once in our sample, this average is 13.5% in non-default years, and increases to 14.5% of bank assets during default years. Panel A further shows that bondholdings are much larger in financially less developed countries, as the average bondholdings is 8.4% of assets in OECD countries and 12.4% in non-OECD countries. Panel B reports similar, albeit somewhat smaller figures in the constant-continuing sample that we use in our regression analysis.

To conclude, consider our data on the realized returns of public bonds. Table AIII in the Appendix contains descriptive statistics on these returns. The average annual return of public bonds is 9.81%, with a large standard deviation of 21.37%. Countries that experience at least one default episode in the sample have average annual returns of 14.46%, as compared with 9.70% for countries that do not experience any defaults. OECD countries have average annual returns of 7.62%, much lower than the non-OECD annual returns of 11.61%.

Bond returns vary substantially over time. To show this, Figure 1 plots sovereign bond prices for six countries that experienced at least one default over 1998-2012. The Figure depicts a window centered on the day of the default, and bond prices are standardized to begin at 100.

Across these six countries, bond prices exhibit the characteristic V-shaped pattern: in particular, prices deteriorate steadily in the year prior to the default, they reach a minimum in the months immediately after the default, and they pick up thereafter.

Finally, we comment briefly on our two-stage process for the construction of a series of expected returns. Table AIV in the Appendix shows the results of the

Table II Banks' Holdings of Government Bonds – Comparing the EU Stress Tests and Bankscope

	Mean	Median	Std Deviation	No Countries	No Banks	No Obs.
Panel A – Full Sample						
E.U. Bonds	7.11	6.26	4.94	20	79	119
Own Bonds	5.39	4.61	4.78	20	79	119
PIIGS Bonds	3.52	2.02	4.15	20	79	119
Panel B – Constant Sample						
E.U. Bonds	6.75	6.06	4.57	18	57	79
Own Bonds	5.37	4.46	4.68	18	57	79
PIIGS Bonds	4.09	3.38	4.67	18	57	79
Panel C – Bankscope data, Constant Sample						
Bondholdings Bankscope	7.94	7.42	4.84	18	57	79
Panel D – Banks in Selected Countries, Constant Sample						
Greece						
E.U. Bonds	13.72	11.64	6.37	1	6	9
Own Bonds	12.87	10.78	6.84	1	6	9
PIIGS Bonds	12.90	10.78	6.83	1	6	9
Bondholdings Bankscope	16.05	14.89	6.43	1	6	9
Ireland						
E.U. Bonds	4.59	5.03	1.39	1	3	2
Own Bonds	2.32	2.18	0.43	1	3	2
PIIGS Bonds	2.83	2.89	0.81	1	3	2
Bondholdings Bankscope	8.12	7.59	1.49	1	3	2
Italy						
E.U. Bonds	7.06	7.00	1.94	1	5	10
Own Bonds	6.13	6.44	2.28	1	5	10
PIIGS Bonds	6.24	6.47	2.28	1	5	10
Bondholdings Bankscope	8.58	7.52	2.22	1	5	10
Portugal						
E.U. Bonds	5.58	4.74	2.75	1	4	5
Own Bonds	4.00	4.08	2.20	1	4	5
PIIGS Bonds	5.01	4.34	3.21	1	4	5
Bondholdings Bankscope	8.46	7.31	3.97	1	4	5
Spain						
E.U. Bonds	4.39	4.93	2.16	1	15	20
Own Bonds	4.04	4.75	2.03	1	15	20
PIIGS Bonds	4.27	4.93	2.16	1	15	20
Bondholdings Bankscope	5.48	6.09	3.02	1	15	20

The table reports summary statistics of bank bondholdings as a percentage of total assets for various samples over 2010-2011. Panel A reports statistics from the EU stress tests of 2010 and 2011 on the full sample of banks involved in the EU stress tests; Panel B reports statistics from the EU stress tests of 2010 and 2011 on the constant sample, defined as the sample for which data is available from both Bankscope and the EU stress tests; Panel C reports statistics from Bankscope on the constant sample; Panel D reports statistics from both Bankscope and EU stress tests on the constant sample for selected countries.

160

Table III Banks' Holdings of Government Bonds Around the World

Panel A – Bondholdings – Bankscope population

	Overall	Non-Defaulting Countries	Defaulting Countries		OECD	Non-OECD
			Non-Default Yrs	Default Yrs		
Mean	9.28	9.06	13.49	14.49	8.43	12.39
Median	5.15	5.02	8.94	9.15	4.47	8.11
Std Deviation	11.24	11.03	13.90	15.35	10.60	12.85
No Banks	20,337	19,714	542	501	16,401	3,976
No Countries	191	157	34	24	34	157
No Bank-Year Ob	99,328	94,744	3,161	1,225	78,118	21,210

Panel B – Bondholdings – Constant-Continuing Sample

	Overall	Non-Defaulting Countries	Defaulting Countries		OECD	Non-OECD
			Non-Default Yrs	Default Yrs		
Mean	6.67	6.19	12.96	14.87	4.61	12.63
Median	2.81	2.57	8.89	11.17	1.92	8.79
Std Deviation	9.37	8.84	12.94	13.87	7.13	12.12
No Banks	7,391	6,935	414	264	5,334	2,058
No Countries	160	144	26	17	32	128
No Bank-Year Obs.	36,449	34,030	1,784	635	27,074	9,375

The table reports summary statistics of the banks' holdings of government bonds, computed as a percentage of total assets. Panel A reports statistics on the Bankscope universe and Panel B on the constant-continuing sample.

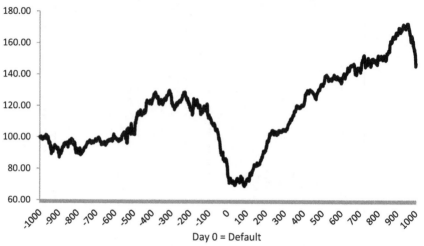

Figure 1 **Sovereign Bond Prices in Defaulting Countries**. The figure plots the average bond prices over 7 default episodes in 6 countries (Argentina 2001-2004, Russia 1998-2000, Cote d'Ivoire 2000-2004, Ecuador 1998-2000, Ecuador 2009, Nigeria 2002, Greece 2012), from day -1,000 to +1,000, whereby day 0 is the day in which default is announced.

first-stage estimation of Equation (1), in which we regress bond returns on country risk-ratings. As the first three columns of the table shows, there is a strong negative correlation between the risk ratings at time t and realized returns at time $t + 1$.[15] Taking into account that these ratings are decreasing in risk, this result is exactly what one would expect from theory: the positive coefficients are consistent with the notion that high bond returns compensate investors for economic, financial, and political risk. In the second stage, we define expected returns as the fitted values of this first-stage regression.[16] This is the series that we use in our regressions.

2.2 Summary Statistics of other Bank-Level Variables

We consider the distribution of bank characteristics in BANKSCOPE, focusing on: (i) bank size as measured by total assets, (ii) non-cash assets, measured as the investment in assets other than cash and other liquid securities, (iii) leverage as measured by one minus shareholders' equity as a share of assets, (iv) loans outstanding as a share of assets, (v) profitability as measured by operating income over assets, (vi) exposure to the Central Bank as measured by deposits in the Central Bank over assets, (vii) balances in the interbank market, and (viii) government ownership, a dummy that equals one if the government owns more than

50% of the bank's equity. To neutralize the impact of outliers, all variables are winsorized at the 1st and 99th percentile. Table IV provides descriptive statistics for these variables in our sample.

Panel A shows that there is a fairly large variation in bank characteristics within the BANKSCOPE sample. The average bank invests roughly 96% of its resources in non-cash assets (60% of which are loans, and the rest includes government bonds, debentures and other securities), obtains 91% of its financing in the form of debt, which includes deposits (for an average leverage ratio assets/ equity of about 10), and holds 3% of its assets in central bank reserves.[17] Table AV in the appendix reports the correlations between different bank characteristics in our sample. All correlations are statistically significant. Bank profitability is positively correlated with size, exposure to the central bank and interbank balances, while it is negatively correlated with non-cash assets, leverage, and loans outstanding.

3. Determinants of Banks' Bondholdings

This section addresses our first question: what determines bank bondholdings? We have already mentioned that average bondholdings are high in our data: they account for 9.3% of bank assets in the entire sample. Moreover, there is also substantial variation in bondholdings over time. In countries that experience at least one default, average bondholdings during default years represent 14.5% of assets as opposed to 13.5% in non-default years. Figure 2 illustrates this by depicting the average evolution of bondholdings across six defaulting countries, during a seven-year window centered on the year of default.

The figure shows that bondholdings follow a V-shaped pattern. Starting from their initial level, they first decrease gradually as the default is approached. From there, bondholdings rise after reaching a minimum on the year of the default itself.

Thus, the raw data already provides two interesting facts regarding bondholdings: banks hold substantial amounts of public bonds in non-default years and they hold even more bonds during sovereign defaults. To delve deeper into these facts and see how they relate to bank- and country-characteristics, we turn to regression analysis.

3.1. Methodology

Let $B_{i,c,t}$ denote the ratio of government bonds over assets held at time t by bank i located in country c. We think of $B_{i,c,t}$ as being chosen by banks in period $t-1$, so that bondholdings at time t are a function of the bank's balance sheet and of the state of the economy at time $t-1$.[18] We then run the following regression:

$$B_{i,c,t} = \alpha_0 + \alpha_1 \cdot X_{i,c,t-1} + \alpha_2 \cdot X_{c,t-1} + \alpha_3 \cdot Def_{c,t-1}$$
$$+ \alpha_4 \cdot Def_{c,t-1} \cdot X_{i,c,t-1} + \alpha_5 \cdot Def_{c,t-1} \cdot X_{c,t-1} + \epsilon_{i,c,t}, \tag{2}$$

163

Table IV Descriptive Statistics

Panel A – Bankscope, Constant-continuing sample

	Mean	Median	Std Deviation	No Countries	No Observations
Assets ($/M)	9,922.0	725.6	81,400.0	160	36,449
Non-cash assets	95.8	97.6	5.6	160	36,449
Leverage	91.0	93.3	8.4	160	36,449
Loans	57.1	60.0	17.0	160	36,449
Profitability	0.9	0.7	2.1	160	36,449
Exposure to Central Bank	3.3	1.5	4.9	160	36,449
Interbank Balances	12.2	9.2	12.5	160	36,449
Government Owned	2.5	0.0	15.7	160	36,449

Panel B – EU banks involved in the EU stress test 2010

	Mean	Median	Std Deviation	No Countries	No Observations
Assets ($/M)	394,000.0	130,000.0	618,000.0	18	79
Non-cash assets	97.6	98.3	1.9	18	79
Leverage	93.3	93.8	4.2	18	79
Loans	64.8	67.2	13.9	18	79
Profitability	-0.1	0.3	1.9	18	79
Exposure to Central Bank	1.7	1.0	1.9	11	40
Interbank Balances	5.9	4.7	4.7	18	79
Government Owned	0.0	0.0	0.1	18	79

The table reports summary statistics of the main variables used in the empirical analysis. Assets is the total book value in million $ of intangible, tangible and other fixed assets; non-cash assets is total assets minus cash and due from banks, divided by total assets; leverage is one minus book value of equity (issued share capital plus other shareholders fund) divided by total assets; loans is total loans outstanding divided by total assets; profitability is operating income divided by total assets; exposure to central bank is total exposure to central bank divided by total assets; interbank balances is interest-earning balances with central and other banks divided by total assets; government owned is a dummy that equals one if the government owns more than 50% of the bank's equity. Panel A reports statistics on the Bankscope universe and Panel B on banks involved in the EU stress test of 2010. For details on the construction of all variables see Table AI in the Appendix.

164

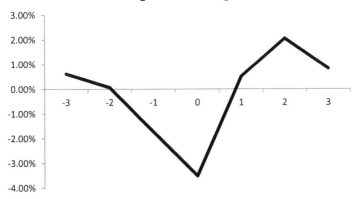

Figure 2 **Bondholdings in Defaulting Countries.** The figure plots the average annual bondholdings in seven default episodes in six countries (Argentina 2001-2004, Russia 1998-2000, Cote d'Ivoire 2000-2004, Ecuador 1998-2000, Ecuador 2009, Nigeria 2002, Greece 2012), from three years prior to default to three years after. The within-country averages are normalized at 0. Year 0 is the first year of default.

where $Def_{c,t-1}$ is a dummy variable taking value 1 if country c is in default at $t-1$ and value 0 otherwise, $X_{i,c,t-1}$ is a vector of bank characteristics, and $X_{c,t-1}$ is a vector of country characteristics. We run this regression in specifications that include country dummies, time dummies, and also their interaction. Standard errors are clustered at the bank level throughout.[19]

Coefficients α_1 and α_2 respectively capture the effect of bank- and country-factors on a bank's holdings of public bonds when the government is not in default (i.e., in "normal times"). Coefficient α_3 captures the average impact of default on bondholdings, while α_4 and α_5 indicate whether the association between default and bonds is heterogeneous across banks and countries. Equation (2) thus allows us to test whether bondholdings behave differently in years of default relative to all other years. For example, if $\alpha_3 > 0$, all banks tend to increase their bondholdings during default events.

Vector $X_{i,c,t-1}$ includes bank characteristics that may affect the demand for bonds, such as loans outstanding (which proxies for a bank's investment opportunities), non-cash assets, exposure to central bank, interbank balances, profitability, size, whether or not the bank is owned by the government, and lagged bondholdings to control for persistence. Vector $X_{c,t-1}$ includes instead country-level factors that may affect the demand for bonds, such as a country's financial development (as measured by Private Credit to GDP and banking crises), GDP growth, and inflation. One interesting variable to consider is the expected return of public bonds denoted by $R^e_{c,t}$, which captures the expectation (at time $t-1$)

of the time-t return of public bonds of country c. As explained in Section 2, we proxy this variable with the fitted value of realized returns when regressed on lagged country-specific risk factors, and we estimate the two-stage model with GMM.

3.2. Results

Table V reports the estimates of different specifications of Equation (2). Columns (1)-(3) assess the patterns of bondholdings without accounting for the interactive effects of default and by using only time dummies. Column (4) includes interactive effects, column (5) includes country dummies, and finally column (6) includes country*time dummies. The inclusion of dummies is important because it allows us to control – among other things – for variations in the supply of government bonds in a country.[20] Table V only reports coefficients of variables that are systematically significant.

Consider first columns (1) and (2). Bondholdings decrease with outstanding loans, while they increase with bank size and government ownership. In terms of country factors, bondholdings fall with private credit and GDP growth, and increase with banking crises. The variables with greatest explanatory power in terms of marginal R^2 are private credit and outstanding loans. Column (3) adds expected returns to the regression.[21] We do so in a separate column because bond returns are available only for a subset of countries, so the number of observations drops accordingly. Over the full sample, expected bond returns are negatively and significantly correlated with bondholdings. If we think of expected returns as a compensation for risk, this means that bondholdings are higher when bonds are safest.

Next, we examine whether these patterns differ in default relative to non-default years. To assess the importance of default, we include our default dummy in columns (4)-(6). These columns teach us two critical features of the data.

First, columns (4)-(6) show that the accumulation of bonds during default years is very unequal across banks. Relative to non-default years, large banks are systematically more likely to increase their exposure to public bonds, while banks with more outstanding loans are less likely to do so. The non-interacted default dummy is often insignificant (or even negative in column (6)), implying that the average increase in bondholdings during defaults entirely comes from a selected set of banks. Column (6) shows that these results hold when controlling also for country and country*year fixed effects. Quite strikingly, this indicates that within-country-year bank heterogeneity is critical in explaining the variations in the data. Quantitatively, this heterogeneity across banks is large. During a default year, for instance, banks in the lowest size decile decrease their bondholdings by 4.2% of assets, while banks in the highest decile increase their bondholdings by 4.5% of assets.[22]

The second and perhaps most interesting message of columns (4)-(6) is that bondholdings behave differently during default and non-default years. Consider

Table V Banks' Demand for Government Bonds

	(1)	(2)	(3)	(4)	(5)	(6)
$Size_{t-1}$	0.001*	0.001***	0.001	0.001***	-0.000	0.000
	(0.000)	(0.000)	(0.000)	(0.000)	(0.001)	(0.000)
$Loans_{t-1}$	-0.020***	-0.026***	-0.030***	-0.027***	-0.045***	-0.041***
	(0.003)	(0.005)	(0.007)	(0.004)	(0.007)	(0.004)
Government Owned$_{t-1}$	0.008***	0.003	0.005	0.002	-0.003	0.003
	(0.002)	(0.004)	(0.006)	(0.004)	(0.005)	(0.002)
Expected Sov. Bond Return$_{t-1}$			-0.015**		-0.029***	
			(0.006)		(0.009)	
GDP Growth$_{t-1}$		-0.243***	-0.204***	-0.164**	-0.208**	
		(0.052)	(0.053)	(0.066)	(0.101)	
Banking Crisis$_{t-1}$		0.036***	0.026***	0.030***	0.025	
		(0.004)	(0.006)	(0.005)	(0.020)	
Private Credit$_{t-1}$		-0.022***	-0.007*	-0.021***	0.018	
		(0.004)	(0.004)	(0.004)	(0.016)	
Sovereign Default$_{t-1}$				-0.123	-0.242	-0.091*
				(0.158)	(0.247)	(0.055)
Sovereign Default$_{t-1}$ * Size$_{t-1}$				0.009***	0.012***	0.007***
				(0.003)	(0.003)	(0.003)
Sovereign Default$_{t-1}$ * Loans$_{t-1}$				-0.013	-0.056	-0.041
				(0.032)	(0.038)	(0.029)
Sovereign Default$_{t-1}$ * Government Owned$_{t-1}$				0.008	0.033	0.016
				(0.022)	(0.024)	(0.021)
Sovereign Default$_{t-1}$ * Expected Sov. Bond Return$_{t-1}$					0.067**	
					(0.027)	
Sovereign Default$_{t-1}$ * GDP Growth$_{t-1}$				0.027	0.224	
				(0.170)	(0.226)	
Sovereign Default$_{t-1}$ * Banking Crisis$_{t-1}$				0.035*	0.018	
				(0.021)	(0.035)	
Sovereign Default$_{t-1}$ * Private Credit$_{t-1}$				0.448*	0.730**	
				(0.230)	(0.321)	

(Continued)

167

Table V Continued

	(1)	(2)	(3)	(4)	(5)	(6)
Other controls?	Yes	Yes	Yes	Yes	Yes	Yes
Year Dummies?	Yes	Yes	Yes	Yes	Yes	Yes
Country Dummies?					Yes	Yes
Country × Year Dummies?						Yes
No Observations	36,449	13,082	5,341	13,082	5,341	26,549
No Banks	7,391	2,912	2,103	2,912	2,103	5,124
No Countries	160	40	29	40	29	157
R-squared	0.772	0.797	0.715	0.801	0.735	0.814

The table presents coefficient estimates from pooled OLS regressions. The dependent variable is bank bondholdings, and it is computed as bondholdings divided by total assets. Size is the natural logarithm of total assets; non-cash assets is total assets minus cash and due from banks, divided by total assets; leverage is one minus book value of equity (issued share capital plus other shareholders fund) divided by total assets; loans is total loans outstanding divided by total assets; profitability is operating income divided by total assets; exposure to central bank is total exposure to central bank divided by total assets; interbank balances is interest-earning balances with central and other banks divided by total assets; government owned is a dummy that equals one if the government owns more than 50% of the bank's equity. Sovereign default is a binary variable that equals 1 if the sovereign is in default in year $t-1$ and 0 otherwise; GDP growth is natural logarithm of GDP in year t minus natural logarithm of GDP in year $t-1$; aggregate leverage is the country-year average of bank leverage; banking crisis is a binary variable that equals 1 if the country is in a banking crisis in year $t-1$ and 0 otherwise, private credit is the ratio of credit from deposit taking financial institutions to the private sector to GDP, expressed as a percentage. Standard errors (in parentheses below the coefficient estimates) are adjusted for heteroskedasticity using the Huber (1967) and White (1980) correction, as well as for clustering at the bank level using the Huber (1967) correction. *** indicates significance at the 1% level; ** indicates significance at the 5% level; * indicates significance at the 10% level.

168

the role of expected returns in column (5). While in non-default years expected bond returns are associated with lower bondholdings, this correlation is reversed during default years. A similar reversal arises with respect to Private Credit to GDP. Columns (4) and (5) show that banks in countries with more developed financial markets, as measured by Private Credit to GDP, hold fewer bonds in normal times but pile up more bonds during default events.

How can we interpret Table V? The evidence suggests a simple narrative. In non-default years, the demand for bonds is consistent with their role as providers of liquidity. Banks that already have many good investment opportunities available (i.e., banks with many outstanding loans) do not need safe and liquid public bonds to 'store' their funds. Banks that operate in financially developed economies do not need to buy many public bonds because private alternatives are available. Finally, bondholdings are low when expected bond returns are high, because high-risk, high-return bonds do not provide a good store of liquidity.

One caveat to this interpretation is that bondholdings in the year immediately before default need not necessarily represent banks' "normal" demand for bonds. Indeed, they may already reflect some risk taking if signs of future default have already materialized. Prima facie, this possibility seems unlikely. As shown in Figure 1, the main defaults that we consider are characterized by abrupt drops in bond prices that take place when the defaults are just 3-4 months away, on average. Additionally, as Figure 2 shows, average bondholdings tend – if anything – to slightly decrease as a default approaches (consistent with them being decreasing in expected bond returns in normal times). In this respect, our representative default is very different from the Greek default of 2012, as Greek bond spreads started to rise already in 2009 and Greek banks accumulate public bonds during these years. Figure 3 indeed shows the different paths of bondholdings in Greece with respect to the main defaulters in our sample.[23]

As Table V and Figure 3 show, in fact, during default episodes bondholdings change behavior. In those times, high expected returns correlate with higher bondholdings, implying that demand for high-risk, high-return bonds is higher during years of default. Moreover, higher bondholdings in default years are largely concentrated in the hands of large banks. This is consistent with the possibility that these banks have an incentive to take risk in the sovereign bond market owing to implicit government bailout guarantees or to direct moral suasion.[24]

The analysis of this provides a general overview of the behavior of bank bondholdings. But do these bondholdings matter for bank lending? We turn to this question next.

4. Default, Bondholdings and Loans

Equipped with the results of the previous section, we now address our second question: what is the relationship between bondholdings and lending during default events?

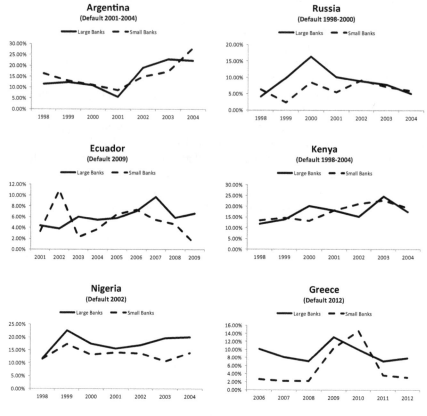

Figure 3 **Bondholdings in Selected Defaulting Countries by Bank Size**. The figure plots the average bondholdings by large (above-median total assets) and small (below-median total assets) banks in selected countries.

4.1. Methodology

Let $\Lambda_{i,c,t}$ denote the change in loans over assets made by bank i in country c between time $t-1$ and t. We run the following regression:

$$\Lambda_{i,c,t} = \gamma_0 + \gamma_1 \cdot B_{i,c,t-1} + \gamma_2 \cdot Def_{c,t-1} + \gamma_3 \cdot Def_{c,t-1} \cdot B_{i,c,t-1} + \gamma_4 \cdot X_{i,c,t-1}$$

$$+ \gamma_5 \cdot Def_{c,t-1} \cdot X_{i,c,t-1} + \gamma_6 \cdot X_{c,t-1} + \gamma_7 \cdot Def_{c,t-1} \cdot X_{c,t-1} + \mu_{i,c,t}. \tag{3}$$

Coefficient γ_2 captures the average effect of default on bank loans. A negative value of γ_2 suggests that, all else equal, sovereign defaults are associated with a subsequent reduction in bank lending. The main focus of our analysis is on coefficient γ_3. A negative value of γ_3 is consistent with the hypothesis that default reduces bank lending through government bondholdings: it implies that, when governments are in default, banks that hold more public bonds are the ones that reduce their lending the most.

Once again, controlling for vectors $X_{i,c,t-1}$ and $X_{c,t-1}$ and for their interactions with the sovereign default dummy allows us to control for cross-bank and cross-country variation in the proclivity of banks to make loans. Together with country and country*time dummies, these controls reduce the likelihood that our results are due to omitted variables, like recession-induced drops in the demand for loans by firms. They also reduce the likelihood of identifying spurious correlations, like the ones that would arise if larger banks both hold more bonds *and* make more loans during default years.

The interpretation of coefficient γ_3 raises an interesting question. If higher bonds are indeed associated with a stronger drop in loans (i.e. $\gamma_3 < 0$) in default years, is this drop related to the bonds that banks normally purchase in non-default years or to the bonds purchased during the default events themselves? As we discuss in Section 5, this distinction is important: shedding light on whether the dangerous embrace between the government and banks originates in normal times or in the proximity of sovereign defaults has important positive and normative implications. We address this question in three alternative ways.

First, we run a cross sectional version of Equation (3) focusing on the change in loans around default episodes. In this regression, the dependent variable is the change in a bank's loan-to-asset ratio occurring in the first two years of default, while the main explanatory variable is the bank's bondholdings in the year prior to default. This is the simplest way to check whether pre-default bondholdings matter. One shortcoming here is that bondholdings in the year before default may be influenced by the anticipation of default by the bank. As a result, we perform a second test in which the explanatory variable is a bank's *average bondholdings in the three years prior to the default.* This test allows us to establish whether or not the change in a bank's lending behavior around a default event is related to the public bonds that the bank has *well before* the default event, before sovereign risk materializes.

While useful, this last test has still two shortcomings. First, its cross sectional nature does not allow us to control for a full set of country*time dummies. Second, by considering only bonds accumulated for the most part well before default, this test does not allow us to properly assess the impact of bondholdings accumulated in the run-up to and during the default itself, which may be an important part of the story.

We address these concerns by running yet another specification of Equation (2), in which we decompose a bank's holdings of public bonds $B_{i,t}$ into: (i) a "normal-times" average component $b_{i,n,t}$ measuring a bank's average bond-holdings in all non-default years up to year t, and; (ii) a "residual" component $b_{i,t} = B_{i,t} - b_{i,n,t}$, which captures any differential take-up in public bonds relative to the normal-times average. We then use these components as separate explanatory variables in Equation (2). Because this regression uses the full panel structure of our data, it can include a full set of country*time dummies.

To interpret this regression, we view the component $b_{i,n,t}$ as capturing a bank's average demand for bonds in the course of its everyday business activity. Hence, the interaction of $b_{i,n,t}$ with the default dummy proxies for the effect of sovereign defaults that is transmitted through the bonds that are normally held by bank i for its regular operations.[25] According to this interpretation, the residual $b_{i,t}$ captures any discrepancy between observed bondholdings and typical bondholdings in normal times. This discrepancy may be due to a number of reasons, including – as we have mentioned – distorted incentives to accumulate bonds precisely when they are risky.

4.2. Results

Table VI reports our estimates. Columns (1)-(4) include as explanatory variables the total bondholdings of bank i in year $t-1$, $B_{i,c,t-1}$, as well as our sovereign default dummy, various bank-level controls, the realized return of bonds,[26] and their interactions. Column (1) report results of a specification without any fixed effects. It shows that bondholdings have a large negative effect on subsequent lending during default years.

Column (2) presents estimation results with year dummies but without country dummies; column (3) presents results with year and country dummies, to control for time-invariant country-level differences in the quality of economic policy and other institutional differences; column (4) presents estimation results with year, country, and country*year dummies, to control for uniform demand shocks at the country-year level. The results confirm a strong negative effect of bondholdings on subsequent lending during default years. Column (5) repeats this test in the full sample, i.e., including also the countries for which we do not observe sovereign bond returns, and shows that our result is, if anything, stronger. Remarkably, columns (4) and (5) show that within *the same* defaulting country-year, it is the banks most loaded with government bonds that reduce their lending the most. This is the basic result of this section. This raises a question: is this association driven by the bonds accumulated in non-default years or by those accumulated during the default event itself?

Columns (6) and (7) address this question by looking at the cross-sectional variation in changes in loans around a default and seeing how it correlates with bonds held before the default. Column (6) shows that the bonds held in the year before the default have a strong negative association with the subsequent decrease in lending during the first two years of a default event. This finding suggests that the bonds accumulated prior to default matter for the decrease in lending. However, it could still be that bank purchases of bonds in the year prior to default reflect the deteriorating prospects of sovereign risk and not their regular business activity.

To address this possibility, in column (7) we focus on the average bondholdings held by the banks in the three years prior to the beginning of default, to attempt to better capture the effect of bondholdings held during the course of banks' 'normal' business activity. Column (7) shows a strong negative association between

Table VI Bondholdings and Changes in Loans

	(1)	(2)	(3)	(4)	(5)	(6)	(7)	(8)	(9)
Bank Bondholdings$_{t-1}$ * Sovereign Defaults$_{t-1}$	-0.126** (0.057)	-0.129** (0.057)	-0.095* (0.058)	-0.148** (0.060)	-0.133*** (0.045)				
Pre-Default Bank Bondholdings						-0.281*** (0.080)			
Avg Pre-Default Bank Bondholdings							-0.361*** (0.028)		
Bank avg non-default years Bonds$_{t-1}$ * Sovereign Defaults$_{t-1}$								-0.201** (0.100)	-0.213** (0.088)
Bank time-varying Bondholdings$_{t-1}$ * Sovereign Defaults$_{t-1}$								0.197*** (0.072)	-0.206*** (0.068)
Sovereign Bond Return$_{t-1}$ * Sovereign Defaults$_{t-1}$	0.072*** (0.014)	0.068*** (0.015)	0.071*** (0.015)					0.128*** (0.031)	
Bank Bondholdings$_{t-1}$	0.032*** (0.009)	0.034*** (0.009)	0.009 (0.011)	0.009 (0.011)	0.002 (0.016)				
Bank avg non-default years Bonds$_{t-1}$								0.035 (0.022)	-0.006 (0.017)
Bank time-varying Bondholdings$_{t-1}$								0.029 (0.026)	-0.002 (0.020)
Sovereign Defaults$_{t-1}$	-0.038 (0.026)	-0.035 (0.025)	-0.019 (0.024)	-0.057 (35.69)	0.122** (0.055)			0.052 (0.070)	0.075 (0.143)
Sovereign Bond Return$_{t-1}$	0.005 (0.005)	0.011* (0.006)	0.004 (0.007)					0.003 (0.007)	
Bank-Level Controls and Interactions?	Yes	Yes	Yes	Yes	Yes	Yes	Yes	Yes	Yes
Year Dummies?		Yes	Yes	Yes	Yes	Yes	Yes	Yes	Yes
Country Dummies?			Yes	Yes	Yes	Yes	Yes	Yes	Yes
Country × Year Dummies?				Yes	Yes				Yes

(*Continued*)

173

Table VI Continued

	(1)	(2)	(3)	(4)	(5)	(6)	(7)	(8)	(9)
Constant	0.041**	0.030*	-0.026	-0.069	-0.280	0.780**	0.874**	-0.052*	0.027
	(0.018)	(0.018)	(0.021)	(283.3)	(178.6)	(0.275)	(0.272)	(0.028)	(93.0)
No Observations	14,074	14,074	14,074	14,074	27,408	105	105	13,347	26,006
No Banks	3,722	3,722	3,722	3,722	5,218	105	105	3,553	4,972
No Countries	60	60	60	60	158	5	5	60	158
R-squared	0.061	0.072	0.106	0.204	0.224	0.439	0.442	0.113	0.229

The table presents coefficient estimates from pooled OLS regressions. The dependent variable changes in loans is computed as loans outstanding in year t minus loans outstanding in year t-1, divided by total assets. The main independent variables are bank bondholdings, computed as bondholdings divided by total assets; pre-default bank bondholdings, computed as bondholdings in the year prior to the first year of a sovereign default, divided by total assets; average pre-default bank bondholdings, computed as the average of bondholdings divided by total assets in the last three years prior to the first year of a sovereign default; bank average non-default years bondholdings, computed as the average of bank bondholdings in all the non-default years prior to and including year $t-1$, bank time-varying bondholdings, computed as bank bondholdings minus bank average non-default years bondholdings. Standard errors (in parentheses below the coefficient estimates) are adjusted for heteroskedasticity using the Huber (1967) and White (1980) correction, as well as for clustering at the bank level using the Huber (1967) correction. *** indicates significance at the 1% level; ** indicates significance at the 5% level; * indicates significance at the 10% level.

a bank's *average* bondholdings in the three years prior to a default and its change in loans during the first two years of a default event. The effects are quantitatively large: a 10% increase in the average level of bondholdings in the three years before default is associated with a 3.6% cumulative reduction in loans during the first two years in default. This result is consistent with a standard balance sheet effect, whereby losses on pre-existing government bonds reduce bank capital, forcing the bank to deleverage and thus reducing its ability to intermediate funds towards investment. It is important to stress that these tests require bank data for a five-year window around a default, so that they effectively focus on large banks in large defaulting countries such as for example Argentina, Greece, and Ecuador. These results suggest that the effects of bondholdings on lending are pervasive, long-lasting and not limited to small banks that may go bust during the crisis.

Finally, columns (8) and (9) address this question in an alternative way, by splitting bonds into their "normal-times" and "residual components" as defined in Section 4.1. Column (8) introduces both variables while controlling for country dummies, time dummies, bank controls, and expected returns, as well as for their interactions with default. Thus, column (8) effectively amounts to a 'decomposed version' of column (3). Column (9) then adds country*year fixed effects, so it effectively amounts to a decomposed version of column (5). We obtain two important results.

First, higher normal-times bonds are indeed associated with significantly fewer loans during default events. Second, the interaction of the residual component of bonds and the default dummy is also negative and significant, indicating that banks holding abnormally many bonds during default years are systematically less likely to make new loans. This negative association is interesting because, as we documented in Section 3, it is the large banks that are most likely to accumulate bonds during default years. Presumably, these banks also face strong investment opportunities. As a result, the drop in their loans during default seems likely to be induced by the bonds that they hold, and not by a drop in their relative demand for credit.

The estimates of column (7) may be contaminated by country-level unobserved shocks, though, such as a pre-existent decline in demand for credit by firms in the country. To rule out this possibility, column (8) adds a full set of country*time dummies. The coefficients of both components of bondholdings remain economically large and strongly statistically significant.

The economic effects of both the normal-time and residual component of bondholdings are large. A 10% annual increase in the normal-time component of bondholdings within a defaulting country is associated with a 2.1% decrease in lending; and a 10% annual increase in the residual component of bondholdings within a defaulting country is associated with a 2.0% decrease in lending.

The estimated marginal effects of the normal-time and the residual component of bondholdings on loans are thus similar in magnitude. To properly assess the contribution of these components, however, one needs to consider that in our sample banks tend to accumulate a much larger proportion of bonds in the years prior to default relative to those accumulated in the default years. In particular, in our sample of defaulting countries, average bank bondholdings during non-default years (13% of assets) represent 87% of their average bondholdings during default years (14.9% of assets). Coupled with the fact that in our sample banks loans as a share of assets are four times larger than bondholdings (in particular, loans represent approximately 53% of total assets), our estimates imply that a one-dollar increase in bonds translate into a 60-cent decrease in lending during default years; and that about 90% of this effect is due to the normal-time component of bondholdings, i.e. to the average bondholdings held by banks before the default took place.

Our data thus shows that, when a default takes place, there is a strong negative correlation between a bank's bondholdings and the loans that it extends. In our sample, though, the bulk of the correlation is explained by the bonds accumulated in normal times. We discuss the economic implications of these findings in Section 5.

Before concluding our statistical tests, we mention two robustness tests that address important concerns regarding the results of this section. A first concern is that these results may be driven by relatively "unimportant" defaults, because approximately one half of the default episodes in our sample involve either small countries, or countries with a small banking sector, or both. We address this concern thoroughly by redoing our estimation in various possible ways: (i) we exclude the smaller defaulting countries in our sample, both as measured by GDP per capita, and by the economic magnitude of the debt defaulted, and; (ii) we exclude the defaulting countries with fewer than 5, 10, and 15 banks, respectively in our sample. As Table VII shows in columns (1)-(10), these exercises strongly confirm our main results, which – if anything – become both statistically and economically stronger. A second concern is that our default dummy is too blunt a variable to capture default crises. We repeat our analysis using the haircut measure of default constructed by Cruces and Trebesch (2013) and Zettelmeyer et al. (2012), which capture the severity of a default. As Table VII, column (11) shows, our main results are again confirmed and if anything the economic magnitude of the results is stronger. Finally, we repeat our analysis using the augmented measure of default that, in addition to the default identified by S&P, includes defaults identified as situations in which sovereign spreads exceed 1,000 basis points.[27] As Table VII, columns (13)-(14) show, our main results are again confirmed.

5 Interpretations and Implications of our Findings

What do we learn from our empirical analysis? While the main goal of our paper is descriptive, the correlations that we document are consistent with a simple narrative of the sovereign default-banking crisis nexus. As we already discussed at the end of Section 3, the demand for public bonds behaves differently in default and non-default years. During non-default years, banks' bondholdings are consistent with the liquidity services of public bonds (Holmström and Tirole (1998)):

Table VII Bondholdings and Changes in Loans: Robustness Tests

	Largest defaults only		Large defaults only		No defaults with <5 banks		No defaults with <10 banks		No defaults with <15 banks		Haircut measure of default		Spread or Default measure of default	
	(1)	(2)	(3)	(4)	(5)	(6)	(7)	(8)	(9)	(10)	(11)	(12)	(13)	(14)
Bank avg non-default years Bonds$_{t-1}$ *	-0.263*	-0.268**	-0.223**	-0.259**	-0.222**	-0.224**	-0.219**	-0.223**	-0.219**	-0.260**	-0.321**	-0.334**	-0.211*	-0.224*
Sovereign Default$_{t-1}$	(0.123)	(0.123)	(0.107)	(0.108)	(0.107)	(0.090)	(0.107)	(0.090)	(0.107)	(0.108)	(0.160)	(0.159)	((0.122))	((0.122))
Bank time-varying Bondholdings$_{t-1}$ *	-0.236***	-0.260***	-0.189***	-0.234***	-0.190***	-0.210***	-0.190***	-0.211***	-0.193***	-0.234***	-0.286***	-0.322***	-0.216***	-0.244***
Sovereign Default$_{t-1}$	(0.072)	(0.071)	(0.073)	(0.070)	(0.073)	(0.069)	(0.073)	(0.069)	(0.073)	(0.070)	(0.093)	(0.092)	(0.073)	(0.071)
Sovereign Bond Return$_{t-1}$ *	0.117***		0.142***		0.127***		0.109***		0.109***		0.162***		0.118***	
Sovereign Default$_{t-1}$	(0.031)		(0.032)		(0.031)		(0.032)		(0.032)		(0.040)		(0.031)	
Bank avg non-default years Bonds$_{t-1}$	0.008	0.017**	0.006	0.015*	0.009	0.017**	0.008	0.017**	0.007	0.015*	-0.008	0.005	-0.011	0.004
	(0.011)	(0.009)	(0.012)	(0.009)	(0.011)	(0.008)	(0.011)	(0.008)	(0.011)	(0.008)	(0.009)	(0.007)	(0.009)	(0.007)
Bank time-varying Bondholdings$_{t-1}$	0.010	0.025*	0.001	0.022	0.003	0.019	0.002	0.021	0.005	0.022	-0.006	0.013	0.000	0.018
	(0.019)	(0.014)	(0.019)	(0.014)	(0.018)	(0.014)	(0.018)	(0.014)	(0.018)	(0.014)	(0.017)	(0.013)	(0.017)	(0.014)
Sovereign Bond Return$_{t-1}$	0.006		0.000		0.003		0.015**		0.015**		0.002		0.005	
	(0.008)		(0.008)		(0.007)		(0.007)		(0.007)		(0.006)		(0.007)	
Bank-Level Controls and Interactions?	Yes	Yes	Yes	Yes	Yes	Yes	Yes	Yes	Yes	Yes	Yes	Yes	Yes	Yes
Year Dummies?	Yes	Yes	Yes	Yes	Yes	Yes	Yes	Yes	Yes	Yes	Yes	Yes	Yes	Yes
Country Dummies?	Yes	Yes	Yes	Yes	Yes	Yes	Yes	Yes	Yes	Yes	Yes	Yes	Yes	Yes
Country × Year Dummies?		Yes		Yes		Yes		Yes		Yes		Yes		Yes
Constant	-0.042*	0.211	-0.039*	0.411	-0.027	0.378	-0.050**	-1.259	-0.071**	0.580**	-0.015	0.163***	-0.008	0.150***
	(0.023)	(.)	(0.023)	(0.292)	(0.023)	(0.286)	(0.023)	(.)	(0.028)	(0.292)	(.)	(0.023)	(0.022)	(0.021)
No Observations	12,742	25,017	12,951	25,371	13,312	25,857	12,957	25,501	12,827	25,307	17,048	29,899	16,470	28,956
No Banks	3,388	4,729	3,425	4,795	3,532	4,923	3,445	4,835	3,396	4,784	5,343	6,768	5,175	6,525
No Countries	55	147	56	148	58	151	55	148	54	147	61	160	56	149
R-squared	0.118	0.229	0.112	0.221	0.113	0.226	0.118	0.227	0.117	0.227	0.112	0.221	0.115	0.220

The table presents coefficient estimates from pooled OLS regressions. The dependent variable changes in loans is computed as loans outstanding in year t minus loans outstanding in year $t-1$, divided by total assets. The main independent variables are bank average non-default years bondholdings, computed as the average of bank bondholdings in all the non-default years prior to and including year $t-1$, bank time-varying bondholdings, computed as bank bondholdings minus bank average non-default years bondholdings. Largest defaults are Argentina's, Russia's, Ukraine's and Greece's; Large defaults are Argentina's, Russia's, Greece's, Ecuador's, Nigeria's, and Kenya's. Standard errors (in parentheses below the coefficient estimates) are adjusted for heteroskedasticity using the Huber (1967) and White (1980) correction, as well as for clustering at the bank level using the Huber (1967) correction. *** indicates significance at the 1% level; ** indicates significance at the 5% level; * indicates significance at the 10% level.

banks demand low-risk public bonds when they have few investment opportunities, particularly in less financially-developed countries. During sovereign crises, instead, bondholdings patterns change. In those times, it is predominantly large banks that accumulate high-risk public bonds, consistent with an important role of bailout guarantees or moral suasion.

The evidence analyzed in Section 4 then seems to indicate that all bondholdings, regardless of their origin, hurt the ability or willingness of banks to extend new loans when sovereign default materializes. On the one hand, banks holding on average more bonds in the pre-default years significantly contract their loans during the default event. These banks may be cutting their loans for one or more of the following reasons: (i) losses on their existing public bonds force them to deleverage, or relatedly; (ii) they deliberately choose to remain exposed to sovereign risk, or finally because; (iii) the unavailability of safe public bonds prevents them from efficiently managing their liquidity. Either way, this correlation suggests that banks' regular demand for bonds during normal times induces an adverse effect on bank lending once default strikes. On the other hand, banks with high bondholdings during the default years also significantly contract their loans. Regardless of whether these high bondholdings are due to banks reaching for yield or to government intervention, this correlation suggests that the banks' demand for bonds during sovereign defaults is also detrimental to lending. The typical explanation for this effect is that purchases of bonds crowd out new loans on the asset side of banks.

One important feature of our dataset is that, by covering a wide sample of default and non-default years, it allows us to quantitatively evaluate the relative importance of these different bondholdings in transmitting sovereign defaults. In this respect, our data provide a rather clear result: in the countries and periods that we consider, average bondholdings in non-default years, which reflect banks' normal activity, play a significantly larger role than bonds accumulated in the run-up to and during default years. First, the marginal adverse effect of bonds accumulated in non-default years is slightly larger than the marginal adverse effect of bonds bought during crises. Second, and most important, banks in our sample of defaulting countries hold many bonds in normal times (13.0%), and the average increase in bondholdings during crises is rather small by comparison (less than 2%).

These results provide a new perspective on the mechanisms whereby the sovereign default-banking crisis nexus comes into existence and operates. Fueled by the recent European sovereign crisis, much of the work on this nexus has focused on risk-taking by European banks (e.g., see Acharya and Steffen (2013)). Although this may well be the right strategy for the European context, our panoramic view of sovereign debt crises calls for paying close attention also to the bonds held by banks in normal times: average bondholdings of banks during non-default years appear to play a very important role in sovereign crises, and neglecting them might be problematic. This insight has both positive and, potentially, normative implications.

From a positive standpoint, our analysis suggests that the unfolding of sovereign crises is qualitatively different in emerging and advanced economies. In emerging economies, financial markets are less developed and banks hold a large amount of bonds in normal times (12.7% of assets in non-OECD countries). It is only natural that these bondholdings generate a large fraction of the adverse effects of sovereign defaults on bank lending. In developed economies, banks hold substantially fewer bonds in normal times (5% of assets in OECD countries). As a result, in these countries, banks' take-up of public bonds during crises is likely to be more important relative to their total bondholdings. The patterns of bondholdings in our sample confirm this hypothesis. In the defaults by emerging countries in our sample, such as for example Argentina and Russia, banks hold many bonds before the default; if anything, they slightly decrease their bondholding as default approaches and, after default happens, large banks accumulate even more bonds. By contrast, banks in Europe's more troubled economies held few bonds before 2008, but they accumulated large quantities of them as sovereign risk increased. In our sample, bondholdings between 2008 and 2010 went from 4.4% to 12.3% in Greek banks; from 6.7% to 11% in Irish banks; and from 3% to 8.1% in Portuguese banks.[28] It thus seems highly likely that, in more advanced economies, the accumulation of bonds during crises (either due to a search for yield or to moral suasion) is responsible for a substantially larger portion of the adverse costs of default.

Our results also carry some potentially important normative implications. In the context of recent events, conventional wisdom holds that the European sovereign crisis became a banking crisis due to the specifics of bank regulation. In particular, the fact that regulation assigns a low risk weight to sovereign bonds even in times of crisis made it possible for banks to gamble in the sovereign bond market without being penalized by the regulator. This consideration is important, but our results suggest that the link between sovereign risk and banking crisis might result from deeper forces. If banks demand a sizeable amount of government bonds to carry out their normal business activities, as seems to be particularly the case in emerging economies but also in developed ones, sovereign defaults will undermine the functioning of the banking sector and bank lending over and above its risk taking during the crisis itself. In this context, proposed regulations to increase the risk weight of government bonds during sovereign crises may backfire, because they might exacerbate the pro-cyclicality of bank balance sheets without having much of an effect on the link between sovereign risk and the banking sector.

We are grateful for helpful suggestions from seminar participants at the Norwegian School of Economics, the Stockholm School of Economics, Wharton conference on Liquidity, Banque de France/Sciences Po/CEPR conference on "The Economics of Sovereign Debt and Default," the ECGI workshop on Sovereign Debt, the Barcelona GSE Summer Forum, and the conference on macroeconomic fragility at the University of Chicago Booth School of Business. We have received helpful comments from Kenneth Singleton (the editor), three anonymous referees, Andrea Beltratti, Stijn Claessens (discussant), Mariassunta Giannetti, Sebnem Kalemli-Ozcan (discussant), Colin Mayer (discussant), Camelia Minou, Paolo Pasquariello, Hélène Rey (discussant), Sergio Schmukler, and Michael Weber (discussant). Jacopo Ponticelli and Xue Wang provided excellent research assistantship. Gennaioli thanks the European Research Council (grant ERC-GA 241114). Martin acknowledges support from the Spanish Ministry of Science and Innovation (grant Ramon y Cajal RYC-2009-04624), the Spanish Ministry of Economy and Competitivity (grant ECO2011-23192), the Generalitat de Catalunya-AGAUR (grant 2009SGR1157), the Ramon Areces Grant and the IMF Research Fellowship.

Notes

1 *The Economist,* December 17th 2011.

2 Mengus (2013) has used a related model with nondiscriminatory default to study bank bailouts; Acharya and Rajan (2013) study the incentives of myopic governments to service their debts.

3 Other work documents the link between public defaults and private credit. Arteta and Hale (2008) show that defaults are accompanied by a decline in syndicated foreign credit to domestic firms. Borensztein and Panizza (2008) show that defaults are accompanied by larger contractions in GDP when they happen together with banking crises. To the best of our knowledge, ours is the first empirical exercise to highlight the role of bank bondholdings. In ongoing research, Baskaya and Kalemli-Ozcan (2014) also study the link from government solvency to the banking sector. In particular, they find that the 1999 Marmara earthquake in Turkey had a larger effect on lending by banks that were highly exposed to government debt.

4 Although very different in scope, our paper is also related to work estimating the demand for government bonds (e.g. Krishnamurthy and Vissing-Jorgensen (2012), and Greenwood and Vayanos (2014)). This work, however, does not specifically consider the role of banks.

5 Bonds are typically recorded at the historic cost of purchase. Fair value adjustments have been limited to a few developed countries in more recent years, and we understand they are not a systematic feature of the data.

6 The relevance of book value reporting is also confirmed by our regression results, both those dealing with bondholdings and with loans, which are economically intuitive.

7 This strategy yields two advantages relative to obtaining all data at once from the web interface. First, we avoid the survivorship bias that would occur because the web interface does not retain accounting information on banks after they delist. Second, our strategy allows us to obtain a time series of all relevant variables, while in some cases the BANKSCOPE interface only keeps the most recent information. For example, the web interface reports only the most recent ownership structure (including any government ownership), and by assembling the annual updates we are thus able to obtain time variation in the ownership structure.

8 Importantly, by filtering out banks with total assets smaller than $100,000 we are effectively filtering out also the banks with incomplete accounting information on the most basic variables such as loans.

9 To preserve space, Table AI only reports defaults for which we observe bank-level information in the constant-continuing sample. BANKSCOPE starts covering some

defaulting countries such as Nicaragua, Paraguay and others only after their default events. For some other defaulting countries (Antigua in 2002-2003, Dominican Republic in 2005, Iraq in 2004, Madagascar in 1998-2002, Moldova in 2002, Pakistan in 1998-1999, and Yemen in 1999-2001), we do observe bondholdings for a number of banks but we do not observe other bank characteristics. For a full list of countries in default up to 2005 see Gennaioli et al. (2014) and Borensztein and Panizza (2008).

10 More details are found at www.prsgroup.com.

11 See, for instance, Classens and Laeven (2004), and Kalemli-Ozcan, Sorensen, and Yesiltas (2012).

12 The highest bondholdings in the sample are above 65% for selected banks in Argentina, Japan, and Venezuela in 2003; the lowest bondholdings are 0% (e.g., several U.S. banks).

13 This variable reports the net positions of commercial banks, defined as holdings of securities plus direct lending minus government deposits, and it can be interpreted as a proxy for the bondholdings of banks. Other papers using this measure are Gennaioli et al. (2014) and Kumhof and Tanner (2008).

14 While BANKSCOPE also counts non-EU bonds, the bondholdings of European banks consist primarily of EU bonds – the very reason of the stress test in the first place.

15 All three risk scores are suitable instruments for expected returns, as the F-test in the univariate regressions are close to 10 or above, mitigating concerns that the instruments are weak (see Stock and Yogo (2005)). By comparison, column (4) in Table AIV presents the result of regressing government bond returns at t on returns at t-1. While there is also a negative and significant univariate correlation, the F-test is around 3, indicating that past government bond returns is likely to be a weak instrument. As a result, we do not use it in our analysis.

16 Specifically, we use as instruments the economic score and the political score, and we include time dummies to capture variations in the global riskless interest rate. Column 5 of Table AIV presents the results for the specification that we use in the empirical analysis as the first-stage estimation of the expected returns used in Table V, columns 3 and 5. Our results in Table V are not sensitive to the choice of instruments within the three risk scores of the ICRG.

17 Panel B of Table III shows the characteristics of banks involved in the stress test. These banks are much larger and extend more loans than the median BANKSCOPE bank. They also have lower exposure to the Central Bank and to other banks. Leverage and cash are instead of similar magnitude to those observed in BANKSCOPE.

18 The use of lagged independent variables is preferable to the use of independent variables that are contemporaneous to bondholdings for two reasons. First, bank-level explanatory variables are determined jointly with bondholdings within each year. As a result, a contemporaneous formulation of Equation (1) would suffer from severe endogeneity problems. Second, the bank does not observe the aggregate final state of the economy at t until the end of period t itself. As a result, the forecast of macro variables performed by the bank or by the market at time t will depend on the state of the economy as measured at time $t - 1$.

19 In a previous draft we clustered standard errors at the country level and obtained very similar results.

20 It could be, for instance, that governments in poorer and less financially developed countries have higher debt levels for reasons that have nothing to do with the demand of bonds by banks. The inclusion of country dummies and country*time dummies allows us to mitigate these and other omitted variables concerns.

21 Table AIV in the appendix reports the first stage estimation used to compute expected government returns, as well as a detailed discussion of the estimation results.

22 This implies that it is crucial to control for bank characteristics when assessing the link between bondholdings and subsequent lending. We have shown that large banks are the most likely to accumulate public bonds during defaults; they are also the ones that lend the most. Thus, without controlling for bank size, we might spuriously find a positive correlation between bondholdings and loans during defaults. We shall return to this important point in Section 4.

23 In Section 4 we further mitigate this concern by analyzing the behavior of average bondholdings outside of default episodes, which are presumably more representative of banks' normal business activities. As we discuss in the next section and show in the Appendix, average bondholdings in non-default years behave very similarly to total bondholdings in the same years: they are larger in financially less developed countries, when expected bond returns are smaller, and for banks that have fewer outstanding loans.

24 One important caveat here is that the effect of the default dummy in columns (4)-(6) should be viewed as capturing a lower bound on the role of risk taking during crises. Indeed, even if bank bondholdings did not increase at all during sovereign crises (so that the estimated effects of default were all zero), banks could still be taking on excessive risk by maintaining their pre-crisis bondholdings despite the increase in sovereign risk.

25 The effect of $b_{i,n,t}$ on loans during defaults could capture both the fact that default exerts an adverse balance sheet effect on banks with higher average bondholdings in normal times, and the fact that defaults reduce the appeal of bonds as liquid assets and this is costly for banks that normally use bonds for that reason.

26 We do not include other country-level controls because doing so drastically reduces the number of observations. To control for all country-level, time-varying factors, columns (4) and (5) also include country*year dummies.

27 As discussed before, for this exercise we are limited by the availability of data on spreads, so we are effectively limited to examining the larger, economically more important defaults. In addition to the defaults in Argentina in 2001-2004, Russia in 1998-2000, Ukraine in 1998-2000, Greece in 2012, and Seychelles in 2010 identified also by S&P, the additional defaults we examine here are Ireland in 2011, Portugal in 2011 and 2012, Greece in 2011, and Ukraine in 2001.

28 Over the same period, the increase in bondholdings was much smaller in Spanish (from 4.6% to 6%) and Italian (from 11.8% to 12.4%) banks.

References

Acharya, Viral V., Itamar Drechsler, and Philipp Schnabl, 2013, A Pyrrhic victory? Bank bailouts and sovereign credit risk, *Journal of Finance, forthcoming*.

Acharya, Viral V., and Raghuram G. Rajan, 2013, Sovereign debt, government myopia, and the financial sector, *Review of Financial Studies* 26, 1526-1560.

Acharya, Viral V., and Sascha Steffen, 2013, The greatest carry trade ever? Understanding Eurozone bank risks, NBER working paper 19039.

Andritzky, Jochen R. 2012, Government bonds and their investors: What are the facts and do they matter?, IMF working paper.

Arellano, Cristina, 2008, Default risk and income fluctuations in emerging economies, *American Economic Review* 98, 690-712.

Arteta, Carlos, and Galina Hale, 2008, Sovereign debt crises and credit to the private sector, *Journal of International Economics* 74, 53-69.

Baskaya, Yusuf Soner, and Sebnem Kalemli-Ozcan, 2014, Government debt and financial repression: Evidence from a rare disaster, University of Maryland working paper.

Battistini, Niccolò, Marco Pagano, and Saverio Simonelli, 2013, Systemic risk, sovereign yields and bank exposures in the Euro crisis, mimeo, Università di Napoli Federico II.

Beck, Thorsten, Asli Demirgüç-Kunt, and Ross Levine, 2000, A new database on financial development and structure, *World Bank Economic Review* 14, 597-605.

Berger, Allen, Christa Bouwman, Thomas Kick, and Klaus Schaeck, 2012, Bank risk taking and liquidity creation following regulatory interventions and capital support, mimeo, Case Western Reserve University.

Borensztein, Eduardo, and Ugo Panizza, 2008, The costs of sovereign default, IMF working paper.

Broner, Fernando, Alberto Martin, and Jaume Ventura, 2010, Sovereign risk and secondary markets, *American Economic Review* 100, 1523-1555.

Broner, Fernando, and Jaume Ventura, 2011, Globalization and risk sharing, *Review of Economic Studies* 78, 49-82.

Brutti, Filippo, and Philip Sauré, 2013, Repatriation of Debt in the Euro Crisis: Evidence for the Secondary Market Theory, mimeo, University of Zurich.

Claessens, Stijn, and Luc Laeven, 2004, What drives bank competition? Some international evidence, *Journal of Money, Credit and Banking* 36, 563-583.

Comelli, Fabio, 2012, Emerging market sovereign bond spreads: Estimation and back-testing, IMF working paper.

Cruces, Juan J., and Christoph Trebesch, 2013, Sovereign defaults: The price of haircuts, *American Economic Journal: Macroeconomics* 5, 85-117.

Eaton, Jonathan, and Mark Gersovitz, 1981, Debt with potential repudiation: Theoretical and empirical analysis, *Review of Economic Studies* 48, 289-309.

Gelos, R. Gaston, Sahay Ratna and Guido Sandleris, 2011, Sovereign borrowing by developing countries: What determines market access?, *Journal of International Economics* 83(2), pages 243-254.

Gennaioli, Nicola, Alberto Martin, and Stefano Rossi, 2014, Sovereign default, domestic banks, and financial institutions, *Journal of Finance* 69, 819-866.

Greenwood, Robin, and Dimitri Vayanos, 2014, Bond supply and excess bond returns, *Review of Financial Studies* 27, 663-713.

Hannoun, Hervé, 2011, Sovereign risk in bank regulation and supervision: Where do we stand?, Bank for International Settlements.

Holmström, Bengt, and Jean Tirole, 1993, Market liquidity and performance monitoring, *Journal of Political Economy* 101, 678-709.

Kalemli-Ozcan, Sebnem, Bent E. Sorensen and Sevcan Yesiltas, 2012, Leverage across banks, firms and countries, *Journal of International Economics* 88, 284-298.

Kim, Gloria, 2010, EMBI Global and EMBI Global Diversified, rules and methodology, Global Research Index Research, J.P. Morgan Securities Inc.

Krishnamurthy, Arvind and Annette Vissing-Jorgensen, 2012, The aggregate demand for treasury debt, *Journal of Political Economy* 120, 233-267.

Kumhof, Michael, and Evan Tanner, 2008, Government debt: A key role in financial intermediation, in Carmen M. Reinhart, Carlos Végh, and Andres Velasco, eds.: *Money, Crises and Transition, Essays in Honor of Guillermo A. Calvo.*

Levy-Yeyati, Eduardo, Maria Soledad Martinez Peria, and Sergio Schmukler, 2010, Depositor behavior under macroeconomic risk: Evidence from bank runs in emerging economies, *Journal of Money, Credit, and Banking* 42, 585-614.

Livshits, Igor, and Koen Schoors, 2009, Sovereign default and banking, mimeo, University of Western Ontario.

Mengus, Eric, 2012, Foreign borrowing, portfolio allocation, and bailouts, mimeo, University of Toulouse.

Opler, Tim, Lee Pinkowitz, Réné Stulz, and Rohan Williamson, 1999, The determinants and implications of corporate cash holdings, *Journal of Financial Economics* 52, 3-46.

Ozer-Balli, Hatice, and Bent E. Sorensen, 2013, Interaction effects in econometrics, *Empirical Economics, forthcoming.*

Pescatori Andrea, and Amadou N.R. Sy, 2007, Are debt crises adequately defined? IMF Staff Papers 54(2), 306-337.

Reinhart, Carmen M., and M. Belen Sbrancia, 2011, The liquidation of government debt, NBER working paper 16893.

Sandleris, Guido, 2012, The costs of sovereign defaults: theory and empirical evidence, mimeo, Universidad DiTella.

Stock, James, and Motohiro Yogo, 2005, Testing for Weak Instruments in Linear IV Regression. In: Andrews DWK Identification and Inference for Econometric Models. New York: Cambridge University Press; pp. 80-108.

Sturzenegger, Federico, and Jeromin Zettelmeyer, 2008, Haircuts: Estimating investor losses in sovereign debt restructurings, 1998-2005, *Journal of International Money and Finance* 27, 780-805.

Tomz, Michael, 2007, *Reputation and international cooperation,* Princeton University Press.

Zettelmeyer, Jeromin, Christoph Trebesch, and G. Mitu Gulati, 2012, The Greek debt exchange: An autopsy, *Economic Policy* 28, 513-569.

Appendix

This Appendix reports tables that are referred to in the main text. Table AI lists the default events that we consider in our empirical analysis. Table AII describes our variables and their sources. Table AIII reports descriptive statistics on realized sovereign bond returns.

Table AIV presents results related to the estimation of Equation (1) in the paper, namely, the first stage of our estimation of expected sovereign bond returns, whereby realized sovereign returns are regressed on economic, financial, and political risk scores provided by the ICRG that in the literature have been found to predict sovereign returns.

The purpose of this exercise is very narrow, as we simply want to determine whether, in our sample, the country risk measures provided by the ICRG constitute valid instruments and can thus be used to construct our proxy of expected government bond returns. Our purpose is not to determine whether future government bond returns are predictable using current information publicly available to investors, which is discussed for example in Comelli (2012) and others. As a result, among other things, we are not concerned about the out-of-sample properties of our instruments.

Table AIV present the results of the first stage estimation of sovereign returns. The first three columns present the univariate correlation of annual government bond returns at year t with the economic, political, and financial risk score

Table AI Default Episodes and Bank-Years in Default in our Sample

Country	Default S&P	Haircut	Spread or Default	No Bank-Years	No Banks
Argentina	2001-2004	76.8%	2001-2004	231	87
Ecuador	1998-2000; 2009	38.3%		8	8
Ethiopia	1998-1999	92.0%		2	1
Greece	2012	64.8%	2011-2012	12	9
Guyana	1998-2004	91.0%		20	3
Honduras	1998-2004	82.0%		79	21
Indonesia	1998-2000; 2002			17	13
Ireland			2011	7	7
Jamaica	2010			5	5
Kenya	1998-2004	45.7%		160	33
Nigeria	2002			41	41
Portugal			2011-2012	24	15
Russia	1998-2000	51.1%	1998-2000	40	31
Serbia	1998-2004	70.9%		2	2
Seychelles	2000-2002; 2010	56.2%	2010	1	1
Sudan	1998-2004			2	1
Tanzania	2004	88.0%		1	1
Ukraine	1998-2000	14.8%	1998-2001	17	8
Zimbabwe	2000-2004			6	3
No Banks				675	290
No Countries	17	12	7		
No Episodes	20	13	7		

The table reports episodes of sovereign defaults over 1998-2012 for which we observe bank-level data from Bankscope. A default episode is an uninterrupted sequence of years in default by a country. Default S&P reports the years in which a country is in default according to the definition of sovereign default by Standard & Poor's, which is based on whether an outstanding debt issue is not repaid in full, or is renegotiated with worse terms for the creditors. Haircut is the average creditors' haircuts from the work of Cruces and Trebesch (2013) and Zettelmeyer, Trebesch, and Gulati (2012). Spread or Default considers countries with available data on sovereign spreads and reports the years in which a country is in default according to whether at least once in a given year the spreads of the sovereign bond with the corresponding U.S. or German bonds exceed a given threshold; or it is in default according to the S&P definition.

measured at year t-1, respectively. The correlations are large and strongly statistically significant. A higher score implies less risk, so for example, a 1-percent increase in the economic risk score translates into a 0.31% lower government return; and a 1-percent increase in the economic risk score translates into a 0.27% lower government return.

Importantly for our purposes, the F-test in these three columns is very high, around 10 or higher, which suggests that our instruments are unlikely to be weak according to the 'rule-of-thumb' proposed by Stock and Yogo (2005). By comparison, column (4) present the result of regressing government bond returns at t on past returns at t-1. While there is also a negative and significant univariate correlation, the F-test is around 3, indicating that past government bond returns is a likely weak instrument, and as a result we do not use it in our analysis.

Table AII Definition of the Variables used in the Analysis

Variable	Definition
Bank-level variables	
Assets	Total book value of intangible, tangible and other fixed assets. Source: Bankscope.
Bondholdings	Total holding of government securities, including treasury bills, bonds and other government securities, divided by total assets. Source: Bankscope.
Size	Natural logarithm of total assets. Source: Bankscope.
Non-cash assets	Total assets minus cash and due from banks, divided by total assets. Source: Bankscope.
Leverage	One minus book value of equity (issued share capital plus other shareholders fund) divided by total assets. Source: Bankscope.
Loans	Total loans outstanding divided by total assets. Source: Bankscope.
Profitability	Operating income divided by total assets. Source: Bankscope.
Exposure to Central Bank	Total exposure to central bank divided by total assets. Source: Bankscope.
Interbank Balances	Interest-earning balances with central and other banks, excluding impairment allowance, but including amounts due under reverse repurchase agreements, divided by total assets. Source: Bankscope.
Government Owned	Dummy variable that equals 1 if the government owns more than 50% of the bank's equity. Source: Bankscope.
Country-level variables	
Sovereign Default	Dummy variable that equals 1 if the sovereign issuer is in default. Sovereign default is defined as the failure to meet a principal or interest payment on the due date (or within the specified grace period) contained in the original terms of the debt issue. In particular, each issuer's debt is considered in default in any of the following circumstances: (i) For local and foreign currency bonds, notes and bills, when either scheduled debt service is not paid on the due date, or an exchange offer of new debt contains terms less favorable than the original issue; (ii) For central bank currency, when notes are converted into new currency of less than equivalent face value; (iii) For bank loans, when either scheduled debt service is not paid on the due date, or a rescheduling of principal and/or interest is agreed to by creditors at less favorable terms than the original loan. Such rescheduling agreements covering short and long term debt are considered defaults even where, for legal or regulatory reasons, creditors deem forced rollover of principal to be voluntary. Source: Standard & Poor's (2008)
Sovereign Bond Return	Index aggregating the realized returns of sovereign bonds of different maturities and denominations in each country. Returns are expressed in dollars. The index takes into account the change in the price of the bonds and it assumes that any cash received from coupons or pay downs is reinvested in the bond. Source: the J.P. Morgan's Emerging Market Bond Index Plus file (EMBIG+) for emerging countries; and the J.P. Morgan's Global Bond Index (GBI) file for developed countries.

(Continued)

Table AII Continued

Variable	Definition
GDP Growth	Logarithm of gross domestic product per capita (Atlas method). Source: World Development Indicators.
Aggregate Leverage	Country-year average of bank-level leverage. Source: Bankscope.
Banking Crisis	Dummy variable that equals 1 if the country is experiencing a banking crisis. Banking crisis is defined as a situation in which the net worth of the banking system has been almost or entirely eliminated. Source: Caprio and Klingebiel (2001) and the updated data by Caprio et al. (2005).
Unemployment Growth	Annual percentage change in unemployment. Source: World Development Indicators (September 2008).
Inflation	Annual percentage inflation, GDP deflator. Source: World Development Indicators (September 2008).
Private Credit	Ratio of credit from deposit taking financial institutions to the private sector (International Financial Statistics lines 22d and 42d) to GDP (International Financial Statistics line 99b), expressed as a percentage. Line 22d measures claims on the private sector by commercial banks and other financial institutions that accept transferable deposits such as demand deposits. Line 42d measures claims on the private sector given by other financial institutions that do not accept transferable deposits but that perform financial intermediation by accepting other types of deposits or close substitutes for deposits (e.g., savings and mortgage institutions, post office savings institutions, building and loan associations, certain finance companies, development banks, and offshore banking institutions). Source: International Monetary Fund, International Financial Statistics (September 2008).
Economic Score	Rating of economic risk that reflects indicators such as GDP, GDP growth, inflation, and current account balance. It ranges between 0 and 50, where 0 represents the highest risk. Source: ICRG (2013).
Political Score	Rating of political risk that reflects sociopolitical indicators including government stability, socioeconomic conditions, internal or external conflict, corruption, law and order, and public accountability. It ranges between 0 and 100, where 0 represents the highest risk. Source: ICRG (2013).
Financial Score	Rating of financial risk that combines variables such foreign debt as a share of GDP, foreign debt services as a share of exports, and exchange rate stability. It ranges between 0 and 50, where 0 represents the highest risk. Source: ICRG (2013).

Table AIII Sovereign Bond Returns in Defaulting and non-Defaulting Countries

	Default	No Default	OECD	No OECD	Overall
Mean	14.46%	9.70%	7.62%	11.61%	9.81%
Std Deviation	58.61%	19.76%	12.34%	26.47%	21.37%
Variance	34.35%	3.90%	1.52%	7.01%	4.57%
No Countries	6	70	27	43	70
No Country-year obs.	18	764	353	429	782

The table presents descriptive statistics of realized government bond returns.

Table AIV First-Stage Estimation of Government Bond Returns

	(1)	(2)	(3)	(4)	(5)	(6)	(7)	(8)
Economic Score$_{c,t-1}$	-0.311***				-0.251**	-0.477**	-0.363*	-0.451**
	(0.090)				(0.110)	(0.202)	(0.224)	(0.196)
Political Score$_{c,t-1}$		-0.221***			-0.148*	-0.416**	-0.435**	-0.553***
		(0.075)			(0.081)	(0.185)	(0.184)	(0.205)
Financial Score$_{c,t-1}$			-0.270***				-0.198	
			(0.082)				(0.186)	
Return$_{c,t-1}$				-0.143*				-0.184**
				(0.078)				(0.076)
Constant	0.328***	0.257***	0.300***	0.121***	0.189**	0.515***	0.611***	0.896***
	(0.070)	(0.059)	(0.064)	(0.013)	(0.087)	(0.151)	(0.185)	(0.194)
Time dummies?					Yes	Yes	Yes	Yes
Country dummies?						Yes	Yes	Yes
F-test	12.02	8.69	10.91	3.37	11.37			
No Observations	766	766	766	719	766	766	766	712
R-squared	0.020	0.018	0.013	0.022	0.239	0.290	0.292	0.336

The Table presents results from the first stage estimation of government bond returns. The instruments are the economic score, a rating of economic risk provided by the ICRG and normalized to be between 0 and 1; the political score, a rating of political risk provided by the ICRG and normalized to be between 0 and 1; and the financial score, a rating of financial risk provided by the ICRG and normalized to be between 0 and 1. Standard errors (in parentheses below the coefficient estimates) are adjusted for heteroskedasticity using the Huber (1967) and White (1980) correction. *** indicates significance at the 1% level; ** indicates significance at the 5% level; * indicates significance at the 10% level.

188

Table AV Pair-wise Correlations

	Bonds	Bank Size	Non-cash Assets	Leverage	Loans	Profitability	Exposure	Balances
Banks size	-0.063***							
Non-cash assets	-0.835***	0.202***						
Leverage	-0.141***	0.335***	0.207***					
Loans	-0.376***	0.016***	0.202***	0.238***				
Profitability	0.102***	0.059***	-0.071***	-0.286***	-0.100***			
Exposure to Central Bank	0.096***	0.209***	-0.374***	-0.218***	-0.231***	0.140***		
Interbank Balances	-0.136***	-0.087***	0.117***	-0.173***	-0.553***	0.061***	0.367***	
Government Owned	0.082***	0.141***	-0.026***	-0.031***	-0.073***	0.009***	0.027***	0.022***

The table reports pair-wise correlations among the main variables used in the empirical analysis. *** indicates significance at the 1% level; **indicates significance at the 5% level; *indicates significance at the 10% level.

Column (5) presents the specification that we use in the empirical analysis as the first stage of Table V, in Columns 3 and 5. We use as instruments the economic score and the political score, and we include time dummies to capture variations in the global riskless interest rate. It turns out that our results in Table V are not sensitive to the choice of any combination of instruments, within the three risk scores of ICRG.

The remainder of the Table shows that in-sample predictability comes from both the cross section and the time series, that is, our coefficients of interest remain strongly significant when adding time dummies and country dummies; and our main specification is also robust to the inclusion of past returns as an additional explanatory variable.

Finally, Table AV presents pair-wise correlations among the variables used in the analysis.

54

HEDGE FUND CONTAGION AND LIQUIDITY SHOCKS

Nicole M. Boyson, Christof W. Stahel, and René M. Stulz

Source: *Journal of Finance* LXV, 5, 2010, 1789–1816.

ABSTRACT

Defining contagion as correlation over and above that expected from economic fundamentals, we find strong evidence of worst return contagion across hedge fund styles for 1990 to 2008. Large adverse shocks to asset and hedge fund liquidity strongly increase the probability of contagion. Specifically, large adverse shocks to credit spreads, the TED spread, prime broker and bank stock prices, stock market liquidity, and hedge fund flows are associated with a significant increase in the probability of hedge fund contagion. While shocks to liquidity are important determinants of performance, these shocks are not captured by commonly used models of hedge fund returns.

USING MONTHLY HEDGE FUND INDEX DATA for the period January 1990 to October 2008, we find that the worst hedge fund returns, defined as returns that fall in the bottom 10% of a hedge fund style's monthly returns, cluster across styles. Further, using both parametric and semi-parametric analyses, we show that this clustering cannot be explained by risk factors commonly used to explain hedge fund performance. Bekaert, Harvey, and Ng (2005 p. 40) define contagion as "correlation over and above what one would expect from economic fundamentals." With this definition, the clustering we observe is contagion. To our knowledge, this is the first study to test for and document the existence of hedge fund contagion.

To understand the determinants of hedge fund contagion, we turn to a recent paper by Brunnermeier and Pedersen (2009) for theoretical motivation. In their model, an adverse shock to speculators' funding liquidity (the availability of funding) forces them to reduce their leverage and provide less liquidity to the markets, which reduces asset liquidity (the ease with which assets trade). When the impact of the funding liquidity shock on asset liquidity is strong enough, the decrease in asset liquidity makes funding even tighter for speculators, causing a self-reinforcing liquidity spiral in which both funding liquidity and asset liquidity continue to deteriorate. An important implication of their study is that these liquidity spirals affect all assets held by speculators that face funding liquidity constraints, leading to commonality in the performance of these assets. Discussions of the recent credit crisis emphasize the role of liquidity spirals, such as the impact of the subprime crisis on margins that led to a sharp reduction in liquidity in many if not most asset markets by the second half of 2008, when the clustering of hedge fund worst returns we document is most dramatic.[1] Because hedge funds are quintessential speculators of the type envisaged by Brunnermeier and Pedersen (2009), their model can be used to guide an investigation of contagion among hedge fund styles. Their model predicts that shocks to asset liquidity and hedge fund funding liquidity lead to poor performance of assets in which hedge funds are marginal investors, and hence to hedge fund contagion. While the predictions of their model may be most significant during a severe financial crisis like the credit crunch that began in 2007, we study periods of coincident poor performance in hedge funds since 1990 and show that large adverse shocks to asset and hedge fund funding liquidity make hedge fund contagion more likely.

We use monthly hedge fund index return data from Hedge Fund Research (HFR) for eight different hedge fund styles to investigate the existence of hedge fund contagion. Since hedge fund returns are autocorrelated and affected by a number of risk factors, we first filter the raw hedge fund returns using AR(1) models augmented with factors from Fama and French (1993), Fung and Hsieh (2004), and Agarwal and Naik (2004). We then use the residuals (i.e., "filtered returns") from these models in our analysis. Using the filtered returns should strongly reduce the possibility that we attribute to contagion clustering due to exposure to commonly known risk factors or to autocorrelation in monthly returns, but it does so at the cost of perhaps making our analysis too conservative. In particular, the analysis would be too conservative if the factors themselves were affected by contagion, so that through our filtering we eliminate part of the effect of contagion. Consistent with this concern, we find that our results are typically stronger without the filtering.

Our first test of contagion uses the filtered data in a quantile regression analysis. The quantile regression estimates the conditional probability that a variable falls below a given threshold (quantile) when another random variable is also below this same quantile. Advantages to this approach are that it puts no distributional assumptions on the data, it may be estimated for a large range of possible quantiles, and it allows for heteroskedasticity. Using this approach, we show that for all quantiles below the median, the conditional probability that a given hedge fund style's returns will be in the same quantile as the equally weighted average of all other hedge fund styles' returns is much higher than would be expected if there were no dependence, providing strong evidence of clustering in filtered below-median returns. Strikingly, there is no evidence of clustering for above-median returns.

Next, we implement a parametric test of contagion, a logit model that has been previously used in the literature (see Eichengreen, Rose, and Wyplosz (1996), and Bae, Karolyi, and Stulz (2003)). Our analysis, which is performed separately for each hedge fund style index, uses as the dependent variable an indicator variable set to one if the index of interest has a return in the bottom decile (a "worst return") of that index's entire time series of returns, and zero otherwise. The key independent variable for this analysis is *COUNT*, which ranges in value from zero to seven and is defined as the number of *other* hedge fund styles that have worst returns in the same month. The logit results are consistent with the quantile analysis in that the coefficients on *COUNT* are positive and statistically significant for all eight hedge fund style indices. Hence, both the semi-parametric and para-metric approaches provide evidence of clustering in worst returns that cannot be attributed to autocorrelation in returns or to changes in factors commonly used to explain hedge fund returns, or in other words, contagion.

The second part of the paper investigates whether shocks to asset liquidity and hedge fund funding liquidity increase the probability of contagion. For this investigation, we identify variables for which an extreme adverse realization is likely associated with a tightening of asset liquidity and hedge fund funding liquidity. We call these variables contagion channel variables. These variables include the Chordia, Sarkar, and Subrahmanyam (2005) measure of stock market liquidity, a measure of credit spreads, the TED spread, returns to banks and prime brokers, changes in repo volume, and flows to hedge funds. We investigate whether extreme adverse shocks to the contagion channel variables can explain hedge fund contagion using a multinomial regression analysis. The dependent variable is a measure of the intensity of contagion. To model extreme adverse shocks for each of the contagion channel variables, we create dummy variables set to one when the corresponding channel variable experiences a large adverse shock that decreases liquidity (defined as a realization in the worst 25th percentile for that variable) and zero otherwise. Since we use monthly data, it is not obvious how quickly shocks to contagion channel variables will be reflected in hedge fund performance. We therefore perform two separate analyses for each of the contagion channel shock dummy variables, one in which the shock is measured contemporaneously and one in which the shock is lagged one month. We find that both contemporaneous and lagged channel shock dummies are linked to high levels of contagion intensity across hedge fund styles.

Since we show that liquidity *shocks* are strongly related to hedge fund contagion, our final analysis examines whether our finding of contagion could be due to an omitted liquidity risk factor in the initial filtering regressions. The idea of liquidity as a risk factor is consistent with work by Amihud (2002), Pástor and Stambaugh (2003), Acharya and Pedersen (2005), and Chordia et al. (2005). To test this idea, we add to the initial filtering process innovations to the continuous measures of the contagion channel variables. We find that while most of the coefficients on the innovation factors are statistically insignificant, the coefficient on TED spread innovations is negative and significant for five of the eight hedge fund indices, indicating that hedge fund returns are negatively impacted by widening TED spreads. However, despite the addition of these new factors to the filtering process, results from the logit models (that use the residuals from this process) still provide strong evidence of contagion, and results from the multinomial regressions still indicate a strong relationship between shocks to liquidity and contagion, with the exception that shocks to the TED spread have a somewhat weaker effect. Thus, while commonly used models of hedge fund returns do not capture the exposure of hedge funds to large shocks to liquidity, this exposure cannot be accounted for by simply adding changes in liquidity proxies to these models.

To our knowledge, we are the first to document the existence of contagion in hedge fund returns, after controlling for autocorrelation and common risk factors. Additionally, we are the first to link hedge fund contagion to liquidity shocks, and thus to provide an initial test of the Brunnermeier and Pedersen (2009) model. In a related paper, Adrian and Brunnermeier (2009) use quantile regressions to document the increase in a measure of the risk of financial institutions, that is, value-at-risk (VaR), conditional on other financial institutions experiencing financial distress. They explain financial institution VaR contagion using various factors including credit spreads, repo spreads, and returns on the main markets. In a recent paper, Dudley and Nimalendran (2009) investigate correlations among hedge fund styles conditional on extreme returns of hedge fund styles and find support for a role for funding liquidity. Consistent with our finding that shocks to bank stock performance increase the probability of hedge fund contagion, Chan et al. (2006) find a positive correlation between bank returns (measured using a broad-based bank index from CRSP) and hedge fund returns. Billio, Getmansky, and Pelizzon (2009) examine hedge fund risk exposures in a regime switching model and show that when volatility is high, the four strategies they examine have exposures to proxies for liquidity and credit risk, consistent with our results that shocks to credit spreads increase the probability of hedge fund contagion. Finally, while we use index data and find contagion across hedge fund styles, Klaus and Rzepkowski (2009) use individual fund data and provide evidence of contagion effects within hedge fund styles.

The paper is organized as follows. In Section I we describe the data for the hedge fund index returns and the explanatory variables. Section II uses monthly hedge fund indices and documents contagion within the hedge fund sector. Section III examines possible economic explanations for hedge fund contagion using a number of contagion channel variables. Section IV examines the possibility that our contagion results are driven by an omitted variable. We attempt to interpret our results and conclude in Section V.

I. Hedge Fund Data

The hedge fund style returns are the monthly style index returns provided by HFR. The returns are equally weighted and net of fees. The indices include both domestic and offshore funds. These data extend from January 1990 to October 2008 for a total of 226 monthly observations. There are eight single-strategy indices: Convertible Arbitrage, Distressed Securities, Event Driven, Equity Hedge, Equity Market Neutral, Global Macro, Merger Arbitrage, and Relative Value Arbitrage.[2] These indices include over 1,600 funds, with no required minimum track record or asset size. Additionally, these indices are not directly investible; that is, they include some funds that are closed to new investors. To address backfilling and survivorship bias, when a fund is added to an index, the index is not recomputed with past returns of that fund. Similarly, when a fund is dropped from an index, past returns of the index are left unchanged. We use the HFR database for the analyses we report in the paper, but we also repeat all our tests using the Credit Suisse/Tremont indices, since recent research suggests that funds sometimes migrate from one database to another and that no database provides comprehensive coverage of all funds.[3] Results using the latter indices are reported in the Internet Appendix.[4]

II. Tests for Contagion Using HFR Index Data

A. Filtering the Index Data

A preliminary review of the raw hedge fund index data in the Internet Appendix indicates relatively high positive correlations among hedge fund styles, significant autocorrelation within hedge fund styles, and significantly non-normal returns. For example, simple correlations range from a low of 0.27 between Convertible Arbitrage and Global Macro indices to a high of 0.83 between Distressed and Event Driven. In addition, the correlations between the hedge fund indices and the Russell 3000 index are also high, ranging from 0.32 for Equity Market Neutral to 0.75 for Equity Hedge. Ljung-Box autocorrelation tests reject the null hypothesis of no autocorrelation for up to six lags at the 1% level for all indices except Merger Arbitrage, which is significant at the 2% level. Finally, Jarque-Bera tests indicate that for all indices the null hypothesis of normally distributed returns is rejected at the 1% significance level.

To control for the exposure to common risk factors, we regress the returns of each style individually on a number of variables. We use these factors here so that in later tests we do not mistakenly attribute to contagion correlations in returns that are related to common risk factors, consistent with our definition of contagion as correlation over and above that expected based on economic fundamentals. To control for broad market exposure, we use three market factors: an equity market index (the Russell 3000), a broad-based bond index (the Lehman Brothers bond index), and a broad currency index (the change in the trade-weighted U.S. dollar exchange rate index published by the Board of Governors of the U.S. Federal Reserve System), as well as the return on the 3-month T-bill. We include the monthly change in the 10-year constant maturity Treasury yield and the change in the monthly spread of Moody's Baa yield over the 10-year constant maturity

Treasury yield, based on Fama and French (1993) and Fung and Hsieh (2004). We also use ABS (asset-based strategy) factors and a size spread factor (Wilshire Small Cap 1750 monthly return minus Wilshire Large Cap 750 monthly return), both from Fung and Hsieh (2004).[5] The ABS factors are lookback straddles on bonds, currencies, commodities, short-term interest rates, and equities. We also include the negative portion of the S&P 500 to proxy for a put option, based on Agarwal and Naik (2004). We received the ABS factors from William Fung and David Hsieh; all other factors are from Thomson Datastream. Finally, we use an AR(1) term in each model to control for autocorrelation. The residuals from these filtering models are then used in our analyses. The regression results (see the Internet Appendix) indicate that the explanatory variables are relevant in explaining the performance of hedge funds, with adjusted-R^2 values ranging from 0.23 for Equity Market Neutral to 0.79 for Event Driven.

Table I presents summary statistics, autocorrelations, and normality tests for the filtered residuals. Comparing these results to the raw data, there is a significant decrease in correlations among hedge fund indices. The correlations between filtered hedge fund indices and the filtered Russell 3000 index also drop dramatically. Finally, autocorrelation has been reduced greatly as only three of the eight indices exhibit significant autocorrelation, as compared to seven out of eight for raw returns.

B. Contagion Tests Using Quantile Regressions

We next investigate whether hedge fund indices exhibit excess correlations in the tails of the distributions, using the filtered index data. We use two different approaches for the investigation. The first approach uses quantile regressions, which make it possible to estimate the probability of a given hedge fund return conditional on the performance of all other hedge fund indices. The second approach uses logit regressions. The two approaches provide consistent results.

Based on a quantile regression approach, we show visually the existence of contagion among hedge fund styles using a so-called "co-movement box" as in Cappiello, Gérard, and Manganelli (2005).[6] The quantile regression estimates the conditional probability that a random variable y_t falls below a given quantile $q_{Y,\theta}$ conditional on a different random variable x_t also falling below the same quantile $q_{X,\theta}$. In an unconditional setting the probability $\Pr(y_t < q_{Y,\theta})$ is by definition equal to θ, but the conditional probability is different from θ when the two variables are not independent. Other financial studies using the quantile regression approach include Koenker and Bassett (1978), Engle and Manganelli (2004), and Adrian and Brunnermeier (2009). The conditional probability is easily estimated through an OLS regression using quantile co-exceedance indicators.[7] Advantages to this semi-parametric methodology are that OLS estimates are consistent and that no distributional assumptions need be imposed on the data, which allows for heteroskedasticity.

Table I Summary Statistics of Filtered Monthly Returns on HFR Indices and Market Factors: January 1990 to October 2008

	HFR Hedge Fund Indices								Main Market Factors		
	Convertible Arbitrage	Distressed Securities	Event Driven	Equity Hedge	Equity Market Neutral	Merger Arbitrage	Global Macro	Relative Value	Russell 3000 Index	Return on LB bond Index	Δ in FRB Dollar Index
Panel A: Summary Statistics											
Median	-0.040	-0.047	0.022	-0.002	0.006	0.057	0.010	-0.024	0.537	0.098	0.020
Standard deviation	0.906	0.953	0.874	1.268	0.785	0.827	1.750	0.806	4.220	1.006	1.002
Skewness	-0.994	0.330	0.214	-0.098	0.019	-1.219	0.120	0.434	-0.757	-0.445	-0.468
Excess kurtosis	8.956	2.336	1.401	3.842	0.319	5.025	0.571	4.983	1.730	0.650	0.917
Panel B: Simple Correlations											
Convertible arbitrage	1.00										
Distressed securities	0.30*	1.00									
Event driven	0.31*	0.54	1.00								
Equity hedge	0.25*	0.27*	0.34*	1.00							
Equity market neutral	0.15*	0.19*	0.20*	0.35*	1.00						
Merger arbitrage	0.27*	0.33*	0.49*	0.00	0.16*	1.00					
Global macro	0.05	0.27*	0.40*	0.43*	0.14*	0.08	1.00				
Relative value	0.49*	0.49*	0.40*	0.31*	0.25*	0.26*	0.14*	1.00			
Russell 3000 return	0.00	0.00	0.00	0.01	0.00	0.00	-0.01	0.00	1.00		
Return on LB bond Index	-0.03	-0.01	-0.01	0.02	-0.01	-0.03	0.01	-0.02	0.16*	1.00	
Δ in FRB Dollar Index	-0.03	-0.01	0.00	0.01	0.00	0.01	-0.01	-0.03	0.15*	0.22*	1.00

(Continued)

Table I Continued

	HFR Hedge Fund Indices								Main Market Factors		
	Convertible Arbitrage	Distressed Securities	Event Driven	Equity Hedge	Equity Market Neutral	Merger Arbitrage	Global Macro	Relative Value	Russell 3000 Index	Return on LB bond Index	Δ in FRB Dollar Index
Panel C: Autocorrelation Test for Significance at Six Lags											
Ljung-Box test (1–6)	6.7	15.3*	8.8	4.8	16.7*	3.2	16.3*	7.5	–	–	–
p-value	0.35	0.02	0.19	0.57	0.01	0.79	0.01	0.28	–	–	–
Panel D: Jarque Bera Normality Test											
Jarque-Bera Test	747.8*	51.6*	18.5*	130.2*	0.8	277.6*	3.2	226.1*	–	–	–
p-value	0.00	0.00	0.00	0.00	0.68	0.00	0.20	0.00	–	–	–

Summary statistics for monthly data on filtered returns for eight HFR monthly hedge fund indices and three market factors used in the paper are reported below. The indices include Convertible Arbitrage, Distressed Securities, Event Driven, Equity Hedge, Equity Market Neutral, Merger Arbitrage, Global Macro, and Relative Value and are described more fully in Section II. The market factors are from Datastream and include the return on the Russell 3000 Index, the change in the Federal Reserve Bank competitiveness-weighted dollar index (the FRB Dollar Index), and the return on the Lehman Brothers U.S. Bond Index. The number of observations is 224. Correlations between the variables, the autocorrelations, as well as Jarque-Bera test statistics for normality are reported below the summary statistics. A * indicates significance at the 5% level.

The estimated co-dependence is plotted in a co-movement box, which is a square of unit side where the conditional probabilities are plotted against quantiles. When the plot of the conditional probability lies above (below) the 45° line, which represents the unconditional probability of no dependence between the variables, there is evidence of positive (negative) conditional co-movement between x_t and y_t. In our analysis, y_t represents the return on an individual hedge fund index, while x_t is the equally weighted average return on all other hedge fund indices. Results from the analysis are presented in Figure 1. To construct the figure, we calculate the probabilities at the 1st and 99th quantiles, as well as for

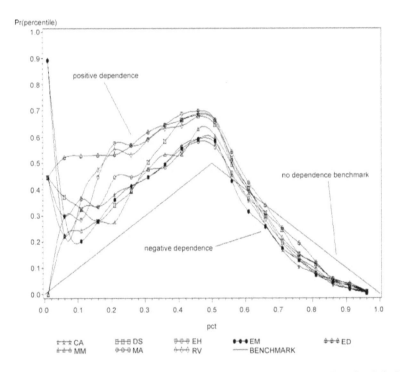

Figure 1 **Co-movement box: Relationship between individual hedge fund index performance and average of all other hedge fund indices.** The estimated co-dependence between the return on an individual hedge fund index and the equally weighted average return on all other hedge fund indices is estimated using a quantile regression approach, and the results are plotted in a co-movement box. This box is a square of unit side that plots the conditional probability that a hedge fund index has a return below or above a certain percentile conditional on the same event occurring in an equally weighted average of all other hedge funds. This plot of conditional probability is graphed for each index at 5th percentile increments. When the plot of the conditional probability lies above (below) the 45° line, which represents the unconditional probability of no dependence between the variables, there is evidence of positive (negative) co-movement between the two variables.

5% increments between the 5th and 95th quantiles. These results provide strong evidence that the conditional probability of a hedge fund index having a return in any quantile below the 50th percentile is increased significantly when the equally weighted index of other hedge fund returns is also below the same quantile. For example, at the 10th quantile, the Event Driven index has about a 55% probability of being in the 10th quantile when the equally weighted index of other hedge fund styles is also in the 10th quantile, compared to an unconditional probability of 10% if there were no dependence.

Importantly, this conditional probability for quantile returns above the 50th percentile is close to (and often lower than) the unconditional probability of no dependence. The co-movement box thus illustrates an asymmetry in the data: when returns are low, dependence among hedge fund indices increases but there is no corresponding increase when returns are high. Although the results hold for all indices, they are strongest for the Equity Hedge and Event Driven styles and weakest for the Equity Market Neutral style.

These results provide preliminary evidence of contagion among poor returns in hedge fund indices. However, it is difficult to interpret the statistical significance of this analysis. We next perform logit analyses to further test for contagion in the sense that we directly estimate the probability of an extreme return in a hedge fund style conditional on whether other hedge fund styles experience extreme returns.

C. Contagion Tests Using a Logit Model

For the logit model tests of contagion, we use a lower 10% cutoff of the overall distribution of returns to identify worst returns among hedge fund styles (i.e., returns that are in the bottom decile of all returns for an index's entire time series). Since there are 224 observations for each style, we have 23 worst returns for each style. A 5% cutoff gives only 11 observations, too few for a meaningful analysis, but the results from Figure 1 indicate that there is nothing special about the 10% cutoff in that we find strong evidence of clustering for all quantiles below the median. The logit model is a parametric test that addresses the issue of contagion by estimating whether a given hedge fund style is more likely to have a worst return when other styles also have worst returns. Logit models have been used extensively in the contagion literature (see, for instance, Eichengreen et al. (1996), and Bae et al. (2003)).

The dependent variable is an indicator variable set to one if the hedge fund index under study has a filtered return in the bottom decile of all returns for that index and zero otherwise. To measure the extent of clustering of worst returns, we add the variable COUNT, which is equal to the number of hedge fund styles— other than the style whose performance is under study—that have a worst return in the same month. A positive and significant coefficient on this variable indicates that worst returns for a particular style cluster with worst returns in the other styles. Results are presented in Table II.[8] The coefficients on COUNT are always

Table II Contagion Tests Using Filtered Return Data

	Convertible Arbitrage	Distressed Securities	Event Driven	Equity Hedge	Equity Market Neutral	Merger Arbitrage	Global Macro	Relative Value
Constant	-2.62***	-2.97***	-3 07***	-2.96***	-2.62***	-2.83***	-2.51***	-3.01***
	(-7.73)	(-7.91)	(-7.16)	(-5.82)	(-8.47)	(-7.16)	(-6.64)	(-8.90)
Other hedge fund index indicator variable								
COUNT	0.46***	0.73***	0.81***	0.73***	0.45***	0.63***	0.36*	0.77***
	(2.70)	(3.82)	(3.71)	(2.78)	(2.94)	(3.19)	(1.86)	(4.45)
R^2 MAX	7.7	18.1	20.3	16.4	8.0	13.8	4.5	20.5

The event of a worst return in each hedge fund style is separately modeled as the outcome of a binary variable and estimated as a logit regression. The independent variable is *COUNT*, which takes a value from zero to seven and is the number of other hedge fund indices that also have worst returns for the month. Below the coefficients are the *t*-statistics in parentheses. R^2 MAX is the scaled coefficient of determination suggested by Nagelkerke (1991). Coefficients with ***, **, and * are statistically significant at the 1%, 5%, and 10% levels, respectively.

positive and statistically significant, providing strong evidence that returns cluster across hedge fund styles. These results are consistent with the co-movement box from Figure 1.[9] In reaching this result, we attempt to explain hedge fund style worst returns using a large number of factors from the literature and controlling for autocorrelation in hedge fund returns, yet these factors do not explain the clustering we observe. As a result, we believe this clustering can be referred to as contagion, where contagion is defined as in Bekaert et al. (2005) as correlation over and above what one would expect based on fundamentals.

We also perform a test to assess the economic significance of our results in Table II. For each of the eight styles, we calculate the probability of observing an extreme negative return conditional on the various realizations of the *COUNT* variable (zero to seven) using the estimated coefficients from the logit regression analyses. The results indicate that when *COUNT* is set to zero, the average probability across the eight hedge fund styles of a worst return is about 6%. However, when *COUNT* is set to seven, the probability of a worst return averaged across hedge fund styles increases dramatically to above 70%.

Since we use hedge fund index data, one concern is that hedge funds might be misclassified in the indices. In this case, we could find that performance of indices is similar because some hedge funds pursue the same strategies even though they are classified into different styles. However, while this explanation could lead to an increase in return correlations across hedge fund indices, there is no reason to believe that this problem would cause contagion of worst returns. As a robustness test, we repeat all our analyses using the Credit Suisse/Tremont hedge fund indices.[10] The results are consistent with those obtained using the HFR database. Hence, we reject this explanation.

III. Channels of Hedge Fund Contagion

Figure 2 shows *COUNT8,* the number of hedge fund styles per month that have simultaneous worst returns over our sample period, using both the raw and the filtered return data. The figure has two striking features. First, the extent of clustering in worst returns during the recent financial crisis is dramatic. Second, the risk factors used in the filtering process explain some of the clustering. The extent of clustering in the recent financial crisis does not explain our results since we presented similar results in the first draft of this paper despite including hedge fund returns up to 2007 only. Besides the most recent crisis, the next two most important episodes of clustering in the figure are August 1998 (the Long Term Capital Management crisis) and April 2005 (the month immediately before Ford and GM lost their investment grade ratings).

To put the magnitude of the clustering of filtered returns into perspective, we conduct a Monte Carlo analysis using the correlations estimated from days without clustering and drawing 1,000 independent multivariate normal samples of eight series of 224 observations.[11] Based on these simulations, we find that our sample exhibits more clustering than we would expect, particularly for larger

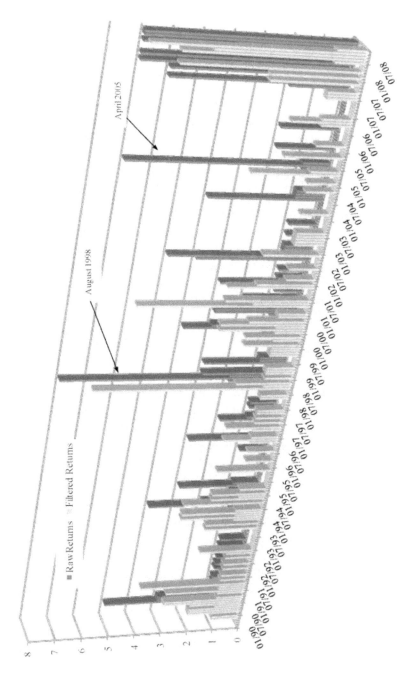

Figure 2 Number of hedge funds experiencing worst returns based on raw and filtered data.

values of *COUNT8*. Specifically, while we observe 20, 7, 6, 5, and 2 incidents with *COUNT8* equal to or larger than three, four, five, six, or seven, respectively, the Monte Carlo analysis indicates that we should expect to find 15.9, 4.6, 1.1, 0.2, and 0 incidents, respectively.

We are interested in identifying factors that explain the contagion we observe. Brunnermeier and Pedersen (2009) provide a theoretical framework from which to conduct our investigation. They argue that speculators, notably hedge funds, help smooth price fluctuations in markets that are caused by order imbalances across buyers and sellers by providing liquidity. In order to provide liquidity, speculators must finance their trades through collateralized borrowing from financiers, including commercial and investment banks. As a result, speculators can face funding liquidity constraints, either through higher margins, a decline in the value of the assets they hold, or both. For example, in the case of a liquidity shock, a financier may raise its margin rate, forcing the speculator to delever in a time of crisis, reducing prices and market liquidity even further (a margin liquidity spiral).[12] Concurrently, any large positions that the speculator holds will lose value, which can lead to margin calls at the now higher margin rate, causing further delevering in a weak market (a loss liquidity spiral). As a result, both funding liquidity and asset liquidity are diminished.

One implication of Brunnermeier and Pedersen (2009) is that liquidity has commonality across securities because shocks to funding liquidity (capital constraints) affect all securities in which speculators are marginal investors.[13] Empirically, there is support for the hypothesis that there is commonality in liquidity: Chordia et al. (2005) document commonality in stock and bond market liquidity; Acharya, Schaefer, and Zhang (2008) document an increase in co-movement in CDS spreads during the GM/Ford downgrade period when dealers faced liquidity shocks; and Coughenour and Saad (2004) show that commonality in liquidity across stocks is higher for stocks handled by NYSE specialist firms that face funding constraints. Another implication is that since most market makers have net long positions, liquidity will tend to dry up most quickly when markets perform poorly, and will have a stronger relationship with asset prices during these times than during normal times.

To test the predictions of Brunnermeier and Pedersen (2009) for hedge fund contagion, we identify seven contagion channel variables, that is, variables whose extreme adverse realizations are associated with a tightening of asset and hedge fund funding liquidity, and then test whether large adverse shocks to these variables can explain the hedge fund contagion we document. These variables include the Baa–10-year Treasury constant maturity yield spread (*CRSPRD*), the Treasury–Eurodollar (*TEDSPRD*) spread, the difference between overnight repo and reverse overnight repo volume (*REPO*), the liquidity measure of Chordia et al. (2005) (*STKLIQ*), a stock index for commercial banks (*BANK*), a stock index for prime brokers (*PBI*) and, finally, hedge fund redemptions (*FLOW*). The construction of these variables, their foundation in the literature, and their relationship to liquidity is detailed in Table III.

Table III Contagion Channel Variables

Variable and Source	Basis for Inclusion	Prior Literature Using This Variable	Relationship with Liquidity
CRSPRD: Change in Baa-10-year Constant Maturity Treasury credit spread from the Federal Reserve Board's website.	Increased spreads imply higher borrowing costs and/or counterparty risk.	Longstaff, Mithal, and Neis (2005), Dick-Nielsen, Feldhütter, and Lando (2009)	Inverse
TEDSPRD: Change in Treasury-Eurodollar (TED) spread from the Federal Reserve Board's website.	Increased spreads imply higher borrowing costs and/or higher credit risk.	Gupta and Subrahmanyam (2000), Campbell and Taksler (2003), Taylor and Williams (2009)	Inverse
REPO: Change in the difference between overnight repurchase and reverse repurchase volume since 1994, constructed using weekly data from John Kambhu and Tobias Adrian of the Federal Reserve Bank of New York.	Reduced volume indicates tighter availability of funding liquidity and low repo volume is related to hedge fund distress.	Kambhu (2006)	Direct
	Net repo volume is related to dealer leverage.	Adrian and Fleming (2005)	Direct
STKLIQ: Change in average round-trip cost of a trade on the NYSE within a month; calculated as the monthly average of daily changes of the NYSE stock market liquidity after removing deterministic day-of-the-week effects and effects related to changes in tick size. The daily changes are calculated from daily cross-sectional value-weighted averages of individual stock proportional bid-ask spreads.	Higher trading costs imply lower liquidity. Other common liquidity measures include Amihud (2002), Pástor and Stambaugh (2003), and Acharya and Pedersen (2005); we choose the measure based on recent work by Goyenko, Holden, and Trzcinka (2009) suggesting that bid-ask spreads are the most appropriate measure of liquidity.	Chordia et al. (2005), Goyenko et al. (2009)	Inverse

(*Continued*)

Table III Continued

Variable and Source	Basis for Inclusion	Prior Literature Using This Variable	Relationship with Liquidity
BANK: Monthly change in the equally weighted stock price index of large commercial banks from Datastream.	Shocks that decrease the financial strength of hedge fund intermediaries could be transmitted to hedge funds through increased margin requirements as they curtail their lending.	Chan et al. (2006)	Direct
PBI: Monthly change in the equally weighted stock price index of prime broker firms including Goldman Sachs, Morgan Stanley, Bear Stearns, UBS AG, Bank of America, Citigroup, Merrill Lynch, Lehman Brothers, Credit Suisse, Deutsche Bank, and Bank of New York Mellon, adjusted for mergers and including bankruptcy returns. Data are from CRSP.	Shocks that decrease the financial strength of hedge fund intermediaries could be transmitted to hedge funds through increased margin requirements as they curtail their lending.	N/A	Direct
FLOW: Monthly change in hedge fund outflows as a percentage of assets under management calculated from individual hedge fund data from Lipper TASS and matched to HFR index data based on style description. We use both contemporaneous $FLOW_t$ and one-month-ahead $FLOW_{t+1}$ since many hedge funds have redemption notice periods.	Redemption requests force hedge funds to liquidate more assets than required to meet redemptions if they are levered, and make it harder for hedge funds to borrow. Redemption requests may come about from poor performance, shifts in sentiment, or other reasons. An alternative to accepting redemption requests is to put up redemption gates, which are unpopular.	N/A	Direct

This table presents details on the contagion channel variables from Section III.

Table IV presents summary statistics for the liquidity proxies. For all variables, the number of observations is the same as for the hedge fund indices (with the exception of the percent change in repo volume, which is only available since August 1994 for 171 unfiltered or 169 filtered observations). To remove autocorrelation, each contagion channel variable is filtered using a univariate AR(1) model. The correlations between the variables are positive and significant among *CRSPRD, TEDSPRD,* and *STKLIQ* and between *PBI* and *BANK.* The high correlation between *PBI* and *BANK* is not too surprising, since the firms in these indices are all in the financial services industry. Correlations among the other variables are generally insignificant and the signs vary.

Also calculated, and reported in the Internet Appendix, are correlations between each of the hedge fund indices' filtered returns and the contagion channel variables. As would be expected, the correlations between *TEDSPRD, CRSPRD, FLOW,* and *STKLIQ* and hedge fund returns are generally negative, although fairly small and typically statistically insignificant. Similarly, the correlations between *PBI, BANK,* and *REPO* and hedge fund indices are generally positive. The correlations are never statistically significant for *BANK* and *REPO,* and are rarely significant for *PBI.* The correlation results using lagged realizations of the contagion channel variables are weaker for most measures, with the exception that the correlations between lagged *BANK* and the hedge fund indices are somewhat stronger.

To test whether large adverse shocks to liquidity can help explain hedge fund contagion, we create indicator variables for each of the seven contagion channel variables. These indicators are set to one if the contagion channel variable has a realization in its lowest (highest) quartile over the time series and zero otherwise for variables that are positively (negatively) related to liquidity shocks. To distinguish these variables from their continuous measures, we add the prefix *"IND"* (for indicator) to each. Hence, *INDPBI, INDFLOW$_t$, INDFLOW$_{t+1}$, INDBANK,* and *INDREPO* are set to one if the changes in their corresponding contagion channel variables are in the bottom 25% of all respective values, and *INDSTKLIQ, INDCRSPRD,* and *INDTEDSPRD* are set to one if the realizations are in the top 25% of all respective values.

To perform this analysis, we create a categorical dependent variable *OCCUR* that indicates the severity of contagion, estimate a multinomial logistic regression model following Bae et al. (2003), and then calculate the likelihood of observing each category of *OCCUR.*[14] We set *OCCUR$_t$* equal to zero in a given month *t*, which we call "base case" or "no" contagion, if zero or one hedge fund style indices have a worst return during the month; equal to one, which we call "low" contagion, if two or three hedge fund style indices have worst returns during the month; and equal to two, which we call "high" contagion, if four or more hedge fund style indices have worst returns during the month.

Since contemporaneous as well as lagged liquidity shocks could affect hedge fund returns, we investigate these effects in two separate tables. Regressions are performed separately for each contagion channel variable, for a total of seven

Table IV Summary Statistics for Filtered Contagion Channel Variables: January 1990 to October 2008

	Baa-10-year CMT Spread	TED Spread	CSS Liquidity Measure	Repo Volume	Contemporaneous Hedge Fund Flows	Bank Index	Prime Broker Index
Panel A: Summary Statistics							
Median	0.00	-0.61	-0.16	-0.05	-0.02	0.08	-0.14
Standard deviation	0.18	10.70	0.76	4.29	2.19	6.02	7.37
Skewness	1.67	1.84	2.38	0.26	-0.11	-0.54	-0.19
Excess kurtosis	11.53	10.29	9.32	0.61	16.11	2.03	1.46
Panel B: Correlations							
Baa-10y Treasury CMT Spread	1.00						
TED spread	0.27*	1.00					
CSS liquidity measure	0.37*	0.26*	1.00				
Repo Volume	-0.06	0.00	-0.10	1.00			
Contemporaneous Hedge fund flows	-0.19*	-0.11	-0.12	0.02	1.00		
Bank index	-0.15*	-0.04	-0.31*	0.01	0.06	1.00	
Prime broker index	-0.32*	-0.13*	-0.43*	0.02	0.05	0.78*	1.00
Panel C: Autocorrelation Test for Significance at Six Lags							
Ljung-Box test (1–6)	5.0	35.6*	14.0*	13.7*	10.5	4.6	5.2
p-value	0.54	0.00	0.03	0.03	0.11	0.59	0.52
Panel D: Jarque-Bera Normality Test							
Jarque-Bera test	1,283.3*	1,064.4*	978.9*	4.1	2,307.6*	46.5*	19.5*
p-value	0.00	0.00	0.00	0.13	0.00	0.00	0.00

Summary statistics for monthly data on seven contagion channel variables are described below. The variables include: the monthly percent change in the Baa-10-year CMT spread, the monthly percent change in the Treasury-Eurodollar (TED) spread, the monthly percent change in the Chordia et al. (2005) liquidity measure, the monthly percent change in repo volume, the monthly percent change in hedge fund flows as a percentage of assets (contemporaneous), the monthly returns from the Datastream Bank Index, and the monthly returns from the Prime Broker Index. The liquidity variables are filtered using an AR(1) approach. Further description of these variables is in Section III. The number of filtered observations is 224, except for repo volume, which is only available as of January 1994 and has 169 observations. Correlations between the variables are reported below the summary statistics. A * indicates significance at the 5% level.

regressions for each of the contemporaneous and lagged analyses. The seven regressions in Table V include the relevant continuous contemporaneous contagion channel variables, winsorized at the 25th percentile lower tail to avoid double counting extreme realizations, and the relevant *contemporaneous* measures of the channel indicator variable (for hedge fund flows, we include both $INDFLOW_t$ and $INDFLOW_{t+1}$, since, as we argued earlier, flows in the subsequent period are likely related to a tightening of funding liquidity in the current period). The seven regressions in Table VI are identical to the regressions in Table V except these regressions use the one-month *lagged* measure of the channel indicator variable instead of the contemporaneous measure (for the flow proxy, we include both $INDFLOW_{t-1}$ and $INDFLOW_t$). While we would prefer using decile realizations of these variables, using decile indicator variables in the multivariate setting creates quasi-complete separation problems in the regressions, so we resort to using quartiles. Finding a positive and significant coefficient on a contagion channel indicator variable means that the variable is associated with an increased probability that hedge fund worst returns exhibit contagion relative to the base case.

The multinomial logistic approach simultaneously estimates the parameters of the model for the low and high contagion categories of $OCCUR_t$ relative to the base case. The results in Table V provide evidence that several of the indicator variables are related to high levels of contagion. Specifically, the credit spread indicator variable ($INDCRSPRD_t$), the TED spread indicator variable ($INDTEDSPRD_t$), the contemporaneous and leading hedge fund flows indicator variables ($INDFLOW_{t+1}$ and $INDFLOW_t$), and the bank index indicator variable ($INDBANK_t$) all have positive and statistically significant coefficients for high realizations of the dependent variable, while the TED spread indicator variable ($INDTEDSPRD_t$) and the contemporaneous hedge fund flows indicator variable ($INDFLOW_t$) both have positive and significant coefficients for the low realizations of the dependent variable.

To understand the economic significance of these results, we perform the following analysis for each of the seven regression specifications (one for each contagion channel). We set the continuous contemporaneous contagion channel variable to its time-series mean and calculate the probability associated with each of the three possible realizations of $OCCUR_t$ (zero, one, or two representing no, low, or high contagion) conditional on the contagion channel indicator variable taking on either zero or one. We then calculate the change in the probability of each realization of $OCCUR_t$ when the contagion channel indicator variable changes from zero to one. For the above results that are statistically significant, the economic significance is as follows. A shock to the credit spread increases the probability of a high realization of $OCCUR_t$ from 1% to an impressive 15%. While a shock to the TED spread increases the probability of a low realization of $OCCUR_t$ from a 13% probability with no shock to a 23% probability with a shock, the same shock increases the probability of a high realization of $OCCUR_t$ from 2% to 7%. For a shock to hedge fund flows, the probability of a low realization of $OCCUR_t$ increases from 13% to 23%, and the probability of a high

Table *V* Liquidity Shocks and Hedge Fund Contagion, Contemporaneous Contagion Channel Variables

Dependent Variable: OCCUR

	Channel Variable = CRSPRD	Channel Variable = TEDSPRD	Channel Variable = STKLIQ	Channel Variable = REPO	Channel Variable = FLOW	Channel Variable = BANK	Channel Variable = PBI
Constant *(LOW)*	-1.66***	-1.99***	-1.70***	-1.72***	-1.95***	-1.86***	-1.88***
	(-9.40)	(-10.10)	(-7.64)	(-8.18)	(-10.91)	(-9.30)	(-9.65)
Constant *(HIGH)*	-4.89***	-3.91***	-3.14***	-3.01***	-4.53***	-3.99***	-3.60***
	(-6.79)	(-7.93)	(-6.51)	(-7.92)	(-8.04)	(-7.76)	(-8.23)
Winsorized Continuous Channel Variables							
Cont. Chan. Winsorized variable$_t$ *(LOW)*	-0.33	-0.04	-0.11	-0.07	0.09	0.07*	0.05
	(-0.24)	(-1.57)	(-0.22)	(-1.11)	(1.21)	(1.88)	(1.65)
Cont. Chan. Winsorized variable$_t$ *(HIGH)*	-5.72**	-0.01	1.62	-0.03	-0.07	0.18***	0.02
	(-1.96)	(-0.21)	(1.04)	(-0.26)	(-0.20)	(2.55)	(0.26)
Indicator Variables							
Indicator$_{t+1}$ *(LOW)*					0.23		
					(0.77)		
Indicator$_{t+1}$ *(HIGH)*					1.06*		
					(1.90)		

Indicator$_t$ (LOW)	-0.15	0.83**	-0.01	-0.50	0.68**	0.36	0.48
	(-0.41)	(2.31)	(-0.02)	(-1.02)	(2.10)	(0.88)	(1.26)
Indicator$_t$ (HIGH)	3.10***	1.64**	0.18	-0.69	1.86***	1.49*	0.99
	(3.33)	(2.10)	(0.23)	(-0.72)	(2.43)	(1.66)	(1.29)
Pseudo R^2	8.2	5.9	1.7	1.4	11.4	4.4	2.4

The co-occurrence of worst returns in hedge fund style indices is modeled as the outcome of a variable ($OCCUR_t$) that takes the value of zero if zero or one hedge fund indices have a worst return during a given month (*base case*), one if two or three hedge fund indices have a worst return during a given month (low), and two if four or more hedge fund indices have a worst return in a given month (high), and is estimated as a multinomial logistic regression. A monthly return is classified as a "worst return" if it belongs to the bottom 10% of all returns of that style. The regressions also include the continuous contagion channel variables (winsorized at the 25th percentile) and indicator variables corresponding to contemporaneous negative quartile realizations of the contagion channel variables. The contagion channel variables and their corresponding indicator variables include: the change in the Baa-10-year CMT Credit Spread (*CRSPRD*), the change in the Treasury-Eurodollar spread (*TEDSPRD*), the change in the Chordia et al. (2005) Liquidity Measure (*STKLIQ*), the change in Repo Volume (*REPO*), flows from other hedge funds, both contemporaneous and one month in the future (*FLOW*), the monthly change in the Datastream Bank Index (*BANK*), and the monthly change in the Prime Broker Index (PBI). The t-statistics are shown below the coefficients in parentheses. The pseudo R^2 is McFadden's likelihood ratio index. Coefficients with ***, **, and * are statistically significant at the 1%, 5%, and 10% levels, respectively.

Table VI Liquidity Shocks and Hedge Fund Contagion, Lagged Contagion Channel Variables

Dependent Variable: $OCCUR_t$

	Channel Variable = CRSPRD	Channel Variable = TEDSPRD	Channel Variable = STKLIQ	Channel Variable = REPO	Channel Variable = FLOW	Channel Variable = BANK	Channel Variable = PBI
Constant (LOW)	-1.56***	-1.96***	-1.63***	-1.91***	-1.85***	-2.02***	-1.85***
	(-1027)	(-11.68)	(-9.73)	(-9.62)	(-10.60)	(-11.09)	(-11.08)
Constant (HIGH)	-3.26***	-3.33***	-3.64***	-3.60***	-4.28***	-3.72***	-3.83***
	(-9.93)	(-10.44)	(-8.49)	(-824)	(-7.91)	(-9.38)	(-9.04)
Winsorized Continuous Channel Variables							
Cont. Chan. Winsorized variable$_t$ (LOW)	-1.21	0.01	-0.24	-0.05	0.12	0.04	0.02
	(-1.00)	(0.41)	(-0.58)	(-0.89)	(1.48)	(1.46)	(0.95)
Cont. Chan. Winsorized variable$_t$ (HIGH)	3.23	0.09	1.85*	0.01	-0.09	0.09*	-0.04
	(1.00)	(1.58)	(1.80)	(0.16)	(-024)	(1.69)	(-0.74)
Indicator Variables							
Indicator$_t$ (LOW)					0.86***		
					(2.63)		
Indicator$_t$ (HIGH)					2.00***		
					(2.43)		

212

Indicator$_{t-1}$ (LOW)	-0.80**	0.97***	-0.47	0.01	-0.45	0.96***	0.51*
	(-2.12)	(3.46)	(-1.30)	(0.02)	(-1.37)	(325)	(1.71)
Indicator$_{t-1}$ (HIGH)	0.23	0.50	1.53***	1.16*	0.29	0.96*	1.56***
	(0.38)	(0.84)	(2.66)	(1.87)	(0.51)	(1.61)	(2.74)
Pseudo R^2	3.4	7.1	6.4	2.9	10.8	8.4	5.6

The co-occurrence of worst returns in hedge fund style indices is modeled as the outcome of a variable ($OCCUR_t$) that takes the value of zero if zero or one hedge fund indices have a worst return during a given month (base case), one if two or three hedge fund indices have a worst return during a given month (low), and two if four or more hedge fund indices have a worst return in a given month (high), and is estimated as a multinomial logistic regression. A monthly return is classified as a "worst return" if it belongs to the bottom 10% of all returns of that style. The regressions also include the continuous contagion channel variables (winsorized at the 25th percentile) and indicator variables corresponding to lagged negative quartile realizations of the contagion channel variables. The contagion channel variables and their corresponding indicator variables include: the change in the Baa-10-year CMT Credit Spread ($CRSPRD$), the change in the Treasury-Eurodollar spread ($TEDSPRD$), the change in the Chordia et al. (2005) Liquidity Measure ($STKLIQ$), changes in Repo Volume ($REPO$), flows from other hedge funds both contemporaneous and one month in the future ($FLOW$), the monthly change in the Datastream Bank Index ($BANK$), and the monthly change in the Prime Broker Index (PBI). The t-statistics are shown below the coefficients in parentheses. The pseudo R^2 is McFadden's likelihood ratio index. Coefficients with ***, **, and * are statistically significant at the 1%, 5%, and 10% levels, respectively.

213

realization of $OCCUR_t$ increases from 1% to 13%. Finally, a shock to bank stock returns increases the probability of a high realization of $OCCUR_t$ from 2% to 7%. Clearly, these results for statistically significant coefficients are also economically relevant.

The exact timing of the impact of liquidity shocks is not known. It could be the case that a shock in month t takes place towards the end of the month, in which case it would mostly impact the probability of contagion in the next month. To account for this possibility, we also estimate the regressions of Table V lagging the contagion channel indicator variables. Table VI reports the results. Here, the TED spread indicator variable ($INDTEDSPRD_{t-1}$) and the bank index indicator variable ($INDBANK_{t-1}$) have positive and significant coefficients for the low realizations of $OCCUR_t$, while the coefficient on the stock illiquidity indicator variable ($INDSTKLIQ_{t-1}$) and the coefficient on the repo indicator variable ($INDREPO_{t-1}$) are each significant for the high realizations of $OCCUR_t$. Further, for both the low and the high realizations of $OCCUR_t$, the coefficients on the prime broker indicator variable are positive and significant. In sum, Tables V and VI indicate that all the contagion channel indicator variables have positive and statistically significant coefficients for at least one regression specification. We take this finding as strong evidence that shocks to asset liquidity and hedge fund funding liquidity are important in explaining hedge fund contagion.

We perform the same tests for economic significance for the lagged channel indicator variables as for the contemporaneous indicator variables. A lagged shock to the TED spread increases the probability of a low realization of $OCCUR_t$ from 12% to 26%. A shock to stock market liquidity (repo volume) in the previous month increases the probability of a high realization of $OCCUR_t$ from 1% to 7% (2% to 7%). A lagged shock to hedge fund flows increases the probability of a low realization of $OCCUR_t$ from 14% to 18%. Finally, a lagged shock to bank and prime broker stock returns increases the probability of low (high) realizations of $OCCUR_t$ from approximately 13% to around 20% (2% to around 6%). Again, these results for the statistically significant coefficients are economically relevant.

As robustness tests of our results and methodology, we perform several additional analyses, for which all results are reported in the Internet Appendix. We first repeat all analyses of the paper using raw returns rather than filtered returns. In these analyses we include the common risk factors from the filtering stage directly in the logit and multinomial logit analyses. The results are strongly consistent with and sometimes stronger than the results using filtered data. However, because using raw returns does not control for autocorrelation and common risk factors in the raw return data, we believe the results reported in the paper are more conservative. We next perform the multinomial logit analyses using the Credit Suisse/Tremont indices. These results are consistent with the HFR results. In a third test we repeat all the analyses in Tables V and VI using an OLS specification with the dependent variable taking a value ranging from zero to eight, which captures the number of hedge fund indices that experience worst returns (COUNT8). The results are broadly consistent with the multinomial regressions reported in Tables V and VI. As a fourth robustness test, we create a count variable for shocks to contagion channel variables (*LIQSHOCK6*) that equals the sum of the values of the channel indicator variables.[15] The Pearson (Spearman rank) correlation between *COUNT8* and *LIQSHOCK6* is 0.20 (0.09), significant at the 1% (19%) level.[16] We then estimate an OLS regression of *COUNT8* on the continuous liquidity variables and either the contemporaneous *LIQSHOCK6* or the lagged *LIQSHOCK6*. For the contemporaneous regression the coefficient on *LIQSHOCK6* is 0.29 with a *t*-statistic of 3.85, and for the lagged regression the coefficient on lagged *LIQSHOCK6* is 0.17 with a *t*-statistic of 2.80, indicating that shocks to a large number of contagion channel variables increase the probability of hedge fund contagion. Fifth, we repeat all our tests by splitting the sample period into two equal subperiods. The results from this analysis indicate that the coefficients are fairly stable over time, although perhaps not surprisingly, the statistical significance of the coefficients is generally stronger for the second half of the sample period. Finally, we perform a principal components analysis and extract eight principal components (PCs) from the filtered hedge fund return indices to determine whether these indices contain a common factor that we can interpret as a driver for clustering. We find that the first PC explains about 38% of the correlation between the indices with positive loadings for all styles, although the PC with the largest loading for each style varies across styles. We then perform a correlation analysis between the first PC and the continuous contagion channel variables and find that the first PC is negatively correlated with all but one of our contagion channel variables with an average of –0.07 and values ranging from –0.21 to 0.02. This result suggests that shocks to our liquidity variables are reflected to some extent in this common component of style returns. However, since we are interested in the effect of "large shock" events of the contagion channel variables on the probability of extreme negative returns, the low average correlation may simply confirm the known issue that correlations, on which the principal components analysis is based, are often poor measures of tail dependence.

An important concern with our contagion channel variables is that they could also be related to a flight to safety or panic effect. As investors become more risk averse, risk premia increase across a wide range of assets, which hurts hedge funds if hedge funds are net long on average. It is quite possible that such an effect could explain some of the success of our contagion channel variables. However, there are two limitations to this explanation for our results. First, there is little evidence of contagion from the main markets to hedge funds, but the panic explanation would imply such contagion. Second, the panic explanation would explain a contemporaneous effect much more than a lagged effect. The VIX index is sometimes used as a proxy for a panic effect. We estimate our multinomial regressions using the VIX as a channel variable. These results indicate that contemporaneous large shocks to the VIX significantly increase the probability of a low realization of *OCCUR*. Hence, these results suggest that our contagion channel variables measure something other than a panic factor for severe contagion when we use contemporaneous shocks, and for any type of contagion when we use lagged variables.

IV. Omitted Factor Tests

Though the prior analyses indicate strong evidence of hedge fund contagion, it could be the case that the models used in the literature to explain hedge fund returns might omit one or more relevant factors. If this is the case, then the inclusion of the omitted factors might preclude or weaken our finding of hedge fund contagion. While it is impossible to identify all potential omitted factors, our multinomial logit analysis that links contagion channel variables to hedge fund contagion, as well as prior literature by Amihud (2002), Pástor and Stambaugh (2003), Acharya and Pedersen (2005), Chordia et al. (2005), and Sadka (2010), among others, that proposes liquidity as a possible risk factor provide a starting point. In this section, we test (and report in the Internet Appendix) whether including in the filtering process the contagion channel variables themselves (as opposed to the shocks to the channel variables that we use in the multinomial logit model) changes our results.

To do so, we first repeat the filtering analysis including the continuous measures of the contagion channel variables. Since the credit spread measure is already included in the filtering analysis, as it is one of the Fung and Hsieh (2004) factors, and since the *REPO* volume is only available as of August 1994, we add the other five channel variables (*TEDSPRD, STKLIQ, BANK, PBI,* and *FLOW*). The results indicate that the coefficients on *BANK, PBI, STKLIQ,* and *FLOW* are inconsistent in sign and rarely significant, while the coefficient on *TEDSPRD* is negative and significant in five of the eight regression specifications, providing evidence that an increase in the TED spread is negatively related to hedge fund performance. Hence, it is possible that the TED spread is an omitted factor in our filtering analysis.

We next use the residuals from this analysis in a logit model to test for hedge fund contagion. The results indicate that six of the eight coefficients on the *COUNT* variable remain significant, still providing strong evidence of contagion consistent with the results presented in Table II. Finally, we re-run the multinomial analysis of contagion as in Tables V and VI. Since the contagion channel variables are included in the filtering process, they are not included in the multinomial logit analysis to avoid double counting. Results from the multinomial analysis presented in the Internet Appendix provide strong evidence that shocks to contagion channel variables are positively correlated with hedge fund contagion, consistent with the results in Tables V and VI. The only possible exception is for shocks to the TED spread. The results from Tables V and VI (where the filtering process does not include the contagion channel variables) indicate that the coefficient on the TED spread shock indicator variable is positive and significant for three of the four analyses performed: for the low and high cases of the contemporaneous shock analysis in Table V and for the low case of the lagged shock in Table VI. By contrast, the results in the Internet Appendix, where the filtering process does include the contagion channel variables, indicate that shocks to the TED spread are significant in only one of the four cases: the high case for the lagged shock variable.

Hence, the results from this section indicate that although one of the contagion channel variables, the TED spread, appears to be a possible omitted factor in the filtering regression, its inclusion does not change the main results of the paper that hedge funds exhibit contagion and that this contagion is linked to shocks in contagion channel variables.

V. Implications and Conclusions

In this paper, we use quantile, binomial logit, and multinomial logit regression models to study contagion among worst returns in the hedge fund industry. We define contagion following Bekaert et al. (2005) as correlation that cannot be explained by economic fundamentals. We seek to answer the following questions. First, when we control for common risk factors in hedge fund performance, is there evidence of contagion among worst returns of hedge fund styles? Second, is this contagion in worst returns systematically linked to shocks to liquidity?

To answer these questions, the first part of the paper performs a filtering analysis where hedge fund index returns are regressed against a number of common risk factors in an AR(1) model that also controls for autocorrelation in hedge fund returns. We then use the residuals from these filtering models to study contagion across hedge fund indices using both a quantile regression approach and a logit model. Results from both of these analyses indicate very strong evidence of contagion in hedge fund returns. Given these results, the second part of the paper examines whether this contagion is linked to shocks in liquidity, as in the model of Brunnermeier and Pedersen (2009). In their model, shocks to asset liquidity can lead to funding constraints that force hedge funds to reduce their leverage. As a result of this deleveraging, asset liquidity worsens, which leads to further deleveraging. Alternatively, a shock to funding liquidity leads to deleveraging, which reduces asset liquidity. These spirals affect all assets for which hedge funds are the marginal investors, not only the assets affected directly by the initial shock. Therefore, their model explains contagion.

Based on their model, we perform a multinomial logit analysis and show that liquidity shocks to a number of contagion channel variables help explain the hedge fund contagion we document. One possible alternative explanation for this result is that liquidity itself is a risk factor in hedge fund performance, and that its inclusion in models explaining hedge fund returns could explain the existence of hedge fund contagion. We test this idea and find little evidence to support it. Thus, we conclude that while small changes to liquidity are not associated with hedge fund contagion, large shocks to liquidity are associated with it. Further, hedge funds appear to share a common exposure to large liquidity shocks, and existing models used to explain hedge fund returns do not capture this exposure.

We wish to thank Nick Bollen, Stephen Brown, William Greene, Cam Harvey, David Hsieh, Andrew Karolyi, Andy Lo, Marno Verbeek, an Associate Editor, two referees, and participants at seminars and conferences at the CREST-Banque de France conference on contagion, the ECB, the FDIC, Imperial College, Maastricht University, The Ohio State University, RSM Erasmus University, UCLA, the 2009 AFA annual meeting, the 2009 WFA annual meeting, Villanova University, and Wharton for useful comments. We are also grateful to Rose Liao and Jerome Taillard for research assistance. We thank Lisa Martin at Hedge Fund Research for assistance regarding her firm's products.

Notes

1 See Brunnermeier (2009).
2 See www.hedgefundresearch.com for definitions of each style category.
3 See Fung and Hsieh (2009).
4 An Internet Appendix for this article is available online in the "Supplements and Datasets" section at http://www.afajof.org/supplements.asp.
5 See, for example, Fung and Hsieh (1997, 1999, 2001, 2004), Ackermann, McEnally, and Ravenscraft (1999), Liang (2004), Mitchell and Pulvino (2001), and Agarwal and Naik (2004).
6 Much of the following description of the model follows Cappiello et al. (2005). For further detail on quantile regressions and the co-movement box, see Cappiello et al. (2005).
7 Co-exceedance occurs when both random variables exceed a pre-specified threshold (i.e., quantile).
8 We relax the distributional assumptions underlying the logit models and allow for overdispersion by adjusting the standard errors when estimating the regressions.
9 As a robustness check, we also perform an analysis that includes as an independent variable the 10% winsorized equally weighted return on all other hedge fund indices except the index under study. We also include indicator variables based on the main market variables from the filtering exercise (stocks, bonds, and currencies) that are set to one if the main market variable has a 10% negative tail return, and we include measures of volatility from the main markets since prior literature suggests that volatility itself may be related to clustering. Coefficients on the main market indicator variables are not consistent in sign or significance, indicating no evidence of contagion from main markets to hedge funds. Also, coefficients on the volatility variables and the equally weighted hedge fund variable are rarely significant. Most important, seven of the eight coefficients on the *COUNT* variable remain positive and statistically significant at the 5% level. These results are available in the Internet Appendix.
10 The Credit Suisse/Tremont index family does not contain a separate relative value strategy. Further, the Credit Suisse/Tremont indices only date back to 1994 and are value-weighted. We therefore restrict this analysis to seven hedge fund styles and the period January 1994 to October 2008. Summary statistics and logit results from the Credit Suisse/Tremont index analysis are presented in the Internet Appendix.
11 We recognize that our return series are not normally distributed. Our results should thus be interpreted with this in mind.
12 Brunnermeier and Pedersen (2009) note that the liquidity shock could be caused by a shock to liquidity demand, fundamentals, or volatility.
13 In addition, a large literature shows that shocks to liquidity and liquidity risk affect asset returns and that there is co-movement in liquidity and liquidity risk across asset classes (e.g., Amihud and Mendelson (1986), Amihud (2002), Pástor and Stambaugh (2003), Chordia et al. (2005), and Acharya and Pedersen (2005)).
14 For a general exposition on multinomial logistic regression models see, for example, Maddala (1986) or Hosmer and Lemeshow (1989).

15 We exclude *REPO* from this analysis because it is only available since 1994. Results including *REPO* are similar.

16 We also create a categorical contagion channel variable (*LIQOCCUR*) that takes on a value of zero if zero or one of the contagion channel variables has an extreme shock, one if two or three of the contagion channel variables have an extreme shock, and two if four or more contagion channel variables have an extreme shock and perform a correlation test between this variable and the *OCCUR* variable used in the paper. This Pearson (Spearman rank) correlation is 0.17 (0.11) and significant at the 1% (11%) level.

REFERENCES

Acharya, Viral V., and Lasse H. Pedersen, 2005, Asset pricing with liquidity risk, *Journal of Financial Economics* 77, 375–410.

Acharya, Viral V., Stephen M. Schaefer, and Yili Zhang, 2008, Liquidity risk and correlation risk: A clinical study of the General Motors and Ford downgrade of 2005, Working paper, London Business School.

Ackermann, Carl, Richard McEnally, and David Ravenscraft, 1999, The performance of hedge funds: Risks, returns, and incentives, *Journal of Finance* 54, 833–874.

Adrian, Tobias, and Markus K. Brunnermeier, 2009, CoVar, Working paper, Princeton University.

Adrian, Tobias, and Michael J. Fleming, 2005, What financing data reveal about dealer leverage, *Current Issues in Economics and Finance* 11, 1–7.

Agarwal, Vikas, and Narayan J. Naik, 2004, Risk and portfolio decisions involving hedge funds, *Review of Financial Studies* 17, 63–98.

Amihud, Yakov, 2002, Illiquidity and stock returns: Cross-section and time-series effects, *Journal of Financial Markets* 5, 31–56.

Amihud, Yakov, and Haim Mendelson, 1986, Asset pricing and the bid-ask spread, *Journal of Financial Economics* 17, 223–249.

Bae, Kee Hong, G. Andrew Karolyi, and René M. Stulz, 2003, A new approach to measuring financial contagion, *Review of Financial Studies* 16, 717–764.

Bekaert, Geert, Campbell R. Harvey, and Angela Ng, 2005, Market integration and contagion, *Journal of Business* 78, 39–69.

Billio, Monica, Mila Getmansky, and Loriana Pelizzon, 2009, Crises and hedge fund risk, Working paper, University of Massachusetts.

Brunnermeier, Markus K., 2009, Deciphering the 2007–2008 liquidity and credit crunch, *Journal of Economic Perspectives* 23, 77–100.

Brunnermeier, Markus K., and Lasse Heje Pedersen, 2009, Market liquidity and funding liquidity, *Review of Financial Studies* 22, 2201–2238.

Campbell, John Y., and Glen B. Taksler, 2003, Equity volatility and corporate bond yields, *Journal of Finance* 58, 2321–2350.

Cappiello, Lorenzo, Bruno Gérard, and Simon Manganelli, 2005, Measuring comovements by regression quantiles, Working paper 501, European Central Bank.

Chan, Kevin Nicholas, Mila Getmansky, Shane Haas, and Andrew W. Lo, 2006, Systemic risk and hedge funds, in Mark Carey, and René M. Stulz, eds.: *The Risks of Financial Institutions* (University of Chicago Press, Chicago, IL).

Chordia, Tarun, Asani Sarkar, and Avinidhar Subrahmanyam, 2005, An empirical analysis of stock and bond market liquidity, *Review of Financial Studies* 18, 85–129.

Coughenour, Jay F., and Mohsen Saad, 2004, Common market makers and commonality in liquidity, *Journal of Financial Economics* 73, 37–70.

Dick-Nielsen, Jens, Peter Feldhütter, and David Lando, 2009, Corporate bond liquidity before and after the onset of the subprime crisis, Working paper, Copenhagen Business School.

Dudley, Evan, and Mahendrarajah Nimalendran, 2009, Liquidity spirals and hedge fund contagion, Unpublished working paper, University of Florida, Gainesville, FL.

Eichengreen, Barry, Andrew Rose, and Charles Wyplosz, 1996, Contagious currency crises: First tests, *Scandinavian Journal of Economics* 98, 463–484.

Engle, Robert F., and Simone Manganelli, 2004, CAViaR: Conditional autoregressive value at risk by regression quantiles, *Journal of Business and Economic Statistics* 22, 367–381.

Fama, Eugene F., and Kenneth R. French, 1993, Common risk factors in the returns on stocks and bonds, *Journal of Financial Economics* 33, 3–56.

Fung, William, and David A. Hsieh, 1997, Empirical characteristics of dynamic trading strategies, *Review of Financial Studies* 10, 275–302.

Fung, William, and David A. Hsieh, 1999, A primer on hedge funds, *Journal of Empirical Finance* 6, 309–331.

Fung, William, and David A. Hsieh, 2001, The risk in hedge fund strategies: Theory and evidence from trend followers, *Review of Financial Studies* 10, 313–341.

Fung, William, and David A. Hsieh, 2004, Hedge fund benchmarks: A risk-based approach, *Financial Analyst Journal* 60, 65–80.

Fung, William, and David. A. Hsieh, 2009, Perspectives: Measurement biases in hedge fund performance data, *Financial Analysts Journal* 65, 36–38.

Goyenko, Ruslan Y., Craig W. Holden, and Charles A. Trzcinka, 2009, Do liquidity measures measure liquidity? *Journal of Financial Economics* 92, 153–181.

Gupta, Anurag, and Marti G. Subrahmanyam, 2000, An empirical examination of the convexity bias in the pricing of interest rate swaps, *Journal of Financial Economics* 55, 239–279.

Hosmer, David W., and Stanley Lemeshow, 1989, *Applied Logistic Regression* (John Wiley and Sons, Hoboken, NJ).

Kambhu, John, 2006, Trading risk, market liquidity, and convergence trading in the interest rate swap spread, *FRBNY Economic Policy Review* 12, 1–13.

Klaus, Benjamin, and Bronka Rzepkowski, 2009, Risk spillovers among hedge funds: The role of redemptions and fund failures, European Central Bank working paper no. 1112.

Koenker, Roger, and Gilbert Bassett, 1978, Regression quantiles, *Econometrica* 46, 33–50.

Liang, Bing, 2004, Alternative investments: CTAs, hedge funds, and funds-of-funds, *Journal of Investment Management* 3, 76–93.

Longstaff, Francis A., Sanjay Mithal, and Eric Neis, 2005, Corporate yield spreads: Default risk or liquidity? New evidence from the credit default swap market, *Journal of Finance* 60, 2213–2253.

Maddala, G.S., 1986, *Limited Dependent and Qualitative Variables in Econometrics* (Cambridge University Press, Cambridge).

Mitchell, Mark L., and Todd C. Pulvino, 2001, Characteristics of risk and return in risk arbitrage, *Journal of Finance* 56, 2135–2175.

Nagelkerke, N. J. D, 1991, A note on a general definition of the coefficient of determination, *Biometrika* 78, 691–692.

Pástor, Lubos, and Robert F. Stambaugh, 2003, Liquidity risk and expected returns, *Journal of Political Economy* 111, 642–685.

Sadka, Ronnie, 2010, Liquidity risk and the cross-section of hedge fund returns, *Journal of Financial Economics* (forthcoming).

Taylor, John B., and John C. Williams, 2009, A black swan in the money market, *American Economic Journal: Macroeconomics* 1, 58–83.

55

MARKET LIQUIDITY AND FUNDING LIQUIDITY

Markus K. Brunnermeier and Lasse Heje Pedersen

Source: *Review of Financial Studies* 22, 6, 2009, 2201–2238.

We provide a model that links an asset's market liquidity (i.e., the ease with which it is traded) and traders' funding liquidity (i.e., the ease with which they can obtain funding). Traders provide market liquidity, and their ability to do so depends on their availability of funding. Conversely, traders' funding, i.e., their capital and margin requirements, depends on the assets' market liquidity. We show that, under certain conditions, margins are destabilizing and market liquidity and funding liquidity are mutually reinforcing, leading to liquidity spirals. The model explains the empirically documented features that market liquidity (i) can suddenly dry up, (ii) has commonality across securities, (iii) is related to volatility, (iv) is subject to "flight to quality," and (v) co-moves with the market. The model provides new testable predictions, including that speculators' capital is a driver of market liquidity and risk premiums.

Trading requires capital. When a trader (e.g., a dealer, hedge fund, or investment bank) buys a security, he can use the security as collateral and borrow against it, but he cannot borrow the entire price. The difference between the security's price and collateral value, denoted as the margin or haircut, must be financed with the trader's own capital. Similarly, short-selling requires capital in the form of a margin; it does not free up capital. Therefore, the total margin on all positions cannot exceed a trader's capital at any time.

Our model shows that the funding of traders affects—and is affected by—market liquidity in a profound way. When funding liquidity is tight, traders become reluctant to take on positions, especially "capital intensive" positions in high-margin securities. This lowers market liquidity, leading to higher volatility. Further, under certain conditions, low future market liquidity increases the risk of financing a trade, thus increasing margins. Based on the links between funding and market liquidity, we provide a unified explanation for the main empirical features of market liquidity. In particular, our model implies that market liquidity (i) can suddenly dry up, (ii) has commonality across securities, (iii) is related to volatility, (iv) is subject to "flight to quality," and (v) co-moves with the market. The model has several new testable implications that link margins and dealer funding to market liquidity: We predict that (i) speculators' (mark-to-market) capital and volatility (as, e.g., measured by VIX) are state variables affecting market liquidity and risk premiums; (ii) a reduction in capital reduces market liquidity, especially if capital is already low (a nonlinear effect) and for high-margin securities; (iii) margins increase in illiquidity if the fundamental value is difficult to determine; and (iv) speculators' returns are negatively skewed (even if they trade securities without skewness in the fundamentals).

Our model is similar in spirit to Grossman and Miller (1988) with the added feature that speculators face the real-world funding constraint discussed above. In our model, different customers have offsetting demand shocks, but arrive sequentially to the market. This creates a temporary order imbalance. Speculators smooth price fluctuations, thus providing market liquidity. Speculators finance their trades through collateralized borrowing from financiers who set the margins to control their value-at-risk (VaR). Since financiers can reset margins in each period, speculators face funding liquidity risk due to the risk of higher margins or losses on existing positions. We derive the competitive equilibrium of the model and explore its liquidity implications. We define market liquidity as the difference between the transaction price and the fundamental value, and funding liquidity as speculators' scarcity (or shadow cost) of capital.

We first analyze the properties of margins, which determine the investors' capital requirement. We show that margins can increase in illiquidity when margin-setting financiers are unsure whether price changes are due to fundamental news or to liquidity shocks, and volatility is time varying. This happens when a liquidity shock leads to price volatility, which raises the financier's expectation about future volatility, and this leads to increased margins. Figure 1 shows that margins did increase empirically for S&P 500 futures during the liquidity crises of 1987, 1990, 1998, and 2007. More generally, the October 2007 IMF Global Stability Report documents a significant widening of the margins across most asset classes during the summer of 2007. We denote margins as "destabilizing" if they can increase in illiquidity, and note that anecdotal evidence from prime brokers suggests that margins often behave in this way. Destabilizing margins force speculators to de-lever their positions in times of crisis, leading to pro-cyclical market liquidity provision.[1]

In contrast, margins can theoretically decrease with illiquidity and thus can be "stabilizing." This happens when financiers know that prices diverge due to temporary market illiquidity and know that liquidity will be improved shortly as complementary customers arrive. This is because a current price divergence from fundamentals provides a "cushion" against future adverse price moves, making the speculators' position less risky in this case.

Turning to the implications for market liquidity, we first show that, as long as speculators' capital is so abundant that there is no risk of hitting the funding

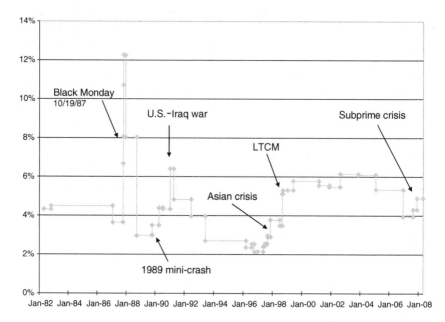

Figure 1 Margins for S&P 500 futures. The figure shows margin requirements on S&P 500 futures for members of the Chicago Mercantile Exchange as a fraction of the value of the underlying S&P 500 index multiplied by the size of the contract. (Initial or maintenance margins are the same for members.) Each dot represents a change in the dollar margin.

constraint, market liquidity is naturally at its highest level and is insensitive to marginal changes in capital and margins. However, when speculators hit their capital constraints—or risk hitting their capital constraints over the life of a trade—then they reduce their positions and market liquidity declines. At that point prices are more driven by funding liquidity considerations rather than by movements in fundamentals, as was apparent during the quant hedge fund crisis in August 2007, for instance.

When margins are destabilizing or speculators have large existing positions, there can be multiple equilibria and liquidity can be *fragile*. In one equilibrium, markets are liquid, leading to favorable margin requirements for speculators, which in turn helps speculators make markets liquid. In another equilibrium, markets are illiquid, resulting in larger margin requirements (or speculator losses), thus restricting speculators from providing market liquidity. Importantly, any equilibrium selection has the property that small speculator losses can lead to a discontinuous drop of market liquidity. This "sudden dry-up" or fragility of market liquidity is due to the fact that with high levels of speculator capital, markets must be in a liquid equilibrium, and, if speculator capital is reduced enough, the market must eventually switch to a low-liquidity/high-margin equilibrium.[2] The events following the Russian default and LTCM collapse in 1998 are a vivid example of fragility of liquidity since a relatively small shock had a large impact. Compared to the total market capitalization of the U.S. stock and bond markets, the losses due to the Russian default were minuscule but, as Figure 1 shows, caused a shiver in world financial markets. Similarly, the subprime losses in 2007–2008 were in the order of several hundred billion dollars, corresponding to only about 5% of overall stock market capitalization. However, since they were primarily borne by levered financial institutions with significant maturity mismatch, spiral effects amplified the crisis so, for example, the overall stock market losses amounted to more than 8 trillion dollars as of this writing (see Brunnermeier 2009).

Further, when markets are illiquid, market liquidity is highly sensitive to further changes in funding conditions. This is due to two liquidity spirals, as illustrated in Figure 2. First, a *margin spiral* emerges if margins are increasing in market illiquidity. In this case, a funding shock to the speculators lowers market liquidity, leading to higher margins, which tightens speculators' funding constraint further, and so on. For instance, Figure 1 shows how margins gradually escalated within a few days after Black Monday in 1987. The subprime crisis that started in 2007 led to margin increases at the end of August and end of November 2007 for the S&P futures contract. For other assets, margins and haircuts widened significantly more (see, for example, IMF Global Stability Report, October 2007). The margin spiral forces traders to de-lever during downturns and recently, Adrian and Shin (2009) found consistent evidence for investment banks. Second, a *loss spiral* arises if speculators hold a large initial position that is negatively correlated with customers' demand shock. In this case, a funding shock increases market illiquidity, leading to speculator losses on their initial position, forcing speculators to sell more, causing a further price drop, and so on.[3] These liquidity spirals

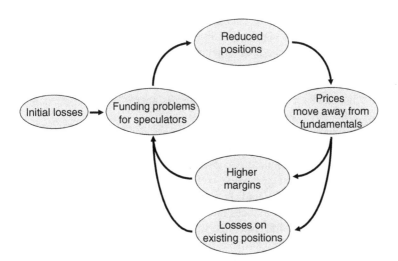

Figure 2 Liquidity spirals. The figure shows the loss spiral and the margin/haircut spiral.

reinforce each other, implying a larger total effect than the sum of their separate effects. Paradoxically, liquidity spirals imply that a larger shock to the customers' demand for immediacy leads to a reduction in the provision of immediacy during such times of stress. Consistent with our predictions, Mitchell, Pedersen, and Pulvino (2007) find significant liquidity-driven divergence of prices from fundamentals in the convertible bond markets after capital shocks to the main liquidity providers, namely convertible arbitrage hedge funds. Also, Garleanu, Pedersen, and Poteshman (2008) document that option market makers' unhedgeable risk is priced, especially in times following recent losses.

In the cross section, we show that the ratio of illiquidity to margin is the same across all assets for which speculators provide market liquidity. This is the case since speculators optimally invest in securities that have the greatest expected profit (i.e., illiquidity) per capital use (determined by the asset's dollar margin). This common ratio is determined in equilibrium by the speculators' funding liquidity (i.e., capital scarcity). Said differently, a security's market illiquidity is the product of its margin and the shadow cost of funding. Our model thus provides a natural explanation for the *commonality* of liquidity across assets since shocks to speculators' funding constraint affect all securities. This may help explain why market liquidity is correlated across stocks (Chordia, Roll, and Subrahmanyam 2000; Hasbrouck and Seppi 2001; and Huberman and Halka 2001), and across stocks and bonds (Chordia, Sarkar, and Subrahmanyam 2005). In support of the idea that commonality is driven at least in part by our funding-liquidity mechanism, Chordia, Roll, and Subrahmanyam (2005) find that "money flows . . . account for part of the commonality in stock and bond market liquidity." Moreover, their finding that "during crisis periods, monetary expansions are associated with increased liquidity" is consistent with our model's prediction that the effects are largest when traders are near their constraint. Acharya, Schaefer, and Zhang (2008) document a substantial increase in the co-movement among credit default swaps (CDS) during the GM/Ford rating downgrade in May 2005 when dealer funding was stretched. Coughenour and Saad (2004) provide further evidence of the funding-liquidity mechanism by showing that the co-movement in liquidity among stocks handled by the same NYSE specialist firm is higher than for other stocks, commonality is higher for specialists with less capital, and decreases after a merger of specialists.

Next, our model predicts that market liquidity declines as fundamental volatility increases, which is consistent with the empirical findings of Benston and Hagerman (1974) and Amihud and Mendelson (1989).[4] Further, the model can shed new light on "flight to quality," referring to episodes in which risky securities become especially illiquid. In our model, this happens when speculators' capital deteriorates, which induces them to mostly provide liquidity in securities that do not use much capital (low-volatility stocks with lower margins), implying that the liquidity differential between high-volatility and low-volatility securities increases. This capital effect means that illiquid securities are predicted to have more liquidity risk.[5] Recently, Comerton-Forde, Hendershott, Jones, Moulton and

Seasholes (2008) test these predictions using inventory positions of NYSE specialists as a proxy for funding liquidity. Their findings support our hypotheses that market liquidity of high-volatility stocks is more sensitive to inventory shocks and that this is more pronounced at times of low funding liquidity. Moreover, Pastor and Stambaugh (2003) and Acharya and Pedersen (2005) document empirical evidence consistent with flight to liquidity and the pricing of this liquidity risk.

Market-making firms are often net long in the market. For instance, Ibbotson (1999) reports that security brokers and speculators have median market betas in excess of one. Therefore, capital constraints are more likely to be hit during market downturns, and this, together with the mechanism outlined in our model, helps to explain why sudden liquidity dry-ups occur more often when markets decline. Further, capital constraints affect the liquidity of all securities, leading to co-movement as explained above. The fact that this effect is stronger in down markets could explain that co-movement in liquidity is higher during large negative market moves, as documented empirically by Hameed, Kang, and Viswanathan (2005).

Finally, the very risk that the funding constraint becomes binding limits speculators' provision of market liquidity. Our analysis shows that speculators' optimal (funding) risk management policy is to maintain a "safety buffer." This affects initial prices, which increase in the covariance of future prices with future shadow costs of capital (i.e., with future funding illiquidity).

Our paper is related to several literatures.[6] Traders rely both on (equity) investors and counterparties, and, while the limits to arbitrage literature following Shleifer and Vishny (1997) focuses on the risk of investor redemptions, we focus on the risk that counterparty funding conditions may worsen. Other models with margin-constrained traders are Grossman and Vila (1992) and Liu and Longstaff (2004), which derive optimal strategies in a partial equilibrium with a single security; Chowdhry and Nanda (1998) focus on fragility due to dealer losses; and Gromb and Vayanos (2002) derive a general equilibrium with one security (traded in two segmented markets) and study welfare and liquidity provision. We study the endogenous variation of margin constraints, the resulting amplifying effects, and differences across high- and low-margin securities in our setting with multiple securities. Stated simply, whereas the above-cited papers use a fixed or decreasing margin constraint, say, $5000 per contract, we study how market conditions lead to changes in the margin requirement itself, e.g., an increase from $5000 to $15,000 per futures contract as happened in October 1987, and the resulting feedback effects between margins and market conditions as speculators are forced to de-lever.

We proceed as follows. We describe the model (Section 1) and derive our four main new results: (i) margins increase with market illiquidity when financiers cannot distinguish fundamental shocks from liquidity shocks and fundamentals have time-varying volatility (Section 2); (ii) this makes margins destabilizing, leading to sudden liquidity dry-ups and margin spirals (Section 3); (iii) liquidity crises simultaneously affect many securities, mostly risky high-margin securities, resulting in commonality of liquidity and flight to quality (Section 4); and (iv) liquidity risk matters even before speculators hit their capital constraints (Section 5). Then we outline how our model's new testable predictions may be helpful for a novel line of empirical work that links measures of speculators' funding conditions to measures of market liquidity (Section 6). Section 7 concludes. Finally, we describe the real-world funding constraints for the main liquidity providers, namely market makers, banks, and hedge funds (Appendix A), and provide proofs (Appendix B).

1. Model

The economy has J risky assets, traded at times $t = 0, 1, 2, 3$. At time $t=3$, each security j pays off v^j, a random variable defined on a probability space $(\Omega, \mathcal{F}, \mathcal{P})$. There is no aggregate risk because the aggregate supply is zero and the risk-free interest rate is normalized to zero, so the fundamental value of each stock is its conditional expected value of the final payoff $v_t^j = E_t[v^j]$. Fundamental volatility has an autoregressive conditional heteroscedasticity (ARCH) structure. Specifically, v_t^j evolves according to

$$v_{t+1}^j = v_t^j + \Delta v_{t+1}^j = v_t^j + \sigma_{t+1}^j \varepsilon_{t+1}^j,\tag{1}$$

where all ε_t^j are i.i.d. across time and assets with a standard normal cumulative distribution function Φ with zero mean and unit variance, and the volatility σ_t^j has dynamics

$$\sigma_{t+1}^j = \underline{\sigma}^j + \theta^j \left| \Delta v_t^j \right|,\tag{2}$$

where $\underline{\sigma}^j, \theta^j \geq 0$. A positive θ^j implies that shocks to fundamentals increase future volatility.

There are three groups of market participants: "customers" and "speculators" trade assets while "financiers" finance speculators' positions. The group of customers consists of three risk-averse agents. At time 0, customer $k = 0, 1, 2$ has a cash holding of W_0^k bonds and zero shares, but finds out that he will experience an endowment shock of $z^k = \{z^{1,k}, \ldots, z^{J,k}\}$ shares at time $t=3$, where z are random variables such that the aggregate endowment shock is zero, $\sum_{k=0}^2 z^{j,k} = 0$.

With probability $(1-a)$, all customers arrive at the market at time 0 and can trade securities in each time period 0, 1, 2. Since their aggregate shock is zero, they can share risks and have no need for intermediation.

The basic liquidity problem arises because customers arrive sequentially with probability a, which gives rise to order imbalance. Specifically, in this case customer 0 arrives at time 0, customer 1 arrives at time 1, and customer 2 arrives at time 2. Hence, at time 2 all customers are present, at time 1 only customers 0 and 1 can trade, and at time 0 only customer 0 is in the market.

Before a customer arrives in the marketplace, his demand is $\mathbf{y}_t^k = 0$, and after he arrives he chooses his security position each period to maximize his exponential utility function $U(W_3^k) = -\exp\{-\gamma W_3^k\}$ over final wealth. Wealth W_t^k, including the value of the anticipated endowment shock of $\mathbf{z}^k$ shares, evolves according to

$$W_{t+1}^k = W_t^k + \left(\mathbf{p}_{t+1} - \mathbf{p}_t\right)' \left(\mathbf{y}_t^k + \mathbf{z}^k\right). \tag{3}$$

The vector of total demand shock of customers who have arrived in the market at time t is denoted by $Z_t := \sum_{k=0}^{t} \mathbf{z}^k$.

The early customers' trading need is accommodated by speculators who provide liquidity/immediacy. Speculators are risk-neutral and maximize expected final wealth W_3. Speculators face the constraint that the total margin on their position $\mathbf{x}_t$ cannot exceed their capital W_t:

$$\sum_j \left(x_t^{j+} m_t^{j+} + x_t^{j-} m_t^{j-}\right) \le W_t, \tag{4}$$

where $x_t^{j+} \ge 0$ and $x_t^{j-} \ge 0$ are the positive and negative parts of $x_t^j = x_t^{j+} - x_t^{j-}$, respectively, and $m_t^{j+} \ge 0$ and $m_t^{j-} \ge 0$ are the dollar margin on long and short positions, respectively. The institutional features related to this key constraint for different types of speculators like hedge funds, banks, and market makers are discussed in detail in Appendix A.

Speculators start out with a cash position of W_0 and zero shares, and their wealth evolves according to

$$W_t = W_{t-1} + \left(\mathbf{p}_t - \mathbf{p}_{t-1}\right)' \mathbf{x}_{t-1} + \eta_t, \tag{5}$$

where η_t is an independent wealth shock arising from other activities (e.g., a speculator's investment banking arm). If a speculator loses all his capital, $W_t \le 0$, he can no longer invest because of the margin constraint (4), i.e., he must choose $x_t = 0$. We let his utility in this case be $\varphi_t W_t$, where $\varphi_t \ge 0$. Limited liability corresponds to $\varphi_t = 0$, and a proportional bankruptcy cost (e.g., monetary, reputational, or opportunity costs) corresponds to $\varphi_t > 0$. We focus on the case in which $\varphi_2 = 1$, that is, negative consumption equal to the dollar loss in $t=2$. We discuss φ_1 in Section 5. Our results would be qualitatively the same with other bankruptcy assumptions.

We could allow the speculators to raise new capital as long as this takes time. Indeed, the model would be the same if the speculators could raise capital only at time 2 (and in this case we need not assume that the customers' endowment shocks z^j aggregate to zero). Hence, in this sense, we can view our model as one of "slow moving capital," consistent with the empirical evidence of Mitchell, Pedersen, and Pulvino (2007).

Each financier sets the margins to limit his counterparty credit risk. Specifically, each financier ensures that the margin is large enough to cover the position's π-value-at-risk (where π is a non-negative number close to zero, e.g., 1%):

$$\pi = \Pr\left(-\Delta p_{t+1}^j > m_t^{j+} \,\middle|\, \mathcal{F}_t\right), \tag{6}$$

$$\pi = \Pr\left(\Delta p_{t+1}^j > m_t^{j-} \,\middle|\, \mathcal{F}_t\right). \tag{7}$$

Equation (6) means that the margin on a long position m^+ is set such that price drops that exceed the amount of the margin only happen with a small probability π. Similarly, Equation (7) means that price increases larger than the margin on a short position only happen with small probability. Clearly, the margin is larger for more volatile assets. The margin depends on financiers' information set $\mathcal{F}_t$. We consider two important benchmarks: "informed financiers," who know the fundamental value and the liquidity shocks $\mathbf{z}$, $\mathcal{F}_t = \sigma\{\mathbf{z}, \mathbf{v}_0,\ldots, \mathbf{v}_t, \mathbf{p}_0,\ldots,\mathbf{p}_t, \eta_1,\ldots,\eta_t\}$, and "uninformed financiers," who only observe prices, $\mathcal{F}_t = \sigma\{\mathbf{p}_0,\ldots,\mathbf{p}_t\}$. This margin specification is motivated by the real-world institutional features described in Appendix A. Theoretically, Stiglitz and Weiss (1981) show how credit rationing can be due to adverse selection and moral hazard in the lending market, and Geanakoplos (2003) considers endogenous contracts in a general-equilibrium framework of imperfect commitment.

We let Λ_t^j be the (signed) deviation of the price from fundamental value:

$$\Lambda_t^j = p_t^j - v_t^j, \tag{8}$$

and we define our measure of market illiquidity as the absolute amount of this deviation, $\left|\Lambda_t^j\right|$. We consider competitive equilibria of the economy:

Definition 1. An *equilibrium* is a price process $\mathbf{p}_t$ such that (i) $\mathbf{x}_t$ maximizes the speculators' expected final profit subject to the margin constraint (4); (ii) each $\mathbf{y}_t^k$ maximizes customer k's expected utility after their arrival at the marketplace and is zero beforehand; (iii) margins are set according to the VaR specification (6–7); and (iv) markets clear, $\mathbf{x}_t + \sum_{k=0}^2 \mathbf{y}_t^k = 0$.

Equilibrium. We derive the optimal strategies for customers and speculators using dynamic programming, starting from time 2, and working backwards. A customer's value function is denoted Γ and a speculator's value function is denoted J. At time 2, customer k's problem is

$$\Gamma_2\left(W_2^k, p_2, v_2\right) = \max_{y_2^k} - E_2\left[e^{-\gamma W_3^k}\right] \tag{9}$$

$$= \max_{y_2^k} - e^{-\gamma\left(E_2\left[W_3^k\right] - \frac{\gamma}{2}Var_2\left[w_j^k\right]\right)}, \tag{10}$$

which has the solution

$$y_2^{j,k} = \frac{v_2^j - p_2^j}{\gamma\left(\sigma_3^j\right)^2} - z^{j,k}.$$ (11)

Clearly, since all customers are present in the market at time 2, the unique equilibrium is $p_2 = v_2$. Indeed, when the prices are equal to fundamentals, the aggregate customer demand is zero, $\sum_k y_2^{j,k} = 0$, and speculators also has a zero demand. We get the customer's value function $\Gamma_2(W_2^k, p_2 = v_2, v_2) = -e^{-\gamma W_2^k}$, and the speculator's value function $J_2(W_2, p_2 = v_2, v_2) = W_2$.

The equilibrium before time 2 depends on whether the customers arrive sequentially or simultaneously. If all customers arrive at time 0, then the simple arguments above show that $p_t = v_t$ at any time $t = 0, 1, 2$.

We are interested in the case with sequential arrival of the customers such that the speculators' liquidity provision is needed. At time 1, customers 0 and 1 are present in the market, but customer 2 has not arrived yet. As above, customer $k = 0, 1$ has a demand and value function of

$$y_1^{j,k} = \frac{v_1^j - p_1^j}{\gamma\left(\sigma_2^j\right)^2} - z^{j,k}$$ (12)

$$\Gamma_1\left(W_1^k, p_1, v_1\right) = -\exp\left\{-\gamma\left[W_1^k + \sum_j \frac{\left(v_1^j - p_1^j\right)^2}{2\gamma\left(\sigma_2^j\right)^2}\right]\right\}.$$ (13)

At time 0, customer $k = 0$ arrives in the market and maximizes $E_0[\Gamma_1(W_1^k, p_1, v_1)]$.

At time $t = 1$, if the market is perfectly liquid so that $p_1^j = v_1^j$ for all j, then the speculators are indifferent among all possible positions x_1. If some securities have $p_1 \neq v_1$, then the risk-neutral speculators invest all his capital such that his margin constraint binds. The speculators optimally trade only in securities with the highest expected profit per dollar used. The profit per dollar used is $(v_1^j - p_1^j)/m_1^{j+}$ on a long position and $-(v_1^j - p_1^j)/m_1^{j-}$ on a short position. A speculators' shadow cost of capital, denoted ϕ_1, is 1 plus the maximum profit per dollar used as long as he is not bankrupt:

$$\phi_1 = 1 + \max_j\left\{\max\left(\frac{v_1^j - p_1^j}{m_1^{j+}}, \frac{-\left(v_1^j - p_1^j\right)}{m_1^{j-}}\right)\right\},$$ (14)

231

where the margins for long and short positions are set by the financiers, as described in the next section. If the speculators are bankrupt, $W_1 < 0$, then $\phi_1 = \varphi_1$. Each speculator's value function is therefore

$$J_1\left(W_1, p_1, v_1, p_0, v_0\right) = W_1\phi_1. \tag{15}$$

At time $t=0$, the speculator maximizes $E_0[W_1\phi_1]$ subject to his capital constraint (4).

The equilibrium prices at times 1 and 0 do not have simple expressions but we can characterize their properties, starting with a basic result from which much intuition derives:

Proposition 1 (market and funding liquidity). *In equilibrium, any asset j's market illiquidity $\left|\Lambda_1^j\right|$ is linked to its margin m_1^j and the common funding illiquidity as measured by the speculators' marginal value of an extra dollar ϕ_1:*

$$\left|\Lambda_1^j\right| = m_1^j\left(\phi_1 - 1\right), \tag{16}$$

where $m_1^j = m_1^{j+}$ if the speculator is long and $m_1^j = m_1^{j-}$ otherwise. If the speculators have a zero position for asset j, the equation is replaced by $\leq$.

We next go on to show the (de-)stabilizing properties of margins, and then we further characterize the equilibrium connection between market liquidity and speculators' funding situation, and the role played by liquidity risk at time 0.

2. Margin Setting and Liquidity (Time 1)

A key determinant of speculators' funding liquidity is their margin requirement for collateralized financing. Hence, it is important to determine the margin function, m_1, set by, respectively, informed and uninformed financiers. The margin at time 1 is set to cover a position's value-at-risk, knowing that prices equal the fundamental values in the next period 2, $p_2 = v_2$.

We consider first informed financiers who know the fundamental values v_1 and, hence, price divergence from fundamentals Λ_1. Since $\Lambda_2 = 0$, they set margins on long positions at $t=1$, according to

$$\pi = \Pr\left(-\Delta p_2^j > m_1^{j+}\middle|\mathcal{F}_1\right)$$

$$= \Pr\left(-\Delta v_2^j + \Lambda_1^j > m_1^{j+}\middle|\mathcal{F}_1\right) \tag{17}$$

$$= 1 - \Phi\left(\frac{m_1^{j+} - \Lambda_1^j}{\sigma_2^j}\right),$$

which implies that

$$m_1^{j+} = \Phi^{-1}(1-\pi)\sigma_2^j + \Lambda_1^j$$

$$= \bar{\sigma}^j + \bar{\theta}\left|\Delta v_1^j\right| + \Lambda_1^j, \tag{18}$$

where we define

$$\bar{\sigma}^j = \underline{\sigma}^j \Phi^{-1}(1-\pi), \tag{19}$$

$$\bar{\theta}^j = \theta^j \Phi^{-1}(1-\pi). \tag{20}$$

The margin on a short position can be derived similarly and we arrive at the following surprising result:

Proposition 2 (stabilizing margins and the cushioning effect). *When the financiers are informed about the fundamental value and knows that prices will equal fundamentals in the next period, $t=2$, then the margins on long and short positions are, respectively,*

$$m_1^{j+} = \max\left\{\bar{\sigma}^j + \bar{\theta}^j\left|\Delta v_1^j\right| + \Lambda_1^j, 0\right\}, \tag{21}$$

$$m_1^{j-} = \max\left\{\bar{\sigma}^j + \bar{\theta}^j\left|\Delta v_1^j\right| - \Lambda_1^j, 0\right\}. \tag{22}$$

The more prices are below fundamentals $\Lambda_1^j < 0$, the lower is the margin on a long position m_1^{j+}, and the more prices are above fundamentals $\Lambda_1^j > 0$, the lower is the margin on a short position m_1^{j-}. Hence, in this case illiquidity reduces margins for speculators who buy low and sell high.

The margins are reduced by illiquidity because the speculators are expected to profit when prices return to fundamentals at time 2, and this profit "cushions" the speculators from losses due to fundamental volatility. Thus, we denote the margins set by informed financiers at $t=1$ as *stabilizing margins*.

Stabilizing margins are an interesting benchmark, and they are hard to escape in a theoretical model. However, real-world liquidity crises are often associated with increases in margins, not decreases. To capture this, we turn to the case of a in which financiers are uninformed about the current fundamental so that he must set his margin based on the observed prices p_0 and p_1. This is in general a complicated problem since the financiers need to filter out the probability that customers arrive sequentially, and the values of z_0 and z_1. The expression becomes simple, however, if the financier's prior probability of an asynchronous arrival of endowment shocks is small so that he finds it likely that $p_t^j = v_t^j$, implying a common margin $m_1^j = m_1^{j+} = m_1^{j-}$ for long and short positions in the limit:

Proposition 3 (destabilizing margins). *When the financiers are uninformed about the fundamental value, then, as $a \rightarrow 0$, the margins on long and short positions approach*

$$m_1^j = \bar{\sigma}^j + \bar{\theta}^j \left| \Delta p_1^j \right| = \bar{\sigma}^j + \bar{\theta}^j \left| \Delta v_1^j + \Delta \Lambda_1^j \right|. \tag{23}$$

Margins are increasing in price volatility and market illiquidity can increase margins.

Intuitively, since liquidity risk tends to increase price volatility, and since uninformed financiers may interpret price volatility as fundamental volatility, this increases margins.[7] Equation (23) corresponds closely to real-world margin setting, which is primarily based on volatility estimates from past price movements. This introduces a procyclicality that amplifies funding shocks—a major criticism of the Basel II capital regulation. (See Appendix A.2 for how banks' capital requirements relate to our funding constraint.) Equation (23) shows that illiquidity increases margins when the liquidity shock $\Delta \Lambda_1^j$ has the same sign as the fundamental shock Δv_1^j (or is greater in magnitude), for example, when bad news and selling pressure happen at the same time. On the other hand, margins are reduced if the nonfundamental z-shock counterbalances a fundamental move. We denote the phenomenon that margins can increase as illiquidity rises by *destabilizing margins*. As we will see next, the information available to the financiers (i.e., whether margins are stabilizing or destabilizing) has important implications for the equilibrium.

3. Fragility and Liquidity Spirals (Time 1)

We next show how speculators' funding problems can lead to liquidity spirals and fragility—the property that a small change in fundamentals can lead to a large jump in illiquidity. We show that funding problems are especially escalating with uninformed financiers (i.e., destabilizing margins). For simplicity, we illustrate this with a single security $J = 1$.

3.1 Fragility

To set the stage for the main fragility proposition below, we make a few brief definitions. Liquidity is said to be *fragile* if the equilibrium price $p_t(\eta_t, v_t)$ cannot be chosen to be continuous in the exogenous shocks, namely η_t and Δv_t. Fragility arises when the excess demand for shares $x_t + \sum_{k=0}^{1} y_1^k$ can be non-monotonic in the price. While under "normal" circumstances, a high price leads to a low total demand (i.e., excess demand is decreasing), binding funding constraints along with destabilizing margins (margin effect) or speculators' losses (loss effect) can lead to an increasing demand curve. Further, it is natural to focus on *stable* equilibria in which a small negative (positive) price perturbation leads to excess demand (supply), which, intuitively, "pushes" the price back up (down) to its equilibrium level.

Proposition 4 (fragility). *There exist $\underline{x}, \underline{\theta}, \underline{a} > 0$ such that:*

    (i)   *With informed financiers, the market is fragile at time 1 if speculators' position $|x_0|$ is larger than $\underline{x}$ and of the same sign as the demand shock Z_1.*

    (ii)   *With uninformed financiers the market is fragile as in (i) and additionally if the ARCH parameter θ is larger than $\underline{\theta}$ and the probability, a, of sequential arrival of customers is smaller than $\underline{a}$.*

Numerical example. We illustrate how fragility arises due to destabilizing margins or dealer losses by way of a numerical example. We consider the more interesting (and arguably more realistic) case in which the financiers are uninformed, and we choose parameters as follows.

The fundamental value has ARCH volatility parameters $\bar{\sigma} = 10$ and $\theta = 0.3$, which implies clustering of volatility. The initial price is $p_0 = 130$, the aggregate demand shock of the customers who have arrived at time 1 is $Z_1 = z_0 + z_1 = 30$, and the customers' risk aversion coefficient is $\gamma = 0.05$. The speculators have an initial position of $x_0 = 0$ and a cash wealth of $W_1 = 900$. Finally, the financiers use a VaR with $\pi = 1\%$ and customers learn their endowment shocks sequentially with probability $a = 1\%$.

Panel A of Figure 3 illustrates how the speculators' demand x_1 and the customers' supply (i.e., the negative of the customers' demand as per Equation (12)) depend on the price p_1 when the fundamental value is $v_1 = 120$ and the speculators' wealth shock is $\eta_1 = 0$. Customers' supply is given by the upward sloping dashed line since, naturally, their supply is greater when the price is higher. Customers supply $Z_1 = 30$ shares, namely the shares that they anticipate receiving at time $t = 3$, when the market is perfectly liquid, $p_1 = v_1 = 120$ (i.e., illiquidity is $|\Lambda_1| = 0$). For lower prices, they supply fewer shares.

The speculators' demand, x_1, must satisfy the margin constraints. It is instructive to consider first the simpler limiting case $a \to 0$ for which the margin requirement is simply $m = \bar{\sigma} + \bar{\theta}|\Delta p_1| = 2.326(10 + 0.3|\Delta p_1|)$. This implies that speculators demand $|x_1| \leq W_1 / (\bar{\sigma} + \bar{\theta}|\Delta p_1|)$. Graphically, this means that their demand must be inside the "hyperbolic star" defined by the four (dotted) hyperbolas (that are partially overlaid by a solid demand curve in Figure 3). At the price $p_1 = p_0 = 130$, the margin is smallest and hence the constraint is most relaxed. As p_1 departs from

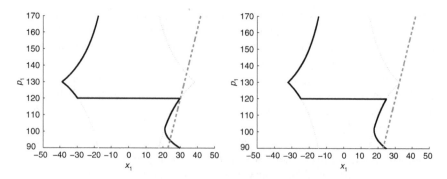

Figure 3 Speculator demand and customer supply. This figure illustrates how margins can be destabilizing when financiers are uninformed and the fundamentals have volatility clustering. The solid curve is the speculators' optimal demand for $a=1\%$. The upward sloping dashed line is the customers' supply, that is, the negative of their demand. In panel A, the speculators experience a zero wealth shock, $\eta_1 = 0$, while in panel B they face a negative wealth shock of $\eta_1 = -150$, otherwise everything is the same. In panel A, perfect liquidity $p_1 = v_1 = 120$ is one of two stable equilibria, while in panel B the unique equilibrium is illiquid.

$p_0 = 130$, margins increase and speculators become more constrained—the horizontal distance between two hyperbolas shrinks.

After establishing the hyperbolic star, it is easy to derive the demand curve for $a \to 0$: For $p_1 = v_1 = 120$, the security's expected return is zero and each speculator is indifferent between all his possible positions on the horizontal line. For price levels $p_1 > v_1$ above this line, the risk-neutral speculators want to short-sell the asset, $x_1 < 0$, and their demand is constrained by the upper-left side of the star. Similarly, for prices below v_1, speculators buy the asset, $x_1 > 0$, and their demand is limited by the margin constraint. Interestingly, the speculators' demand is upward sloping for prices below 120. As the price declines, the financiers' estimate of fundamental volatility, and consequently of margins, increase.

We now generalize the analysis to the case where $a > 0$. The margin setting becomes more complicated since uninformed financiers must filter out to what extent the equilibrium price change is caused by a movement in fundamentals Δv_1 and/or an occurrence of a liquidity event with an order imbalance caused by the presence of customers 0 and 1, but not customer 2. Since customers 0 and 1 want to sell ($Z_1 = 30$), a price increase or modest price decline is most likely due to a change in fundamentals, and hence the margin setting is similar to the case of $a = 0$. This is why speculators' demand curve for prices above 100 almost perfectly overlays the relevant part of the hyperbolic star in Figure 3. However, for a large price drop, say below 100, financiers assign a larger conditional probability that a liquidity event has occurred. Hence, they are willing to set a lower margin (relative to the one implying the hyperbolic star) because they expect the speculator to profit as the price rebounds in period 2—hence, the cushioning effect discussed above reappears in the extreme here. This explains why the speculators' demand curve is backward bending only in a limited price range and becomes downward sloping for p_1 below roughly 100.[8]

Panel A of Figure 3 shows that there are two stable equilibria: a perfect liquidity equilibrium with price $p_1 = v_1 = 120$ and an illiquid equilibrium with a price of about 94 (and an uninteresting unstable equilibrium with p_1 just below 120).

Panel B of Figure 3 shows the same plot as panel A, but with a negative wealth shock to speculators of $\eta_1 = -150$ instead of $\eta_1 = 0$. In this case, perfect liquidity with $p_1 = v_1$ is no longer an equilibrium since the speculators cannot fund a large enough position. The unique equilibrium is highly illiquid because of the speculators' lower wealth and, importantly, because of endogenously higher margins.

This "disconnect" between the perfect-liquidity equilibrium and the illiquid equilibrium and the resulting fragility is illustrated more directly in Figure 4. Panel A plots the equilibrium price correspondence for different exogenous funding shocks η_1 (with fixed $\Delta v_1 = -10$) and shows that a marginal reduction in funding cannot always lead to a smooth reduction in market liquidity. Rather, there must be a level of funding such that an infinitesimal drop in funding leads to a discontinuous drop in market liquidity.

The dark line in Figure 4 shows the equilibrium with the highest market liquidity and the light line shows the equilibrium with the lowest market liquidity. We note that the financiers' filtering problem and, hence, the margin function depend on the equilibrium selection. Since the margin affects the speculators' trades, the

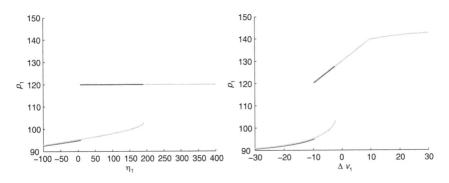

Figure 4 Fragility due to destabilizing margins. The figure shows the equilibrium price as a function of the speculators' wealth shock η_1 (panel A) and of fundamental shocks Δv_1 (panel B). This is drawn for the equilibrium with the highest market liquidity (light line) and the equilibrium with the lowest market liquidity (dark line). The margins are destabilizing since financiers are uninformed and fundamentals exhibit volatility clustering. The equilibrium prices are discontinuous, which reflects *fragility* in liquidity since a small shock can lead to a disproportionately large price effect.

equilibrium selection affects the equilibrium outcome everywhere—prices are slightly affected even outside the η region (v_1 region) with fragility.

Panel B of Figure 4 plots the equilibrium price correspondence for different realizations of the fundamental shock Δv_1 (with fixed $\eta_1 = 0$) and shows the same form of discontinuity for adverse fundamental shocks to v_1. The discontinuity with respect to Δv_1 is most easily understood in conjunction with panel A of Figure 3. As Δv_1 falls, the horizontal line of speculator demand shifts downward, and the customer supply line moves downward. As a result, the perfect liquidity equilibrium vanishes. Panel B of Figure 4 also reveals the interesting asymmetry that negative fundamental shocks lead to larger price movements than corresponding positive shocks (for $Z_1 := z_0 + z_1 > 0$). This asymmetry arises even without a loss effect since $x_0 = 0$.

Fragility can also arise because of shocks to customer demand or volatility. Indeed, the market can also be suddenly pushed into an illiquid equilibrium with high margins due to an increase in demand and an increase in volatility. Paradoxically, a marginally larger demand for liquidity by customers can lead to a drastic reduction of liquidity supply by the speculators when it pushes the equilibrium over the edge.

While the example above has speculators with zero initial positions, $x_0 = 0$, it is also interesting to consider $x_0 > 0$. In this case, lower prices lead to losses for the speculators, and graphically this means that the constraints in the "hyperbolic star" tighten (i.e., the gap between the hyperbolas narrows) at low prices. Because of this "loss effect," the discontinuous price drop associated with the illiquid equilibrium is even larger.

In summary, this example shows how destabilizing margins and dealer losses give rise to a discontinuity in prices, which can help to explain the sudden market liquidity dry-ups observed in many markets. For example, Russia's default in 1998 was in itself only a trivial wealth shock relative to global arbitrage capital. Nevertheless, it had a large effect on liquidity in global financial markets, consistent with our fragility result that a small wealth shock can push the equilibrium over the edge.

3.2 Liquidity Spirals

To further emphasize the importance of speculators' funding liquidity, we now show how it can make market liquidity highly sensitive to shocks. We identify two amplification mechanisms: a "margin spiral" due to increasing margins as speculator financing worsens, and a "loss spiral" due to escalating speculator losses.

Figure 2 illustrates these "liquidity spirals." A shock to speculator capital ($\eta_1 < 0$) forces speculators to provide less market liquidity, which increases the price impact of the customer demand pressure. With uninformed financiers and

ARCH effects, the resulting price swing increases financiers' estimate of the fundamental volatility and, hence, increases the margin, thereby worsening speculator funding problems even further, and so on, leading to a "margin spiral." Similarly, increased market illiquidity can lead to losses on speculators' existing positions, worsening their funding problem and so on, leading to a "loss spiral." Mathematically, the spirals can be expressed as follows:

Proposition 5. (i) *If speculators' capital constraint is slack, then the price p_1 is equal to v_1 and insensitive to local changes in speculator wealth.*

(ii) (**Liquidity spirals**) *In a stable illiquid equilibrium with selling pressure from customers, Z_1, $x_1 > 0$, the price sensitivity to speculator wealth shocks η_1 is*

$$\frac{\partial p_1}{\partial \eta_1} = \frac{1}{\dfrac{2}{\gamma(\sigma_2)^2}m_1^+ + \dfrac{\partial m_1^+}{\partial p_1}x_1 - x_0} \tag{24}$$

and with buying pressure from customers, Z_1, $x_1 < 0$

$$\frac{\partial p_1}{\partial \eta_1} = \frac{-1}{\dfrac{2}{\gamma(\sigma_2)^2}m_1^- + \dfrac{\partial m_1^-}{\partial p_1}x_1 + x_0}. \tag{25}$$

*A **margin/haircut spiral** arises if $\dfrac{\partial m_1^+}{\partial p_1} < 0$ or $\dfrac{\partial m_1^-}{\partial p_1} > 0$, which happens with positive probability if financiers are uninformed and a is small enough. A **loss spiral** arises if speculators' previous position is in the opposite direction as the demand pressure, $x_0 Z_1 > 0$.*

This proposition is intuitive. Imagine first what happens if speculators face a wealth shock of $1, margins are constant, and speculators have no inventory $x_0 = 0$. In this case, the speculator must reduce his position by $1/m_1$. Since the slope of each of the two customer demand curves is[9] $1/(\gamma(\sigma_2)^2)$, we get a total price effect of $1/\left(\dfrac{2}{\sqrt{\gamma(\sigma_2)^2}}m_1\right)$.

The two additional terms in the denominator imply amplification or dampening effects due to changes in the margin requirement and to profit/losses on the speculators' existing positions. To see that, recall that for any $k > 0$ and l with $|l| < k$, it holds that $\dfrac{1}{k-l} = \dfrac{1}{k} + \dfrac{l}{k^2} + \dfrac{l^2}{k^3} + \ldots$; so with $k = \dfrac{2}{\gamma(\sigma_2)^2}m_1$ and $l = -\dfrac{\partial m_1^+}{\partial p_1}x_1 \pm x_0$, each term in this infinite series corresponds to one loop around the circle in

Figure 2. The total effect of the changing margin and speculators' positions amplifies the effect if $l>0$. Intuitively, with $Z_1>0$, then customer selling pressure is pushing down the price, and $\dfrac{\partial m_1^+}{\partial p_1}<0$ means that as prices go down, margins increase, making speculators' funding tighter and thus destabilizing the system. Similarly, when customers are buying, $\dfrac{\partial m_1^-}{\partial p_1}>0$ implies that increasing prices leads to increased margins, making it harder for speculators to short-sell, thus destabilizing the system. The system is also destabilized if speculators lose money on their previous position as prices move away from fundamentals.

Interestingly, the total effect of a margin spiral together with a loss spiral is greater than the sum of their separate effects. This can be seen mathematically by using simple convexity arguments, and it can be seen intuitively from the flow diagram of Figure 2.

Note that spirals can also be "started" by shocks to liquidity demand Z_1, fundamentals v_1, or volatility. It is straightforward to compute the price sensitivity with respect to such shocks. They are just multiples of $\dfrac{\partial p_1}{\partial \eta_1}$. For instance, a fundamental shock affects the price both because of its direct effect on the final payoff and because of its effect on customers' estimate of future volatility—and both of these effects are amplified by the liquidity spirals.

Our analysis sheds some new light on the 1987 stock market crash, complementing the standard culprit, portfolio insurance trading. In the 1987 stock market crash, numerous market makers hit (or violated) their funding constraint:

> "By the end of trading on October 19, [1987] thirteen [NYSE specialist] units had no buying power," —SEC (1988, chap. 4, p. 58)

While several of these firms managed to reduce their positions and continue their operations, others did not. For instance, Tompane was so illiquid that it was taken over by Merrill Lynch Specialists and Beauchamp was taken over by Spear, Leeds & Kellogg (Beauchamp's clearing broker). Also, market makers outside the NYSE experienced funding troubles: the Amex market makers Damm Frank and Santangelo were taken over; at least 12 OTC market makers ceased operations; and several trading firms went bankrupt.

These funding problems were due to (i) reductions in capital arising from trading losses and defaults on unsecured customer debt, (ii) an increased funding need stemming from increased inventory, and (iii) increased margins. One New York City bank, for instance, increased margins/haircuts from 20% to 25% for certain borrowers, and another bank increased margins from 25% to 30% for all specialists (SEC, 1988, pp. 5–27 and 5–28). Other banks reduced the funding period by making intraday margin calls, and at least two banks made intraday margin calls based on assumed 15% and 25% losses, thus effectively increasing the haircut by 15% and 25%. Also, some broker-dealers experienced a reduction in their line of credit and—as Figure 1 shows—margins at the futures exchanges also drastically increased (SEC 1988 and Wigmore 1998). Similarly, during the ongoing liquidity and credit crunch, the margins and haircuts across most asset classes widened significantly starting in the summer of 2007 (see IMF Global Stability Report, October 2007).

In summary, our results on fragility and liquidity spirals imply that during "bad" times, small changes in underlying funding conditions (or liquidity demand) can lead to sharp reductions in liquidity. The 1987 crash exhibited several of the predicted features, namely capital-constrained dealers, increased margins, and increased illiquidity.

4. Commonality and Flight to Quality (Time 1)

We now turn to the cross-sectional implications of illiquidity. Since speculators are risk-neutral, they optimally invest all their capital in securities that have the greatest expected profit $|\Lambda^j|$ per capital use, i.e., per dollar margin m^j, as expressed in Equation (14). That equation also introduces the shadow cost of capital ϕ_1 as the marginal value of an extra dollar. The speculators' shadow cost of capital ϕ_1 captures well the notion of funding liquidity: a high ϕ means that the available funding—from capital W_1 and from collateralized financing with margins m_1^j—is low relative to the needed funding, which depends on the investment opportunities deriving from demand shocks z^j.

The market liquidity of all assets depends on the speculators' funding liquidity, especially for high-margin assets, and this has several interesting implications:

Proposition 6. *There exists $c > 0$ such that, for $\theta^j < c$ for all j and either informed financiers or uninformed with $a < c$, we have:*

(i) **Commonality of market liquidity.** *The market illiquidities $|\Lambda|$ of any two securities, k and l, co-move,*

$$\mathrm{Cov}_0\left(\left|\Lambda_1^k\right|, \left|\Lambda_1^l\right|\right) \geq 0, \tag{26}$$

and market illiquidity co-moves with funding illiquidity as measured by speculators' shadow cost of capital, ϕ_1,

$$\mathrm{Cov}_0\left[\left|\Lambda_1^k\right|, \phi_1\right] \geq 0. \tag{27}$$

(ii) **Commonality of fragility.** *Jumps in market liquidity occur simultan-eously for all assets for which speculators are marginal investors.*

(iii) **Quality and liquidity.** *If asset l has lower fundamental volatility than asset k, $\underline{\sigma}^l < \underline{\sigma}^k$, then l also has lower market illiquidity,*

$$\left|\Lambda_1^l\right| \leq \left|\Lambda_1^k\right|,\tag{28}$$

if $x_1^k \neq 0$ or $\left|Z_1^k\right| \geq \left|Z_1^l\right|$.

(iv) **Flight to quality.** *The market liquidity differential between high- and low-fundamental-volatility securities is bigger when speculator funding is tight, that is, $\underline{\sigma}^l < \underline{\sigma}^k$ implies that $\left|\Lambda_1^k\right|$ increases more with a negative wealth shock to the speculator,*

$$\frac{\partial\left|\Lambda_1^l\right|}{\partial\left(-\eta_1\right)} \leq \frac{\partial\left|\Lambda_1^k\right|}{\partial\left(-\eta_1\right)},\tag{29}$$

if $x_1^k \neq 0$ or $\left|Z_1^k\right| \geq \left|Z_1^l\right|$. Hence, if $x_1^k \neq 0$ or $\left|Z_1^k\right| \geq \left|Z_1^l\right|$ a.s., then

$$\text{Cov}_0\left(\left|\Lambda_1^l\right|, \phi_1\right) \leq \text{Cov}_0\left(\left|\Lambda_1^k\right|, \phi_1\right)\tag{30}$$

Numerical example, continued. To illustrate these cross-sectional predictions, we extend the numerical example of Section 3 to two securities. The two securi-ties only differ in their long-run fundamental volatility: $\bar{\sigma}^1 = 7.5$ and $\bar{\sigma}^2 = 10$. The other parameters are as before, except that we double W_1 to 1800 since the specu-lators now trade two securities, the financiers remain uninformed, and we focus on the simpler limited case with $a \rightarrow 0$.

Figure 5 depicts the assets' equilibrium prices for different values of the funding shock η_1. First note that as speculator funding tightens and our funding illiquidity measure ϕ_1 rises, the market illiquidity measure $\left|\Lambda_1^j\right|$ rises for both assets. Hence, for random η_1, we see our commonality in liquidity result $\text{Cov}_0[|\Lambda_1^k|, |\Lambda_1^l|] > 0$.

The "commonality in fragility" cannot directly be seen from Figure 5, but it is suggestive that both assets have the same range of η_1 with two equilibrium prices p_1^j. The intuition for this result is the following. Whenever funding is uncon-strained, there is perfect market liquidity provision for all assets. If funding is constrained, then it cannot be the case that speculators provide perfect liquidity for one asset but not for the other, since they would always have an incentive to

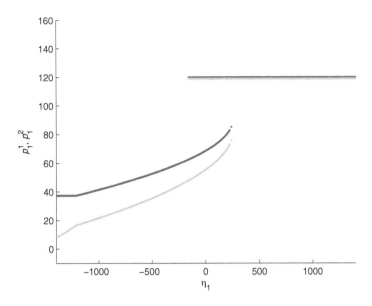

Figure 5 Flight to quality and commonality in liquidity. The figure plots the prices p_1^j of assets 1 and 2 as functions of speculators' funding shocks η_1. Asset 1 (darker curve) has lower long-run fundamental risk than asset 2 (lighter cunve), $\bar{\sigma}^1 = 7.5 < 10 - \bar{\sigma}^2$.

shift funds toward the asset with non-perfect market liquidity. Hence, market illiquidity jumps for both assets at exactly the same funding level.

Our result relating fundamental volatility to market liquidity ("quality and liquidity") is reflected in p_1^2 being below p_1^1 for any given funding level. Hence, the high-fundamental-volatility asset 2 is always less liquid than the low-fundamental-volatility asset 1.

Figure 5 also illustrates our result on "flight to quality." To see this, consider the two securities' relative price sensitivity with respect to η_1. For large wealth shocks, market liquidity is perfect for both assets, i.e., $p_1^1 = p_1^2 = v_1^1 = v_1^2 = 120$, so in this high range of funding, market liquidity is insensitive to marginal changes in funding. On the lower branch of the graph, market illiquidity of both assets increases as η_1 drops since speculators must take smaller stakes in both assets. Importantly, as funding decreases, p_1^2 decreases more steeply than p_1^1, that is, asset 2 is more sensitive to funding declines than asset 1. This is because speculators cut back more on the "funding-intensive" asset 2 with its high margin requirement. Speculators want to maximize their profit per dollar margin, $|\Lambda^j|/m^j$, and therefore $|\Lambda^2|$ must be higher than $|\Lambda^1|$ to compensate speculators for using more capital for margin.

Both price functions exhibit a kink around $\eta = -1210$, because, for sufficiently low funding levels, speculators put all their capital into asset 2. This is because the customers are more eager to sell the more volatile asset 2, leading to more attractive prices for the speculators.

5. Liquidity Risk (Time 0)

We now turn attention to the initial time period, $t=0$, and demonstrate that (i) funding liquidity risk matters even before margin requirements actually bind; (ii) the pricing kernel depends on future funding liquidity, ϕ_{t+1}; (iii) the conditional distribution of prices p_1 is skewed due to the funding constraint (inducing fat tails *ex ante);* and (iv) margins m_0 and illiquidity Λ_0 can be positively related due to liquidity risk even if financiers are informed.

The speculators' trading activity at time 0 naturally depends on their expectations about the next period and, in particular, the time 1 illiquidity described in detail above. Further, speculators risk having negative wealth W_1 at time 1, in which case they have utility $\varphi_t W_t$. If speculators have no dis-utility associated with negative wealth levels ($\varphi_t = 0$), then they go to their limit already at time 0 and the analysis is similar to time 1.

We focus on the more realistic case in which the speculators have dis-utility in connection with $W_1 < 0$ and, therefore, choose not to trade to their constraint at time $t=0$ when their wealth is large enough. To understand this, note that while most firms legally have limited liability, the capital W_t in our model refers to pledgable capital allocated to trading. For instance, Lehman Brothers' 2001 Annual Report (p. 46) states:

"The following must be funded with cash capital: Secured funding 'haircuts,' to reflect the estimated value of cash that would be advanced to the Company by counterparties against available inventory, Fixed assets and goodwill, [and] Operational cash..."

Hence, if Lehman suffers a large loss on its pledgable capital such that $W_t<0$, then it incurs monetary costs that must be covered with its unpledgable capital like operational cash (which could also hurt Lehman's other businesses). In addition, the firm incurs non-monetary cost, like loss in reputation and in goodwill, that reduces its ability to exploit future profitable investment opportunities. To capture these effects, we let a speculator's utility be $\phi_1 W_1$, where ϕ_1 is given by the right-hand side of Equation (14) both for positive and negative values of W_1. With this assumption, equilibrium prices at time $t=0$ are such that the speculators do not trade to their constraint at time $t=0$ when their wealth is large enough. In fact, this is the weakest assumption that curbs the speculators' risk taking since it makes their objective function linear. Higher "bankruptcy costs" would lead to more cautious trading at time 0 and qualitatively similar results.[10]

If the speculator is not constrained at time $t=0$, then the first-order condition for his position in security j is $E_0[\phi_1(p_1^j - p_0^j)] = 0$. (We leave the case of a constrained time-0 speculator for Appendix B.) Consequently, the funding liquidity, ϕ_1, determines the pricing kernel $\phi_1/E_0[\phi_1]$ for the cross section of securities:

$$p_0^j = \frac{E_0\left[\phi_1 p_1^j\right]}{E_0\left[\phi_1\right]} = E_0\left[p_1^j\right] + \frac{Cov_0\left[\phi_1, p_1^j\right]}{E_0\left[\phi_1\right]}. \tag{31}$$

Equation (31) shows that the price at time 0 is the expected time-1 price, which already depends on the liquidity shortage at time 1, further adjusted for liquidity risk in the form of a covariance term. The liquidity risk term is intuitive: The time-0 price is lower if the covariance is negative, that is, if the security has a low payoff during future funding liquidity crises when ϕ_1 is high.

An illustration of the importance of funding-liquidity management is the "LTCM crisis." The hedge fund Long Term Capital Management (LTCM) had been aware of funding liquidity risk. Indeed, they estimated that in times of severe stress, haircuts on AAA-rated commercial mortgages would increase from 2% to 10%, and similarly for other securities (HBS Case N9-200-007(A)). In response to this, LTCM had negotiated long-term financing with margins fixed for several weeks on many of their collateralized loans. Other firms with similar strategies, however, experienced increased margins. Due to an escalating liquidity spiral, LTCM could ultimately not fund its positions in spite of its numerous measures to control funding risk, it was taken over by fourteen banks in September 1998. Another recent example is the funding problems of the hedge fund Amaranth in September 2006, which reportedly ended with losses in excess of USD 6 billion. The ongoing liquidity crisis of 2007–2008, in which funding based on the asset-backed commercial paper market suddenly eroded and banks were reluctant to lend to each other out of fear of future funding shocks, provides a nice out-of-sample test of our theory.[11]

Numerical example, continued. To better understand funding liquidity risk, we return to our numerical example with one security, $\eta_1 = 0$ and $a \to 0$. We first consider the setting with uninformed financiers and later turn to the case with informed financiers.

Figure 6 depicts the price p_0 and expected time-1 price $E_0[p_1]$ for different initial wealth levels, W_0, for which the speculators' funding constraint is not binding at $t = 0$. The figure shows that even though the speculators are unconstrained at time 0, market liquidity provision is limited with prices below the fundamental value of $E_0[v] = 130$. The price is below the fundamental for two reasons: First, the expected time-1 price is below the fundamental value because of the risk that speculators cannot accommodate the customer selling pressure at that time. Second, p_0 is even below $E_0[p_1]$, since speculators face liquidity risk: Holding the security leads to losses in the states of nature when speculators are constrained and investment opportunities are good, implying that $Cov[\phi_1, p_1] < 0$. The additional compensation for liquidity risk is $\dfrac{Cov_0[\phi_1, P_1^j]}{E_0[\phi_1]}$, as seen in Equation (31), which is the difference between the solid line p_1 and the dashed $E_0[p_1]$.

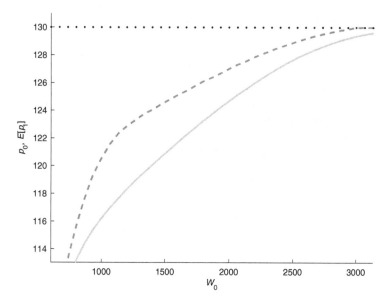

Figure 6 Illiquidity at time 0. This graph shows the price p_0 at time 0 (solid line), the expected time-1 price $E_0[p_1]$ (dashed line), and the fundamental value $E_0[v] = 130$ (dotted line) for different levels of speculator funding W_0. The price p_0 is below the fundamental value due to illiquidity, in particular, because of customer selling pressure and the risk that speculators will hit their capital constraints at time 1, even though speculators are not constrained at time 0 for the depicted wealth levels.

The funding constraint not only affects the price level, it also introduces skewness in the p_1-distribution conditional on the sign of the demand pressure. For $Z_1 > 0$, speculators take long positions and, consequently, negative v_1-shocks lead to capital losses with resulting liquidity spirals. This amplification triggers a sharper price drop than the corresponding price increase for positive v_1-shocks. Figure 7 shows this negative skewness for different funding levels W_0. The effect is not monotone—zero dealer wealth implies no skewness, for instance.

When customers want to buy (not sell as above), and funding constraints induce a positive skewness in the p_1-distribution. The speculator's return remains negatively skewed, as above, since it is still its losses that are amplified. This is consistent with the casual evidence that hedge fund return indexes are negatively skewed, and it can help explain why FX carry trade returns are negatively skewed (see Brunnermeier, Nagel, and Pedersen 2009). It also suggests that from an *ex ante* point of view (i.e., prior to the realization of Z_1), funding constraints lead to higher kurtosis of the price distribution (fat tails).

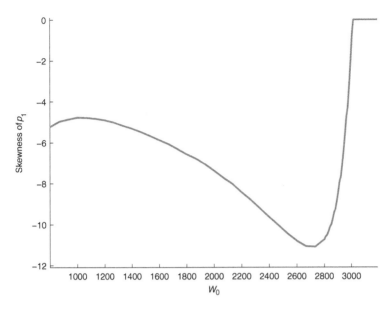

Figure 7 Conditional price skewness. The figure shows the conditional skewness of p_1 for different funding levels W_0. While the funding constraint is not binding at time 0, it can become binding at time 1, leading to large price drops due to liquidity spirals. Price increases are not amplified, and this asymmetry results in skewness.

Finally, we can also show numerically that unlike at time $t=1$, margins can be positively related to illiquidity at time 0, even when financiers are fully informed.[12] This is because of the liquidity risk between time 0 and time 1. To see this, note that if we reduce the speculators' initial wealth W_0, then the market becomes less liquid in the sense that the price is further from the fundamental value. At the same time, the equilibrium price in $t=1$ is more volatile and thus equilibrium margins at time 0 can actually increase.

6. New Testable Predictions

Our analysis provides a theoretical framework that delivers a unified explanation for a host of stylized empirical facts. Our analysis further suggests a novel line of empirical work that tests the model at a deeper level, namely, its prediction that speculator funding is a driving force underlying these market liquidity effects.

First, it would be of interest to empirically study the determinants of margin requirements (e.g., using data from futures markets or from prime brokers). Our model suggests that both fundamental volatility and liquidity-driven volatility affect margins (Propositions 2 and 3). Empirically, fundamental volatility can be captured using price changes over a longer time period, while the sum of fundamental and liquidity-based volatility can be captured by short-term price changes as in the literature on variance ratios (see, for example, Campbell, Lo, and MacKinlay 1997). Our model predicts that, in markets where it is harder for financiers to be informed, margins depend on the total fundamental and liquidity-based volatility. In particular, in times of liquidity crises, margins increase in such markets, and, more generally, margins should co-move with illiquidity in the time series and in the cross section.[13]

Second, our model suggests that an exogenous shock to speculator capital should lead to a reduction in market liquidity (Proposition 5). Hence, a clean test of the model would be to identify exogenous capital shocks, such as an unconnected decision to close down a trading desk, a merger leading to reduced total trading capital, or a loss in one market unrelated to the fundamentals of another market, and then study the market liquidity and margin around such events.

Third, the model implies that the effect of speculator capital on market liquidity is highly nonlinear: a marginal change in capital has a small effect when speculators are far from their constraints, but a large effect when speculators are close to their constraints—illiquidity can suddenly jump (Propositions 4 and 5).

Fourth, the model suggests that a cause of the commonality in liquidity is that the speculators' shadow cost of capital is a driving state variable. Hence, a measure of speculator capital tightness should help explain the empirical co-movement of market liquidity. Further, our result "commonality of fragility" suggests that especially sharp liquidity reductions occur simultaneously across several assets (Proposition 6(i)–(ii)).

Fifth, the model predicts that the sensitivity of margins and market liquidity to speculator capital is larger for securities that are risky and illiquid on average. Hence, the model suggests that a shock to speculator capital would lead to a reduction in market liquidity through a spiral effect that is stronger for illiquid securities (Proposition 6(iv)).

Sixth, speculators are predicted to have negatively skewed returns since, when they hit their constraints, they incur significant losses because of the endogenous liquidity spirals, and, in contrast, their gains are not amplified when prices return to fundamentals. This leads to conditional skewness and unconditional kurtosis of security prices (Section 5).

7. Conclusion

By linking funding and market liquidity, this paper provides a unified framework that explains the following stylized facts:

(1) Liquidity suddenly dries up; we argue that fragility in liquidity is in part due to destabilizing margins, which arise when financiers are imperfectly informed and the fundamental volatility varies.

(2) Market liquidity and fragility co-moves across assets since changes in funding conditions affects speculators' market liquidity provision of all assets.

(3) Market liquidity is correlated with volatility, since trading more volatile assets requires higher margin payments and speculators provide market liquidity across assets such that illiquidity per capital use, i.e., illiquidity per dollar margin, is constant.

(4) Flight to quality phenomena arise in our framework since when funding becomes scarce speculators cut back on the market liquidity provision especially for capital intensive, i.e., high margin, assets.

(5) Market liquidity moves with the market since funding conditions do.

In addition to explaining these stylized facts, the model also makes a number of specific testable predictions that could inspire further empirical research on margins. Importantly, our model links a security's market illiquidity and risk premium to its margin requirement (i.e. funding use) and the general shadow cost of funding.

Our analysis also suggests policy implications for central banks. Central banks can help mitigate market liquidity problems by controlling funding liquidity. If a central bank is better than the typical financiers of speculators at distinguishing liquidity shocks from fundamental shocks, then the central bank can convey this information and urge financiers to relax their funding requirements—as the Federal Reserve Bank of New York did during the 1987 stock market crash. Central banks can also improve market liquidity by boosting speculator funding conditions during a liquidity crisis, or by simply stating the intention to provide extra funding during times of crisis, which would loosen margin requirements as financiers' worst-case scenarios improve.

Appendix A: Real-World Margin Constraints

A central element of our paper is the capital constraints that the main providers of market liquidity face. In this section, we review the institutional features that drive the funding constraints of securities firms such as hedge funds, banks' proprietary trading desks, and market makers.

A.1 Funding requirements for hedge funds

We first consider the funding issues faced by hedge funds since they have relatively simple balance sheets and face little regulation. A hedge fund's capital consists of its equity capital supplied by the investors, and possible long-term debt financing that can be relied upon during a potential funding crisis. The investors can withdraw their capital at certain times so the equity is not locked into the firm indefinitely as in a corporation,[14] but, to ensure funding, the withdrawal is subject to initial lock-up periods and general redemption notice periods before specific redemption dates (typically at least a month, often several months or even years). Also, hedge funds use a variety of other contractual arrangements to manage their funding liquidity: "Side pocket" determines that a proportion of each investor's capital, for example, 10%, can only be redeemed when the designated assets (e.g., a privately held firm) are sold. A "gate" limits the fraction of the total capital that can leave the fund during any redemption period. Individual investors' redemptions are typically prorated in case of excess demand for outflows. "Withdrawal suspensions" (or *force majeure* terms) temporarily suspend withdrawals completely.

Hedge funds usually do not have access to unsecured debt financing, but a few large hedge funds have managed to obtain medium-term bank loans, a guaranteed line of credit,[15] or even issued bonds (see, for example, *The Economist* 1/27/2007, p. 75).

The main sources of leverage for hedge funds are (i) collateralized borrowing financed through the repo market; (ii) collateralized borrowing financed by the hedge fund's prime broker(s); and (iii) implicit leverage using derivatives, either exchange traded or over the counter (OTC). Real-world financing contracts are complex, opaque (i.e., negotiated privately and hence unobservable to an outsider), different across market participants, and change over time, so our description is somewhat stylized and we discuss some caveats below. Nevertheless, all three forms of financing are based on the same general principle, which we describe first, and then we outline a few specific issues.

The guiding principle for margin setting on levered positions is that the hedge fund's counterparty should be relatively immune to the hedge fund's possible losses. In particular, if a hedge fund buys at time t a long position of $x_t^j > 0$ shares of a security j at price p_t^j, it has to come up with $x_t^j p_t^j$ dollars. The security can, however, be used as collateral for a new loan of, say, l_t^j dollars. The difference between the price of the security and the collateral value is denoted as the margin requirement $m_t^{j+} = p_t^j - l_t^j$. Hence, this position uses $x_t^j m_t^{j+}$ dollars of the fund's capital. The collateralized funding implies that the cash use depends on margins, not notional amounts. The margins are typically set so as to make the loan almost risk-free for the counterparty, that is, such that it covers the largest possible price drop with a certain degree of confidence (i.e., it covers the VaR).[16] Hence, if the price drops and the hedge fund defaults, the counterparty can still recover its loan by selling the security.

Similarly, if the hedge fund wants to sell short a security, $x^j < 0$, then the fund asks one of its brokers to locate a security that can be borrowed, and then the fund sells the borrowed security. Duffie, Gârleanu, and Pedersen (2002) describe in detail the institutional arrangements of shorting. The broker keeps the proceeds of the short sale and, additionally, requires that the hedge fund posts a margin m_t^{j-} that covers the largest possible price increase with a certain degree of confidence (in case the hedge fund defaults when the price increases, in which case the broker needs enough cash to buy the security back at a higher price).

This stylized description of collateralized financing portrays well the repo market for fixed-income securities (e.g., government and corporate bonds) and the prime brokerage that banks offer hedge funds for financing equities and convertible bonds, among other things. However, these forms of financing have different implementation. Prime brokerage is an ongoing service provided by banks in which they finance a whole portfolio of the hedge funds' securities on an ongoing basis (as well as providing other services), whereas in the repo market, a hedge fund will often get bids from multiple counterparties each time they make a new repo transaction. The portfolio nature of the prime brokerage business means that the prime broker can take diversification among securities into account and therefore lower the margin using so-called cross-margining, as we describe further below.

As an aside, margins on U.S. equities are in principle subject to Regulation T, which stipulates that non-brokers/dealers must put down an initial margin (down payment) of 50% of the market value of the underlying stock, both for new long and short positions. Hedge funds can, however, get around Regulation T in various ways and therefore face significantly lower stock margins. For example, their prime broker can organize the transaction offshore or as a total return swap, which is a derivative that is functionally equivalent to buying the stock.

With derivatives, the principle is similar, although the hedge fund does not "borrow against" the security, it must simply post margins to enter into the derivative contract in the first place. Suppose, for instance, that a hedge fund buys an OTC forward contract. The forward contract initially has a market value of zero (so in this sense the contract has leverage built in), but this does not mean that you can buy the forward without cash. To enter into the forward contract, which obviously has risk, the hedge fund must post margins corresponding to the largest adverse price move with a certain confidence. To ease netting long and short positions, unwinding, and other things, many OTC derivatives are structured using standardized swaps provided by the International Swaps and Derivatives Association (ISDA).

For exchange-traded derivatives such as futures and options, a hedge fund trades through a clearing broker (sometimes referred to as a futures clearing merchant). The exchange requires margins from the broker, and these margins are set using the same principle as described above, that is, the margin is set to make the exchange almost immune to losses and hence riskier contracts have larger margins. The broker, in turn, typically passes the margin requirement on to the hedge fund. Sometimes, the broker requires higher margins from the hedge fund or lower margins (the latter is considered granting the hedge fund a risky loan, usually at an interest rate spread). While the broker margins are opaque as mentioned above, the exchange margins are usually publicly available. Figure 1 depicts the exchange margins charged by the CME for the S&P 500 futures contract.

A hedge fund must finance all of its positions, that is, the sum of all the margin requirements on long and short positions cannot exceed the hedge fund's capital. In our model, this is captured by the key Equation (4) in Section 1.

At the end of the financing period, time $t+1$, the position is "marked-to-market," which means that the hedge fund is credited any gains (or pays any losses) that have occurred between t and $t+1$, that is, the fund receives $x_t^j(p_{t+1}^j - p_t^j)$ and pays interest on the loan at the funding rate. If the trade is kept on, the broker keeps the margin to protect against losses going forward from time $t+1$. The margin can be adjusted if the risk of the collateral has changed, unless the counterparties have contractually fixed the margin for a certain period.

Instead of posting risk-free assets (cash), a hedge fund can also post other risky assets, say asset k, to cover its margin on position, say x^j. However, in this case, a "haircut," h_t^k, is subtracted from asset k's market value to account for the riskiness of the collateral. The funding constraint becomes $x_t^j m_t^j \le W_t - x_t^k h_t^k$. Moving the haircut term to the left-hand side reveals that the haircut is equivalent to a margin, since the hedge fund could alternatively have used the risky security to raise cash and then used this cash to cover the margins for asset j. We therefore use the terms "margins" and "haircuts" interchangeably.

We have described how funding constraints work when margins and haircuts are set separately for each security position. As indicated earlier, it is, however, increasingly possible to "cross-margin" (i.e., to jointly finance several positions). This leads to a lower total margin if the risks of the various positions are partially offsetting. For instance, much of the interest rate risk is eliminated in a "spread trade" with a long position in one bond and a short position in a similar bond. Hence, the margin/haircut of a jointly financed spread trade is smaller than the sum of the margins of the long and short bonds. For a strategy that is financed jointly, we can reinterpret security j as such a strategy. Prime brokers compete (especially when credit is as loose as in early 2007) by, among other things, offering low margins and haircuts, a key consideration for hedge funds, which means that it has become increasingly easy to finance more and more strategies jointly. It is by now relatively standard to cross-margin an equity portfolio or a portfolio of convertible bonds, and so-called cross-product-margining, which attempts to give diversification benefits across asset classes, is becoming more common although it is associated with some issues that make some hedge funds avoid it.[17] In the extreme, one can imagine a joint financing of a hedge fund's total position such that the "portfolio margin" would be equal to the maximum portfolio loss with a certain confidence level. Currently, it is often not practical to jointly finance a large portfolio with all the benefits of diversification. This is because a large hedge fund finances its trades using several brokers; both a hedge fund and a broker can consist of several legal entities (possibly located in different jurisdictions); certain trades need separate margins paid to exchanges (e.g., futures and options) or to other counterparties of the prime broker (e.g., securities lenders); prime brokers may not have sufficiently sophisticated models to evaluate the diversification benefits (e.g., because they do not have enough data on the historical performance of newer products such as CDOs); and because of other practical difficulties in providing joint financing. Further, if the margin requirement relies on assumed stress scenarios in which the securities are perfectly correlated (e.g., due to predatory trading, as in Brunnermeier and Pedersen 2005), then the portfolio margin constraint coincides with position-by-position margins.

A.2 Funding requirements for commercial and investment banks

A bank's capital consists of equity capital plus its long-term borrowing (including credit lines secured from commercial banks, alone or in syndicates), reduced by assets that cannot be readily employed (e.g., goodwill, intangible assets, property, equipment, and capital needed for daily operations), and further reduced by uncollateralized loans extended by the bank to others (see, for example, Goldman Sachs's 2003 Annual Report). Banks also raise money using short-term uncollateralized loans, such as commercial paper and promissory notes, and, in the case of commercial banks, demand deposits. These sources of financing cannot, however, be relied on in times of funding crisis since lenders may be unwilling to continue lending, and therefore this short-term funding is often not included in measures of capital.

The financing of a bank's trading activity is largely based on *collateralized* borrowing. Banks can finance long positions using collateralized borrowing from corporations, other banks, insurance companies, and the Federal Reserve Bank, and can borrow securities to short-sell from, for instance, mutual funds and pension funds. These transactions typically require margins that must be financed by the bank's capital, as captured by the funding constraint in Equation (4).

The financing of a bank's trading is more complicated than that of a hedge fund, however. For instance, banks may negotiate zero margins with certain counterparties, and banks can often sell short shares held in-house, that is, held in a customer's margin account (in "street name") such that the bank does not need to use capital to borrow the shares externally. Further, a bank receives margins when financing hedge funds (i.e., the margin is negative from the point of view of the bank). In spite of these caveats, in times of stress, banks face margin requirements and are ultimately subject to a funding constraint in the spirit of Equation (4). Bear Stearns's demise is a vivid reminder that banks' funding advantage from clients' margin accounts can quickly evaporate. In March of 2008, Bear Stearns's clients terminated their brokerage relationships and ran on the investment bank. Only an orchestrated merger with JPMorgan Chase avoided a bankruptcy.

Banks must also satisfy certain regulatory requirements. Commercial banks are subject to the Basel Accord, supervised by the Federal Reserve System for U.S. banks. In short, the Basel Accord of 1988 requires that a bank's "eligible capital" exceeds 8% of the "risk-weighted asset holdings," which is the sum of each asset holding multiplied by its risk weight. The risk weight is 0% for cash and government securities, 50% for mortgage-backed loans, and 100% for all other assets. The requirement posed by the 1988 Basel Accord corresponds to Equation (4) with margins of 0%, 4%, and 8%, respectively. In 1996, the accord was amended, allowing banks to measure market risk using an internal model based on portfolio VaRs rather than using standardized risk weights. To outmaneuver the Basel

Accord, banks created a shadow banking system, which allowed them to off-load assets to off-balance sheet vehicles like SIVs and conduits. For details, see Brunnermeier (2009).

Broker-speculators in the United States, including banks acting as such, are subject to the Securities and Exchange Commission's (SEC's) "net capital rule" (SEC Rule 15c3-1). This rule stipulates, among other things, that a broker must have a minimum "net capital," which is defined as equity capital plus approved subordinate liabilities minus "securities haircuts" and operational charges. The haircuts are set as security-dependent percentages of the market value. The standard rule requires that the net capital exceeds at least $6\frac{2}{3}\%$ (15:1 leverage) of aggregate indebtedness (broker's total money liabilities) or alternatively 2% of aggregate debit items arising from customer transactions. This constraint is similar in spirit to Equation (4).[18] As of August 20, 2004, SEC amended the net capital rule for Consolidated Supervised Entities (CSEs) such that CSEs may, under certain circumstances, use their internal risk models to determine whether they fulfill their capital requirement (SEC Release No.34-49830).

A.3 Funding requirements for market makers

There are various types of market-making firms. Some are small partnerships, whereas others are parts of large investment banks. The small firms are financed in a similar way to hedge funds in that they rely primarily on collateralized financing; the funding of banks was described in Section A2.

Certain market makers, such as NYSE specialists, have an obligation to make a market; and a binding funding constraint means that they cannot fulfill this requirement. Hence, avoiding the funding constraint is especially crucial for such market makers.

Market makers are in principle subject to the SEC's net capital rule (described in Section A2), but this rule has special exceptions for market makers. Hence, market makers' main regulatory requirements are those imposed by the exchange on which they operate. These constraints are often similar in spirit to Equation (4).

Appendix B: Proofs

Proof of Propositions 1–3

These results follow from the calculations in the text.

Proof of Proposition 4

We prove the proposition for $Z_1 > 0$, implying $p_1 \leq v_1$ and $x_1 \geq 0$. The complementary case is analogous. To see how the equilibrium depends on the exogenous shocks, we first combine the equilibrium condition $x_1 = -\sum_{k=0}^{1} y_1^k$ with the speculator funding constraint to get

$$m_1^+ \left(Z_1 - \frac{2}{\gamma(\sigma_2)^2}(v_1 - p_1) \right) \leq b_0 + p_1 x_0 + \eta_1, \tag{B1}$$

that is,

$$G(p_1) := m_1^+ \left(Z_1 - \frac{2}{\gamma(\sigma_2)^2}(v_1 - p_1) \right) - p_1 x_0 - b_0 \leq \eta_1. \tag{B2}$$

For η_1 large enough, this inequality is satisfied for $p_1 = v_1$, that is, it is a stable equilibrium that the market is perfectly liquid. For η_1 low enough, the inequality is violated for $p_1 = \dfrac{2v_1}{\gamma(\sigma_2)^2} - Z_1$, that is, it is an equilibrium that the speculator is in default. We are interested in intermediate values of η_1. If the left-hand side G of (B2) is increasing in p_1, then p_1 is a continuously increasing function of η_1, implying no fragility with respect to η_1.

Fragility arises if G can be decreasing in p_1. Intuitively, this expression measures speculator funding needs at the equilibrium position, and fragility arises if the funding need is greater when prices are lower, that is, further from fundamentals. (This can be shown to be equivalent to a non-monotonic excess demand function.)

When the financiers are informed, the left-hand side G of (B2) is

$$\left(\bar{\sigma} + \bar{\theta}|\Delta v_1| + p_1 - v_1 \right) \left(Z_1 + \frac{2}{\gamma(\sigma_2)^2}(p_1 - v_1) \right) - p_1 x_0 - b_0. \tag{B3}$$

The first product is a product of two positive increasing functions of p_1, but the second term, $-p_1 x_0$, is decreasing in p_1 if $x_0 > 0$. Since the first term does not depend on x_0, there exists $\underline{x}$ such that, for $x_0 > \underline{x}$, the whole expression is decreasing.

When the financier is uninformed, we first show that there is fragility for $a = 0$. In this case, the left-hand side G of (B2) is

$$G^0(p_1) := \left(\bar{\sigma} + \bar{\theta}|\Delta p_1| \right) \left(Z_1 + \frac{2}{\gamma(\sigma_2)^2}(p_1 - v_1) \right) - p_1 x_0 - b_0. \tag{B4}$$

When $p_1 < p_0$, $\bar{\theta}|\Delta p_1| = \bar{\theta}(p_0 - p_1)$ decreases in p_1 and, if $\bar{\theta}$ is large enough, this can make the entire expression decreasing. (Since $\bar{\theta}$ is proportional to θ, this clearly translates directly to θ.) Also, the expression is decreasing if x_0 is large enough.

Finally, on any compact set of prices, the margin function converges uniformly to (23) as a approaches 0. Hence, G converges uniformly to G^0.

Since the limit function G^0 has a decreasing part, choose $p_1^a < p_1^b$ such that $\varepsilon := G^0(p_1^a) - G^0(p_1^b) > 0$. By uniform convergence, choose $\underline{a} > 0$ such that for $a < \underline{a}$, G differs from G^0 by at most $\varepsilon/3$. Then we have

$$G\left(p_1^a\right) - G\left(p_1^b\right) = G^0\left(p_1^a\right) - G^0\left(p_1^b\right) + \left[G\left(p_1^a\right) - G^0\left(p_1^a\right)\right]$$
$$- \left[G\left(p_1^b\right) - G^0\left(p_1^b\right)\right] \tag{B5}$$

$$\geq \varepsilon - \frac{\varepsilon}{3} - \frac{\varepsilon}{3} = \frac{\varepsilon}{3} > 0, \tag{B6}$$

which proves that G has a decreasing part.

It can be shown that the price cannot be chosen continuously in η_1 when the left-hand side of (B2) can be decreasing.

Proof of Proposition 5

When the funding constraint binds, we use the implicit function theorem to compute the derivatives. As above, we have

$$m_1^+\left(Z_1 - \frac{2}{\gamma(\sigma_2)^2}(v_1 - p_1)\right) = b_0 + p_1 x_0 + \eta_1. \tag{B7}$$

We differentiate this expression to get

$$\frac{\partial m_1^+}{\partial p_1}\frac{\partial p_1}{\partial \eta_1}\left(Z_1 - \frac{2}{\gamma(\sigma_2)^2}(v_1 - p_1)\right) + m_1^+\frac{2}{\gamma(\sigma_2)^2}\frac{\partial p_1}{\partial \eta_1} = \frac{\partial p_1}{\partial \eta_1}x_0 + 1, \tag{B8}$$

which leads to Equation (24) after rearranging. The case of $Z_1 < 0$ (i.e., Equation (25)) is analogous.

Finally, spiral effects happen if one of the last two terms in the denominator of the right-hand side of Equations (24) and (25) is negative. (The total value of the denominator is positive by definition of a stable equilibrium.) When the speculator is informed, $\frac{\partial m_1^+}{\partial p_1} = 1$ and $\frac{\partial m_1^-}{\partial p_1} = -1$ using Proposition 2. Hence, in this case, margins are stabilizing.

If the speculators are uninformed and a approaches 0, then using Proposition 3, we find that $\frac{\partial m_1^+}{\partial p_1} = \frac{\partial m_1^+}{\partial \Lambda_1}$ approaches $-\bar{\theta} < 0$ for $v_1 - v_0 + \Lambda_1 - \Lambda_0 < 0$ and $\frac{\partial m_1^-}{\partial p_1} = \frac{\partial m_1^-}{\partial \Lambda_1}$ approaches $\bar{\theta} > 0$ for $v_1 - v_0 + \Lambda_1 - \Lambda_0 < 0$. This means that there is a margin spiral with positive probability. The case of a loss spiral is immediately seen to depend on the sign on x_0.

Proof of Proposition 6

We first consider the equation that characterizes a constrained equilibrium. When there is selling pressure from customers, $Z_1^j > 0$, it holds that

$$\left|\Lambda_1^j\right| = -\Lambda_1^j = v_1^j - p_1^j = \min\left\{(\phi_1 - 1)m_1^{j+}, \frac{\gamma(\sigma_2^j)^2}{2}Z_1^j\right\},$$ (B9)

and if customers are buying, $Z_1^j < 0$, we have

$$\left|\Lambda_1^j\right| = \Lambda_1^j = p_1^j - v_1^j = \min\left\{(\phi_1 - 1)m_1^{j-}, \frac{\gamma(\sigma_2^j)^2}{2}(-Z_1^j)\right\}.$$ (B10)

We insert the equilibrium condition $x_1^j = -\sum_k y_1^{j,k}$ and Equation (12) for $y_1^{j,k}$ into the speculators' funding condition to get

$$\sum_{Z_1^j > \frac{2(\phi_1 - 1)m_1^{j+}}{\gamma(\sigma_2^j)^2}} m_1^{j+}\left(Z_1^j - \frac{2(\phi_1 - 1)m_1^{j+}}{\gamma(\sigma_2^j)^2}\right)$$

$$+ \sum_{-Z_1^j > \frac{2(\phi_1 - 1)m_1^{j-}}{\gamma(\sigma_2^j)^2}} m_1^{j-}\left(-Z_1^j - \frac{2(\phi_1 - 1)m_1^{j-}}{\gamma(\sigma_2^j)^2}\right)$$ (B11)

$$= \sum_j x_0^j p_1^j + b_0 + \eta_1,$$

where the margins are evaluated at the prices solving Equations (B9)–(B10). When ϕ_1 approaches infinity, the left-hand side of Equation (B11) becomes zero, and when ϕ_1 approaches one, the left-hand side approaches the capital needed to make the market perfectly liquid. As in the case of one security, there can be multiple equilibria and fragility (Proposition 4). On a stable equilibrium branch, ϕ_1 increases as η_1 decreases. Of course, the equilibrium shadow cost of capital $(\phi_1 - 1)$ is random since $\eta_1, \Delta v_1^1, \ldots, \Delta v_1^j$ are random. To see the commonality in liquidity, we note that $|\Lambda^j|$ is increasing in ϕ_1 for each $j = k, l$. To see this, consider first the case $Z_1^j > 0$. When the financiers are uninformed, $a = 0$, and $\theta^j = 0$, then, $m_1^{j+} = \bar{\sigma}^k$, and, therefore, Equation (B9) shows directly that $\left|\Lambda_1^j\right|$ increases in ϕ_1 (since the minimum of increasing functions is increasing). When financiers are informed and $\theta^j = 0$ then $m_1^{j+} = \bar{\sigma}^k + \Lambda_1^j$, and, therefore, Equation (B9) can be solved to be $\left|\Lambda_1^j\right| = \min\left\{\dfrac{\phi_1 - 1}{\phi_1}\bar{\sigma}^j, \dfrac{\gamma\left(\sigma_2^k\right)^2}{2}Z_1^k\right\}$, which increases in ϕ_1. Similarly, Equation (B10) shows that $|\Lambda^j|$ is increasing in ϕ_1 when $Z_1^j < 0$.

Now, since $|\Lambda^j|$ is increasing in ϕ_1 and does not depend on other state variables under these conditions, $\text{Cov}(|\Lambda^k(\phi)|, |\Lambda^l(\phi)|) > 0$ because any two functions that are both increasing in the same random variable are positively correlated (the proof of this is similar to that of Lemma 1 below). Since $|\Lambda^j|$ is bounded, we can use dominated convergence to establish the existence of $c > 0$ such that part (i) of the proposition applies for any θ^j, $a < c$.

To see part (ii) of the proposition, note that, for all j, $|\Lambda^j|$ is a continuous function of ϕ_1, which is locally insensitive to ϕ_1 if and only if the speculator is not marginal on security j (i.e., if the second term in Equation (B9) or (B10) attains the minimum). Hence, $|\Lambda^j|$ jumps if and only if ϕ_1 jumps.

To see part (iii), we write illiquidity using Equations (B9)–(B10) as

$$\left|\Lambda_1^j\right| = \min\left\{\left(\phi_1 - 1\right)m_1^{j, \text{sign}\left(z_1^j\right)}, \frac{\gamma\left(\sigma_2^j\right)^2}{2}\left|Z_1^j\right|\right\}. \tag{B12}$$

Hence, using the expression for the margin, if the financier is uninformed and $\theta^j = a = 0$, then

$$\left|\Lambda_1^j\right| = \min\left\{\left(\phi_1 - 1\right)\bar{\sigma}_1^j, \frac{\gamma\left(\sigma_2^j\right)^2}{2}\left|Z_1^j\right|\right\} \tag{B13}$$

and, if the financiers are informed and $\theta^j = 0$, then

$$\left|\Lambda_1^j\right| = \min\left\{\frac{\phi_1 - 1}{\phi_1}\bar{\sigma}_1^j, \frac{\gamma\left(\sigma_2^j\right)^2}{2}\left|Z_1^j\right|\right\}. \tag{B14}$$

In the case of uninformed financiers as in Equation (B13), we see that, if $x_1^k \neq 0$,

$$\left|\Lambda_1^k\right| = (\phi_1 - 1)\bar{\sigma}_1^k > (\phi_1 - 1)\bar{\sigma}_1^l \geq \left|\Lambda_1^k\right| \tag{B15}$$

and, $\left|Z_1^k\right| \geq \left|Z_1^l\right|$,

$$\left|\Lambda_1^k\right| = \min\left\{(\phi_1 - 1)\bar{\sigma}_1^k, \frac{\gamma\left(\sigma_2^k\right)^2}{2}\left|Z^k\right|\right\}$$

(B16)

$$> \min\left\{(\phi_1 - 1)\bar{\sigma}_1^l, \frac{\gamma\left(\sigma_2^l\right)^2}{2}\left|Z^l\right|\right\} = \left|\Lambda_1^l\right|.$$

Since Λ^k and Λ^l converge to these values as θ^i, a approach zero, we can choose c so that inequality holds for θ^i, a below c. With informed financiers, it is seen that $\left|\Lambda_1^k\right| \geq \left|\Lambda_1^l\right|$ using similar arguments.

For part (iv) of the proposition, we use that

$$\frac{\partial\left|\Lambda_1^j\right|}{\partial\left(-\eta_1\right)} = \frac{\partial\left|\Lambda_1^j\right|}{\partial\phi_1}\frac{\partial\phi_1}{\partial\left(-\eta_1\right)}.$$

(B17)

Further, $\dfrac{\partial\phi_1}{\partial\left(-\eta_1\right)} \geq 0$ and, from Equations (B13)–(B14), we see that $\dfrac{\partial\left|\Lambda_1^k\right|}{\partial\phi_1} \geq \dfrac{\partial\left|\Lambda_1^l\right|}{\partial\phi_1}$.

The result that $\text{Cov}(\Lambda^k, \phi) \geq \text{Cov}(\Lambda^l, \phi)$ now follows from Lemma 1 below.

Lemma 1. *Let X be a random variable and g_i, $i = 1, 2$, be weakly increasing functions of X, where g_1 has a larger derivative than g_2, that is, $g_1'(x) > g_2'(x)$ for all x and $g_1'(x) > g_2'(x)$ on a set with nonzero measure. Then*

$$\text{Cov}\left[X, g_1(X)\right] > \text{Cov}\left[X, g_2(X)\right].$$

(B18)

Proof. For $i = 1, 2$ we have

$$\text{Cov}\left[X, g_i(X)\right] = E\left[(X - E[X])g_i(X)\right]$$

(B19)

$$= E\left[(X - E[X])\left(\int_{E[X]}^{X} g_i'(y)\,dy\right)\right].$$

(B20)

The latter expression is a product of two terms that always have the same sign. Hence, this is higher if g_i' is larger. ∎

Liquidity Risk (Time 0). Section 5 focuses on the case of speculators who are unconstrained at $t = 0$. When a speculator's problem is linear and he is constrained at time 0, then he invests only in securities with the highest expected profit per capital use, where profit is calculated using the pricing kernel $\phi_1^i/E_0[\phi_1^i]$. In this case, his time-0 shadow cost of capital is

$$\phi_0^i = E_0\left[\phi_1^i\right]$$

$$\left\{1+\max_j\left(\frac{E_0\left[\dfrac{\phi_1^i}{E_0\left[\phi_1^i\right]}p_1^j\right]-p_0^j}{m_0^+}, -\frac{E_0\left[\dfrac{\Phi_1^i}{E_0\left[\phi_1^i\right]}p_1^j\right]-p_0^j}{m_0^-}\right)\right\} \qquad \text{(B21)}$$

We are grateful for helpful comments from Tobias Adrian, Franklin Allen, Yakov Amihud, David Blair, Bernard Dumas, Denis Gromb, Charles Johns, Christian Julliard, John Kambhu, Markus Konz, Stefan Nagel, Michael Brennan, Martin Oehmke, Ketan Patel, Guillaume Plantin, Felipe Schwartzman, Hyun Shin, Matt Spiegel (the editor), Jeremy Stein, Dimitri Vayanos, Jiang Wang, Pierre-Olivier Weill, and from an anonymous referee and Filippos Papakonstantinou and Felipe Schwartzman for outstanding research assistantship. We also thank seminar participants at the New York Federal Reserve Bank, the New York Stock Exchange, Citigroup, Bank for International Settlement, University of Zurich, INSEAD, Northwestern University, Stockholm Institute for Financial Research, Goldman Sachs, IMF, the World Bank, UCLA, LSE, Warwick University, Bank of England, University of Chicago, Texas A&M, University of Notre Dame, HEC, University of Maryland, University of Michigan, Virginia Tech, Ohio State University, University of Mannheim, ECB-Bundesbank, MIT, and conference participants at the American Economic Association Meeting, FMRC conference in honor of Hans Stoll at Vanderbilt, NBER Market Microstructure Meetings, NBER Asset Pricing Meetings, NBER Risks of Financial Institutions conference, the Five Star conference, and American Finance Association Meeting. Brunnermeier acknowledges financial support from the Alfred P. Sloan Foundation.

Notes

1 The pro-cyclical nature of banks' regulatory capital requirements and funding liquidity is another application of our model, which we describe in Appendix A.2.
2 Fragility can also be caused by asymmetric information on the amount of trading by portfolio insurance traders (Gennotte and Leland 1990), and by losses on existing positions (Chowdhry and Nanda 1998).
3 The loss spiral is related to the multipliers that arise in Grossman (1988); Kiyotaki and Moore (1997); Shleifer and Vishny (1997); Chowdhry and Nanda (1998); Xiong

(2001); Kyle and Xiong (2001); Gromb and Vayanos (2002); Morris and Shin (2004); Plantin, Sapra, and Shin (2005); and others. In Geanakoplos (2003) and in Fostel and Geanakoplos (2008), margins increase as risk increases. Our paper captures the margin spiral—i.e., the adverse feedback loop between margins and prices—and the interaction between the margin and loss spirals. Garleanu and Pedersen (2007) show how a risk management spiral can arise.

4 The link between volatility and liquidity is shared by the models of Stoll (1978); Grossman and Miller (1988); and others. What sets our theory apart is that this link is connected with margin constraints. This leads to testable differences since, according to our model, the link is stronger when speculators are poorly financed, and high-volatility securities are more affected by speculator wealth shocks—our explanation of flight to quality.

5 In Vayanos (2004), liquidity premiums increase in volatile times. Fund managers become effectively more risk-averse because higher fundamental volatility increases the likelihood that their performance falls short of a threshold, leading to costly performance-based withdrawal of funds.

6 Market liquidity is the focus of market microstructure (Stoll 1978; Ho and Stoll 1981, 1983; Kyle 1985; Glosten and Milgrom 1985; Grossman and Miller 1988), and is related to the limits of arbitrage (DeLong et al. 1990; Shleifer and Vishny 1997; Abreu and Brunnermeier 2002). Funding liquidity is examined in corporate finance (Shleifer and Vishny 1992; Holmström and Tirole 1998, 2001) and banking (Bryant 1980; Diamond and Dybvig 1983; Allen and Gale 1998, 2004, 2005, 2007). Funding and collateral constraints are also studied in macroeconomics (Aiyagari and Gertler 1999; Bernanke and Gertler 1989; Fisher 1933; Kiyotaki and Moore 1997; Lustig and Chien 2005), and general equilibrium with incomplete markets (Geanakoplos 1997, 2003). Finally, recent papers consider illiquidity with constrained traders (Attari, Mello, and Ruckes 2005; Bernardo and Welch 2004; Brunnermeier and Pedersen 2005; Eisfeldt 2004; Morris and Shin 2004; Weill 2007).

7 In the analysis of time 0, we shall see that margins can also be destabilizing when price volatility signals future liquidity risk (not necessarily fundamental risk).

8 We note that the cushioning effect relies on the financiers' knowledge that the market will become liquid in period $t = 2$. This is not the case in the earlier period 0, though. In an earlier version of the paper, we showed that the cushioning effect disappears in a stationary infinite horizon setting in which the "complementary" customers arrive in each period with a constant arrival probability.

9 See Equation (12).

10 We note that risk aversion also limits speculators' trading in the real world. Our model based on margin constraints differs from one driven purely by risk aversion in several ways. For example, an adverse shock that lowers speculator wealth at $t = 1$ creates a profitable investment opportunity that one might think partially offsets the loss—a natural "dynamic hedge." Because of this dynamic hedge, in a model driven by risk-aversion, speculators (with a relative-risk-aversion coefficient larger than one) increase their $t = 0$ hedging demand, which in turn, lowers illiquidity in $t = 0$. However, exactly the opposite occurs in a setting with capital constraints. Capital constraints prevent speculators from taking advantage of investment opportunities in $t = 1$ so they cannot exploit this "dynamic hedge." Hence, speculators are reluctant to trade away the illiquidity at $t = 0$.

11 See Brunnermeier (2009) for a more complete treatment of the liquidity and credit crunch that started in 2007.

12 The simulation results are available upon request from the authors.

13 One must be cautious with the interpretation of the empirical results related to changes in Regulation T since this regulation may not affect speculators but affects the demanders of liquidity, namely the customers.

14 A few hedge funds have in fact raised some amount of permanent equity capital.
15 A line of credit may have a "material adverse change" clause or other covenants subject to discretionary interpretation of the lender. Such covenants imply that the line of credit may not be a reliable source of funding during a crisis.
16 An explicit equation for the margin is given by Equation (6) in Section 1. Often brokers also take into account the delay between the time a failure by the hedge fund is noticed, and the time the security is actually sold. Hence, the margin of a one-day collateralized loan depends on the estimated risk of holding the asset over a time period that is often set as five to ten days.
17 For instance, cross-product margining means that the broker effectively can move extra cash from one margin account to cover a loss elsewhere, even if the hedge may dispute the loss. Also, collecting all positions with one broker may mean that the hedge fund cannot get a good pricing on the trades, e.g., on repos, and may expose the hedge fund to predatory trading.
18 Let L be the lower of $6\frac{2}{3}\%$ of total indebtedness or 2% of debit items and h^j the haircut for security j; then the rule requires that $L \le W - \sum_j h^j x^j$ that is, $\sum_j h^j x^j \le W - L$.

References

Abreu, D., and M. K. Brunnermeier. 2002. Synchronization Risk and Delayed Arbitrage. *Journal of Financial Economics* 66:341–60.

Acharya, V. V., and L. H. Pedersen. 2005. Asset Pricing with Liquidity Risk. *Journal of Financial Economics* 77:375–410.

Acharya, V. V., S. Schaefer, and Y. Zhang. 2008. Liquidity Risk and Correlation Risk: A Clinical Study of the General Motors and Ford Downgrade of 2005. Working Paper, London Business School.

Adrian, T., and H. S. Shin. 2009. Liquidity and Leverage. *Journal of Financial Intermediation.*

Aiyagari, S. R., and M. Gertler. 1999. "Overreaction" of Asset Prices in General Equilibrium. *Review of Economic Dynamics* 2:3–35.

Allen, F., and D. Gale. 1998. Optimal Financial Crisis. *Journal of Finance* 53:1245–84.

Allen, F., and D. Gale. 2004. Financial Intermediaries and Markets. *Econometrica* 72:1023–61.

Allen, F., and D. Gale. 2005. Financial Fragility, Liquidity, and Asset Prices. *Journal of the European Economic Association* 2:1015–48.

Allen, F., and D. Gale. 2007. *Understanding Financial Crises.* Clarendon Lectures in Economics. Oxford, UK: Oxford University Press.

Amihud, Y., and H. Mendelson. 1989. The Effects of Beta, Bid-Ask Spread, Residual Risk, and Size on Stock Returns. *Journal of Finance* 44:479–86.

Attari, M., A. S. Mello, and M. E. Ruckes. 2005. Arbitraging Arbitrageurs. *Journal of Finance* 60:2471–511.

Benston, G. J., and R. L. Hagerman. 1974. Determinants of the Bid-Ask Spread in the Over-the-Counter Market. *Journal of Financial Economics* 1:353–64.

Bernanke, B., and M. Gertler. 1989. Agency Costs, Net Worth, and Business Fluctuations. *American Economic Review* 79:14–31.

Bernardo, A. E., and I. Welch. 2004. Liquidity and Financial Markets Run. *Quarterly Journal of Economics* 119:135–58.

Brunnermeier, M. K. 2009. Deciphering the Liquidity and Credit Crunch 2007–08. *Journal of Economic Perspectives.* 2009, Issue 1.

Brunnermeier, M. K., S. Nagel, and L. H. Pedersen. 2009. Carry Trades and Currency Crashes, in Daron Acemoglu, Kenneth Rogoff, and Michael Woodford (eds.), *NBER Macroeconomics Annual 2008,* vol. 23. Cambridge, MA: MIT Press.

Brunnermeier, M. K., and L. H. Pedersen. 2005. Predatory Trading. *Journal of Finance* 60:1825–63.

Bryant, J. 1980. A Model of Reserves, Bank Runs, and Deposit Insurance. *Journal of Banking and Finance* 4:335–44.

Campbell, J. Y., A. W. Lo, and A. C. MacKinlay. 1997. *The Econometrics of Financial Markets.* Princeton, NJ: Princeton University Press.

Chordia, T., R. Roll, and A. Subrahmanyam. 2000. Commonality in Liquidity. *Journal of Financial Economics* 56:3–28.

Chordia, T., A. Sarkar, and A. Subrahmanyam. 2005. An Empirical Analysis of Stock and Bond Market Liquidity. *Review of Financial Studies* 18:85–129.

Chowdhry, B., and V. Nanda. 1998. Leverage and Market Stability: The Role of Margin Rules and Price Limits. *Journal of Business* 71:179–210.

Comerton-Forde, C., T. Hendershott, C. M. Jones, P. C. Moulton, and M. S. Seasholes. 2008. Time Variation in Liquidity: The Role of Market Maker Inventories and Revenues. Working Paper, Columbia University.

Coughenour, J. F., and M. M. Saad. 2004. Common Market Makers and Commonality in Liquidity. *Journal of Financial Economics* 73:37–69.

DeLong, J. B., A. Shleifer, L. H. Summers, and R. J. Waldmann. 1990. Noise Trader Risk in Financial Markets. *Journal of Political Economy* 98:703–38.

Diamond, D., and P. Dybvig. 1983. Bank Runs, Deposit Insurance, and Liquidity. *Journal of Political Economy* 91:401–19.

Duffie, D., N. Gârleanu, and L. H. Pedersen. 2002. Securities Lending, Shorting, and Pricing. *Journal of Financial Economics* 66:307–39.

Eisfeldt, A. 2004. Endogenous Liquidity in Asset Markets. *Journal of Finance* 59:1–30.

Fisher, I. 1933. The Debt-Deflation Theory of Great Depression. *Econometrica* 1:337–57.

Fostel, A., and J. Geanakoplos. 2008. Leverage Cycles and The Anxious Economy. *American Economic Review* 98:1211–44.

Garleanu, N., and L. H. Pedersen. 2007. Liquidity and Risk Management. *The American Economic Review (Papers & Proceedings)* 97:193–97.

Garleanu, N., L. H. Pedersen, and A. Poteshman. 2008. Demand-Based Option Pricing. *Review of Financial Studies.*

Geanakoplos, J. 1997. Promises, Promises, in W.B. Arthur, S. Durlauf and D. Lane (eds.), *The Economy as an Evolving Complex System II* 1997: 285–320. Addison-Wesley, Reading MA.

Geanakoplos, J. 2003. Liquidity, Default and Crashes: Endogenous Contracts in General Equilibrium, in Mathias Dewatripont, Lars Peter Hansen, and Stephen J. Turnovsky (eds.), *Advances in Economics and Econometrics: Theory and Applications II, Eighth World Congress,* vol. 2, pp. 170–205. Econometric Society Monographs. Cambridge, UK: Cambridge University Press.

Gennotte, G., and H. Leland. 1990. Market Liquidity, Hedging, and Crashes. *American Economic Review* 80:999–1021.

Glosten, L. R., and P. R. Milgrom. 1985. Bid, Ask, and Transaction Prices in a Specialist Market with Heterogeneously Informed Traders. *Journal of Financial Economics* 14:71–100.

Gromb, D., and D. Vayanos. 2002. Equilibrium and Welfare in Markets with Financially Constrained Arbitrageurs. *Journal of Financial Economics* 66:361–407.

Grossman, S. J. 1988. An Analysis of the Implications for Stock and Futures Price Volatility of Program Trading and Dynamic Hedging Strategies. *Journal of Business* 61:275–98.

Grossman, S. J., and M. H. Miller. 1988. Liquidity and Market Structure. *Journal of Finance* 43:617–33.

Grossman, S. J., and J.-L. Vila. 1992. Optimal Dynamic Trading with Leverage Constraints. *Journal of Financial and Quantitative Analysis* 27:151–68.

Hameed, A., W. Kang, and S. Viswanathan. 2005. Asymmetric Comovement in Liquidity. Mimeo, Duke University.

Hasbrouck, J., and D. Seppi. 2001. Common Factors in Prices, Order Flows, and Liquidity. *Journal of Financial Economics* 59:383–411.

Ho, T. S. Y., and H. R. Stoll. 1981. Optimal Dealer Pricing under Transactions and Return Uncertainty. *Journal of Financial Economics* 9:47–73.

Ho, T. S. Y., and H. R. Stoll. 1983. The Dynamics of Dealer Markets under Competition. *Journal of Finance* 38:1053–74.

Holmström, B., and J. Tirole. 1998. Private and Public Supply of Liquidity. *Journal of Political Economy* 106:1–39.

Holmström, B., and J. Tirole. 2001. LAPM: A Liquidity-Based Asset Pricing Model. *Journal of Finance* 56:1837–67.

Huberman, G., and D. Halka. 2001. Systematic Liquidity. *Journal of Financial Research* 24:161–78.

Ibbotson. 1999. *Cost of Capital Quarterly, 1999 Yearbook,* 2nd ed. Chicago: Ibbotson Associates, 1976.

International Monetary Fund. 2007. *Global Financial Stability Report.* October.

Kiyotaki, N., and J. Moore. 1997. Credit Cycles. *Journal of Political Economy* 105:211–48.

Kyle, A. S. 1985. Continuous Auctions and Insider Trading. *Econometrica* 53:1315–35.

Kyle, A. S., and W. Xiong. 2001. Contagion as a Wealth Effect. *Journal of Finance* 56:1401–40.

Liu, J., and F. A. Longstaff. 2004. Losing Money on Arbitrages: Optimal Dynamic Portfolio Choice in Markets with Arbitrage Opportunities. *Review of Financial Studies* 17:611–41.

Lustig, H., and Y. Chien. 2005. The Market Price of Aggregate Risk and Wealth Distribution. NBER Working Paper 11132.

Mitchell, M., L. H. Pedersen, and T. Pulvino. 2007. Slow Moving Capital. *American Economic Review (Papers & Proceedings)* 97:215–20.

Morris, S., and H. Shin. 2004. Liquidity Black Holes. *Review of Finance* 8:1–18.

Pastor, L., and R. F. Stambaugh. 2003. Liquidity Risk and Expected Stock Returns. *Journal of Political Economy* 111:642–85.

Plantin, G., H. Sapra, and H. S. Shin. 2005. Marking-to-Market: Panacea or Pandora's Box? *Journal of Accounting Research* 46:435–60.

Shleifer, A., and R. W. Vishny. 1992. Liquidation Values and Debt Capacity: A Market Equilibrium Approach. *Journal of Finance* 47:1343–66.

Shleifer, A., and R. W. Vishny. 1997. The Limits of Arbitrage. *Journal of Finance* 52:35–55.

Stiglitz, J. E., and A. Weiss. 1981. Credit Rationing in Markets with Imperfect Information. *American Economic Review* 71:393–410.

Stoll, H. R. 1978. The Supply of Dealer Services in Securities Markets. *Journal of Finance* 33:1133–51.

Vayanos, D. 2004. Flight to Quality, Flight to Liquidity, and the Pricing of Risk. Working Paper, London School of Economics.

Weill, P.-O. 2007. Leaning Against the Wind. *Review of Economic Studies* 74:1329–54.

Wigmore, B. 1998. Revisiting the October 1987 Crash. *Financial Analysts Journal* 54:36–48.

Xiong, W. 2001. Convergence Trading with Wealth Effects: An Amplification Mechanism in Financial Markets. *Journal of Financial Economics* 62(2): 247–92.

56

HOW DO OFFICIAL BAILOUTS AFFECT THE RISK OF INVESTING IN EMERGING MARKETS?

Giovanni Dell'Ariccia, Isabel Schnabel
and Jeromin Zettelmeyer

Source: *Journal of Money, Credit and Banking* 38, 7, 2006, 1689–1714.

We analyze the effects of bailout expectations on sovereign bond spreads in emerging markets. The non-bailout of Russia in August 1998 is interpreted as an event that decreased the perceived probability of future crisis lending to emerging markets. If official rescues are expected to mitigate the losses of investors in the event of a crisis, such an event should raise the cross-country dispersion of spreads, because investors pay more attention to differences in risk characteristics across countries. We find strong evidence for such an effect. This is consistent with the existence of "investor moral hazard," at least prior to 1998.

No SUBJECT IN THE DEBATE ON GLOBALIZATION and international institutions has suffered from a greater disconnect between policy debate and empirical literature than that of the "moral hazard" supposedly caused by international official rescues. Ever since the Mexican bailout of 1995, IMF critics have claimed that large-scale crisis lending might encourage excessive risk-taking by investors and imprudent policies in debtor countries, and nowadays this concern is shared by a large part of the official community, including the IMF itself.[1] This has given rise to a range of policy initiatives seeking to offset the assumed effects of crisis lending on the risks perceived by private creditors—from "private sector involvement" in official rescue packages, to more explicit criteria that regulate and limit large-scale crisis lending, to the proposal to establish a "Sovereign Debt Restructuring Mechanism" as an alternative approach for resolving debt crises. Yet, there is no empirical evidence so far that indicates that IMF-led interventions have had *any* systematic effect on international capital markets, let alone that they have distorted the incentives faced by international investors or country authorities.

This paper takes a fresh look at the effects of the anticipation of official crisis lending on emerging market default premia. If bailouts are expected to reduce investors' losses in case of a crisis, a change in the likelihood of a bailout should translate into changes in emerging market bond spreads. In contrast to the existing literature, we examine not only the *levels* of spreads, but also their cross-country *variance*. To the extent that an official safety net insulates investors from country vulnerabilities, spreads should react less sensitively to differences in the riskiness of fundamentals across countries. Hence, an event that strengthens (or weakens) the perceived safety net should result in a decrease (or increase) in the cross-sectional dispersion of spreads.

We apply our tests to a particular, highly unanticipated event—the August 1998 Russian "non-bailout." We argue that this event is much better suited to test for the impact of changing bailout expectations on spreads than the events studied by other authors, such as the 1995 Mexican crisis, which has figured prominently in the literature.[2] We check the robustness of our results by applying our testing procedures to two distinct datasets: J.P. Morgan's dataset of secondary market bond spreads contained in the "EMBI Global" Bond Index, as well as a dataset of launch bond spreads based on Dealogic "Bondware." In order to separate the structural effects of perceptions regarding official lending from short-term market turbulence after the Russian default, we focus on the long-term behavior of emerging market bond spreads, after market volatility had returned to normal levels.

Our main result is that the Russian crisis was followed by a permanent, significant increase in the cross-sectional dispersion of spreads (controlling for fundamentals), indicating that investors paid more attention to differences in country characteristics after the crisis than they had done before. We also observe significant increases in the levels of spreads in many—but not all—countries studied, in particular in countries with relatively weak fundamentals. The implication is that, prior to 1998, official crisis lending must have mitigated the perceived risk of holding emerging market debt, an effect sometimes referred to as "investor moral hazard." Our results do not imply that this was necessarily inefficient. Official crisis lending may have provided efficient insurance—less costly and perhaps less likely crises; but it may also have had adverse incentive effects, leading, for example, to overborrowing on the side of countries. Hence, this paper demonstrates only the presence of an insurance effect, without inferring its welfare consequences. This said, there is evidence suggesting that public debt levels may be unsustainably high in many emerging market countries (International Monetary Fund 2003), and high levels of debt have played an important role in most recent emerging market crises. This suggests that official policies encouraging cheaper and larger debt flows to emerging markets prior to 1998 were probably not all efficient, and that some of the policy initiatives taken in subsequent years in response to worries about moral hazard may in fact have been justified.

Only four studies—Zhang (1999), Lane and Phillips (2000), Kamin (2004), and Brealey and Kaplanis (2004)—study the effects of IMF or IMF-led crisis lending on emerging market default premia. Their conclusions are mostly negative, either rejecting the presence of any impact on emerging market debt values, or finding weak and inconsistent effects. We argue that the literature's failure to find a clear-cut insurance effect is primarily a consequence of the methodologies used so far: in particular, these papers focus on anticipated or ambiguous events, and their tests rely only on changes in the levels of spreads.

Zhang (1999) regresses emerging market bond spreads before and after the Mexican crisis on a number of macroeconomic fundamentals and a dummy variable for the period after the crisis. The latter turns out to have an insignificant positive coefficient, contrary to what one would expect if the Mexican bailout had created moral hazard. However, the Mexican crisis also led to a general reassessment of the risks associated with emerging market lending, as investors learned that even a country with a recent track record of reform and relatively sound fundamentals was vulnerable to a sudden capital flow reversal (Calvo and Mendoza 1996). Any reduction in spreads due to the IMF/U.S. intervention may have been offset by this effect. Lane and Phillips (2000) examine the short-term reactions of the spread of an emerging market bond index to 22 events that might have changed expectations of future international crisis lending. With few exceptions, these events fail to produce statistically significant reactions of spreads in the expected direction. But, as Lane and Phillips themselves point out, this could just be due to the fact that most events were anticipated. They do find a significant reaction to the event considered in this study, namely the Russian default. However, their event-study methodology merely captures the market turbulence shortly after the Russian crisis, and not the structural long-term effect. In a similar vein, Brealey and Kaplanis (2004) analyze the short-term impact of IMF-related announcements in a broader range of countries and asset classes, and find no significant effects, apart from one important exception: announcements that IMF support would *not* be forthcoming lead to negative abnormal returns. These results suggest that IMF intervention is generally anticipated, so that only "bad news" triggers noticeable reactions. However, that paper only looks at the wealth effects of IMF interventions on the involved country, and not at the effects of the intervention on bailout expectations, and hence bond spreads, in *other* countries. Finally, the paper by Kamin (2004) relies largely on the methodology developed in our paper, but it presents a less formal analysis. It finds that there was no significant moral hazard in emerging market finance in the years *after* 1998. This does not contradict the results of this paper, which finds evidence consistent with the presence of investor moral hazard *prior* to the 1998 crisis.

The remainder of the paper is organized as follows. Section 1 presents our tests and discusses the empirical implementation of these tests. This is followed by a description of, and look at, the raw data in Section 2. Section 3 presents the results, and Section 4 discusses the results and concludes the paper.

1. METHODOLOGY

1.1 Testable Implications

To the extent that official bailouts insulate investors from the effects of emerging market crises, the expectation of such bailouts should lower the *levels* of spreads on emerging market debt (conditioning on country fundamentals). This is the main prediction used in the existing literature to test for "investor moral hazard." By the same logic, in a multi-country setting, the anticipation of an official bailout should lead to a reduction in the cross-country *variance* of spreads (again conditioning on country fundamentals). The intuition is simple: if official crisis lending mitigates the blow of future crises from an investor perspective, this will reduce the spreads of countries with relatively weak fundamentals more than those of relatively safe countries. This is almost the same argument as that underlying the "level test," except that it is applied to the cross-sectional comparison across emerging market borrowers, rather than to the pairwise comparison between the debt of a specific emerging market country and a risk-free alternative investment.

To derive these implications as simply as possible, consider a world with risk-neutral investors who can either hold a risk-free asset delivering a gross return R^*, or sovereign debt of emerging market country i promising a return R_i if there is no crisis. However, with probability θ_i (assumed to depend on country specific fundamentals, i.e. $\theta_i = \theta(\mathbf{x}_i)$), the country suffers a crisis, which leads to an expected loss of l percent. In order to obtain an expected return of R^*, investors demand

$$R_i = \frac{R^*}{1 - l\theta_i},$$

or equivalently, in terms of spreads over the risk free rate,

$$s_i = R_i - R^* = R^* \cdot \frac{l\theta_i}{1 - l\theta_i}. \tag{1}$$

We would like to know how the spreads change if the expected loss l in a crisis depends inversely on the presence and size of an official bailout package b (i.e. $l = l(b)$ with $l'(b) < 0$). Furthermore, following Cook and Spellman (1996), assume that $l\theta_i$ is small, which implies that the expected repayment is large. This is clearly not a good assumption for emerging market countries facing a crisis, though it may be a reasonable assumption in normal times. We impose it only for expositional purposes (see Dell'Ariccia, Schnabel, and Zettelmeyer 2002 for a more general treatment). Then we can approximate the spreads by

$$s_i \approx R^* l(b)\theta(\mathbf{x}_i).$$

Hence, the spread of any country i decreases in b for given $\mathbf{x}_i$. Moreover, $Var(s_i) \approx R^{*2}l(b)^2Var[\theta(\mathbf{x}_i)]$, so the variance of spreads across countries decreases in b as well, holding $\mathbf{x}_i$, constant.

Compared to the *level test*, the *variance test* has two important advantages. The first is that it provides a single measure to test for the potential insurance effect of official bailouts in the entire sample of emerging market countries. Therefore, it is easier to interpret than the level test, which is applied country by country and could lead to mixed overall results. The second advantage of the variance test is that it is subject to a smaller bias when the analyzed event contains additional information, unrelated to official intervention policies, which affects all countries more or less in the same way. Such information would increase or decrease all spreads by the same amount, while it would leave the variance of spreads unchanged.

1.2 Econometric Implementation

To derive our econometric tests, we consider a standard model of the determination of bond spreads,

$$s_{it} = \mathbf{x}_{it}\beta + u_{it}, \tag{2}$$

where s_{it} denotes the bond spread of country i at time t, and $\mathbf{x}_{it}$ is a $1 \times k$-vector containing the country's fundamentals, which determine the spreads of sovereign bonds, u represents a random error. This equation will be the basis of all our tests.

Consider an event that *reduces* the perceived probability of future bailouts. Since we are looking at the unexpected *absence* of a further international rescue package for Russia in August of 1998, this is the relevant case for our empirical analysis. The general estimation procedure consists in estimating a pooled model over the whole period, i.e. before and after the event, allowing for a structural break at the time of the event. For the ease of exposition, assume that there are only two points in time: "before" the event ($t=0$) and "after" the event ($t=1$).

Then, bond spreads before the event can be described by the model

$$s_{i0} = \mathbf{x}_{i0}\beta^0 + u_{i0}, \tag{3}$$

whereas the model changes to

$$s_{i1} = \mathbf{x}_{i1}\beta^1 + u_{i1} \tag{4}$$

after the event. All our tests are based on the estimated coefficients β^0 and β^1 from these regressions. Let H_0 denote the null hypothesis, i.e. that official intervention has no impact on default premia. Then the testable implications discussed above can be restated as follows:

1. Level test: Under H_0, the *levels* of spreads should not be affected by an event that reduces expected international crisis lending. Under H_1, the levels of spreads should increase for every country, holding fundamentals constant. More formally, the change in the levels of spreads can be decomposed into three components,

$$s_{i1} - s_{i0} = \mathbf{x}_{i1}\left(\beta^1 - \beta^0\right) + \left(\mathbf{x}_{i1} - \mathbf{x}_{i0}\right)\beta^0 + \left(u_{i1} - u_{i0}\right), \tag{5}$$

or, alternatively,

$$s_{i1} - s_{i0} = \mathbf{x}_{i0}\left(\beta^1 - \beta^0\right) + \left(\mathbf{x}_{i1} - \mathbf{x}_{i0}\right)\beta^1 + \left(u_{i1} - u_{i0}\right). \tag{6}$$

The first term is the change in the levels of spreads induced by the change in β, the second term is the change in the level of spreads caused by the change in the fundamentals, and the third term reflects the impact of a change in the error term.[3] Here, we are only interested in the first term, which captures the effect of a change in the pricing of risks on the levels of spreads. If the event entails the expectation of a reduction in official bailouts, all risks should be priced higher after the event under H_1. Thus, the *level test* takes the following form:

$$H_0 : \mathbf{x}_{it}\left(\beta^1 - \beta^0\right) = 0$$

$$H_1 : \mathbf{x}_{it}\left(\beta^1 - \beta^0\right) > 0$$

The test can be carried out as a linear Wald test in which we compare the fitted spreads that result from the models estimated before and after the event. As shown by the derivation, the above decomposition is not unique: when controlling for fundamentals, one can either use the fundamentals before or after the event. In fact, this choice can affect the results of the test. Therefore, we present the results of both choices. Note that none of the papers cited in the introduction conduct the level test in the way it is presented here; they all rely on changes in *average* spread levels, rather than individual spread levels, as suggested by theory.[4]

2. Variance test: Under H_0, the cross-sectional variance of spreads should remain unchanged after the event. Under H_1, the difference in spreads between each pair of countries should increase, which, in turn, implies an increase in the cross-sectional variance of spreads (controlling for changes in fundamentals). More formally, we can write the variance *across countries* before the event as

$$Var(s_0) = \beta^{0'}Var(\mathbf{X}_0)\beta^0 + \sigma_0^2, \tag{7}$$

and the variance after the event as

$$Var(s_1) = \beta^{1'}Var(\mathbf{X}_1)\beta^1 + \sigma_1^2, \tag{8}$$

where $\mathbf{X}_t$ is the $N \times k$-matrix of the fundamentals of all countries at date t, and σ_0^2 and σ_1^2 are the variances of the error terms. The change in the variance of spreads can be decomposed into three components:

$$
\begin{aligned}
Var(s_1) &- Var(s_0) \\
&= \left[\beta^{1'}Var(\mathbf{X}_1)\beta^1 - \beta^{0'}Var(\mathbf{X}_1)\beta^0 \right] \\
&\quad + \left[\beta^{0'}Var(\mathbf{X}_1)\beta^0 - \beta^{0'}Var(\mathbf{X}_0)\beta^0 \right] + \left[\sigma_1^2 - \sigma_0^2 \right] \\
&= \left[\beta^{1'}Var(\mathbf{X}_0)\beta^1 - \beta^{0'}Var(\mathbf{X}_0)\beta^0 \right] \\
&\quad + \left[\beta^{1'}Var(\mathbf{X}_1)\beta^1 - \beta^{1'}Var(\mathbf{X}_0)\beta^1 \right] + \left[\sigma_1^2 - \sigma_0^2 \right]
\end{aligned}
\tag{9}
$$

The first term is the change in the variance induced by the change in β; the second term is the change in the variance caused by the change in the fundamentals; and the third term reflects the impact of a change in the variance of the error term.[5] Again, we are mainly interested in the first term, which captures the effect of a change in the pricing of risks on the variance of spreads. Thus, if the event entails an expected reduction in official bailouts, the *variance test* takes the following form:

$$H_0 : \beta^{1'}Var(\mathbf{X}_t)\beta^1 = \beta^{0'}Var(\mathbf{X}_t)\beta^0$$

$$H_1 : \beta^{1'}Var(\mathbf{X}_t)\beta^1 > \beta^{0'}Var(\mathbf{X}_t)\beta^0$$

The test is carried out as a nonlinear Wald test (see Appendix for statistical details). Again, the decomposition is not unique: the choice of $\mathbf{X}_t$ can affect the results of the test, and we report the results for both alternatives (i.e. conditioning on the state of fundamentals both before and after the event). As we shall see, this does not affect the results.[6]

1.3 The Russian Crisis as a Valid Event

In order to implement the proposed tests, we need an event that satisfies three conditions: it has to change investors' perceptions about the likelihood of future official bailouts; it has to be unexpected; and it must not lead to a reassessment of risks, other than through the expectations of future rescues.

The Russian default in August 1998 meets all three criteria fairly well. Judging by the extent of the immediate market reactions following the announcement of a moratorium on foreign debt repayments, it clearly constituted a surprise. This surprise was not due to news about the state of the Russian economy, which was well known. The real surprise was that the international community did not prevent the default of a country that was believed to be "too big and too nuclear to fail."[7] The absence of international support during the Russian crisis was widely interpreted as a sign of a higher reluctance of the international community to support crisis countries.[8] On this basis, the first two of the above conditions seem to be satisfied.

Whether the third condition is satisfied is more debatable. In addition to sending a signal about future bailouts, the crisis may have "reminded" investors of the risks existing in emerging economies, leading to a general repricing of risks (the "wake-up call" interpretation); moreover, it may have taught the world new lessons about the risks in emerging market lending, unrelated to official sector policies. However, this argument, which has some plausibility in the case of the Mexican and the Asian crises, seems less convincing in the case of Russia. First, the two preceding emerging market crises should have been sufficient to "wake up" investors. Second, while both the Tequila crisis and the Asian crisis taught investors new lessons about the risks of investing in emerging markets (by demonstrating the possibility of a "sudden stop" in international capital flows, the power of contagion, and the dangers of "crony capitalism"), it is not clear that the Russian default, which resulted from an old-fashioned fiscal sustainability problem, was a new type of crisis.

If there was anything new about the Russian crisis—other than the unexpected official sector response, it would have been an even more forceful demonstration of the extent of contagion and global interdependence than in the previous two crises, as the crisis in Russia had major repercussions not only for countries as distant and different as Brazil, Mexico, and Chile, but (after the collapse of LTCM) even for the United States. However, if this was a common vulnerability of countries with different fundamentals, it would bias only the level test (making it more likely that the null hypothesis of no change would be rejected), but not the variance test. If, instead, it was expected to increase risks especially in countries with good fundamentals—which had been thought to be immune to contagion—it would still bias the level test in the same direction, but it would also bias the variance test, making it *less* likely that the null hypothesis of equal variances would be rejected. In this sense, the variance test is more conservative than the level test in our application.

1.4 Estimation Strategy

In applying our tests to the Russian crisis, a complication arises from the fact that the crisis was followed by a prolonged period of financial market turbulence, including the LTCM crisis and the Brazilian currency crisis in early 1999. During this period, one cannot reasonably assume a stable relationship between macroeconomic fundamentals and bond spreads, as is necessary in the models used in the literature on emerging market bond spreads.[9] Including the post-crisis turbulence in our estimation will bias our results, making the rejection of the null hypothesis more likely, as both the levels and the cross-sectional variance of spreads rose sharply in the immediate aftermath of the default, before returning to more normal levels.

We deal with this problem by excluding a large period after the crisis from our regressions, namely, the second half of 1998 and the first quarter of 1999. We checked whether the results are sensitive to the precise definition of the exclusion period; this is not the case. Using a simple measure of financial turbulence, it is easy to see the reason for this insensitivity. Figure 1 graphs the predicted conditional variance of changes in the EMBI Global index, using a GARCH (1,1) model estimated from daily data over the period January 1998 until August 2002.[10] The main lesson from the figure is that periods of high market volatility literally stand out; they are easy to identify and to relate to reported events. The figure also shows that by March of 1999, conditional volatility was essentially down to pre-August 1998 levels. So even though conditional volatility is indeed persistent, the persistence does not seem large enough to influence volatility much

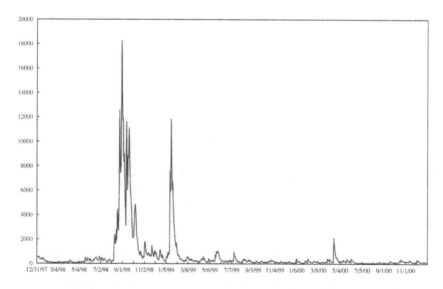

Figure 1 Estimated Conditional Volatility of Changes in the EMBIG Composite Spread, 1998–2000.

beyond the crisis events, and the exact choice of the exclusion period has no impact on the results.

2. DATA

We use two different sources of data for bond spreads. The first are country-level *secondary-market* spreads from J.P. Morgan's Emerging Markets Global Bond Index (EMBI Global, or EMBIG). While its predecessors (EMBI, EMBI+) have been used extensively in the academic literature on emerging market bond spreads (Cline and Barnes, 1997, Zhang, 1999, Lane and Phillips, 2000), the much broader—albeit shorter—EMBIG dataset does not appear to have been used so far.[11] It is made up of U.S.-dollar denominated sovereign or "quasi-sovereign"[12] bonds that satisfy certain criteria, e.g. a sufficient liquidity. Spreads have been available daily for 21 countries since January 1, 1998.[13] The instruments in the index are mainly Brady bonds and Eurobonds, but the index also contains a small number of traded loans as well as local market instruments. The spread of a bond is calculated as the difference between the bond's yield and the yield of a U.S. government bond with a comparable issue date and maturity. A country's bond spread is then calculated as the weighted average of the spreads of all bonds, which satisfy the above-mentioned criteria, where the weighting is done according to market capitalization. In the case of Brady bonds, "stripped" spreads (i.e. spreads that abstract from any collateral backing these bonds) are provided.[14]

An alternative data source is the Dealogic Bondware dataset, which contains *launch* spreads of sovereign and public foreign currency bonds of 54 emerging countries.[15] The spread of a bond is calculated as the difference between the bond's yield and the yield of a government bond of the country issuing the respective currency with a similar issue date and maturity. In contrast to the EMBIG, the Bondware dataset does not include Brady bonds. Therefore, the two datasets are almost disjoint. The main advantage of the Bondware dataset is that it covers a much broader range of countries. However, the use of the Bondware dataset is more complicated, since it contains *primary* spreads that are observed only at the time of issue. Thus, this dataset is a highly unbalanced panel, which raises econometric problems due to a potential selection bias. The selection problem can be tackled by estimating a standard Heckman correction model.

Figure 2 shows the evolution of daily bond spreads for the emerging market countries contained in the EMBIG between January 1998 and December 2000, excluding the two countries (Russia and Ecuador) that suffered major financial crises in this period. The basic pattern is well known: in August 1998, virtually all spreads shot up, and their cross-sectional variance widened sharply. By the beginning of 1999, most spreads had come down from the high levels reached directly after the crisis, but they did not return to their pre-crisis levels. Also, the cross-sectional variance of spreads appears to be larger in the post-crisis period. This is confirmed in Table 1 (left column), which shows the cross-sectional mean and standard deviation of spreads, based on monthly data, for the pre-crisis, crisis,

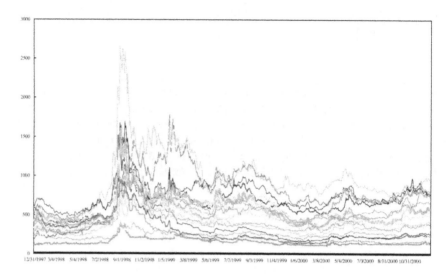

Figure 2 EMBI Global Daily Strip Spreads, 1998–2000, 18 countries (excludes Russia and Ecuador) (in basic points).

and post-crisis periods. Relative to the pre-crisis period, the mean spread rises by about 100 basis points after the crisis, and the standard deviation nearly doubles (excluding Russia and Ecuador).

The evolution of launch spreads contained in the Bondware database is not as easily graphed, since the data consist of single datapoints for each issue, rather than a continuous time series. Moreover, the selection problem makes the raw data more difficult to interpret. For example, the average level of spreads after the Russian crisis is biased downward by the fact that Russia does not issue any bonds in that period. Nevertheless, after excluding Russia and Ecuador from the sample, the raw data confirm the pattern suggested by the EMBIG spreads (right column of Table 1). In particular, both the cross-sectional mean and the cross-sectional standard deviation of spreads remain at substantially higher levels in the post-crisis period than they were in the pre-crisis period. The question is to what extent these changes are attributable to changes in fundamentals, and whether they are statistically significant when controlling for changes in fundamentals.

On the right-hand side of the regressions, we use a rich set of macroeconomic fundamentals, following the literature on bond pricing[16] (see Table 2 for a complete list of variables and their sources). In choosing the set of right-hand-side variables, we tried to capture the most important aspects of a country's macroeconomic performance, such as domestic economic condition, external sector, international interest rates, and political variables. In addition, we included credit ratings, which have been shown to be crucial even when macroeconomic fundamentals are included (Cantor and Packer, 1996, Eichengreen and Mody, 2000).

Table 1 Mean and Cross-sectional Dispersion of Spreads before and after the Russian Crisis: Summary Statistics

Period		18 EMBIG countries (excluding Russia and Ecuador)[a]		39 Bondware countries (excluding Russia and Ecuador)[b]		
		Mean	Std. dev.[c]	Mean	Std. dev.[d]	No. of countries
Pre-crisis	1998:Q1	354	108	330	178	11
	1998:Q2	393	122	272	154	16
Crisis	1998:Q3	776	333	302	292	7
	1998:Q4	668	295	437	214	18
	1999:Q1	561	237	419	222	19
Post-crisis	1999:Q2	532	258	370	194	31
	1999:Q3	567	283	416	179	26
	1999:Q4	438	217	387	182	22
	2000:Q1	406	207	379	188	28
	2000:Q2	479	230	325	209	17
	2000:Q3	447	211	387	182	22
	2000:Q4	532	261	341	212	12

[a]Argentina, Bulgaria, Brazil, China, Colombia, Croatia, Korea, Morocco, Mexico, Malaysia, Panama, Peru, Philippines, Poland, Thailand, Turkey, Venezuela, South Africa.
[b]Argentina, Brazil, Bulgaria, Chile, China, Colombia, Costa Rica, Croatia, Cyprus, Czech Republic, El Salvador, Estonia, Hong Kong, Hungary, India, Israel, Jamaica, Kazakhstan, Korea, Latvia, Lebanon, Lithuania, Malaysia, Malta, Mexico, Morocco, Philippines, Poland, Romania, Singapore, Slovak Republic, Slovenia, South Africa, Taiwan, Thailand, Tunisia, Turkey, Uruguay, and Venezuela. Dominican Republic, Ecuador, Egypt, Guatemala, Indonesia, Jordan, Mauritius, Oman, Pakistan, Panama, Peru, and Saudi Arabia did not issue bonds during this period.
[c]Refers to average cross-sectional standard deviation during period.
[d]Refers to standard deviation of all available bonds during period.

We followed Eichengreen and Mody (2000) in including not the ratings themselves, but rather a residual from a regression of the ratings on all included macroeconomic fundamentals.[17] In the regressions based on the EMBIG dataset, we used the whole range of right-hand-side variables, whereas the regressions based on the Bondware dataset use a more parsimonious specification to avoid excluding too many countries from the dataset due to missing data on the right-hand side.

3 RESULTS

3.1 Tests Using Secondary Market Spread Data

We begin by presenting regressions and test results based on the EMBIG dataset. Table 3 shows pre-and post-crisis regression results for three alternative models: first, a standard model of emerging market spreads, based on Eichengreen and Mody (2000), second, a modification of that model that omits the variable "external debt/GDP," which was insignificant in the post-crisis sample, and instead

Table 2 List of Variables

Variable name	Variable Description	Unit	Frequency	Source
Arrears dummy	= 1 if Arrears/total debt > 5% in any of the past 3 years	Dummy	A	GDF
Asia dummy	= 1 if country is in Asia	Dummy		Own calculations
Brady dummy	= 1 if Brady debt > 0 at some point	Dummy		BIS
Current account	Current account/GDP, lagged	%	A	IFS
Debt issued in preceding year	Total amount of bonds issued in the past 4 quarters/total debt at the beginning of the first quarter	Million USD	Q	BIS (locational), Dealogic Bondware
Dummy for Asian crisis countries	= 1 if Asian crisis country (Thailand, Indonesia, Korea, Malaysia, Philippines)	Dummy		Own calculations
External debt/GDP	External debt/GDP, lagged	%	A	BIS, IFS
Fiscal balance	Fiscal balance/GDP, lagged	%	A	IFS
GDP per capita (1993)	Logarithm of PPP adjusted GDP per capita in 1993	GDP in USD		WEO
High yield	Yield of Merrill Lynch JOAO index (US high-yield corporations with below investment grade rating), end of month (EMBIG) or monthly average (Bondware)	% p.a.	M	Bloomberg
Inflation	Consumer price inflation, lagged	%	M	IFS
Latin dummy	= 1 if Western Hemisphere	Dummy		Own calculations
LIBOR	LIBOR, monthly average (EMBIG) or end of month (Bondware)	%	M	IFS, Bloomberg
Number of previous bond issues	Number of bond issues in the past year		Q	Dealogic Bondware

(Continued)

Table 2 Continued

Variable name	Variable Description	Unit	Frequency	Source
Political instability and violence	"Instability and violence" in 1997	Index, –2.5 (very unstable), 2.5 (very stable)		World Bank Governance Database
Rating	= average of available ratings or only available rating	Index (1 = Caa3/CCC-, 19 = Aaa/ AAA)		Standard and Poor's, Moody's
Rating (residual)	Residual from regression of ratings on fundamentals (cf. ratings)			Own calculations
Real credit growth	Real domestic credit growth, lagged	%	M	IFS
Real growth	Real GDP growth, lagged	%	A	IFS
Short-term Debt/Total Debt	Short-term debt/total debt, lagged	%	SA	BIS (consolidated)
Size	Log of nominal GDP in US$ in 1993	GDP in US$	A	IFS
US high-yield bond spread	= High yield – LIBOR	% p.a.	M	Bloomberg
US ten year yield	Yield of 10-year US government bonds, end of month (EMBIG) or monthly average (Bondware)	% p.a.	M	IFS, Bloomberg

BIS = Bank for International Settlements
GDF = Global Development Finance (World Bank)
IFS = International Financial Statistics (IMF)
INS = Information Notice System (IMF)
WEO = World Economic Outlook Database (IMF)

includes fiscal balance and the current account, and finally, a model selected through a general-to-specific procedure, which attempts to make better use of our rich right-hand-side dataset than models (1) and (2) do.[18] All macroeconomic variables enter in lagged form to account for reporting lags and to reduce potential endogeneity problems. In all three cases, we also include the residual from a regression of credit ratings on the country fundamentals. In all regressions, we use robust standard errors.

Table 3 EMBIG Data: Estimation of Alternative Models Before and After Russian Crisis

Variable	(1) Eichengreen-Mody[a]					(2) Alternative specification A[a]					(3) Alternative specification B[a]				
	Before crisis[b]		After crisis[c]		Test for equality p[d]	Before crisis[b]		After crisis[c]		Test for equality p[d]	Before crisis[b]		After crisis[c]		Test for equality p[d]
	Coef.	p	Coef.	p		Coef.	p	Coef.	p		Coef.	p	Coef.	p	
Constant	766.12	0.43	805.08	0.00	0.97	848.94	0.40	775.12	0.00	0.94	3195.00	0.00	1474.04	0.00	0.00
Real growth	-6.44	0.00	-25.40	0.00	0.00	-7.88	0.00	-22.34	0.00	0.00	-3.83	0.00	-10.02	0.00	0.00
Fiscal balance						-12.29	0.00	-24.59	0.00	0.01	-21.26	0.00	-29.93	0.00	0.12
Current account[e]						3.29	0.28	-6.56	0.00	0.01	0.75	0.79	7.17	0.01	0.10
Real credit growth[e]	1.27	0.00	-0.62	0.14	0.00						-2.77	0.00	-5.83	0.00	0.00
External Debt/GDP	113.54	0.00	253.86	0.00	0.00	141.64	0.00	227.81	0.00	0.00					
Arrears dummy															
Asia dummy											72.39	0.01	-79.54	0.00	0.00
Latin dummy											151.06	0.00	227.29	0.00	0.00
Political Instability and Violence											11.42	0.40	14.44	0.27	0.87
Size (log $GDP in 1993)											-35.75	0.00	-40.01	0.00	0.58
Rating (residual)	-34.32	0.00	-70.59	0.00	0.00	-37.75	0.00	-76.88	0.00	0.00	-39.33	0.00	-51.38	0.00	0.01
U.S. 10-year yield	-167.67	0.23	-57.55	0.03	0.44	-171.71	0.24	-65.62	0.01	0.48	-447.13	0.00	-97.00	0.00	0.00
U.S. high-yield bond spread	151.56	0.03	21.38	0.00	0.07	146.52	0.05	16.65	0.02	0.08					
Observations in subsample	108		378			108		378			108		378		
No. of countries[f]	18		18			18		18			18		18		

[a] Estimated on pooled sample 1998:01-2000:12, excluding 1998:07-1999:03, and allowing for different coefficients for pre- and post-crisis periods. All estimations use robust standard errors.
[b] 1998:01-1998:06.
[c] 1999:04-2000:12.
[d] p values based on two-sided tests; boldface indicates rejection of equality at the 10% level in a direction consistent with greater sensitivity of spreads to country risk after 1998.
[e] Lagged, four-year moving average.
[f] Full sample of 18 countries: Argentina, Bulgaria, Brazil, China, Colombia, Croatia, Korea, Morocco, Mexico, Malaysia, Panama, Peru, Philippines, Poland, Thailand, Turkey, Venezuela, South Africa.

Most coefficients have the expected signs. Real growth, a fiscal surplus, and a favorable credit rating are associated with significantly lower spreads. Recent debt arrears increase spreads, as does a high external debt/GDP ratio in the pre-Russia sample. A high spread of U.S. high-yield bonds, measuring the investors' general attitude towards risk-taking, is associated with higher spreads. When regional and political indicators are added to the regressions, the arrears dummy and external debt to GDP become insignificant; instead, being a Latin American country sharply increases spreads. Asian countries show significantly higher spreads in the pre-crisis period, but significantly lower spreads in the post-crisis period; this may reflect the fact that the pre-Russia crisis sample coincides with the aftermath of the Asian crisis.

Some coefficients show signs that are either inconsistent or hard to interpret (such as real credit growth, the current account, and the U.S. 10-year yield). This reflects a common problem in the literature on bond pricing: it is very difficult to explain bond spreads through country fundamentals in a parsimonious model that yields a satisfactory fit and only "correct" signs. However, the specification chosen appears to be of minor importance for our tests, especially for the variance test. The main results from our tests were robust in all specifications we tried, both those reported in Table 3 and others that we are not reporting.

Table 3 also shows that most of the coefficients in the three models change across the two subsamples in a way that is consistent with the perception of a risk increase due to the weakened official safety net after 1998. The absolute size of the coefficients tends to increase: fundamentals that increase country risk—for example, the presence of arrears, a fiscal deficit, or being located in Latin America—now have an even larger upward impact on spreads, while factors that were negatively related to country risk, such as real growth or a high rating, tend to have a larger downward impact. As shown in the columns labeled "test for equality," these changes are statistically significant in many cases.

The results of the two formal tests proposed in Section 1 are presented in the two following tables. Table 4 shows the results for the variance test. As explained above, this test conditions on fundamentals at a specific point in time; hence, with monthly data, each test can be carried out 27 times for each of the three models of Table 3. Table 4 shows that, regardless of which model and which set of fundamentals is used, the test strongly rejects the null hypothesis, i.e. that there is no change in the fitted variance, at high confidence levels. When the model is estimated on the basis of pre-crisis data, the variance of fitted spreads is always significantly lower than when the same model is estimated on the basis of post-crisis data. Thus, the variance test strongly supports the impression obtained on the basis of the raw data, namely that the Russian crisis was associated with a structural break whose overall effect was to significantly increase the cross-sectional variance of spreads, conditioning on fundamentals.

The results of the level test are more mixed (Table 5). Again, there are 27 alternative sets of fundamentals for the purpose of running the test; but in

Table 4 EMBIG Data: Cross-sectional Variances of Fitted Spreads before and after Russian Crisis, and Results for Variance Test

Month	Actual Variance	(1) Eichengreen-Mody			(2) Alternative specification A			(3) Alternative specification B		
		Fitted variance using coefficients estimated			Fitted variance using coefficients estimated			Fitted variance using coefficients estimated		
		Before crisis[3]	After crisis[b]	Test for equality p[c]	Before crisis[3]	After crisis[b]	Test for equality p[c]	Before crisis[3]	After crisis[b]	Test for equality p[c]
1998:01	14474	9710	43731	0.000	10139	42992	0.000	11109	52238	0.000
1998:02	11714	9676	41690	0.000	9892	41513	0.000	11176	52856	0.000
1998:03	8909	9199	38662	0.000	9156	38260	0.000	10643	51417	0.000
1998:04	10099	8549	28118	0.000	7948	30750	0.000	10064	45233	0.000
1998:05	14559	8525	27828	0.000	7913	30764	0.000	10032	43850	0.000
1998:06	20586	8503	27889	0.000	7888	31006	0.000	10003	42743	0.000
1999:04	53108	8216	42717	0.000	9351	39337	0.000	10465	45869	0.000
1999:05	80188	8236	44277	0.000	9447	40460	0.000	10495	47062	0.000
1999:06	67609	8405	46932	0.000	9714	42610	0.000	10778	48586	0.000
1999:07	78276	8006	42754	0.000	9161	38880	0.000	10304	47063	0.000
1999:08	95792	7847	43728	0.000	9062	39696	0.000	10441	48638	0.000
1999:09	66819	8218	46344	0.000	9527	42477	0.000	11200	50501	0.000
1999:10	50033	8361	49467	0.000	9833	45244	0.000	11406	51572	0.000
1999:11	52809	8592	51260	0.000	10158	47080	0.000	11736	53015	0.000
1999:12	38487	8985	53784	0.000	10702	49515	0.000	12400	55338	0.000
2000:01	48464	9272	49832	0.000	10622	51334	0.000	12208	50902	0.000
2000:02	38017	9373	48124	0.000	10587	50158	0.000	12490	50528	0.000
2000:03	42238	9441	46617	0.000	10516	48860	0.000	12677	49575	0.000
2000:04	52401	8119	33336	0.000	8146	40705	0.000	13237	47214	0.000
2000:05	57975	7984	31876	0.000	7932	39272	0.000	13393	46736	0.000

2000:06	47930	7996	31616	0.000	7991	39202	0.000	13498	46753	0.000
2000:07	43618	8000	31526	0.000	8003	38599	0.000	13497	46470	0.000
2000:08	41079	8007	31385	0.000	8015	38377	0.000	13500	46192	0.000
2000:09	49346	8016	31356	0.000	8031	38232	0.000	13518	46476	0.000
2000:10	63240	7984	31981	0.000	8084	39041	0.000	13365	46428	0.000
2000:11	78292	8263	33196	0.000	8413	41037	0.000	13819	47014	0.000
2000:12	64069	8272	33360	0.000	8435	41237	0.000	13831	46846	0.000

[a] Regression coefficients were estimated on basis of 1998:01-1998:06 data.
[b] Regression coefficients were estimated on basis of 1999:04-2000:12 data.
[c] p values based on two-sided tests.

Table 5 EMBIG Data: Summary Results for Level Test

	Eichengreen-Mody Rejections indicating		Alternative model A: Rejections indicating		Alternative model B: Rejections indicating	
	Significant increase in spreads[a]	Significant decline in spreads[b]	Significant increase in spreads[a]	Significant decline in spreads[b]	Significant increase in spreads[a]	Significant decline in spreads[b]
Argentina	5	0	6	0	27	0
Brazil	6	0	6	0	26	0
Bulgaria	6	0	6	0	25	0
China	0	4	0	12	11	9
Colombia	3	0	4	0	26	0
Croatia	0	2	0	1	19	0
Korea	6	2	6	4	12	3
Malaysia	0	4	0	2	14	8
Mexico	5	1	5	1	26	0
Morocco	4	0	5	0	26	0
Panama	0	5	0	1	25	0
Peru	6	0	6	0	26	0
Philippines	4	1	6	1	17	5
Poland	3	2	2	1	24	1
South Africa	6	1	4	1	26	0
Thailand	6	3	6	1	17	2
Turkey	3	0	4	0	26	0
Venezuela	4	0	1	0	27	0
Sum rejections	67	25	67	25	400	28
Number of countries showing rejection	14	10	14	10	18	6

[a]No. of periods in which fitted spread based on post-crisis model is significantly higher than fitted spread based on pre-crisis model (potential maximum: 27, significance level 5%).

[b]No. of periods in which fitted spread based on post-crisis model is significantly lower than fitted spread based on pre-crisis model (potential maximum: 27, significance level 5%).

addition, the test must now be run separately for each emerging market country. For model (3), countries with significant increases in fitted spreads outnumber countries with significant decreases by 3:1, whereas the margin is smaller for the other two models (1.4:1). The group of countries for which the non-bailout of Russia does not seem to have increased perceived country risk includes a number of Asian countries, as well as some strong Eastern European reformers, such as Poland and Croatia. For most other countries, especially those in Latin America, the results support the view that the Russian non-bailout increased perceived country risk.

3.2 Tests Using Launch Spread Data

We now present an analogous set of regressions and test results based on the Bondware data. OLS regressions of launch spreads on country fundamentals may suffer from a selection problem because the decision to issue a bond may depend on the spreads themselves. We follow Eichengreen and Mody (2000) in dealing with this problem by estimating a standard Heckman selection model, i.e. by jointly modeling spreads and the selection decision.[19] Again we present the regression results for three different models, similar to those discussed in the previous section (see Table 6). Model (1) follows Eichengreen and Mody (2000), and models (2) and (3) are variants of model (1), which drop the variable "external debt/GDP," and include additional variables such as inflation, the current account, a measure of political stability, and a measure of the maturity structure of external debt ("short-term debt/total debt").

Looking first at the selection equation (lower panel), we find that the correlation between the residuals in the selection and the spread equation (denoted by ρ) is not significantly different from zero; hence, the selection problem seems to be less severe than expected. The coefficients in the spread equations largely show the expected signs and are generally highly significant for the period after the crisis, but not for the period before the crisis. This may be due to the relatively small number of observations in this dataset in the pre-crisis period, due to the small number of bond issues. The external debt variables ("external debt/total debt" and "short-term debt/total debt") often show the "wrong" signs; this could reflect endogeneity, as foreign debt tends to flow to countries with relatively good fundamentals and, hence, low spreads.

Moreover, almost all coefficients increase in absolute value across the two subsamples, as would be expected if the post-crisis period was associated with a lower degree of perceived insurance; this increase is significant in many cases. Somewhat surprisingly, the coefficient of the U.S. high-yield bond spread, which is positive, but insignificant in the period before the crisis, becomes negative and significant after the crisis. This seems to contradict the conventional wisdom that the evolution of spreads after the Russian crisis can be explained by a general reluctance of investors to take risks, which would suggest a positive correlation of high-yield bond spreads and emerging market spreads.

Table 6 Launch Spread Data: Estimation of Alternative Models Before and After Russian Crisis

Variable	(1) Eichengreen-Mody[a]					(2) Alternative specification A[a]					(3) Alternative specification B[a]				
	Before crisis[b]		After crisis[c]		Test for equality p[d]	Before crisis[b]		After crisis[c]		Test for equality p[d]	Before crisis[b]		After crisis[c]		Test for equality p[d]
	Coef	.p	Coef.	p		Coef.	p	Coef.	p		Coef.	p	Coef.	p	
Constant	-1249.03	0.88	1254.34	0.00	0.77	-2294.99	0.78	1122.59	0.00	0.67	-5091.50	0.58	1131.48	0.00	0.50
Real growth[e]	-5.80	0.78	-47.10	0.00	**0.06**	-1.62	0.93	-41.76	0.00	**0.03**	-1.85	0.93	-33.89	0.00	0.15
Inflation						-0.89	0.34	2.90	0.00	**0.00**					
Current account[e] External Debt/GDP	-0.92	0.33	-0.63	0.04	0.77	-0.93	0.56	-3.77	0.02	0.18	0.33	0.80	-1.29	0.36	0.38
Brady dummy	46.27	0.45	103.86	0.00	0.36	15.66	0.78	62.70	0.01	0.42	25.52	0.64	77.58	0.00	0.36
Political instability + violence											-97.09	0.00	-159.27	0.00	**0.09**
Short-term debt/total debt											1.71	0.40	-0.46	0.60	0.33
Rating (residual)	-31.37	0.00	-53.26	0.00	**0.03**	-48.85	0.00	-68.62	0.00	**0.10**	-28.05	0.02	-53.40	0.00	**0.04**
U.S. 10-year yield	218.37	0.86	-51.27	0.06	0.83	421.44	0.72	-48.63	0.06	0.69	735.27	0.57	-44.61	0.10	0.55
U.S. high-yield bond spread	113.97	0.85	-82.14	0.00	0.74	71.93	0.89	-74.67	0.00	0.78	392.82	0.55	-69.77	0.01	0.48
Observations in subsample	306		1071			306		1071			306		1071		
Observations with bond data[f]	27		158			27		158			27		158		
No. of countries[g]	51		51			51		51			51		51		
Selection Equation[h]	Coef.		p			Coef.		p			Coef.		p		
Debt issued in preceding year	0.16		0.64			0.11		0.76			0.20		0.60		

No. of previous bond issues	0.08	0.00	0.08	0.00	0.08	0.00
GDP per capita (1993)	0.45	0.00	0.34	0.01	0.43	0.00
Dummy for Asian crisis countries	0.24	0.14	0.30	0.09	0.26	0.12
ρ	-0.04	0.86	0.06	0.80	0.00	1.00

[a]Estimated on pooled sample 1998:01-2000:12, excluding 1998:07-1999:03, and allowing for different coefficients for pre- and post-crisis periods. All estimations use robust standard errors.

[b]1998:01-1998:06.

[c]1999:04-2000:12.

[d]p values based on two-sided tests; boldface indicates rejection of equality at the 10% level in a direction consistent with greater sensitivity of spreads to country risk after 1998.

[e]Lagged, four-year moving average.

[f]Number of country-months in which a bond was issued. The relatively small number of observations with bond data during the sample period is due to the fact that bond issuing activity was depressed as a result of the Asian and Russian crises.

[g]Argentina, Brazil, Bulgaria, Chile, China, Colombia, Costa Rica, Croatia, Cyprus, Czech Republic, Dominican Republic, Ecuador, Egypt, El Salvador, Estonia, Guatemala, Hong Kong, Hungary, India, Indonesia, Israel, Jamaica, Jordan, Kazakhstan, Korea, Latvia, Lebanon, Lithuania, Malaysia, Malta, Mauritius, Mexico, Morocco, Oman, Pakistan, Panama, Peru, Philippines, Poland, Romania, Saudi Arabia, Singapore, Slovak Republic, Slovenia, South Africa, Taiwan, Thailand, Tunisia, Turkey, Uruguay, Venezuela.

[h]Reports only coefficients for instruments and correlation coefficient of disturbance terms of the two equations ρ.

Table 7 shows the results of the variance test. The results are again striking: no matter which period is chosen to calculate the fitted variances, the null hypothesis of equal variances is rejected at high confidence levels. Again, the increase is relatively large: the fitted variance increases by a factor of 3 to 4, compared to a factor of 4 to 5 in the EMBIG dataset. This provides convincing evidence of a stronger differentiation among countries after the Russian crisis.

Finally, Table 8 contains the results for the level test. The results turn out to be more clear-cut than in the EMBIG dataset. The overall evidence strongly supports the notion that spreads increased significantly after the Russian crisis (controlling for fundamentals). In each of the three models, most countries (40 or 41, out of 51) display statistically significant increases in spreads for at least one set of fundamentals, whereas no country exhibits a statistically significant decline in spreads. Eight countries do not show a significant increase in any of the three models. Five of these are again Asian countries. Taken together with the EMBIG evidence, this suggests that Asian countries experienced an over-shooting of their spreads after the Asian crisis. The normalization of spreads after 1998 might mask any effect of changing bailout expectations. As before, it is also true that the countries that did not experience a significant increase in spreads tend to have stronger fundamentals. In fact, their average credit rating—between A/A2 and A-/A3—was well above that of the remaining countries (BB+/Ba1). It is also worth noting that the *extent* to which fitted spreads increased is strongly and significantly negatively correlated with the countries' credit ratings. In other words, the increase in spreads was higher in countries with worse ratings.

In combination with the results from the EMBIG dataset, our findings strongly support the view that there was an increase in perceived risk because of the weakening of the official safety net after the Russian non-bailout. Not only do we find that the cross-sectional variance increases after the event, but we also find that the increase in spreads is strongest among countries with weak fundamentals. Thus, there seems to be a much stronger differentiation between "good" and "bad" countries following the Russian crisis.

3.3 Robustness

The above discussion indicates that our test results—particularly the variance test—are very robust with regard to the economic model that is used to relate spreads to economic fundamentals, and with regard to the dataset used for estimation. However, this leaves a number of other dimensions along which the robustness of our results can be explored. As already mentioned, we tested the robustness of the results by using alternative definitions of the exclusion period after the crisis, or by dropping the exclusion period altogether. We also added lagged dependent variables and/or the composite EMBIG index (i.e. the average level of emerging market spreads) to the regression model. Finally, we experimented with alternative estimation techniques, such as assuming a GARCH (1,1)

Table 7 Launch Spread Data: Cross-sectional Variances of Fitted Spreads before and after Russian Crisis, and Results for Variance Test

Month	(1) Eichengreen-Mody			(2) Alternative specification A			(3) Alternative specification B		
	Fitted variance using coefficients estimated		Test for equality p[c]	Fitted variance using coefficients estimated		Test for equality p[c]	Fitted variance using coefficients estimated		Test for equality p[c]
	Before crisis[a]	After crisis[b]		Before crisis[a]	After crisis[b]		Before crisis[a]	After crisis[b]	
1998:01	11266	33661	0.033	26355	93187	0.025	8513	32419	0.000
1998:02	11130	33660	0.032	17889	73368	0.001	8366	32279	0.000
1998:03	11174	33739	0.031	14152	55165	0.000	8367	32351	0.000
1998:04	11115	33371	0.034	13903	53231	0.000	8314	32019	0.000
1998:05	11412	34118	0.031	14447	54715	0.000	8585	32848	0.000
1998:06	11692	34694	0.030	15011	55907	0.000	8757	33511	0.000
1999:04	11708	32264	0.033	14277	43183	0.000	9188	35152	0.000
1999:05	11708	32264	0.033	14207	43226	0.000	9188	35152	0.000
1999:06	11750	32473	0.032	14571	43761	0.001	9281	35376	0.000
1999:07	11748	32222	0.034	14640	43375	0.001	8665	34865	0.000
1999:08	11742	32185	0.034	15122	43653	0.001	8658	34826	0.000
1999:09	11798	32559	0.032	15718	44611	0.001	8751	35204	0.000
1999:10	12220	34110	0.025	15954	46653	0.001	9121	36770	0.000
1999:11	12296	34672	0.023	15976	47362	0.001	9228	37355	0.000
1999:12	11723	33128	0.027	14514	44225	0.001	8771	35750	0.000
2000:01	10726	35025	0.005	14960	45338	0.000	8642	37685	0.000
2000:02	10767	35172	0.005	15137	44914	0.001	8680	37818	0.000
2000:03	10725	35338	0.005	15336	44776	0.001	8707	37989	0.000
2000:04	10102	36656	0.001	14959	45158	0.001	8418	37818	0.000
2000:05	10126	36669	0.001	15181	45048	0.001	8485	37848	0.000

(Continued)

Table 7 Continued

Month	(1) Eichengreen-Mody			(2) Alternative specification A			(3) Alternative specification B		
	Fitted variance using coefficients estimated		Test for equality p[c]	Fitted variance using coefficients estimated		Test for equality p[c]	Fitted variance using coefficients estimated		Test for equality p[c]
	Before crisis[a]	After crisis[b]		Before crisis[a]	After crisis[b]		Before crisis[a]	After crisis[b]	
2000:06	10159	36629	0.001	15437	44891	0.001	8498	37781	0.000
2000:07	10160	36672	0.000	15659	44917	0.001	8910	38001	0.000
2000:08	10386	37624	0.000	15182	45731	0.001	9105	38968	0.000
2000:09	9619	34335	0.001	14820	41362	0.001	8157	35289	0.000
2000:10	9583	34216	0.001	14711	41002	0.001	8293	35303	0.000
2000:11	9766	34869	0.001	15146	42243	0.001	8536	35991	0.000
2000:12	9819	35063	0.001	14994	42876	0.001	8614	36201	0.000

[a]Regression coefficients were estimated on basis of 1998:01-1998:06 data.
[b]Regression coefficients were estimated on basis of 1999:04-2000:12 data.
[c]p values based on two-sided tests.

290

Table 8 Launch Spread Data: Summary Results for Level Test

	Eichengreen-Mody: Rejections indicating		Alternative model A: Rejections indicating		Alternative model B: Rejections indicating	
	Significant increase in spreads[a]	Significant decline in spreads[b]	Significant increase in spreads[a]	Significant decline in spreads[b]	Significant increase in spreads[a]	Significant decline in spreads[b]
Argentina	6	0	6	0	6	0
Brazil	6	0	6	0	6	0
Bulgaria	6	0	6	0	6	0
Chile	0	0	0	0	0	0
China	6	0	6	0	3	0
Colombia	6	0	6	0	6	0
Costa Rica	1	0	2	0	3	0
Croatia	2	0	0	0	0	0
Cyprus	2	0	6	0	1	0
Czech Republic	6	0	5	0	6	0
Dominican Republic	6	0	6	0	6	0
Ecuador	6	0	6	0	1	0
Egypt	6	0	6	0	6	0
El Salvador	6	0	6	0	1	0
Estonia	5	0	6	0	1	0
Guatemala	6	0	6	0	0	0
Hong Kong	0	0	0	0	0	0
Hungary	6	0	6	0	4	0
India	2	0	4	0	6	0
Indonesia	6	0	6	0	6	0
Israel	0	0	0	0	0	0
Jamaica	6	0	6	0	6	0
Jordan	6	0	6	0	6	0

(Continued)

Table 8 Launch Spread Data: Summary Results for Level Test

	Eichengreen-Mody: Rejections indicating		Alternative model A: Rejections indicating		Alternative model B: Rejections indicating	
	Significant increase in spreads[a]	*Significant decline in spreads[b]*	*Significant increase in spreads[a]*	*Significant decline in spreads[b]*	*Significant increase in spreads[a]*	*Significant decline in spreads[b]*
Kazakhstan	6	0	6	0	6	0
Korea	2	0	1	0	2	0
Latvia	6	0	6	0	6	0
Lebanon	6	0	6	0	5	0
Lithuania	6	0	6	0	6	0
Malaysia	0	0	0	0	0	0
Malta	2	0	0	0	0	0
Mauritius	6	0	4	0	2	0
Mexico	6	0	6	0	6	0
Morocco	6	0	6	0	6	0
Oman	6	0	4	0	5	0
Pakistan	6	0	6	0	6	0
Panama	0	0	1	0	2	0
Peru	0	0	0	0	0	0
Philippines	6	0	6	0	6	0
Poland	1	0	2	0	3	0
Romania	6	0	6	0	6	0
Saudi Arabia	6	0	6	0	1	0
Singapore	0	0	0	0	0	0
Slovak Republic	6	0	5	0	5	0
Slovenia	0	0	1	0	0	0
South Africa	6	0	6	0	4	0

Taiwan Province of China	0	0	0	0	0	0
Thailand	6	0	6	0	6	5
Tunisia	6	0	6	0	6	6
Turkey	6	0	6	0	6	6
Uruguay	6	0	6	0	6	1
Venezuela	6	0	6	0	6	6
Sum rejections	215	0	215	0	215	181
No. countries showing rejection	41	0	41	0	41	40
Total no. of countries	51		51		51	51

[a]No. of periods in which fitted spread based on post-crisis model is significantly higher than fitted spread based on pre-crisis model (potential maximum per country: 27, significance level 5%).

[b]No. of periods in which fitted spread based on post-crisis model is significantly lower than fitted spread based on pre-crisis model (potential maximum per country: 27, significance level 5%).

process in the errors, and using a panel GLS estimator that allows for serial correlation and cross-country heteroskedasticity.

The results, which are reported in more detail in a longer version of this paper (Dell'Ariccia, Schnabel, and Zettelmeyer 2002), can be summarized as follows. Variations in the exclusion period by a few months in either direction make virtually no difference to the results. Dropping the exclusion period altogether strengthens the results, as would be expected from Figure 1, which shows that the variance and levels of spreads during the crisis were much higher than in the tranquil period following the crisis. This is true even if the errors are allowed to follow a GARCH (1,1) to allow for a more flexible dynamic modeling of spreads in the turbulent period.

Estimating the models in various GLS variants yields coefficients that are very close to the OLS coefficients, along with slightly narrower standard errors; this results in stronger rejections of the null hypotheses of our tests. Using a GARCH (1,1) error process slightly weakens the results: the level tests reject less frequently, whereas the variance tests continue to reject, and the main conclusions are unchanged. Finally, including the composite EMBIG and/or lagged dependent variables in the model implies that the level test can no longer be used, since the model now conditions on either the average level of spreads or the previous realization of the country spread. However, the variance test can be used, and its results are unchanged, regardless of whether the model is estimated via OLS with robust standard errors, or as a GARCH (1,1) model.

4. CONCLUSION

This paper has proposed a novel statistical test for the effects of official bailout policies on the perceived risk of investing in emerging market countries. We applied this test to the Russian default of 1998, which was widely interpreted as signaling a greater reluctance of the international community to bail out countries with severe debt problems. The key idea behind our test is that, controlling for fundamentals, the perceived weakening of an official safety net should result in a higher dispersion of emerging market spreads across countries, because investors are no longer insulated from differences in country risk. In addition, as other authors have observed before us, a reduction in the perceived guarantee should also lead to an increase in the levels of spreads.

Our main finding is that the cross-country dispersion of spreads rose significantly and strongly after the Russian crisis. By focusing on a time period when market volatility had died down, we show that this finding is not due to the market turbulence in the immediate aftermath of the Russian default. Controlling for fundamentals, the fitted variance is 3–5 times larger in the post-crisis period than in the pre-crisis period. This finding is highly robust, including the use of different datasets to measure spreads (launch spread data versus secondary market data), the model specification, the definition of the exclusion period, and the estimation technique.

We also find that there was an increase in the levels of emerging markets bond spreads, controlling for changes in fundamentals, in most countries. The exceptions are some Asian countries that suffered from turbulence prior to the Russian crisis, as well as some countries with traditionally stronger fundamentals, which experienced constant or even decreasing spreads. One plausible interpretation is that investors did not revise their expectations about future large-scale crisis lending uniformly for all countries, but that these revisions were undertaken only for countries likely to run into solvency problems similar to those that had plagued Russia. Such a change in expectations is also consistent with the results of the variance test.

One should be careful when drawing policy conclusions from these findings. We have demonstrated only the existence of an insurance effect attributable to official policies prior to 1998, not the presence of inefficient moral hazard. We know, however, that under some conditions, which plausibly hold in many emerging market countries, reducing the perceived risk associated with emerging market debt can have adverse welfare effects, by encouraging excessive capital flows to countries with weak fundamentals, and by facilitating overborrowing on the side of sovereign or private emerging market debtors (Jeanne and Zettelmeyer 2005). This does not necessarily imply that international rescues should not take place at all, but it does suggest that policy initiatives that seek to reform or limit crisis lending may be responses to a real problem rather than to an illusion. Advocates of unfettered crisis lending often make their case by arguing that there is no evidence that the anticipation of large scale crisis lending has substantially reduced perceived investor risk (Cline 2001). In view of the results of this paper, we believe that it will be much more difficult to take such a position in the future.

APPENDIX

The Variance Test

The variance test is used to test the equality of variances before and after an event, controlling for fundamentals. The null hypothesis can be written as

$$H_0 : \beta^{1'} Var(X_t)\beta^1 - \beta^{0'} Var(X_t)\beta^0 = 0, \tag{10}$$

which is a nonlinear function of the parameter vector named $\begin{pmatrix} \beta^0 \\ \beta^1 \end{pmatrix}$. This function will be named $f(\beta^0, \beta^1)$ in the following. In order to find the distribution of $f(\hat{\beta}^0, \hat{\beta}^1)$ we approximate it by the Delta method around the true parameter values:

$$f\left(\hat{\beta}^0, \hat{\beta}^1\right) \approx f\left(\beta^0, \beta^1\right) + \partial f / \partial \hat{\beta}^0 \cdot \left(\hat{\beta}^0 - \beta^0\right) + \partial f / \partial \hat{\beta}^1 \cdot \left(\hat{\beta}^1 - \beta^1\right) \tag{11}$$

Since $(\hat{\beta}^0, \hat{\beta}^1)$ are jointly normal under the null hypothesis (at least asymptotically), the above expression is also normal since it is a linear combination of $(\hat{\beta}^0, \hat{\beta}^1)$. The variance of the expression can be easily calculated, leading to the following Wald test statistic:

$$W = f\left(\hat{\beta}^0, \hat{\beta}^1\right)' \left[GVG'\right]^{-1} f\left(\hat{\beta}^0, \hat{\beta}^1\right) \overset{as}{\sim} \chi^2(1) \text{ under } H_0, \tag{12}$$

where

$$G = \left(\partial f / \partial \hat{\beta}^0, \partial f / \partial \hat{\beta}^1\right), \tag{13}$$

$$V = \widehat{Var}\begin{pmatrix} \hat{\beta}^0 \\ \hat{\beta}^1 \end{pmatrix}, \tag{14}$$

and $(\hat{\beta}^0, \hat{\beta}^1)$ are the estimators from the pooled model, allowing for different coefficients before and after the event. In order to account for heteroskedastic errors, one should use robust standard errors in the regressions.

We would like to thank Eduardo Borensztein, Giancarlo Corsetti, Mark Flannery (the Editor), Martin Hellwig, Mathias Hoffmann, Olivier Jeanne, Marcel Peter, Steve Phillips, Carmen Reinhart, Roberto Rigobon, Beatrice Weder, Tom Willett, one anonymous referee, and the participants of the IMF's First Annual Research Conference, the Annual Meeting of the American Economic Association in New Orleans, the Annual Meeting of the European Economic Association in Lausanne, and the Annual Meeting of the German Economic Association for useful comments and suggestions. Moreover, we thank Manzoor Gill, Grace Juhn, and Priya Joshi for helping us compile the data set. All errors are ours. The views expressed in this paper are those of the authors only and do not necessarily reflect the views or policies of the IMF.

Notes

1 For a statement and discussion of the critics' view, see Calomiris (1998), Meltzer (1998), and Willett (1999). For an early official reform proposal that explicitly recognizes "moral hazard for both creditors and debtors," see Group of Ten (1996). These contributions are not, of course, the first statements of concern about moral hazard related to international official lending. Such concerns go back at least to Vaubel (1983).

2 In the working paper version of this study (Dell'Ariccia, Schnabel, and Zettelmeyer 2002), we also report the results of our tests when applied to the Mexican and Asian crises to compare our results to the earlier literature.

3 This is the well-known Oaxaca decomposition that has also been used by Eichengreen and Mody (2000).

4 In addition, Zhang (1999) assumes that the coefficients on fundamentals are unchanged before and after the event, which would not be true if moral hazard were in fact present.

5 This type of decomposition has been used in the labor literature on the evolution of the distribution of incomes over time (Juhn, Murphy, and Pierce, 1993, Dunne, Foster, Haltiwanger, and Troske, 2004).

6 Since the variance test employs the variance of *fitted* spreads, it should not be affected by a change in the volatility of spreads after the event, as long as we use heteroskedasticity-consistent standard errors.

7 See e.g. *The Economist*, "Survey of Global Finance," January 30, 1999. The quote is from Aslund (2000).

8 See e.g. the quotes by David Folkerts-Landau, Global Head of Research at Deutsche Bank and former head of capital market studies at the IMF, and by George Soros, cited in Blustein (2001), pp. 276 and 277.

9 Cantor and Packer (1996), Cline and Barnes (1997), Kamin and Kleist (1999), Eichengreen and Mody (2000).

10 The estimated equation is a first-order autoregression of first differences in the EMBIG, allowing the error term to follow a GARCH (1,1) process.

11 Note that the EMBI and EMBI+ cannot be used in our analysis because the number of countries covered is too small to yield reliable results, especially for the variance test, which relies on a large number of observations in the cross-sectional dimension.

12 "Quasi-sovereign" means that the bond is either guaranteed by a sovereign or that the sovereign is the majority shareholder in the respective corporation.

13 We use only 18 countries in the regression analysis. Russia and Ecuador are excluded because their spreads in this period are dominated by their own financial crises, rather than by the impact of the events in Russia on other emerging markets. In addition, we excluded Nigeria, because of incomplete right-hand-side data. See Table 1 for a list of the included countries.

14 More precisely, stripped yields are the internal rate of return of the uncollateralized portion of the bond. For example, consider an emerging market bond of market price p per 100 units of face value maturing in T periods, and assume that this has collateralized principal but uncollateralized periodic coupon payments of c percent. Then, the stripped yield, s, solves

$$p = \sum_{t=1}^{T-1} \frac{c}{(1+s)^t} + \frac{100}{\left(1 + i_{US,T}\right)^T},$$

where $i_{US,T}$ is the yield of the U.S. zero coupon bond of T periods remaining maturity which was used to collateralize the Brady bond principal. In practice, computing stripped yields is slightly more complicated because Brady bonds typically featured a "rolling interest guarantee" that collateralized some coupon payments in addition to the principal collateral. Stripped spreads are routinely quoted by Bloomberg and other financial new services using a program developed by J.P. Morgan that values this rolling interest guarantee and takes into account other issue-specific features of the bonds.

15 In the regression analysis, we only use 51 countries. See again the list in Table 1.

16 E.g. Cline and Barnes (1997) and Eichengreen and Mody (2000).

17 This assumes that the correlation between the included fundamentals and the ratings is entirely due to the fact that the ratings have been calculated on the basis of these fundamentals. The residual impact of the ratings might be due to either other omitted

macroeconomic fundamentals that are used in the calculation of ratings, or to the ratings themselves.

18 We began with a general empirical model including variables from all the main groups of potential determinants of spreads, and then successively eliminated variables or groups of variables that were statistically insignificant, both step-by-step and jointly with respect to the original model. For a survey on this procedure see Campos, Ericsson, and Hendry (2005).

19 See Dell'Ariccia, Schnabel, and Zettelmeyer (2002) for a detailed description of the estimation method.

LITERATURE CITED

Aslund, Anders (2000). "Russia and the International Financial Institutions." Unpublished paper presented to the International Financial Institution Advisory Commission, available at http://www.ceip.org/people/aslIFIs.htm.

Blustein, Paul (2001). *The Chastening: Inside the Crisis that Rocked the Global Financial System and Humbled the IMF.* New York: Public Affairs.

Brealey, Richard, A., and Evi Kaplanis (2004). "The Impact of IMF Programs on Asset Values." *Journal of International Money and Finance* 23, 253–270.

Calomiris, Charles W. (1998). "The IMF's Imprudent Role as Lender of Last Resort." *The Cato Journal* 17, 275–294.

Calvo, Guillermo A., and Enrique Mendoza (1996). "Mexico's Balance-of-Payments Crisis: A Chronicle of a Death Foretold." *Journal of International Economics* 41, 235–264.

Campos, Julia, Neil R. Ericsson, and David F. Hendry (2005). "General-to-specific Modeling: An Overview and Selected Bibliography." Board of Governors of the Federal Reserve System, International Finance Discussion Paper No. 02/181.

Cantor, Richard, and Frank Packer (1996). "Determinants and Impact of Sovereign Credit Ratings." *Federal Reserve Bank of New York Economic Policy Review* 2, 37–53.

Cline, William R. (2001). "The Role of the Private Sector in Resolving Financial Crises in Emerging Markets." In *Economic and Financial Crises in Emerging Market Economies*, edited by Martin Feldstein, pp. 459–496. Chicago and London: The University of Chicago Press.

Cline, William R., and Kevin J. S. Barnes (1997). "Spreads and Risk in Emerging Markets Lending." Institute of International Finance Research Paper No. 97-1.

Cook, Douglas O., and Lewis J. Spellman (1996). "Firm and Guarantor Risk, Risk Contagion, and the Interfirm Spread Among Insured Deposits." *Journal of Financial and Quantitative Analysis* 31, 265–281.

Dell'Ariccia, Giovanni, Isabel Schnabel, and Jeromin Zettelmeyer (2002). "Moral Hazard and International Crisis Lending: A Test." IMF Working Paper No. 02/181, International Monetary Fund.

Dunne, Timothy, Lucia Foster, John Haltiwanger, and Kenneth R. Troske (2004). "Wage and Productivity Dispersion in the United States Manufacturing: The Role of Computer Investment." *Journal of Labor Economics* 22, 397–429.

Eichengreen, Barry, and Ashoka Mody (2000). "What Explains Changing Spreads on Emerging-Market Debt?" In *Capital Flows and the Emerging Economies: Theory, Evidence and Controversies*, edited by Sebastian Edwards, pp. 107–134. Chicago and London: The University of Chicago Press.

Group of Ten (1996). "The Resolution of Sovereign Liquidity Crises: A Report to the Ministers and Governors Prepared Under the Auspices of the Deputies." Available at http://www.bis.org/publ/other.htm.

International Monetary Fund (2003). "Public Debt in Emerging Markets: Is It Too High?" *World Economic Outlook*, September, chap. III, pp. 113–150. Washington D.C.: International Monetary Fund.

Jeanne, Olivier, and Jeromin Zettelmeyer (2005). "The Mussa Theorem and Other Results on IMF Induced Moral Hazard." IMF *Staff Papers* 52, Special Issue (September), International Monetary Fund, 64–84.

Juhn, Chinhui, Kevin M. Murphy, and Brooks Pierce (1993). "Wage Inequality and the Rise in Returns to Skill." *Journal of Political Economy* 101, 410–442.

Kamin, Steven B. (2004). "Identifying the Role of Moral Hazard in International Financial Markets." *International Finance* 7, 25–59.

Kamin, Steven B., and Karsten von Kleist (1999). "The Evolution and Determinants of Emerging Market Credit Spreads in the 1990s." *BIS Quarterly Review* 0, 36–44.

Lane, Timothy D., and Steven T. Phillips (2000). "Does IMF Financing Result in Moral Hazard?" IMF Working Paper No. 00/168, International Monetary Fund.

Meltzer, Allan H. (1998). "Asian Problems and the IMF." *The Cato Journal* 17, 267–274.

Vaubel, Roland (1983). "The Moral Hazard of IMF Lending." In *International Lending and the IMF—A Conference in Memory of Wilson Schmidt*, edited by Allan H. Meltzer, pp. 65–79. The Heritage Lectures 21, Heritage Foundation: Washington, D.C.

Willett, Thomas D. (1999). "Did the Mexican Bailout Really Cause the Asian Crisis?" Claremont Policy Briefs, No. 99-01.

Zhang, Xiaoming A. (1999). "Testing for 'Moral Hazard' in Emerging Markets Lending." Institute for International Finance Research Paper No. 99–1.

57

ON THE CONTRIBUTION OF GAME THEORY TO THE STUDY OF SOVEREIGN DEBT AND DEFAULT

Rohan Pitchford and Mark L. J. Wright

Source: *Oxford Review of Economic Policy* 29, 4, 2013, 649–667.

Abstract

This paper reviews the lessons learned from the application of the tools of game theory to the theoretical study of sovereign debt and default. We focus on two main questions. First, we review answers to the most fundamental question in the theory of sovereign debt: given that there is no supranational institution for enforcing the repayment of debts, why do countries ever repay their debts? Second, we review theories of the process by which sovereign debts are restructured with a view to answering the following question: why does the process of sovereign debt restructuring appear so inefficient? The first question raises issues in the design of self-enforcing contracts and on the credibility of threats to punish a country in default. The second question involves applications of the theory of bargaining in environments where the parties to a bargain cannot commit to honour the terms of the bargain or even commit to enter into negotiations in the first place.

I. Introduction

Sovereign countries have been borrowing money for thousands of years.[1] For much of this time, sovereign debt appears to have been the most widely traded financial asset, accounting for 76 per cent of the assets listed in the mid-nineteenth century on the London Stock Exchange, the largest financial market of the time (Tomz and Wright, 2013). Today, sovereign debt constitutes about 20 per cent of the world's total financial assets (Roxburgh *et al.*, 2011).

The prominence of sovereign debt as a financial asset is remarkable in light of the doctrine of sovereign immunity, which makes repayment of these debts particularly difficult to enforce. Indeed, as a consequence of the doctrine, the market for sovereign debt can be viewed as the archetypal contract-enforcement problem. To understand why sovereigns ever repay their debts, as well as the nature of the interactions between a sovereign and its creditors in the event of a sovereign default, international economists have turned to the tools of game theory. In this paper, we review what international economists have learned about sovereign debt and default by using these tools.

We emphasize two main strands of the literature. In the first strand, international economists have drawn lessons from the game theoretic literature on the design of self-enforcing agreements in order to understand why sovereign countries ever repay their debts and, hence, why creditors ever lend to them. These tools have also found application in a diverse number of areas in which legal enforcement mechanisms are limited, such as developing country financial markets and the (illegal) collusive behaviour of firms. One key question arising from this literature is the extent to which the threat to impose a punishment, and in particular the threat to stop lending to a country, are truly credible. In light of this question, we review the literature on repeated and dynamic games of sovereign lending, with a particular focus on the design of renegotiation-proof sovereign debt contracts.

A criticism of the literature on renegotiation-proofness is that it appeals to the idea that the parties to a contract might desire to renegotiate, without placing any explicit structure on the renegotiation process itself. After all, if renegotiation is important to the question being asked, why is it not modelled explicitly? In response to this objection, the second strand of the literature that we review concerns the process of bargaining to restructure sovereign debts in the event of a default, which in turn draws on the substantial game theoretic literature on bargaining.

We argue that in the same way that international economists have learned a great deal from game theorists, game theorists can learn a lot from the study of sovereign debt. The market for sovereign debt has existed for a long time. This fact, combined with sovereign debt's prominence as a financial asset, means that there is a wealth of data available on the terms of contracts that are agreed on by sovereigns and their creditors, the prices at which these contracts trade, breaches of these contracts, and the outcomes of negotiations to restructure sovereign debts. These data, combined with the ability of researchers to use archival research to probe the thought processes underlying the decisions made by participants in the market for sovereign debt, form one of the richest sets of observations with which to test the predictions of game theory.

II. Enforcement of sovereign debt obligations

In this section, we review the source of the enforcement problem for sovereign debt, as well as various theories as to how self-enforcing contracts can arise. We pay particular attention to the credibility of the strategies used to enforce repayment of debt, as well as the empirical evidence in support of these theories.

(i) Sovereign immunity

The doctrine of sovereign immunity is derived from the intuitive notion that a sovereign cannot be bound by laws that it makes itself. Traditionally, a sovereign could appeal to the doctrine to make itself immune from suit (and its assets immune from attachment) within its own jurisdiction. As a matter of convention, sovereigns grant this immunity to those foreign sovereigns with which they have friendly diplomatic relations.

Over time and as a result of the increasing involvement of governments in commercial transactions, this absolute version of the doctrine of sovereign immunity has been weakened into a more restrictive doctrine of sovereign immunity. Codified in the United States with the passage of the Foreign Sovereign Immunity Act of 1976, codified in the United Kingdom by the State Immunity Act of 1978, and accepted by the general assembly of the United Nations in the Convention on Jurisdictional Immunities of States and Their Property, the restrictive doctrine limits the immunity of a sovereign to acts of state, excluding its commercial activities. As debt issuance is recognized as a commercial act, foreign creditors now have the ability to bring suit against a sovereign in default on its debts at least in their own and other foreign jurisdictions. However, this ability is of value only to the extent to which the assets of the sovereign can be attached, and a number of recent court cases have suggested that it is difficult to seize the small stocks of assets held abroad by the average debtor nation. In one well-known example, the Swiss company Noga unsuccessfully attempted to enforce contracts with Russia by seizing embassy bank accounts, Russian properties in France, naval ships, fighter jets, uranium shipments, and fine art (Wright, 2001a; Dömeland et al., 2008; Kolb, 2011; Pitchford and Wright, 2012).

Why then do sovereign countries ever repay their debts? International economists have theorized that sovereigns repay in order to retain access to capital markets in the future or to avoid direct sanctions that can be imposed upon by them by members of the international community acting either in concert or individually. We next review the different versions of these theories.

(ii) Sanctions and domestic economic costs

In this sub-section, we review punishments that can be imposed upon a defaulting sovereign by the direct action of creditor country governments, or by the direct actions of creditors themselves. We refer to such direct actions as *sanctions* and note that they come in many forms.

One type of sanction affects the ability of a sovereign government and its citizens to access international capital markets. As noted earlier, market participants commonly refer to the loss of normal financial market access as one of the primary consequences of a country's decision to default. Later, we review theories as to how this might arise in the equilibrium of a game between the sovereign and its creditors. However, here we consider the alternative possibility that the loss of credit market access may be the result of direct actions of creditor country governments. In the past, creditor country governments have imposed financial sanctions in the form of restrictions on the ability of their citizens to engage in financial transactions with the government or residents of a foreign country. One of the best-known examples concerns the U.S. restrictions on financial transactions with Iran. Following the hostage crisis in 1979, President Carter issued executive order 12170 freezing Iranian assets. Some of these assets remain frozen to this day. Likewise, Iranian financial institutions have been barred from directly accessing the US financial system. And although they may access US financial markets by using banks in other countries as intermediaries, in recent years the US government has worked to discourage this either directly through sanctions (for example, on Bank Saderat Iran; see Lawder (2008) for details), or indirectly.

While it is certainly possible that countries may repay their debts out of fear of financial sanctions, such sanctions remain rare and there is little evidence that sanctions of this type have been imposed directly in response to a default. An alternative possibility is that—the doctrine of sovereign immunity not withstanding—creditors may use their own country's courts to limit access of a sovereign to international capital markets. Although in general the ability to seize sovereign assets is limited by the fact that most of these assets are not held in creditor country jurisdictions, one asset that inevitably flows through creditor country jurisdictions is the funds associated with servicing new loans to the country. This approach has been adopted in two prominent recent court cases, both involving the hedge fund Elliott Associates. In the first case, which occurred in the late 1990s and involved Peru (for details, see Alfaro, 2006; Pitchford and Wright, 2012), Elliott Associates obtained a judgment in New York and convinced a Belgian court to halt the flow of debt service payments on Brady bonds, issued as part of Peru's debt restructuring, through Euroclear. Peru—with its funds frozen and faced with the prospect of defaulting on its Brady bonds—agreed to settle out of court. In the second case, which is ongoing at the time of writing this article, Elliott Associates convinced a New York court to rule that Argentina could not pay debt service on bonds issued as part of its debt restructuring in 2004 (following its 2001 default) unless it paid the original defaulted bonds held by Elliott Associates in full (for more on this case, and the *pari passu* bond clause at the heart of the legal arguments, see Gulati and Scott, 2011; Wright, 2011). The outcome of this case is uncertain, and the legal mechanism underlying these two claims may be neutered by rewriting future sovereign debt contracts; however, it is possible that fears of such legal tactics may work to discourage default in the future. It is certain, however, that such concerns played no role in encouraging sovereign countries to repay their debts prior to the modern period.

Other sanctions may be imposed directly on a country and its economy without affecting a country's ability to issue sovereign bonds. One possibility is that default may lead to restrictions on international trade (Bulow and Rogoff, 1989*b*). There is some empirical evidence that countries in default experience a significant decline in foreign trade (Rose, 2005; Borensztein and Panizza, 2010). However, it is not clear whether these declines reflect the imposition of trade sanctions, either explicitly or *sub rosa,* or whether they reflect the state of the economy at the time of default. Martinez and Sandleris (2011) find that default disproportionately depressed trade with non-creditors, suggesting that trade sanctions were not at work. Likewise, Agronovsky and Trebesch (2009) show that exports to creditors rose after debt restructuring. Similarly ambiguous evidence exists for earlier time periods (English, 1996; Tomz, 2007). Alternatively, declines in trade may be the result of lost access to trade credit facilities (Kaletsky, 1985; Kohlscheen and O'Connell, 2007). While it has been documented that commercial credit shrinks in the aftermath of default and that exports of sectors that depend on external credit tend to suffer the most (Zymek, 2012), other authors have concluded that the impact on commercial credit is brief and not sufficient to explain the total drop in trade (Borensztein and Panizza, 2009).

Alternatively, sanctions may affect other aspects of a sovereign's international relations. For example, Cole and Kehoe (1998) model a mechanism in which default leads to the disruption of other kinds of international cooperation, echoing findings from the industrial organization literature on multimarket contact (Bernheim and Whinston, 1990). The concept of reputational spillovers seems plausible, and there is some evidence in favour of this hypothesis in the arena of environmental treaties (Rose and Spiegel, 2009); however, there is little indication that such spillovers exist in the closely related topic of foreign direct investment (Fuentes and Saravia, 2010; Tomz and Wright, 2010; Eden *et al.,* 2012).

Finally, other possible sanctions could be more direct and dramatic. For instance, a country in default could become a target of military intervention. Many scholars have argued that this was common until the early twentieth century. For example, Oosterlinck (2013) writes that 'military interventions to force repayment . . . were common up till the First World War'. Additionally, Finnemore (2003) writes that militarized debt collection was accepted practice until the Second Hague Peace Conference in 1907, while Mitchener and Weidenmier (2010) add that gunboat diplomacy was 'effective and commonly used' before 1913. Others have argued that creditor country governments did not use, or threaten to use, military force on behalf of bondholders. For example, Tomz (2007) maintains that even the most commonly cited example of military intervention to enforce a debt—the 1902 intervention against Venezuela—occurred because of tort claims, rather than debt default. Moreover, investors often lent to countries they had no chance of coercing, and debtors repaid militarily strong and weak creditors equally. We find the evidence presented by Tomz (2007) more convincing. However, regardless of the position one takes on these historical debates, all agree that countries do not use military intervention to enforce debt contracts today.

Besides the threat of various forms of sanctions, sovereigns may repay their debts to avoid costly consequences for their own citizens. There are numerous mechanisms through which this might occur. A default may impose direct costs on the economy of the defaulting country if it damages the domestic financial system by inducing a domestic banking crisis. More subtly, if a sovereign default leads to a cessation of issuance of domestic sovereign debts, and if these debts play an important role as collateral or as a hedging instrument, a sovereign default can lead to less intermediation and risk sharing by domestic residents (for a model of this phenomenon, see D'Erasmo and Mendoza, 2012).

Even absent a domestic financial crisis, if a country cannot discriminate among the holders of its debts, a default can result in large redistributions between domestic residents (see relatedly, Broner and Ventura, 2011). Guembel and Sussman (2009) capture this idea in a model wherein the sovereign is disciplined by the political process through the preferences of the median voter. Debt repayments to foreigners are enforced because the (domestic) median voter is a creditor who wants the sovereign to repay through a tax system that transfers funds from voters who do not hold sovereign debt.

Broner *et al.* (2010) construct a related model in which secondary markets may serve to reallocate bond holdings in such a way as to deter default by making the costs of default fall primarily on domestic residents. Thus far, evidence on this mechanism is mixed. For example, Waldenström (2010) studies bond markets during the Second World War, when capital controls segmented international markets, and finds that yields on Danish bonds were lower in Denmark than in Sweden. This is consistent with a model in which sovereigns can favour domestic over foreign investors. Likewise, sovereigns sometimes transform their debt stocks in ways that permit discrimination, as in Argentina in 2000–1, which induced domestic residents to shift into new instruments, which received better treatment than the bonds foreigners continued to hold. In both cases, the ease with which the sovereign discriminated in favour of domestic residents is inconsistent with a model in which sovereigns repay all debts to avoid hurting domestic residents. In addition, some authors have argued that sovereigns frequently discriminate in favour of foreigners. For example, Erce and Díaz-Cassou (2010) analyse 10 recent defaulters and find that four discriminated against foreign creditors, three adopted a neutral approach, and three afforded preferential treatment to foreign creditors.

In light of the mixed empirical evidence in favour of each of these hypotheses, researchers have tended to focus on enforcement mechanisms driven by the desire of a country to retain future capital market access. We next turn to a study of such theories.

(iii) Retaliatory loss of capital market access

As noted previously, market participants frequently refer to the loss of normal credit market access as the primary cost borne by a sovereign that defaults on its debts. There are two main theories as to why credit market access may be lost, in addition to the adoption of legal tactics by creditors discussed earlier. Somewhat confusingly, both mechanisms are said to represent the loss of a country's 'reputation'.

In the first approach, emphasized in early work on sovereign debt by Eaton and Gersovitz (1981), creditors threaten to retaliate against a country in default by denying it access to financial markets in the future. As the response of creditors is conditioned on the past behaviour of the sovereign, this does capture one notion of reputation, although we refer to it as a *retaliatory* mechanism to avoid confusion with the other usage of the term reputation later (namely, reputational loss modelled as a sovereign being revealed as a 'bad' type). The retaliatory mechanism for supporting repayment has been analysed in a number of contexts, most notably by Kocherlakota (1996) who builds on earlier work by Coate and Ravallion (1993). Kocherlakota studies an environment in which two risk-averse agents face a random endowment and seek to trade with each other to smooth their consumption. Neither agent can commit to honouring promises, so that any trade needs to be self-enforcing for both agents (in the language of the literature, this is a 'two sided limited commitment model'). Kocherlakota showed that in this two-agent world, out-of-equilibrium threats to retaliate by denying future capital market access could support positive amounts of trade and that these threats were credible in the sense of being part of a sub-game perfect equilibrium strategy. Kletzer and Wright (2000) studied a similar model, with one risk-averse sovereign and one risk-neutral international creditor.

Although threatened denials of future trade are credible in the sense of being sub-game perfect, such threats may not be credible in a deeper sense. The problem is that exclusion from financial markets leaves unexploited potential gains from trade in financial assets. As a result, the parties to the original agreement have a mutual incentive to depart from such an outcome. If it is anticipated that they will do so, this renders the initial threat not credible. Such a concern underlies the literature on renegotiation-proofness in repeated and dynamic games, and multiple formulations of the notion of renegotiation-proofness have been advanced in the game theory literature (compare Pearce, 1987; Bernheim and Ray, 1989; Farrell and Maskin, 1989; Ray, 1994).

In the case of sovereign borrowing and lending, concerns about the credibility of threats to deny access to international credit market turn out not to be a problem. Kletzer and Wright (2000), for example, show that the same amount of trade that can be supported by the threatened denial of future trading opportunities can also be supported by strategies satisfying alternative definitions of renegotiation-proofness. Essentially, the problem with threats to deny capital market access is that they leave potential gains from trade unexploited. Kletzer and Wright show, however, that the same incentive for repayment can be generated by strategies that do not waste potential gains from trade. Specifically, if the sovereign defaults (that is, if it deviates from the equilibrium strategy), the creditor can refuse to trade with the sovereign unless the sovereign makes an up-front payment large enough to leave the sovereign with the same level of utility that it would have received if it were excluded from capital markets (an analogous argument works for the case in which a creditor deviates from the equilibrium strategy). As the utility of the country is the same as if it were excluded from future access to capital markets, the same incentive to repay exists. However, these retaliatory threats are credible in the sense of being proof to renegotiation by the players of the sovereign debt game because no gains from trade are being wasted.

A related and more problematic concern arises when there are other creditors that could trade with the sovereign if it is in default. Bulow and Rogoff (1989a) demonstrate a particularly strong version of this argument by establishing conditions under which a country could default, take the payments it would have made to foreign creditors, and invest them with foreign financial institutions to generate a higher level of welfare than they could obtain from future borrowing. Specifically, they show that to avoid the costs of default a country need only be able to save abroad using a rich enough menu of assets to be able to replicate the state-contingent cashflows implied by the original debt contract; it need not have future access to borrowing in international capital markets (it needs only future access to saving in international capital markets). They conclude that the threat of exclusion from future borrowing (as opposed to all future credit market access) is not sufficient to enforce repayment of debts.

A large literature has established the limits of the Bulow–Rogoff critique of retaliatory punishments. Much of the literature focused on whether or not a sufficiently rich set of assets is available. Pesendorfer (1992), for example, argues that it may be necessary to go short in one or more assets in order to obtain a rich enough set of savings opportunities for the Bulow–Rogoff critique to work, so that the threatened denial of access to borrowing (going short) would be sufficient to allow some borrowing in equilibrium. Likewise, Amador (2003, 2006) explores a variety of mechanisms under which a country is unable to commit to save for political economy considerations. In the absence of assets that permit a long-term savings commitment, such a country would not optimally exploit savings opportunities in the event of a default, thus invalidating the critique. Finally, in a version of Kletzer and Wright's (2000) model with multiple risk neutral creditors that can all trade with the sovereign, the authors show that retaliatory threats survive because of the assumption of two-sided limited commitment, which means that creditors cannot commit to honour contracts and hence cannot offer the appropriate savings contracts (see also Cole and Kehoe, 1994).

Other research argues that whether or not sufficiently rich savings opportunities required for the Bulow–Rogoff results are readily observed in markets is irrelevant, because if there is demand, market participants are capable of constructing the appropriate asset. Specifically, because the required richness in assets means that the assets can replicate the cashflows under the original debt contract, and because market participants were able to offer the original debt contract, they should be able to construct the required assets. The question then becomes whether creditors can coordinate to keep these contracts from being available, in equilibrium, to the defaulting sovereign.

To study this question, Wright (2001a) develops a model with a risk-averse sovereign that is unable to commit to honouring contracts and with many risk-neutral creditors that can commit to honouring contracts. In this one-sided limited commitment framework, creditors are able to commit to honouring a full set of savings contracts, making the kind of assets envisaged by Bulow and Rogoff feasible. Wright (2001a) shows that, even if there is intense competition among creditors (so that they all expect to earn zero profits), they can coordinate to credibly exclude a defaulting sovereign from access to credit markets. Coordination is facilitated by the fact that, even in a competitive market in which creditors expect to earn zero profits, lending contracts are associated with streams of payment in the future that have a positive value to creditors. That is, at some point in the future in some state of the world, the sovereign must be expected to repay. Hence, creditors can threaten to disrupt each other's shares of these repayments (by offering the appropriate assets to the sovereign) if other creditors do not cooperate to punish a sovereign in default. For this to work, the creditors must appropriately divide up the cashflows associated with any single loan among all creditors (as in syndicated bank loans), or appropriately divide up the total cashflows associated with the borrowing of other sovereigns in which these creditors are engaged.

In all of the models discussed in this sub-section, default in the sense of a deviation from the equilibrium strategy does not occur in equilibrium. This is a reflection of the fact that sovereigns and their creditors in these models are assumed to be able to design contracts of arbitrary complexity under conditions of perfect information so that payoffs can be tailored to ensure default never occurs in any state of nature. If contracting flexibility is limited, events such as default can emerge in equilibrium (as in the discussion of price wars in the repeated oligopoly model of Rotemberg and Saloner (1986, 395–6)). Specifically, if the cashflows associated with borrowing and lending are limited in the extent to which they can vary across states of the world, default provides a partial (and costly) form of insurance that occurs in equilibrium (see Eaton and Gersovitz (1981) as well as its modern variants such as Aguiar and Gopinath (2006); Tomz and Wright (2007); Arellano (2008)). Likewise, modifications of these models to include asymmetric information may result in periods of limited or no capital flows occurring on the equilibrium path (see Hopenhayn and Werning, 2008; Dovis, 2013; Miller et al., 2013).

Moreover, since the theories primarily differ with respect to the sort of behaviour that can happen out of equilibrium, it is not obvious what empirical evidence can be brought to bear on these models. One approach, in the spirit of Greif et al.'s (1994) analysis of cooperation by members of merchants' guilds, is to undertake archival research of the records of market participants at times when defaults were being contemplated, with a view to isolating the thought processes undertaken and, hence, potentially also the range of strategies considered by these market participants. Wright (2001b) provides one such analysis for the case of Spanish loans in London in the 1860s and argues that institutions that lent to Spain in violation of a market-wide embargo found that their other financial dealings were disrupted by creditors that respected the embargo. Similar evidence about the interactions of private creditors with a sovereign in default is presented by Drelichman and Voth (2011a). Further research exploring other cases of this type would be very valuable.

(iv) Reputation

An alternative reason for the loss of credit market access following a default is that the decision to default reveals something negative about the country's creditworthiness, thus leading creditors to reduce or cut off lending to them. We refer to this cost of default as the loss of a country's reputation. For example, if there is incomplete information about the gains from sovereign borrowing—perhaps because the country's value of future lending or the costs of default are unknown to the creditor—a default will lead creditors to infer that the country is a 'bad type'.

Cole and Kehoe (1998) examine a model where there are two types of sovereign and where only the sovereign can observe its type. The 'bad' type will default whenever the discounted value of doing so exceeds the cost due to the loss of future loans. The 'honest' type suffers a large disutility from breaking contracts in general. This framework views the loss of reputation due to a default as being revealed *not* to be the honest type. Cole and Kehoe first show that, without the ability to save abroad, the loss of reputation and the consequent lack of access to future borrowing are enough to support borrowing in equilibrium as the borrowing horizon becomes infinite and even as the prior probability of an honest sovereign approaches zero. However, they show that the Bulow–Rogoff result of zero sovereign borrowing in the presence of saving with international institutions extends to this environment provided the loss of reputation is limited to the sovereign borrowing arena, which Cole and Kehoe refer to as partial loss of reputation.

If being revealed to be a bad type in one arena reveals the same information in other arenas, such as foreign direct investment or international political cooperation, a general loss of reputation occurs. As noted before when we discussed reputational spillovers, the empirical evidence for this is mixed, with some authors finding support from the arena of environmental treaties, while other authors have found little evidence in the context of foreign direct investment.

Richer versions of these models have also been produced. Tomz (2007) describes an environment in which some countries are 'stalwarts' and always repay their debt, some countries are 'lemons' that never repay, and others repay in an attempt to earn a reputation for repayment. He finds evidence for this pattern in a study of the history of sovereign borrowing over the past three centuries. Cole *et al.* (1995) study a variant of this type of model in which the surplus the sovereign obtains from access to financial markets fluctuates over time with changes in the country's demand for borrowing that are unobservable to creditors. Their model produces a rich set of equilibrium dynamics, with defaults occurring on the equilibrium path and with improvements in the sovereign's position being signalled to creditors via a payment that may be thought of as a debt restructuring settlement.

In all of the models discussed in this sub-section, the country's reputation is understood as referring to beliefs about a fundamental characteristic of that country's government that is related to the benefits and costs in the event of a default.

However, a similar mechanism can work if the private information relates to some other aspect of the country. For example, suppose that the government has information on the true level of productivity of the country (perhaps because it is in charge of compiling economic statistics for the country). Such a government may repay debts in order to signal a country's high level of productivity to creditors so that domestic firms retain access to capital markets, as in the model of Sandleris (2008).

III. Bargaining to restructure sovereign debt

Much of the literature reviewed thus far postulates a particular source of punishments for countries that default on their debts, and studies the extent to which these punishments support borrowing in equilibrium. An alternative literature takes the existence of borrowing as given, generates default in equilibrium by placing restrictions on the types of strategies that can be played by agents (as in Eaton and Gersovitz, 1981), and studies the process by which debts in default are restructured through negotiations between the sovereign and its creditors.

Before studying theories of sovereign debt restructuring, it is useful to summarize the empirical evidence on debt restructuring outcomes that has guided this literature. One of the most striking features of the process of restructuring of sovereign debts is that it is very time consuming. Using a standard definition of default (the one produced by the ratings agency Standard & Poor's), Pitchford and Wright (2007) find that defaults commonly take around 6–8 years to be resolved, with a mean of more than 7 years and a median of a little over 6 years (see also Benjamin and Wright, 2008). Although other studies using different definitions of defaults have found a larger number of defaults of shorter duration, they also find that these defaults are closely correlated in time so that, even if individual defaults have short durations, the period during which access to capital markets is disrupted is far longer (see the review in Tomz and Wright, 2013).

The long periods taken to resolve defaults, along with the associated costly disruptions to capital market access and the domestic economy of the defaulting sovereign, seem very inefficient. This inefficiency appears all the more severe given that both creditors and debtors apparently gain little from debt restructuring. Benjamin and Wright (2008), for example, find that sovereign debtors that restructure their debts tend to exit default with a level of indebtedness at least as high as when they entered default (in terms of ratios of debt to gross domestic product (GDP)). Similarly, Sturzenegger and Zettelmeyer (2006), using a different measure of indebtedness, find that the form of the restructured debts typically implied relatively small gains, and in some cases losses, for the countries that defaulted.

At the same time, a number of researchers have found that creditors lose a substantial amount of the value of their claim following a debt restructuring. In the most careful study to date, Cruces and Trebesch (2013) estimate that creditors lose roughly 40 per cent of the value of their investment as a consequence of debt restructuring. This rises to roughly 50 per cent when losses are compounded across neighbouring default events (Benjamin and Wright, 2008).

Given these findings, researchers have sought to understand why these outcomes are so inefficient. In this section, we review alternative game theoretic formulations of the debt-restructuring process that seek to answer this question.

(i) Asymmetric information

Game theorists have long tried to understand why agents—in contexts as varied as labour disputes, political impasses, and debt restructuring—seem to find it difficult to reach agreements that appear to be mutually beneficial. Indeed, this is one of the greatest puzzles addressed by bargaining theory. Perhaps the most commonly cited explanation is that there is an asymmetry of information between the parties to bargaining. In the case of negotiations to restructure sovereign debt, a debtor country is likely to have more precise information about the political and economic costs it would face by agreeing to a settlement than do the creditors. Likewise, creditors are likely to have more information about the state of their balance sheets and the set of alternative investment opportunities they face. In such a world, neither party knows the value the other party places on agreeing to a settlement.

A number of formulations of bargaining in the presence of so-called two-sided asymmetric information have been presented. Cramton (1992) studies a two-sided asymmetric information version of Admati and Perry's (1987) bargaining model in which the time between offers is chosen endogenously by the bargaining parties. In such a world, delay serves to reveal information about the value each player places on a settlement, with each party becoming more pessimistic about the other party's valuation as time goes on. Delay is informative because the more the player values agreement, the more costly is delay. When offers are eventually made and accepted in such a world, the valuations of both creditor and debtor are revealed.

Delay in these games is socially inefficient, which begs the question of whether there may be less costly alternative means of revealing a player's private information. In a related context, Hörner and Sahuguet (2011) show that the ability to signal one's type by committing resources (other than through the time cost of delay) acts to essentially eliminate delay. One implication for policy-makers is that they should investigate mechanisms that allow for faster, less socially costly means of revealing information.

There has been relatively little empirical research assessing whether information asymmetries appear to be relevant in explaining the observed delays in sovereign debt restructuring. One finding, which is suggestive rather than being definitive, is that delays and creditor losses are partially predictable using information on GDP that is readily available at the beginning of negotiations (Benjamin and Wright, 2008). Although this does not rule out a role for asymmetric information as a cause of delay in bargaining, it does suggest that alternative models that are consistent with this predictability are of value. We now turn to such models.

(ii) Symmetric information models of delays in bargaining

Symmetrically informed parties clearly do not learn anything from their rival by adopting a strategy of delay. Removal of this motive might lead one to think that immediate agreement will ensure. However, Merlo and Wilson (1995) found that it might be efficient to delay reaching agreement if the size of the surplus to be split can grow in the future. The idea that this model might be used to explain delays in sovereign debt restructuring was first postulated by Merlo and Wilson (1998) themselves. However, there was no attempt to connect the (somewhat abstract) bargaining model with the details of the sovereign debt restructuring case. Importantly, in both of these papers, the surplus over which the parties bargain varies exogenously according to a stochastic process. It is the fact that this surplus may grow at a rate faster than the discount rate of the parties to the bargain that generates socially efficient delay in Merlo and Wilson's model.

Efforts to analyse sovereign debt restructuring within a Merlo–Wilson framework were made in a series of papers by Marcus Miller and his co-authors. Miller and García-Fronti (2005) take the exact Merlo and Wilson (1998) model and calibrate parameter values to match Argentina's 2004 restructuring. This argument is further developed in Dhillon et al. (2006). In both papers, the size of the surplus is calibrated to match public statements by the parties on their bargaining positions as to the size of the recovery rate (the resulting surplus amounts to 2.64 per cent of Argentina's GDP). Importantly, the analysis assumes that an early settlement locks in a permanently lower level of output, whereas delay generates a permanently higher level of output. That is, delay is not just privately optimal for the debtor and creditors, it is also socially optimal.

In all of the papers discussed in this sub-section, fluctuations in the surplus from bargaining occurred exogenously, and led to socially efficient delay. This efficiency seems in stark contrast to the data on sovereign debt restructuring outcomes discussed earlier. Several recent papers exploit elements of the Merlo–Wilson framework to produce socially inefficient delays, even though delay is privately optimal for the creditor and sovereign debtor, and we describe them next.

(iii) Limited commitment to honour debt-restructuring agreements

An alternative explanation for delays in bargaining over debt restructuring is based on the limited enforceability of contracts. In particular, if agreement to a debt restructuring produces benefits for the country, both at the time of settlement and in the future (possibly as the result of better future capital market access), creditors will bargain in order to obtain a share of these future benefits. If agents are patient, these future gains are likely to far exceed current gains. However, for the very same reasons that the sovereign is in default in the first place, the sovereign is unable to credibly promise to share these future benefits with creditors. Instead, the debtor can only promise to share these gains with the creditor by issuing debt as part of the settlement. However, such debt may not be very valuable if the creditor perceives that the debtor will likely default on it. Thus it may be privately optimal for creditors to wait until future default risk is low before agreeing to a debt restructuring.

Benjamin and Wright (2008) formalize this intuition. They show that the mechanism is further strengthened by the fact that reaccess to international credit markets is more valuable to the country when future default risk is low (because the country can borrow on better terms), giving the parties another reason to delay. The determinants of future default risk include the evolution of the sovereign's economy, the evolving political trade-offs within the economy, and the evolving institutions governing debt restructuring that affect the relative bargaining powers of the parties. For example, Benjamin and Wright (2008) argue that the development of official lending into private arrears reduced creditor bargaining power and prolonged the 1980s debt crisis. Benjamin and Wright (2008) show that a calibrated version of their model can explain long delays and large haircuts, as well as the fact that the level of indebtedness to private creditors typically does not decline following a settlement.

Relative to the Merlo–Wilson framework, in the Benjamin and Wright (2008) model, the surplus over which the sovereign and its creditors bargain is determined endogenously. In Benjamin and Wright's model, fluctuations in the likelihood of future default risk drive fluctuations in the size of the surplus and, specifically the possibility that future default risk may decline, which in turn drives delay. In a related paper, written contemporaneously, Bi (2008) also modifies the Merlo–Wilson framework with a surplus that endogenously fluctuates with the level of current resources in the economy (in her model, debt is not issued as part of a restructuring, and hence future default risk has no direct impact on the value of the settlement to creditors, although it may indirectly matter by increasing the value of capital market access to the sovereign). Both of these approaches show promise in terms of matching the data on debt restructuring outcomes. Neither speaks to the concerns of policy-makers that it is the inability to coordinate groups of creditors that results in delays. We next turn to a model that does address these concerns.

(iv) Limited commitment to enter bargaining

In the models discussed in the previous sub-section, creditors were assumed to be able to perfectly coordinate when negotiating with a sovereign debtor in default (so that the sovereign bargained with a representative creditor). In practice, creditors often find it difficult to coordinate; some creditors accept a debt restructuring offer, others reject it and wait for a better offer, and still others resort to litigation to encourage full repayment. Direct evidence for the importance of this issue can be found in the large number of recent policy proposals suggesting changes to sovereign bond contracts designed to make the coordination of groups of creditors easier (see, for example, IMF, 2013). Indirect evidence comes from studies of corporate debt restructuring that find that when a large investor such as a private equity fund is involved, debt restructuring proceeds more quickly, with less litigation, and is more likely to result in the survival of the firm than when no large investor is involved (Hotchkiss *et al.*, 2012).

There are at least three reasons why creditors may have an incentive not to coordinate when negotiating with a sovereign, even though collectively all would be better off by coordinating. We refer to this incentive problem as the inability of creditors to commit to entering bargaining.

The first reason why creditors may not coordinate is the possibility of free-riding in the provision of debt relief. This was a major concern during the debt crisis of the 1980s, where it was believed that sovereigns faced a debt overhang problem. Debt overhang refers to a situation in which a country's debt level is too large to be repaid in full, leading to suboptimal decisions by both the country and its creditors. From the perspective of the country, if creditors are able to extract the bulk of any future increase in revenues, the country will have no incentive to make investments that increase its future income and, hence, the value of the creditors' claims. This problem can be removed if creditors write down their debt to the level where the country retains enough of the extra income to be persuaded to make the investment, but still leaves creditors with a more valuable settlement. However, if creditors cannot coordinate in writing down their debts, then individual creditors have an incentive to free ride on the write-downs of other creditors. Models of this phenomenon were provided by Krugman (1988), among others.

A variety of informal mechanisms between creditors arose to deal with this problem, albeit imperfectly. Bank advisory committees were set up in which representatives of the major bank creditors were responsible for convincing smaller banks to participate in the restructuring process, among other things. A number of different methods were used. Devlin (1989), for example, argues that large banks used their contact with these smaller banks in other markets as an inducement to participate. Milivojevic (1985) refers to such incentives as working through the 'network of influence' large banks have on small banks which includes threats to exclude free riders from future syndicates, terminate correspondent banking facilities, or cut interbank lines of credit. In addition, although it is difficult in general to discriminate explicitly, in some cases debtors appear also to have discriminated against free-riding banks during a restructuring (Cline, 1983; more generally, see the discussion in Lipson, 1981, 1985). All of these informal methods are imperfect, and a challenge for any future debt-restructuring process is to ensure full participation in order to remove this incentive to free ride.

More recently, a second reason for lack of coordination has arisen in the aftermath of successful litigation by minority creditors against sovereigns in default, such as the Elliott Associates cases discussed earlier. Recent research has focused on the incentive of some creditors to engage in what has been termed 'strategic holdout', in which a subset of creditors does not participate in a restructuring agreement in order to engage in later litigation. If such litigation is able to hold up the restructuring, these creditors might be able to extract more generous terms from the sovereign, which is likely to slow down the restructuring process more generally.

The result of successful early legal actions against sovereigns has been a substantial increase in such litigation, with more than 50 cases filed by commercial creditors over the past decade against highly indebted poor countries (IMF and World Bank, 2005). Given holdout creditors have earned very high returns (see Singh, 2003) their successes have led to a greater incentive to holdout from the regular restructuring process. A number of policy proposals have been advanced to deal with this problem; the most notable among them is the introduction of collective action clauses that allow a supermajority of creditors to impose common restructuring terms on minority holdouts. These clauses have now become standard in bonds issued under New York law.

Game theoretic models of the strategic holdout incentive have been developed by Pitchford and Wright (2007, 2012). They also use the models to study the effect of changes in the contractual form of sovereign debts, including the introduction of collective action clauses in international bonds designed to bind holdout creditors to accept majority settlements. They find that these models are able to explain the amount of delay observed in the data. Moreover, they find that the implementation of such clauses will, in most cases, reduce the cost of default *ex post* by reducing the socially wasteful costs of default. They also find that the implementation of such clauses may nonetheless raise the welfare of borrowing countries *ex ante* despite adverse effects on the incentive of a country to default.

Pitchford and Wright (2012) also find that, in some cases, collective action clauses will increase delay. This comes about because of a third collective action problem—the potential for free riding on negotiation costs. In particular, when collective action clauses are used to impose common settlement terms on creditors, they also reduce the latitude for discriminatory settlements to be used for compensating creditors that take the lead in negotiations and, by consequence, bear the brunt of the costs for negotiations. Pitchford and Wright (2012) provide evidence that these costs are large—in excess of 3 per cent of the value of a restructuring in some complicated restructuring cases—and are in many cases hard to verify and thus difficult to compensate directly through reimbursement of expenses. Thus collective action clauses may work to remove the ability of creditors to hold out for full repayment, but they may also exacerbate the incentive for creditors to free ride on negotiation costs.

IV. Conclusions and policy implications

As a result of the legal doctrine of sovereign immunity, sovereign debt faces the archetypal enforcement problem. The environment in which trade between sovereigns and their creditors takes place is relatively unstructured, and the issues that arise in thinking about sovereign borrowing and sovereign default are particularly amenable to treatment using the tools of game theory. In this paper, we have reviewed the progress made by theorists on two basic questions from the field of sovereign debt that are amenable to analysis using the tools of game theory, and attempted to assess the empirical evidence relevant to these issues.

Approaches to answering the first question—why do countries repay their debts?— typically take the form of the incentive to repay debts as given and study the strength of that incentive in terms of its ability to support sovereign borrowing. Different theories have been postulated as to why sovereigns repay their debts: trade sanctions, military intervention, and disruption of other forms of international cooperation, as well as threatened denials of future capital market access. Although empirical research into the relevance of each of these mechanisms has not yet been proven conclusively, there is an emerging consensus that the threat of losing future capital market access is the primary incentive for sovereigns to repay, although there remains considerable disagreement as to the mechanism by which this denial of credit is supported.

Approaches to answering the second question—why are the outcomes of sovereign debt restructuring negotiations so inefficient?—typically take the existence of borrowing and default as given and study the effect of different bargaining environments on restructuring outcomes. The leading theories have postulated the following as the primary determinants of delay: asymmetric information, the inability of sovereigns to commit to honouring the outcomes of debt restructuring negotiations, and the inability of creditors to commit to enter into such negotiations in the first place. There has been a significant amount of quantitative theoretical research aimed at assessing the ability of these mechanisms to explain observed restructuring outcomes. At the moment, we have several theories that are consistent with a number of facts, and future work will need to derive and test alternative predictions of these models with a view to discriminating among them.

Game theoretic research into these questions has also generated recommendations for policy-makers. As noted before, game theoretic analyses of sovereign debt restructuring have indicated the potential for collective action clauses to actually *worsen* delays in reaching agreement on a restructuring, although they have been a central component of recent policies to *reduce* delays in sovereign debt restructuring (for example, Eurogroup, 2010). Quantitative applications of this theory have also allowed policy-makers to evaluate the trade-off between policies that reduce the cost of default *ex post,* and the effect they have on the incentive to borrow appropriately and avoid default *ex ante.* These evaluations may help determine the conditions under which collective action clauses may reduce delay and increase welfare.

Moreover, the analysis of incentives using game theory has also pointed to problems with the implementation of some recent policy proposals. For example, recent debt restructurings[2] involving aggregation clauses—which allow a super-majority of creditors holding different debt instruments to form an agreement that binds holders of all debt instruments—have allocated voting rights in proportion to the face value of the outstanding debt securities. But Wright (2012) and Dias *et al.* (2012) have illustrated how creditors and the sovereign may manipulate their debt issuance to maximize voting rights in the face of such clauses, and have proposed alternative allocations of voting rights to correct for this problem. Similarly, Wright (2012) points to the problem of pre-default restructuring in the presence of credit default swaps, which can result in a situation in which some creditors in debt restructuring negotiations are indifferent to the outcome.

Finally, in the same way that researchers in the field of sovereign debt have benefitted from the insights of game theory, we argue that there is much that game theorists can learn from the study of sovereign debt. Most obviously, the importance of sovereign debt as a financial asset has ensured that there is a substantial amount of information available as to the prices and quantities of sovereign debt in existence over a long time period. In addition, the long history of borrowing and default means that we are able to study the effect of slow-moving international institutions on the nature of interactions between sovereign debtors and their creditors. Perhaps more subtly, a study of sovereign debt allows researchers to probe more deeply the underlying strategic rationale for observed actions by the sovereign and its creditors. One of the great challenges to an empirical study of game theory is the fact that much of the theory depends on out-of-equilibrium behaviour by players, and yet by its very definition such behaviour is not observed. The fact that both sovereigns and their creditors have traditionally kept substantial records of their borrowing and lending processes means that careful archival work may be able to inform researchers of the kind of out-of-equilibrium behaviour that players were contemplating when arriving at their equilibrium strategies. Some progress along these lines has already been made (see Drelichman and Voth (2011a,b); much of the work of Flandreau and his co-authors, such as Flandreau and Flores (2009) and Flandreau et al. (2009); and Wright (2001b)).

The views expressed herein are those of the authors and not necessarily those of the Federal Reserve Bank of Chicago or the Federal Reserve System. We thank, without implicating, our discussant, Tim Jenkinson, Rui Esteves, Jagjit Chadha, and other participants at the *Oxford Review's* seminar for comments. Further comments are welcomed. Wright thanks the National Science Foundation for support under grant SES-1059829.

Notes

1 The first recorded sovereign debts were loans made by temple authorities to Greek city states to fund military campaigns in the Peloponnesian War in the fifth century BC. The first recorded sovereign default occurred in 377 BC when 10 of the 13 Greek city states in the Attic Maritime Association defaulted on loans made by the Temple of Delos (Winkler, 1933).

2 The recent Greek debt restructuring is an example where an aggregation clause was used.

References

Admati, A. R., and Perry, M. (1987), 'Strategic Delay in Bargaining', *Review of Economic Studies*, **54**, 345–64.

Agronovsky, A., and Trebesch, C. (2009), 'Trade Credit during Financial Crises: Do Negotiated Agreements Work?', in J. J. Choi and M. G. Papaioannou (eds), *Credit,*

Currency, or Derivatives: Instruments of Global Financial Stability or Crisis?, London, Emerald.

Aguiar, M., and Gopinath, G. (2006), 'Defaultable Debt, Interest Rates and the Current Account', *Journal of International Economics,* **69**, 64–83.

Alfaro, L. (2006), 'Creditor Activism in Sovereign Debt: Vulture Tactics or Market Backbone', Harvard Business School Case 9-706-057.

Amador, M. (2003), '*A Political Economy Model of Debt Repayment'*, Stanford University Working Paper.

_____ (2006), *'Sovereign Debt and the Tragedy of the Commons'*, Stanford University Working Paper.

Arellano, C. (2008), 'Default Risk and Income Fluctuations in Emerging Economies', *American Economic Review,* **98**, 690–712.

Benjamin, D., and Wright, M. L. J. (2008), *'Recovery before Redemption: A Theory of Delays in Sovereign Debt Renegotiations'*, University of California at Los Angeles, mimeo.

Bernheim B. D., and Ray, D. (1989), 'Collective Dynamic Consistency in Repeated Games', *Games and Economic Behavior,* **1**, 295–326.

_____ Whinston, M. D. (1990), 'Multimarket Contact and Collusive Behavior', *RAND Journal of Economics,* **21**, 1–26.

Bi, R. (2008), 'Beneficial Delays in Debt Restructuring Negotiations', *IMF Working Paper,* 08.

Borensztein, E., and Panizza, U. (2009), 'The Costs of Sovereign Default', *IMF Staff Papers,* **56**, 683–741.

_____ (2010), 'Do Sovereign Defaults Hurt Exporters?', *Open Economies Review,* **21**, 393–412.

Broner, F. A., and Ventura, J. (2011), 'Globalization and Risk Sharing', *Review of Economic Studies,* **78**, 49–82.

_____ Martin, A., and Ventura, J. (2010), 'Sovereign Risk and Secondary Markets', *American Economic Review,* **100**(4), 1523–55.

Bulow, J., and Rogoff, K. (1989*a*), 'Sovereign Debt: Is to Forgive to Forget?', *American Economic Review,* **79**, 43–50.

_____ (1989*b*), 'A Constant Recontracting Model of Sovereign Debt', *Journal of Political Economy,* **97**, 155–78.

Cline, W. R. (1983), *International Debt and the Stability of the World Economy*, Washington, DC, and Cambridge, MA, Institute for International Economics; distributed by MIT Press.

Coate, S., and Ravallion, M. (1993), 'Reciprocity Without Commitment: Characterization and Performance of Informal Insurance Arrangements', *Journal of Development Economics,* **40**, 1–24.

Cole, H. L., and Kehoe, P. J. (1994), *'The Role of Institutions in Reputation Models of Sovereign Debt'*, Federal Reserve Bank of Minnesota Working Paper.

_____ (1998), 'Models of Sovereign Debt: Partial versus General Reputations', *International Economic Review,* **39**, 55–70.

_____ Dow, J., and English, W. B. (1995), 'Default, Settlement, and Signaling: Lending Resumption in a Reputational Model of Sovereign Debt', *International Economic Review,* **36**, 365–85.

Cramton, P. C. (1992), 'Strategic Delay in Bargaining with Two-sided Uncertainty', *Review of Economic Studies,* **59**, 205–25.

Cruces, J. J., and Trebesch, C. (2013), *'Pricing Haircuts: Do Markets Punish Low Recovery Values in Sovereign Debt Restructurings?'*, Free University of Berlin, mimeo.

D'Erasmo, P., and Mendoza, E. (2012), *'Optimal Domestic Sovereign Default'*, University of Maryland Working Paper.

Devlin, R. (1989), *Debt and Crisis in Latin America: The Supply Side of the Story*, Princeton, NJ, Princeton University Press.

Dhillon, A., García-Fronti, J., Ghosal, S., and Miller, M. (2006), 'Debt Restructuring and Economic Recovery: Analysing the Argentine Swap', *World Economy*, **29**, 377–98.

Dias, D. A., Richmond, C., and Wright, M. L. J. (2012), 'On the Stock of External Sovereign Debt: Can We Take the Data at "Face Value"', *NBER Working Paper* 17551.

Dömeland, D., Gil Sander, F., and Braga, C. A. P. (2008), *The Economics of Odious Debt*, World Bank Report 402.

Dovis, A. (2013), 'Efficient Sovereign Default', University of Minnesota Working Paper.

Drelichman, M., and Voth, H.-J. (2011a), 'Lending to the Borrower from Hell: Debt and Default in the Age of Philip II', *The Economic Journal*, **121**, 1205–27.

_____ (2011b), 'Risk Sharing with the Monarch: Contingent Debt and Excusable Defaults in the Age of Philip II, 1556–1598', *CEPR Discussion Papers*.

Eaton, J., and Gersovitz, M. (1981), 'Debt with Potential Repudiation: Theoretical and Empirical Analysis', *Review of Economic Studies*, **48**, 289–309.

Eden, M., Kraay, A., and Qian, R. (2012), *'Sovereign Defaults and Expropriations: Empirical Regularities'*, World Bank, mimeo.

English, W. B. (1996), 'Understanding the Costs of Sovereign Default: American State Debts in the 1840s', *American Economic Review*, **86**, 259–75.

Erce, A., and Díaz-Cassou, J. (2010), *Creditor Discrimination during Sovereign Debt Restructurings*, Banco de Espana.

Eurogroup (2010), *Statement by the Eurogroup*, 28 November.

Farrell, J., and Maskin, E. (1989), 'Renegotiation in Repeated Games', *Games and Economic Behavior*, **1**, 327–60.

Finnemore, M. (2003), *The Purpose of Intervention: Changing Beliefs about the Use of Force*, Ithaca, NY, Cornell University Press.

Flandreau, M., and Flores, J. H. (2009), 'Bonds and Brands: Foundations of Sovereign Debt Markets, 1820–1830', *Journal of Economic History*, **69**, 646–84.

_____ Gaillard, N., and Nieto-Parra, S. (2009), 'The End of Gatekeeping: Underwriters and the Quality of Sovereign Bond Markets, 1815–2007', *NBER Working Paper* 15128.

Fuentes, M., and Saravia, D. (2010), 'Sovereign Defaulters: Do International Capital Markets Punish Them?', *Journal of Development Economics*, **91**, 336–47.

Greif, A., Milgrom, P., and Weingast, B. R. (1994), 'Coordination, Commitment, and Enforcement: The Case of the Merchant Guild', *Journal of Political Economy*, **102**, 745–76.

Guembel, A., and Sussman, O. (2009), 'Sovereign Debt without Default Penalties', *Review of Economic Studies*, **76**, 1297–320.

Gulati, G. M., and Scott, R. E. (2011), *The Three and a Half Minute Transaction: Boilerplate and the Limits of Contract Design*, Chicago, IL, University of Chicago Press

Hörner, J., and Sahuguet, N. (2011), 'A War of Attrition with Endogenous Effort Levels', *Journal of Economic Theory*, **47**, 1–27.

Hopenhayn, H. A., and Werning, I. (2008), 'Equilibrium Default', MIT Working Paper.

Hotchkiss, E., Smith, D. C., and Stromberg, P. (2012), 'Private Equity and the Resolution of Financial Distress', SIFR Working Paper.

IMF (2013), 'Sovereign Debt Restructuring: Recent Developments and Implications for the Fund's Legal and Policy Framework', International Monetary Fund Paper, Washington, DC, International Monetary Fund.

_____ World Bank (2005), *Heavily Indebted Poor Countries (HIPC) Initiative: Status of Implementation,* Washington, DC, International Monetary Fund and World Bank.

Kaletsky, A. (1985), *The Costs of Default,* New York, Priority Press.

Kletzer, K. M., and Wright, B. D. (2000), 'Sovereign Debt as Intertemporal Barter', *American Economic Review,* **90**, 621–39.

Kocherlakota, N. R. (1996), 'Implications of Efficient Risk Sharing without Commitment', *Review of Economic Studies,* **63**, 595–609.

Kohlscheen, E., and O'Connell, S. A. (2007), 'A *Sovereign Debt Model with Trade Credit and Reserves',* University of Warwick, mimeo.

Kolb, R. W. (2011), 'Sovereign Debt: Theory, Defaults, and Sanctions', in R. W. Kolb (ed.), *Sovereign Debt: From Safety to Default,* Hoboken, NJ, Wiley.

Krugman, P. (1988), 'Financing vs Forgiving a Debt Overhang', *Journal of Development Economics,* **29**, 253–68.

Lawder, D. (2008), 'US Treasury Tightens Banking Sanctions on Iran', *Reuters,* 6 November.

Lipson, C. (1981), 'The International Organization of Third World Debt', *International Organization,* **35**, 603–31.

_____ (1985), 'Bankers' Dilemmas: Private Cooperation in Rescheduling Sovereign Debts', *World Politics,* **38**, 200–25.

Martinez, J. V., and Sandleris, G. (2011), 'Is it Punishment? Sovereign Defaults and the Decline in Trade', *Journal of International Money and Finance,* **30**, 909–30.

Merlo, A., and Wilson, C. (1995), 'A Stochastic Model of Sequential Bargaining with Complete Information', *Econometrica,* **63**, 371–99.

_____ (1998), 'Efficient Delays in a Stochastic Model of Bargaining', *Economic Theory,* **11**, 39–55.

Milivojevic, M. (1985), *The Debt Rescheduling Process,* New York, St. Martin's Press.

Miller, D., Trebesch, C., and Wright, M. L. J. (2013), 'Debt, Default and Bailouts', UCLA Working Paper.

Miller, M., and García-Fronti, J. (2005), *'Case Study: Restructuring Argentine Debt: A Renegotiation Game?',* CSGR Discussion Paper, February.

Mitchener, K. J., and Weidenmier, M. D. (2010), 'Supersanctions and Sovereign Debt Repayment', *Journal of International Money and Finance,* **29**, 19–36.

Oosterlinck, K. (2013), 'Sovereign Debt Defaults: Lessons from History', *Oxford Review of Economic Policy,* **29**(4), 697–714.

Pearce, D. (1987), *'Renegotiation-proof Equilibria: Collective Rationality and Intertemporal Cooperation',* Yale University, mimeo.

Pesendorfer, W. (1992), 'Sovereign Debt: Forgiving and Forgetting Reconsidered', Center for Mathematical Studies in Economics and Management Science, Northwestern University, Discussion Paper 1016.

Pitchford, R., and Wright, M. L. J. (2007), *'Restructuring the Sovereign Debt Restructuring Mechanism',* University of California at Los Angeles, mimeo.

_____ (2012), 'Holdout Creditors in Sovereign Debt Restructuring: A Theory of Negotiation in a Weak Contractual Environment', *Review of Economic Studies,* **79**, 812–37.

Ray, D. (1994), 'Internally Renegotiation-proof Equilibrium Sets: Limit Behavior with Low Discounting', *Games and Economic Behavior,* **6**, 162–77.

Rose, A. K. (2005), 'One Reason Countries Pay Their Debts: Renegotiation and International Trade', *Journal of Development Economics*, **77**, 189–206.

_____ Spiegel, M. M. (2009), 'Noneconomic Engagement and International Exchange: The Case of Environmental Treaties', *Journal of Money, Credit and Banking*, **41**, 337–63.

Rotemberg J. J., and Saloner, G. (1986), 'A Supergame-theoretic Model of Price Wars during Booms', *American Economic Review*, **76**, 390–407.

Roxburgh, C., Lund, S., and Piotrowski, J. (2011), *Mapping Global Capital Markets 2011*, McKinsey Global Institute.

Sandleris, G. (2008), 'Sovereign Defaults: Information, Investment and Credit', *Journal of International Economics*, **76**, 267–75.

Singh, M. (2003), 'Recovery Rates from Distressed Debt—Empirical Evidence from Chapter 11 Filings, International Litigation, and Recent Sovereign Debt Restructurings', IMF Working Paper 03, Washington, DC, International Monetary Fund.

Sturzenegger, F., and Zettelmeyer, J. (2006), 'Creditors' Losses versus Debt Relief: Results from a Decade of Sovereign Debt Crises', *Journal of the European Economic Association*, **5**, 343–51.

Tomz, M. (2007), *Reputation and International Cooperation: Sovereign Debt across Three Centuries*, Princeton, NJ, Princeton University Press.

_____ Wright, M. L. J. (2007), 'Do Countries Default in "Bad Times"?', *Journal of the European Economic Association*, **5**, 352–60.

_____ (2010), 'Sovereign Theft: Theory and Evidence about Sovereign Default and Expropriation', in W. Hogan and F. Sturzenegger (eds), *The Natural Resources Trap: Private Investment Without Public Commitment*, Cambridge, MA, MIT Press.

_____ (2013), 'Empirical Research on Sovereign Debt and Default', *Annual Reviews of Economics*.

Waldenström, D. (2010), 'Why does Sovereign Risk Differ for Domestic and External Debt? Evidence from Scandinavia, 1938–1948', *Journal of International Money and Finance*, **29**, 387–402.

Winkler, M. (1933), *Foreign Bonds: An Autopsy*, Philadelphia, Roland Swain Co..

Wright, M. L. J. (2001*a*), *'Reputations and Sovereign Debt'*, Stanford University Working Paper.

_____ (2001*b*), 'Creditor Coordination and Sovereign Risk', Stanford University Working Paper.

_____ (2011), 'The Pari Passu Clause in Sovereign Bond Contracts: Evolution or Intelligent Design?', *Hofstra Law Review*, **40**, 103–114.

_____ (2012), 'Sovereign Debt Restructuring: Problems and Prospects', *Harvard Business Law Review*, **2**, 153–98.

Zymek, R. (2012), 'Sovereign Default, International Lending, and Trade', *IMF Economic Review*, **60**, 265–394

INDEX

Note: Page numbers in **bold** type refer to tables. Page numbers in *italic* type refer to figures. Volume number is indicated in Roman numerals.